PHEKARUMA TRAVEL GUIDES

In collaboration with

 tredition

Munich

Strictly Confidential

Phekaruma Travel Guide

Rudolf H. Stehle

Copyright © Rudolf H. Stehle, PhD

All rights reserved throughout the world.

No part of this publication, including its cover, may be reproduced, stored in a retrieval system, or transmitted, in any form or by any means, without the prior written permission of the author.

ISBN Softcover: 978-3-384-20315-1
ISBN Hardcover: 978-3-384-20316-8

First published 2024

Photo Credits
All photos were taken be Rudolf H. Stehle, PhD in HDR Qualität.

Disclaimer
The information provided within this book is for general informational purposes only. Although the author has made every effort to ensure that the information in this book is correct, there are no representations or warranties, express or implied, about the completeness, accuracy, reliability, suitability or availability with respect to the information or related graphics contained in this book for any purpose. The author does not assume and hereby disclaim any liability to any party for any loss, damage, or disruption caused by errors or omissions, whether such errors or omissions result from negligence, accident, or any other cause. Any use of this information is at your own risk.

- ◄ **Cover Page:** Schloss Nymphenburg in the evening.
- ► **Rear Cover:** The Glyptothek at the Königsplatz.

Preface

Munich is not just a city but a living being with a thrilling story. Its heroes have woven their dragons into the fabric of history, creating a tapestry of culture and customs that is as fascinating as it is unique. While every society is challenged by opposites, the way Munich has dealt with conflicts sets it apart. Rather than letting history become tragic, Munich has embraced new ideas and outgrown the past, creating a dynamic and ever-evolving town that is a pleasure to explore.

The guide *Munich: Strictly Confidential* seeks to unveil the historically grown network of this incredible town, making its dynamic visible to all who endeavour to write their own story. As one explores Rothenburg's winding streets and charming architecture, one will discover the mark each period of history has left on the town's morphology. It's a joy to gain insight into Rothenburg's rich history, and it is even more a pleasure to share it with others.

Subjective experience is always individual, and your story of Munich will be different from mine. But that's the beauty of this world - it inspires us to write our own story, to embrace meaningful subjectivity, and to counterbalance with experience our blind faith in objective truth based on facts and figures. So come and explore Munich - feel inspired to create your thrilling chapter in this incredible journey through time.

Rudolf H. Stehle

Content

Introduction 1
    Munich, the Village of a Million 1
    Munich's History 5
    Chronicles of Munich 16
    Theme Parks and Adventure Tours 26
    Travel Points at a Glance 28
    Culinary Delights 40
    Annual Calendar 42
    Highlight Tour 1: The Beginnings of Munich 44
    Highlight Tour 2: Absolutism 46
    Highlight Tour 3: Kingdom of Bavaria 48
    Highlight Tour 4: Munich Boheme 50
    Highlight Tour 5: Nazi Regime 52

Walkabouts 54
    The Munich of the Munichers 55
Altstadt 56
  (1) Marienplatz 60
  (2) Altes Rathaus & Talburgtor 62
  (3) St Peter 64
  (4) Glockenspiel 68
  (5) Mariensäule 70
  (6) Neues Rathaus 72
  (7) Burgstraße 76
  (8) Alter Hof 78
  (9) Am Platzl 82
  (10) Hofbräuhaus 84

◀ The Feldherrnhalle at the Odeonsplatz pretends to be patriotic.

(11)	Isartor	86
(12)	Heilig-Geist-Kirche	88
(13)	Viktualienmarkt	92
(14)	Schrannenhalle	94
(15)	Rindermarkt	96
(16)	Münchner Stadtmuseum	98
(17)	Jüdisches Zentrum	100
(18)	Sendlinger Tor	102
(19)	Asamkirche	104
(20)	Kaufingerstraße & Neuhauser Straße	108
(21)	Frauenkirche	110
(22)	Jagd- und Fischereimuseum	114
(23)	St Michael	116
(24)	Bürgersaalkirche	120
(25)	Karlstor	122
(26)	Promenadeplatz	124
(27)	Kardinal Faulhaber Straße	126
(28)	Salvatorkirche	128
(29)	Platz der Opfer des Nationalsozialismus	130
(30)	Wittelsbacher Platz	132
(31)	Odeonsplatz	134
(32)	Feldherrnhalle	136
(33)	Theatinerkirche St Kajetan	138
(34)	Hofgarten	142
(35)	Bayerische Staatskanzlei	144
(36)	Herkulessaal	146
(37)	Münchner Residenz	148
(38)	Max-Joseph-Platz	154
(39)	Nationaltheater	156

Maxvorstadt, Schwabing and Lehel 158

- ㊵ Wittelsbacher Brunnen 162
- ㊶ Künstlerhaus 164
- ㊷ Alter Botanischer Garten 166
- ㊸ St Bonifaz 168
- ㊹ Königsplatz & Propyläen 170
- ㊺ Glyptothek 174
- ㊻ Antikensammlung 176
- ㊼ Lenbachhaus 178
- ㊽ NS-Dokumentationszentrum 180
- ㊾ Karolinenplatz 182
- ㊿ Museum Ägyptischer Kunst 184
- 51 Technische Universität München 186
- 52 Alte Pinakothek 188
- 53 Neue Pinakothek 192
- 54 Pinakothek der Moderne 194
- 55 Ludwigstraße 196
- 56 Ludwigskirche 198
- 57 Ludwig-Maximilians-Universität 200
- 58 Akademie der Bildenden Künste 202
- 59 Siegestor 204
- 60 Schwabing 206
- 61 Englischer Garten 208
- 62 Archäologische Staatssammlung 212
- 63 Prinzregentenstraße 214
- 64 Bayerisches Nationalmuseum 216
- 65 Haus der Kunst 218
- 66 St Anna im Lehel 220
- 67 Maximilianstraße 222
- 68 Völkerkundemuseum Fünf Kontinente 224

Along the Isar ... 226

- ⑥⑨ Bogenhausen ... 230
- ⑦⓪ Prinzregententheater ... 232
- ⑦① Villa Stuck ... 234
- ⑦② Friedensengel ... 236
- ⑦③ Maximilianeum ... 238
- ⑦④ Praterinsel ... 240
- ⑦⑤ St Lukas ... 242
- ⑦⑥ Wiener Platz ... 244
- ⑦⑦ St Johann Baptist ... 246
- ⑦⑧ Haidhausen ... 248
- ⑦⑨ Ostbahnhof ... 250
- ⑧⓪ Gasteig ... 252
- ⑧① Müllersches Volksbad ... 254
- ⑧② Deutsches Museum ... 256
- ⑧③ Mariahilfplatz ... 260
- ⑧④ Nockherberg ... 262
- ⑧⑤ Gärtnerplatz ... 264
- ⑧⑥ Gärtnerplatztheater ... 266
- ⑧⑦ Glockenbachviertel ... 268
- ⑧⑧ St Maximilian ... 270
- ⑧⑨ Flaucher ... 272
- ⑨⓪ Tierpark Hellabrunn ... 274
- ⑨① Bavaria Filmstadt ... 276
- ⑨② Burg Grünwald ... 278

Greater Munich ... 280

- ⑨③ Hauptbahnhof ... 284
- ⑨④ Oktoberfest ... 286
- ⑨⑤ Bavaria ... 288
- ⑨⑥ Ruhmeshalle ... 290
- ⑨⑦ St Paul ... 292
- ⑨⑧ Donnersbergerbrücke ... 294

⑨⑨	Hirschgarten	296
⑩⑩	Nymphenburger Kanal	298
⑩①	Schloss Nymphenburg	300
⑩②	Botanischer Garten	306
⑩③	Schloss Blutenburg	308
⑩④	Olympiazentrum	310
⑩⑤	BMW Zentrum	314
⑩⑥	Dachau Altstadt	316
⑩⑦	Schloss Dachau	318
⑩⑧	Gedenkstätte KZ Dachau	320
⑩⑨	Schloss Schleißheim	322
⑪⑩	Freising	328
⑪①	St Maria & St Korbinian	330
⑪②	Weihenstephan	334
⑪③	Allianz Arena	336

Structure of the Guide Book

Map
Discover the hidden gems around you with the mini-map! Get inspired to take a walk and uncover exciting destinations waiting to be explored.

Number & Header
The numbers hint at an exciting tour waiting to be taken, but it is not mandatory. It is only one possible path among many. Ultimately, the choice is yours to make.

Facts and Figures
A brief introduction presents essential information about the travel point, including its fascinating history, stunning architecture, or the restructuring it may have undergone. With this well-crafted introduction, you can better appreciate your sights and make the most of your travel experience.

While facts and figures provide valuable information, they cannot replace the emotional impact of experiencing the sights firsthand.

---

① Marienplatz

Facts & Figures

The Marienplatz once was the turntable of the city. The square was called *Schrannenplatz* until 1854. When the prayers of the townspeople to the Virgin Mary, launched at the Marienskule, warded off a cholera epidemic, the magistrate renamed the piazza. The Middle Ages held a market at the city's pulsating heart, and the Munichers turned over any long-distance trade here. The barkers relocated their grain bags, fishing nets, apples and potatoes to the Viktualienmarkt during the 19th century. Merchants traded fine cloth and wine at the 100-meter-wide square until 1850, and local farmers offered meat, milk, cheese, poultry and eggs. The Marienplatz still resonates with chanting and processions, pageants and weddings. It also witnessed the execution of obstinate Protestants and witches. Today, the *FC Bayern Munich* celebrates its numerous football titles here and the Advent jingles with a Christmas fair.

Munich at the *Isar* owed its affluence to the *Salt Goddess* in the Middle Ages. The Marienplatz, the town's main square, distributed the white gold. It was excavated at the Alps and brought on carts to town. Salt was a commodity essential to preserve food. The transport, stamp duty, and the need for untermediaries made salt a luxury product, not the mining itself.

When Emperor Ludwig der Bayer granted Munich stacking rights in 1332, he brought prosperity to the city. The royal decree forced traders to cross the Isar at the Gasteig, and they had to put the white wheels down for sale at the central market for three days.

Munich's monopoly on salt turned into clinking coins. Trading relocated to the Promenadeplatz in the 15th century - the business had become industrious. The population grew fast, and the burghers enlarged their city in the 14th century to loosen the asphyxiating girdle. The second moat ran from the Isartor to the Sendlingertor, Karlstor and the Odeonsplatz.

The Marienplatz also merchandised fine cloth and wine besides salt, and the local farmers of the alpine foreland guaranteed staple food and supplies. They sold eggs and herbs outside the Alte Rathaus, and breeders offered fish at the central fountain, kept in nets for freshness.

Background
Experience the richness of a travel point like never before by delving into its history and cultural background. Immerse yourself in the local community or discover the story of a remarkable individual who has left a lasting mark on the city. Alternatively, the secrets of a defining event are uncovered that have shaped the location into what it is today.

Structure of the Guide Book

Illustration
The illustration provides an initial impression and simplifies identifying the travel point.

Every traveller experiences a different world, and that enriches the community. Sharing one's impressions is the joy of the 3rd millennium. Let us embrace the beauty of diversity and come together to learn, grow, and inspire each other with our travel stories.

References
For the latest information on location, opening hours, tickets, and prices, please check the internet as details may change at short notice.

Diversity adds flavour to life and broadens our perspectives.

Telling Tales
Discover the magic of a location through its tales, anecdotes, and legends. Alternatively, another sight close by may be described.

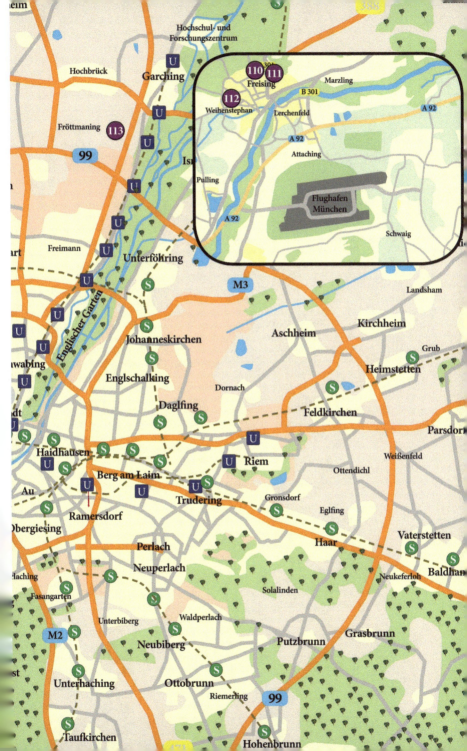

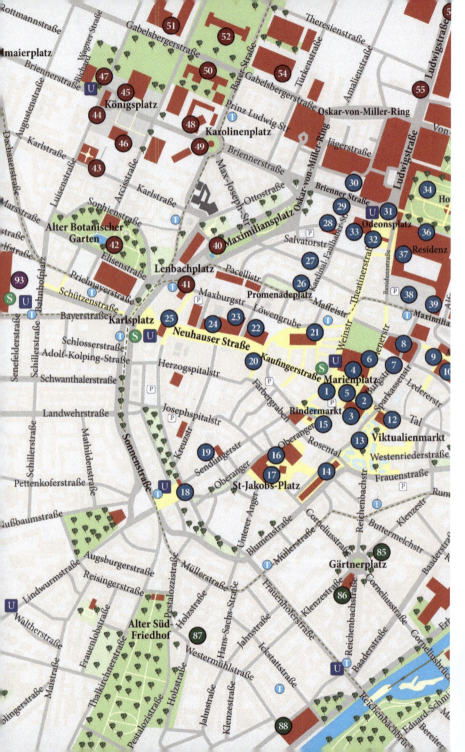

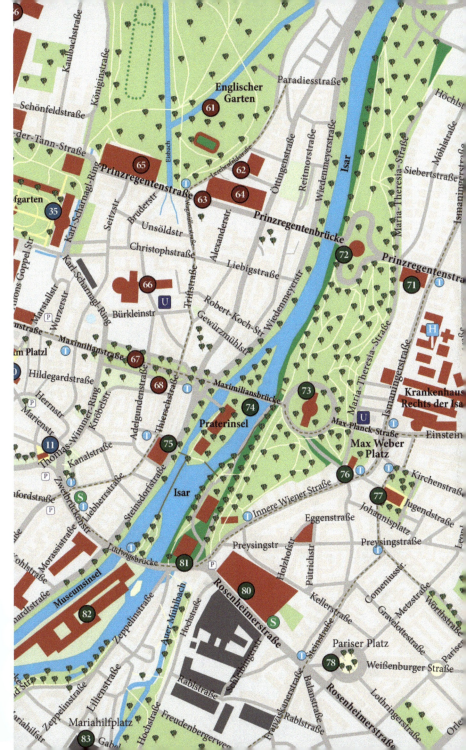

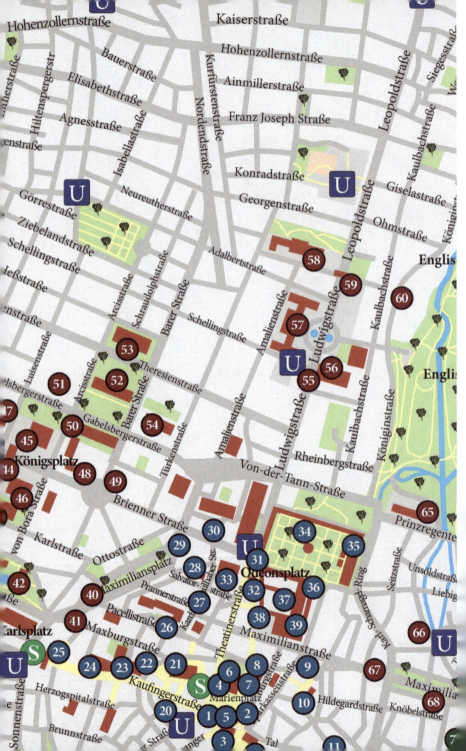

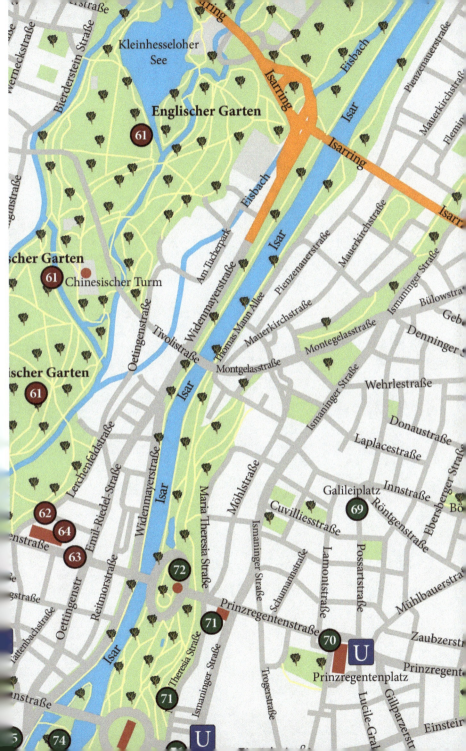

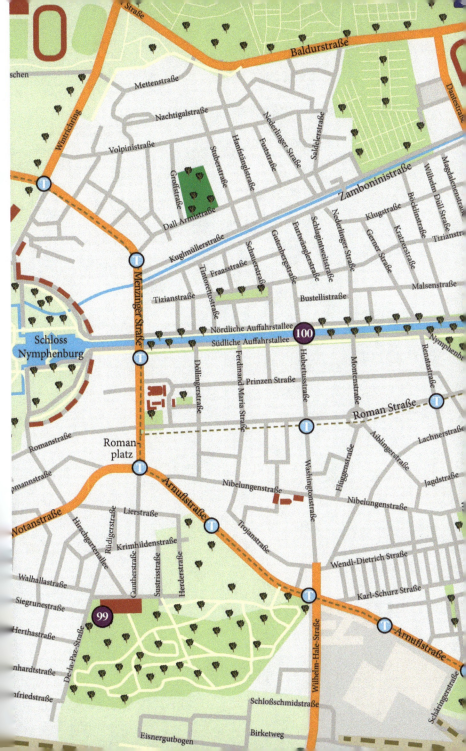

Introduction

Munich, the Village of a Million

Munich is a city of contradictions: it is modern yet conservative, down-to-earth yet trendy; its people are rooted in nationalism yet liberal-minded; the city is urban yet rural, traditional yet cosmopolitan. Munich wallows in melancholy and embraces a sense of *joie de vivre*. The streets are full of life, yet many carry a heavy heart; the people are enthusiastic about technology yet superstitious - "*live and let live*" and "*I am Me*" are their slogans. The list of opposites is long, and any dirndl is aware: "*Many souls live in my chest.*" To explore Munich means confronting the many grimaces, staring into the Gorgon's eye, being haunted by Janus's face.

But tell! How did Munich stroll down the ages? Did Munich swagger fashionably modern across the centuries, slightly twisted, swinging its hip with a cigarette in position? Or did Munich travel through time in a horse-drawn carriage, posing with its legs firmly on the ground, upright and proud, chamois bearded, head in the neck and eyes to the sky? Or perhaps, did Munich dance with a lighthearted step over the aeons of time?

The enigma of Munich has confused the scribes throughout the centuries. Thomas Mann once described Munich as a city that *glared*, yet he never befriended the town. The film director and scriptwriter Helmut Dietl pictured its charm as an *aggressive cosiness*, and the Federal President Roman Herzog believed that "*in Munich, leather trousers and laptop form a symbiotic relationship.*" Heinrich Heine called Munich "*an ocean of little souls and foetid air.*" He added: "*Small-mindedness of the grandest kind.*" The Municher is a smiling, mischievous contradiction, a laughing grump. He constitutes - in fact - the only subspecies of the homo sapiens that manages to scrunch the brow while crunching the lid.

Hans Christian Andersen felt as confused in Munich as most other writers: "*Munich borrows from all cities; one is uncertain if one dwells in the south or the north; at least I was filled with a sense of restlessness, a desire to depart.*"

For many, the mountains and the lake district outshine Munich's glamour, but one may wonder: are the barren rocks and the blue-green billows truly more desirable than Munich's contorted walls and cobbled alleys?

Munich divides opinion as sharply as a swirled walrus moustache twists from starboard to port side. Gottfried Keller described the town as "*a dissolute city ... an immoral dump ... filled with fanaticism, rudeness, calves drivers, holy images, dumplings and radish-hags.*"

The writer Paul Heyse grumbled: "*In Munich, I found ... society to be very unliterary*", and Frank Wedekind complained: "*The Munichers are probably as naive as nowhere in Germany.*"

◄ The Münchner Kindl symbolises the soul of the city.

▲ A knight watches over Munich from the Neue Rathaus.

The daring who surrender their heart to Bavaria's pharynx-mane will enthuse, however; they will feel romantically forsaken, helplessly lost, while sucking milk from Bavaria's motherly wart, joyously burping and wildly flatulating.

A Belgian nobleman idolised the city during the 15th century: *"The prettiest little town I ever saw."* In 1493, Hartmann Schedel wrote: *"Munich exceeds all other cities by the splendour of its public and private buildings."* During the 18th century, Graf Shcherbatov glided through town dressed like a Bavarian angel: *"Everything I observe seems like a dream."* Poets described Munich as *"manna"* and *"a golden saddle on a lean horse."* Yes, *"Munich's sky is painted in blue silk"*, and the keen observer may add: *"Everything has three perspectives in Munich: a positive, a negative and a comical one."*

Munich lies at the feet of the alpine upland. Once, it was a vibrant trading hub. Geographically, the terminal moraine of Upper Bavaria and the hilly countryside of Lower Bavaria squeeze the city in the middle. Munich's climate is haunted by continental heat waves from Russia; at times, snowmen from Scandinavia invade the lands, and falling winds from Italy crush the spirit. Grey and icy winters alternate with hot and humid summers.

Agriculture minted Bavaria's soul; the blades swing to brass bands; the future is rooted in tradition. At the Isar, travellers refilled their stock before Alpine crossings, and in Munich, the long-distance traders from Italy prospered. Trade enriched the city, but the salty gold only powdered a thin social layer - the patricians.

▲ Opposite the Pinakothek, the statue *Present Continuous* surprises with its design.

"I want to shape Munich into a city that will be to the honour of Germany; none may claim to know Germany if he had not visited Munich!" - These were the words of King Ludwig I, the mastermind of the Maxvorstadt! His success proved all critics wrong and justified his ambition. His classicistic monuments at the Königsplatz have left a mark of antiquity on the city, but he could not convert the *beer-bellies* into Greek heroes, however much he tried; once the starry-eyed idealist had preached the Munichers his romantic vision, he had to step down.

The art of the Italian city-states sold well in northern countries, and Bavaria's humanistically educated dukes fashioned the Renaissance. The Baroque crossed the Alps with ease, too, and sprinkled its charm on Munich's bubbly streets and voluptuous churches.

During the Age of Absolutism, Munich submitted to the courtly ideal of France; the electors commissioned Schloss Nymphenburg and Schloss Schleißheim at the outskirts, copying the style of Versailles. During the 19th century, King Maximilian II staggered into the Victorian design, but the critics refused to applaud.

Bottom line! Munich is north and south and both and neither. Munich is artistic, irrational and superstitious; Munich is innovative and rooted in tradition; Munich is a golden saddle and a starving horse; alpine air and frowsty pestilence; blue skies and a pall of smog; cosmopolitan and secluded. Munich is a personification of the *Goddess of Contrast*, a contradiction that requires no resolution! And this is why globetrotters of all nations admire the alpine people so much.

Munich's History

Early Days

When Herzog Heinrich der Löwe (Henry the Lion) founded Munich in the 12th century, the river Isar branched into numerous tributaries along its way. The plains in the south and north, near the Flaucher and close to the university campus in Garching, retain some of the characteristics of the olden days. Every so often, the river bursts its banks and floods the region. Richly wooded and moist, the area offered good hunting and fishing grounds. The water from the Alps was safe to drink, and lush vegetation provided balanced nourishment.

In 2014, during repair work on the sewer system in the Apothekenhof of the Münchner Residenz, workers found the oldest burial site in Munich: the woman was around 50 years old and lived during the late Bronze Age (around 1200 BC). The grave was largely intact - what a surprise! In addition to bone fragments, the archaeologists found grave goods such as dishes and storage containers, pins, a knife and a ferrule made of bronze.

The history of the region dates back even further: the area was already sparsely populated during the Neolithic period. The first people in the region belonged to the Oberlauterbach group. They settled on loessial soils along rivers such as the Donau (Danube) or the Isar. Their pile dwellings were made of wood and covered with clay - straw was used as the roof for their houses.

Celts and Romans

The Celts settled in Bavaria early. The best-known community in the region lived at the Oppidum Manching north of Munich near Ingolstadt. The fortified stronghold was founded around 300 BC and inhabited for about 250 years. Then, the community left for unknown reasons. Between 5,000 and 10,000 people lived there. The town was probably the capital of the Vindelics and a hub for metallurgy and art, as evidenced by the well-known cult tree. The remains of Celtic square enclosures can be found in Oberhaching and Erding. Furthermore, archaeologists discovered burial mounds in Leutstetten near Starnberg and in Pfaffenhofen.

When the Romans crossed the Alps in 15 BC, the area around Munich was sparsely populated, and the Romans incorporated the region into the province of Raetia. Under Emperor Trajan (98–117 AD), Augusta Vindelicum (Augsburg) became the administrative and military centre. The Upper Germanic-Raetian Limes ran through Bavaria. Fortified cities emerged along the wall, such as Regensburg.

When the Alemanni invaded in the 3rd century, the Romans withdrew. With Odoacer's victory over Emperor Romulus Augustulus in 476, his realm dissolved, and in 488 AD, the last Roman soldier left the region north of the Alps.

◄ **Herzog Heinrich der Löwe founded Munich in the 12th century.**

▲ At the Mariensäule, putti are victorious over disbelief, plague and hunger.

Middle Ages

After the fall of the Roman empire, city-like structures survived only in monastic environments like in Freising. Saint Corbinian from the Order of Benedictines established a monastery there in 739. The founding of new cities remained uncommon until the 12th century. Only when new techniques such as the three-field system improved the agricultural yield could the population grow, and cities emerged. Munich was among them. Herzog Heinrich der Löwe founded the city in 1158. The Talburgtor at the Alte Rathaus (Old Town Hall) bears witness to these beginnings.

Legend has it that in 1156, Heinrich burned down the customs bridge in Föhring, run by Freising's bishops. This gave him control over the salt trade, which he redirected to the ford at today's Gasteig. The trade route passed through Munich and became the basis for its prosperity. The enclosure was established at a chapel, today the Church of St Peter at Marienplatz. Monks from Schäftlarn serviced the parish.

The success of a city in the Middle Ages depended on two criteria, both of which Munich fulfilled. On the one hand, significant wealth could only be generated through long-distance trade, which was dangerous and thus expensive. Cities along a long-distance trade route benefited, and Munich was an ideal stopover before and after crossing the Alps.

On the other hand, a city only survived if the region generated a sufficient agricultural surplus. The farmers provided the towns with flour, milk, eggs and everything else.

Munich owes its early success to salt - the white gold of the Alps. What's more, the city developed into a hub for Italian traders.

Munich could rely on an area stretching from the Danube to South Tyrol for the supply of basic foods. Along the Isar, the traders were connected to Venice via Mittenwald, Innsbruck, and Verona. The raftsmen transported wood, beer, wine, grain, and cloth. They were the engine of growth.

The patricians specialised in salt and long-distance trade. Their income enabled the dukes' financial means to govern the country. In return, the traders dominated the Inner Council and the city administration.

After the country's first partition, Herzog Ludwig II chose Munich as his residence in 1255. He settled at the Alter Hof, northeast of the Marienplatz (market square). Herzog Ludwig der Kelheimer had laid the founding stone of the complex in the 12th century.

The guilds also had a say in the city's affairs. Peasants and day labourers were at the bottom of the social hierarchy. Although agriculture was crucial to the city's survival, the geographical fragmentation of the farmers between the Alps and the Danube made it difficult for them to organise into a meaningful political power or revolt.

This social structure (dukes, clergy, patricians, guilds, farmers and day labourers) defined the hierarchy for centuries and determined the fate of Munich during the Middle Ages and beyond.

Reformation

At the beginning of the 16th century, Europe disputed the interpretation of Christian doctrine. The Church had become entangled in a web of contradictions, and dogmatic pressure made matters worse. The understanding of Christian symbolism was at a dead end. The ideas of the Enlightenment, which spread quickly after the invention of printing, were openly discussed on the streets - even in catholic Bavaria. The discovery of the New World by Christopher Columbus enlarged the map of the world, and astronomers like Johannes Kepler and Galileo Galilei expelled the Earth from the centre of the universe.

In 1517, Martin Luther sparked a division within the Church with his 95 Theses. The hierarchy began to grumble over the question of the correct way of living a godly life. The stalemate forced the secular power to take responsibility. In the Peace of Augsburg in 1555, the emperor transferred religious and political responsibility to the sovereigns. In the same year, Herzog Albrecht V banned Protestantism in Bavaria. A year later, he invited the Jesuits to Munich: The order of the Spaniard Ignatius Loyola was to tie Bavaria to Catholicism - forever.

His profoundly religious successor, Herzog Wilhelm V, commissioned the construction of the Jesuit Church of St Michael. He banned the game of dice, punished swearing and shut down the house of the "beautiful daughters". Starting from 1590, anyone accused of witchcraft was burned at the stake. Estimates suggest more than 9,000 died in Bavaria.

Kurfürst Maximilian I turned the country into a fortress of the Virgin Mary. The facade of every house had to be guarded with her statue. Some preserved between the Hofbräuhaus and Isartor. He also forced his court to observe daily devotions; every citizen had to pray the rosary in the morning and evening.

In 1616, the Elector attached the Patrona Bavaria to the west facade of the residence. He submitted to the Virgin Mary, signed the covenant with his blood, and kept his will at the altar of the Black Madonna in Altötting.

In 1609, Kurfürst Maximilian I founded the Catholic League. After the Prague Defenestration, the religious dispute escalated into the Thirty Years' War. The Catholics emerged victorious in the Battle of White Mountain in 1620, then the tide turned against them. Only heartfelt prayers to the Virgin Mary prevented the Swedish King Gustav II Adolf from sacking Munich in 1632. As a thank you, the Elector erected a Mariensäule (Marian column) in the centre of the Marienplatz.

In 1648, the Peace of Westphalia confirmed the previous Peace of Augsburg - nothing was gained either way, and the millions sacrificed were in vain. Bavaria remained Catholic, and Protestants were banned from the country. It was not until 150 years later that followers of the faith of Martin Luther settled in Munich again.

Absolutism

The Thirty Years' War left deep wounds in Bavaria. Under Kurfürst Ferdinand Maria, the country recovered before Europe plunged yet again into a conflict - the war of succession.

Henriette Adelaide von Savoyen, the Elector's wife, brought back joy to Bavaria. Her Italian temperament rekindled Bavaria's spirit. When she gave birth to a successor, she expressed her gratitude by commissioning the construction of a church in Baroque style on the Odeonsplatz: the Theatinerkirche. A new era had begun. The Jesuits had lost their power.

Kurfürst Max Emanuel aspired to become king or emperor. The sacrifices he imposed on the country to achieve his goal were immense. During the Turkish Wars, the soil turned red. The Elector expanded the Münchner Residenz, restructured Schloss Nymphenburg and commissioned Schloss Schleißheim. The court increasingly determined the rhythm of life in Munich. However, any Royal dignity slipped through Max Emanuel's fingers. It was only Kurfürst Karl Albrecht who was crowned emperor in Frankfurt in 1742. The glory was short-lived. Two days later, the Austrians invaded Bavaria and occupied the country. Karl Albrecht had to flee. When he returned to Munich, he died a few months later. Meanwhile, the Asam brothers built a private chapel at the Sendlinger Tor. It is unsurpassed to this day. Historians consider it the most brilliant jewel of the Rococo.

▲ **Kurfürst Maximilian I leads the Catholic League at the Wittelsbacherplatz.**

Kurfürst Max III Joseph accepted Bavaria's military and political limitations. He was like a father to the country; the people loved and admired him. The Elector dedicated himself to rebuilding the country. When he passed away without heirs, a war of succession threatened Bavaria's integrity, but Europe's nobility was tired of war and reestablished a treaty struck in the Middle Ages. After the Bavarian Wittelsbacher dynasty had ended, the Palatinate line took over. Kurfürst Karl Theodor ascended to become the new Elector, although he only reluctantly moved from Mannheim to Munich. Throughout his life, he could not befriend stubborn Bavaria. His dislike of Munich, the Bavarians reciprocated with equal hatred.

When the French Revolution broke out in 1789, Bavaria was under threat, and Kurfürst Karl Theodor had to take action. He followed the advice of Graf Rumford and opened the Englischer Garten to the public, reformed the army, and provided for the poor. His formula was simple: voluntary concessions before the people would rise. The Elector was never popular. When he fell ill in 1798, the country prayed that he would not recover. When he passed away, the people rejoiced.

Once again, the Palatinate line of the Wittelsbacher dynasty had to step in since Kurfürst Karl Theodor had no heirs either. Under Kurfürst Max IV Joseph, Europe fulfilled Bavaria's long-cherished dream: In 1806 during the turmoil of the Coalition Wars, Napoleon embellished Bavaria's proud head with a golden crown.

▲ The Prunkhof at the Neue Rathaus is adorned with Munich's coat of arms.

Kingdom of Bavaria

In Bavaria, the age of absolutism survived into the 19th century. The country sided with France, and Napoleon won the Battle of Austerlitz, probably because a 30,000-strong Bavarian army prevented the Austrians from participating in the bloodbath.

In the Peace of Pressburg, Napoleon granted Bavaria royal dignities. However, the price was high: 30,000 Bavarian soldiers lost their lives during the Russian campaign that followed. The obelisk on the Karolinenplatz commemorates the fallen.

Bavaria changed sides and fought against France in the Battle of Leipzig in 1813. The conflict caused destruction in Europe for two more years. At last, the nations exiled Napoleon in 1815. The Congress of Vienna confirmed Bavaria's royal status, and the country enjoyed territorial gains. Peace had finally returned to Munich and would last until the Franco-Prussian War of 1870/71.

Bavaria was in dire need of reform. The father of the modern state, Maximilian Graf von Montgelas, first minister under King Maximilian I, modernised the state with a sharp mind: he reformed the judiciary system, introduced a Bavarian constitution, and established performance-related pay for civil servants. Montgelas pushed through secularisation and successfully fought corruption. His authority rehabilitated the country.

At this time, the Maxvorstadt north of the old town was designed,

▲ On the eastern bank of the Isar, the Friedensengel rises at the Prinzregentenstraße.

and construction began. Munich grew rapidly. Immigration from all over Bavaria turned the city into a metropolis.

King Ludwig I dedicated himself to structuring and organising the kingdom. He placed regional councils under central administration and invested heavily in the arts. Hardly any other ruler combined necessity with personal inclination so much. The patron of culture was not at home on the battlefields but in Europe's art collections. He visited Italy around 70 times, spent a year in Paris and frequently travelled to France.

The celebrations for his wedding with Therese Charlotte Luise, Princess von Saxony-Hildburghausen, laid the foundation for the Oktoberfest. When the Munichers forced him to step down in 1848, he had accomplished the Maxvorstadt, relocated the university to Munich, and established several museums such as the Glyptothek, the Antikensammlung, the Alte and Neue Pinakothek. He had built the Ludwigskirche, the Allerheiligen Hofkirche and the Church of St Boniface. He had completed the Ludwigstraße and the Königsplatz, expanded the Münchner Residenz with a royal wing, and he had built the Walhalla near Regensburg and the Bavaria at the Ruhmeshalle. Munich still bears the signature of King Ludwig I. None of his successors added much, not even King Maximilian II. His Maximilian style at the Maximilianstraße is often ridiculed by art historians.

King Ludwig II and Prince Regent Luitpold only added final touches

▲ The Pferdebändiger at the Alte Pinakothek is bleeding from his bullet wounds.

to Munich. The time for large-scale royal construction projects had come to an end. At long last, the Wittelsbacher dynasty transferred their treasures to the Bayerische Nationalmuseum and handed over the keys to the city fathers, who ushered in a civic era with the construction of the Neue Rathaus (New Town Hall). New churches emerged in the outskirts. They were mostly financed by bourgeois entrepreneurs. Among them are St Paul and St Maximilian. The financiers had become prosperous in the wake of the Industrial Revolution and now set the tone.

World War I finally put an end to the Wittelsbacher dynasty. In 1918, a few days before the end of the war, the Munichers forced King Ludwig III to step down.

World War I and World War II

In 1914, the Munichers celebrated the outbreak of World War I. Only two years later, their enthusiasm had faded: heroes were piling up in the trenches, cemeteries were at capacity, and hunger gnawed at the morale. The people were increasingly demanding an end to the fighting. Absolutism had run out of time. The writings of the philosopher Karl Marx incited Europe. Pacifists disseminated the slogan *"solidarity among workers."*

Kurt Eisner led a powerful demonstration at the Theresienwiese on November 7, 1918. On this day, Munich discharged King Ludwig III; the people proclaimed the Freistaat Bayern (Free State of Bavaria). The king had run out of options; he fled - even his immediate guards sympathised with the revolutionaries.

A workers' and soldiers' council appointed Kurt Eisner as Bavaria's first Prime Minister. The end of the monarchy was reached. After 800 years of Wittelsbacher dynasty, the country was experimenting with a new form of government.

After World War I, Bavaria collapsed. Radicals from all sides became increasingly more violent. Then, an assassin murdered Kurt Eisner on the way to parliament. Munich succumbed to lynching. Desperation had formed the breeding ground for gunmen from left and right.

Adolf Hitler founded the NSDAP at the Hofbräuhaus in Munich a year later. On November 8, 1923, his Kampfbund (a form of storm troopers) charged into the Bürgerbräukeller and deposed Prime Minister Gustav von Kahr during a political rally. The Bavarian state police intervened, stopped the march to the Feldherrnhalle the following day, and arrested Adolf Hitler. He was sent to prison in Landsberg am Lech.

During the Golden Twenties, Munich was swinging. The global economic crisis following the New York stock market crash 1929 drove the desperate back into the arms of the radicals. In 1933, the people elected Adolf Hitler as Chancellor, and the world plunged into turmoil. Within months, the country turned into a military dictatorship. After the burning of the Reichstag, the Nazi regime abolished the Weimar Constitution, and Adolf Hitler ruled with absolute power.

Militarisation of the country followed, aryanisation, imprisonment of political opponents, persecution of Jews, territorial expansion and much more. In 1938, the Nazis called for the Kristallnacht from the Munich town hall. The people hunted Jews like wolves go after lambs. In the same year, during the Munich Conference, the Allies gave in on the Sudeten crisis. World War II broke out a year later nevertheless, on September 1, 1939. By then, the war had become unavoidable.

Around 1933, the seat of power shifted from Bavaria to Berlin. Adolf Hitler named Munich the *Capital of the NS Movement*. The Maxvorstadt turned into a centre of power, and at the Königsplatz, a temple of honour paid tribute to those killed in the failed coup attempt in 1923.

Architecturally, Adolf Hitler had grandiose plans for Munich. The Haus der Kunst served as a model for the new design. Apartment blocks were to be built along the arterial roads. In the west, the Nazi regime planned a boulevard and a temple to the movement. Luckily, the projects were never executed.

When the troops of the 7th US Army entered Munich on April 30, 1945, the city was so shaken after 70 Allied air raids that all resistance was broken. The Munichers were relieved - the nightmare was over. About half of the city was in ruins - the Maxvorstadt was up to 80% destroyed. Munich coughed up blood and pus. The citizens were looking for a piece of scruffy bread to survive another day.

Present Times

The day after: What had happened? Memories - all just a dream? Look ... look! Munich is a pile of rubble! Reality stabbed illusion. Since the entry of the 7th US Army on April 30, 1945, Bavaria has been under American occupation.

Who explains the unfathomable? What began in the Hofbräuhaus with right-wing slogans ended 25 years later ... who can describe it? The next day, the Americans initiated a program to denazify Bavaria. In doing so, they gave the starting signal for coming to terms with the past. However, the extent to which people had participated in Nazi crimes was so shocking that the project came to nothing. The existential distress of the post-war years was repressed - too big had the evil been for the ego to comprehend - *The Inability to Mourn*. The European economic miracle turned the attention to the future, and with the post-war generation, the immediate connection to World War II was lost. An eternal fire flickers at the site dedicated to the victims of National Socialism, documentation centres commemorate the tears of the innocent, the memorial at the Dachau concentration camp keeps the memory alive, but ... may one ask? ... is it enough?

After World War II, the Allies occupied Germany. The country's influence in foreign policy had faded, and so the population focused on reconstruction.

After World War II, Munich was a heap of rubble - a heap of rubble! It had two options: resignation or reconstruction. "*Rama Dama*" was the slogan. The people cleared the broken glass from the streets with shovels and pickaxes; the Americans provided the trucks. Step by step, the Munichers reconstructed their city with discipline and perseverance - heads down, move arms, don't think. They recovered what could be recovered. Stone by stone, the Munich of the past resurfaced from the ashes.

In 1972, Munich sprinted through the turning loop and invited the world to the Games of the XX Summer Olympiad. After 25 years, the reconstruction was completed. The city fathers converted the Neuhauser Straße into a pedestrian zone and expanded the public transport system. Since 2005, the football club FC Bayern München has been competing in the Allianz Arena, and suburbs curb the housing shortage. The airport moved to the Erdinger Moos, and a new exhibition centre attracts the world to Munich. In Harlaching, environmentalists enforced the naturalisation of the Isar, and the Gasteig Cultural Centre opened in Haidhausen.

At the turn of the millennium, the Munichers ask what the future may hold. Everyone is facing the same challenges: ageing of the population, globalisation, climate change, green energy, social integration, immigration, refugees, combating pandemics, and wars such as in Ukraine or in Gaza - a heavy burden rests on the shoulders of the Munichers - on all peoples around the world.

The Hubertusbrunnen is the endpoint of the Nymphenburger Kanal. ▶

Chronicles of Munich

2000 BC — Archaeological finds hint at the first inhabitants in the region

1250 BC — A grave at the Apothekenhof testifies settlers during the Bronze Age

~300 BC — **Celts establish the Oppidum Manching**
About 60 kilometres north of Munich, the Celts settle and stay until ~50 BC.

25 BC — **The foothills of the Alps become part of the Roman Empire (Raetia)**
In 476, Odoacer overcomes the last Roman emperor, Romulus Augustulus. Shortly after, the Province Raetia collapses.

~500 BC — Alemanni advance into the area north of the Alps

551 — The Bavarian people are mentioned for the first time

750 — **First evidence of today's suburbs of Munich**
Oberföhring (750), Pasing (763), Bogenhausen (768), Schwabing (782)

813 — **A donation attests to the monastery in Freising**
A duke from the Agilolfinger dynasty founds the settlement around 700 AD.

903 — **Bishop Waldo of Freising acquires the market square in Föhring**
The salt trade between Salzburg and Augsburg is flourishing. The income from the bridge toll finances the construction of Freising Cathedral.

1158 — **Augsburger Schied: The contract mentions Munich (by the monks) for the first time**
Emperor Friedrich I Barbarossa confirms Herzog Heinrich der Löwe: the market is moved from Föhring to Munich.

1175 — **The inner city wall is constructed (Heinrichsstadt)**
The city extends from the Talburgtor at the Marienplatz to the Augustinergasse, and from the Marienhof north of the town hall to the Rindermarkt in the south.

1180 — **Emperor Friedrich I Barbarossa accuses Herzog Heinrich der Löwe to be a traitor and deprives him of his privileges**
The Duchy of Bavaria falls to the Bavarian count Herzog Otto I. Munich is governed by the Bishops of Freising.

1225 — The Church of St Peter is mentioned for the first time

1208 — **The Heilig-Geist-Spital is founded east of the city wall**
Herzog Ludwig I expands the city to the Isartor.

1210 — A synagogue is built on Judengasse

1214 — Munich is granted city rights

Chronicles of Munich

1221	Fire devastates Munich
1239	Oldest city seal The city seal shows a monk - the origin of the Münchner Kindl.
1240	Munich passes to the Wittelsbacher dynasty
1255	First partition of Bavaria: Munich becomes residence city
1271	The Marienkirche (Frauenkirche) becomes the second parish
1280	King Rudolf von Hapsburg grants Munich trading privileges
1284	The Order of Franciscans settles in Munich
1285-1337	Construction of a second city wall
1285	67 Jews are murdered during a pogrom
1286	A city council is established
1293	First mention of the leper house St Nikolai at the Gasteig
1294	Rudolfinische Handfeste: Rights and Duties of Citizens The city is granted the right to lower jurisdiction.
1294	The Order of Augustinians settles at the gates of the city
1310	First mention of the Alte Rathaus and the Jakobidult
1313	Herzog Ludwig IV triumphs over Friedrich den Schönen Later, he is proclaimed Emperor Ludwig der Bayer.
1317	An Inner Council and an Outer Council are documented Patricians: Ligsalz, Sendlinger, Schrenck, Ridler, Hundertpfundt
1332	Golden Bull: Munich is granted the staple right for salt Salt must cross the Isar near Munich and be traded in the city.
1340	End of partition: The Lower Bavarian line of dukes ends
1342	Building Regulations: All houses must be built of stone
1385	The Neuveste is built as a refuge for the dukes (seed of the Münchner Residenz)
1349	Outbreak of the Black Death in Munich

Chronicles of Munich

1397-1403	A rise of the guilds reorganises the balance of power
1429	The Hussite War threatens Munich
1435	Schloss Blutenburg is built under Herzog Albrecht III
1442	Herzog Albrecht III banishes the Jews from the city
They return to Munich 350 years later.
1468-1488	The master builder Jörg von Halspach constructs the Frauenkirche
1493	First painting of Munich in the Schedelsche Weltchronik
1500	Munich has 13,500 inhabitants
Köln 45 000, Nürnberg 38 000, Augsburg 30 000, Danzig 30 000, Wien 20 000
1504	Siege of Munich during the Landshut War of Succession
1506	Herzog Albrecht I issues the primogeniture law
1516	Bayerisches Reinheitsgebot (Purity Law): The Munich city ordinance of 1453 is expanded to the entire country
Beer may only be brewed from barley, hops and water.
1520	The Zeughaus (armoury) is built, today the Stadtmuseum
1522	First decrees against Protestants
1527	Members of the Anabaptists are executed
1525	The Weinstadl is built (the oldest surviving town house in Munich)
1530	Emperor Karl V visits Munich
1555	After the Peace of Augsburg, Munich becomes under Herzog Albrecht V the driving force behind the Counter Reformation
1556	The composer Orlando di Lasso arrives in Munich
1559	The Order of Jesuits is called to Munich
1560	Expansion of the Neuveste into the Münchner Residenz
1568	Herzog Wilhelm V marries Renata of Lorraine
The Glockenspiel (carillon) at the Neue Rathaus depicts the elaborate wedding.
1570-1571	Construction of the Antiquarium at the Münchner Residenz

Chronicles of Munich

1583-1597 The Jesuit Church of St Michael and the Alte Akademie are built
The Renaissance arrives in Munich.

1589 Herzog Wilhelm V founds the Hofbräuhaus

1598 Kurfürst Maximilian I takes over the reign in Bavaria
Maximilian I redevelops Bavaria; he builds the Kaiserhof at the Münchner Residenz.

1609 The Catholic League is founded in Munich

1620 With the support of Bavaria, Hapsburg defeats Bohemia in the Battle of White Mountain (Prague)

1623 Bavaria is granted the title Elector
Palatinate had fallen into disgrace because of its Bohemian adventure.

1632 The Swedish King Gustav II Adolf occupies Munich without a fight
The besiegers demand payment of 300,000 Reichstaler.

1634 The Black Death breaks out in Munich
Italian troops under a Spanish banner introduce the disease.

1638 The Mariensäule at the Marienplatz is inaugurated

1648 The Peace of Westphalia confirms Bavaria's electorate status
The era of the absolutism is dawning.

1650 Kurfürst Ferdinand Maria marries Henriette Adelaide von Savoyen
The Italian Baroque arrives in Munich.

1657 Munich's first opera house opens (Salvatortheater)

1663-1675 Construction of the Theatinerkirche at the Odeonsplatz
The Order of Jesuits is disempowered; the Order of Theatines replaces them.

1664 Kurfürst Ferdinand Maria commissions an Italian country villa
The complex is later expanded into Schloss Nymphenburg.

1683 Kurfürst Max Emanuel triumphs over the Turks
The Elector marries Maria Antonia, the daughter of Emperor Leopold I, in 1685. Schloss Lustheim is built.

1701 Construction of Schloss Schleißheim begins

1705-1714 Austria occupies Munich during the War of the Spanish Succession
Max Emanuel flees to France.

Chronicles of Munich

1715	**Kurfürst Max Emanuel returns to Munich** Expansion of Schloss Nymphenburg and Schloss Schleißheim.
1733	**First lighting of the city with oil lamps**
1733-1746	**Construction of the Asamkirche by the Asam brothers**
1742-1743	**Kurfürst Karl Albrecht becomes Emperor of the Holy Roman Empire**
1742-1744	**Austria occupies Munich several times during the War of the Austrian Succession**
1747	**Founding of the Nymphenburger Porzellanmanufaktur**
1750	**Munich becomes the largest city in southern Germany** The city overtakes Nürnberg and catches up with Augsburg.
1753	**Completion of the Cuvilliés Theater at the Münchner Residenz**
1759	**Founding of the Akademie der Wissenschaften**
1775	**The first café opens in Munich at the Hofgarten (Tambosi)**
1777	**With the death of Kurfürst Max III Joseph, the Bavarian line of the Wittelsbacher dynasty ends** Kurfürst Karl Theodor from the Palatinate line takes over the regency. He moves his court from Mannheim to Munich.
1780	**The Hofgarten is opened to the public** Graf Rumford reforms the state and modernises the army. The Englischer Garten is opened to the public.
1791	**Kurfürst Karl Theodor has the city wall demolished**
1795	**Alois Senefelder invents lithography in Munich**
1799-1817	**Graf von Montgelas becomes Prime Minister and reforms Bavaria** A civil code and a criminal code are initiated.
1800	**French troops occupy Munich**
1801	**The wine merchant Johann B. Michel is the first Protestant Citizen of Munich since the 16th century**
1803	**Secularisation: Monasteries and churches are dissolved; the property of the Church passes over to the state**

Chronicles of Munich

1803	The Reichsdeputationshauptschluss incorporates Franconia and Schwabia into Bavaria
1805	Bogenhausen Treaty: Bavaria concludes a secret treaty with Napoleon
1805-1810	Design of the Maxvorstadt under Karl von Fischer and Friedrich Ludwig von Sckell
1806	Bavaria becomes a kingdom
1807	The Heilig-Geist-Spital is closed The market moves from the Marienplatz to the Viktualienmarkt.
1810	Wedding of Crown Prince Ludwig I to Princess Therese von Saxony-Hildburghausen The Oktoberfest develops from a horse race organised in honour of the wedding.
1811-1818	Construction of the Nationaltheater
1813	Flood disaster: More than 100 citizens die
1817	The Archdiocese of Munich & Freising comes into being The Archdiocese in Freising is dissolved. Freising loses it power.
1819	The first Bavarian state parliament is constituted
1825-1848	King Ludwig I rules over Bavaria Munich is turning into an art metropolis. The museum district in the Maxvorstadt, the Ludwigstraße and the universities are created.
1826	The Ludwig-Maximilians-Universität moves to Munich
1830	Inauguration of the Glyptothek
1835	Germany's first railway line between Nürnberg and Fürth opens
1841-1844	The Feldherrnhalle on Ludwigstraße is designed by von Gärtner
1844	Munich beer revolution during the Vormärz
1846	Lola Montez appears as a dancer in Munich The affair forces King Ludwig I to abdicate.
1848	The Münchner Neueste Nachrichten are published

Chronicles of Munich

1848	King Ludwig I abdicates in favour of his son Maximilian II
1850	The city has more than 100,000 inhabitants
1848-1864	The Maximilianstraße is created
1854	1. Allgemeine Deutsche Industrieausstellung in Munich
1855	Founding of the Bayerische Nationalmuseum
1857	The Weißwurst (white sausage) is invented in Munich
1857-1874	The Maximilianeum is built in the Maximilian style
1864	Richard Wagner stays in Munich under King Ludwig II
1864	Richard Strauss is born in Munich
1865	The Gärtnerplatztheater opens
1865	Max von Pettenkofer becomes director of the Institute for Hygiene A pipe from the Mangfalltal guarantees Munich's water supply.
1867-1909	Construction of the Neuen Rathaus at the Marienplatz
1868	King Ludwig II founds the Technische Universität
1871	Bavaria joins the German Reich
1876	The first tram rattles through Munich
1879	Construction of the Armeemuseum (today Bayerische Staatskanzlei)
1880	Tenement houses (Wilhelminian era) built in the Isarvorstadt
1880	The Münchner Rückversicherungs-Gesellschaft is founded
1886	King Ludwig II drowns in the lake Starnberger See
1886-1912	Munich experiences a golden decade under Prince Regent Luitpold
1892	Münchner Secession separates from the artists' cooperative
1890-1901	Construction of the Prinzregentenstraße
1896	The Munich magazine "Die Jugend" gives its name to the Art Nouveau

Chronicles of Munich

1896	The Deutsche Theater opens on Schwanthalerstraße
1900	Gabriel von Seidl designs the Künstlerhaus
1900	500,000 residents live in Munich
1900	The club FC Bayern München is founded
1901	Opening of the Prinzregententheater
1901	The Müllersche Volksbad is the largest swimming arena in the world
1903	Oskar von Miller founds the Deutsche Museum
1906	The Münchner Kammerspiele and the Volkshochschule (adult education centre) are brought to life
1907	Peter Ostermayr launches the Geiselgasteig
1911	Inauguration of the Tierpark Hellabrunn
1911	The artists' association Der Blaue Reiter is founded in Munich
1913	Die Rapp Motorenwerke AG is founded in Munich They later became the Bayerische Motorenwerke (BMW).
1914	Opening of the Botanischer Garten at Schloss Nymphenburg
1914	The Munichers celebrate the outbreak of World War I Munich is the southern hub of mobilisation.
1914-1918	Munich suffers from the impact of the war The arms industry moves to Munich. The population is starving and freezing.
1918	The Munichers protest against hunger There are demonstrations and strikes by workers.
1918	The Spanish flu breaks out in Munich
1918	November Revolution Kurt Eisner proclaims the Free State of Bavaria. King Ludwig III is dismissed.
1919	Anton Graf von Arco murders Kurt Eisner
1919	The airport at the Oberwiesenfeld begins operating
1920s	Workers, employees and pensioners suffer from hyperinflation

Chronicles of Munich

1923	**Hitler Putsch in the Bürgerbräukeller (November 8th/9th)** The coup is suppressed by the Bavarian Police at the Feldherrnhalle.
1929	**Premiere of Bertolt Brecht's Threepenny Opera**
1929	**Global economic crisis: 70,000 unemployed starve in Munich**
1930	**The NSDAP headquarter moves into the Braune Haus**
1931	**A fire destroys the Münchner Glaspalast**
1933	**Reichstag election: NSDAP wins 37% of the vote in Munich** Heinrich Himmler is promoted to police chief of Munich.
1933	**The Dachau concentration camp turns operational on March 22nd**
1933	**Books are burning at the Königsplatz**
1934	**Night of the Long Knives: Adolf Hitler has Schleicher, Röhm and Strasser assassinated**
1934	**Construction of the motorway to Salzburg**
1935-1945	**Adolf Hitler titles Munich "Hauptstadt der Bewegung"**
1937	**Aryanization of German companies**
1938	**Munich Agreement (30. September)** The construct of Czechoslovakia is sacrificed. The Allies want to avoid war at all costs.
1938	**Kristallnacht (November 9th to 10th)** The massacre is started from Munich's Alte Rathaus.
1939	**Munich-Riem Airport opens**
1939	**September 1st: outbreak of World War II**
1939	**Assassination attempt on Adolf Hitler in the Bürgerbräukeller fails** Georg Elser's assassination attempt on Adolf Hitler (November 8th) fails.
1941	**Mass deportation of Jews** Jewish camps are set up in Berg am Laim and Milbertshofen.
1943	**The resistance group Die Weiße Rose is crushed**
1944	**Heavy Allied air raids on Munich**

Chronicles of Munich

1945	**The 7th US Army occupies Munich (April 30, 1945)** General Eisenhower calls Munich the "cradle of the Nazi beast."
1946	**Referendum on the Bavarian constitution**
1948-1960	**Thomas Wimmer becomes mayor of Munich** Reconstruction of the city, currency reform, economic boom.
1956	**Founding of the Münchner Lach- und Schießgesellschaft**
1957	**One million people live in Munich**
1962-1969	**Schwabinger Krawalle (Schwabing riots)** Two people die in Munich.
1968	**Inauguration of the Olympiaturm on the Olympiagelände**
1971	**Opening of Munich's local transport system and pedestrian zone**
1972	**The Games of the XX Summer Olympiads take place in Munich** An attack on Jewish athletes shocks the world.
1974	**World Cup final in Munich**
1980	**The Oktoberfest terror attack claims the lives of 13 people**
1985	**The Gasteig Cultural Centre opens**
1987	**Pope John Paul II beatifies Rupert Mayer SJ**
1992	**Opening of the Franz Josef Strauss Airport**
2000	**Naturalization of the Isar under the slogan "New life for the Isar"**
2002	**Inauguration of the Pinakothek der Moderne**
2005	**FC Bayern München's opening game in the Allianz Arena**
2006	**Inauguration of the main synagogue on Jakobsplatz**
2009	**The Museum Brandhorst opens**
2013	**The Museum Ägyptischer Kunst invites visitors**
2020	**The COVID-19 pandemic paralyses life**
2022	**The War in Ukraine weighs heavily on Munich**

Theme Parks and Adventure Tours

★★ **City Tours:** Munich offers a wide range of city tours that cater to different interests. One may enjoy classic tours, themed sightseeing, evening explorations with a night watchman, and tours designed for families with children. Many museums also offer guided tours of their exhibitions. An overview of the tours is available on the Münchner Stadtportal under "Sehenswürdigkeiten" (https://www.muenchen.de). The program also includes city tours by bike or tram.

★★★ **Music Tours:** The Bavarian Capital is renowned for its musical heritage. The *Munich Music Walks* link famous composers with streets and buildings. (https://musikspaziergang.de)

★ **Bicycle rental:** Radius Tours is an established bicycle rental company in Munich. (https://www.radiustours.com)

★★ **Blade-Nights:** On Mondays, inline skaters race through the city. More information is found at Blade Night Munich. (https://bladenight-muenchen.de)

★★ **Climbing:** The High-East facility in Kirchheim impresses with its professionalism. (https://high-east.de) The Bayerischer Alpenverein organises courses and tours in the Alps. (https://www.alpenverein.de)

★★★ **Swimming and Saunas:** Water lovers are drawn to swimming pools. The attraction of the Cosimabad is waves like those in the Caribbean. The Therme Erding pampers its visitors with a huge sauna area. (https://www.therme-erding.de) The Olympic swimming hall allows jumping from the towers. The Münchner Stadtportal provides an overview. (https://www.muenchen.de/freizeit/schwimmbaeder.html)

★★ **Munich from above:** München Adventures not only offer canyoning and rafting in the Alps but also skydiving, balloon sailing, paragliding and much more. (https://www.muenchen-adventures.com)
A helicopter ride? Turn to helicopter flights. (https://www.hubschrauberflug.de)

★★ **Gondola rides:** In Nymphenburg, the Gondel Nymphenburg offers rides. (https://www.gondel-nymphenburg.de). La Barocca offers culinary gondola rides at Schloss Schleißheim. (https://www.la-gondola-barocca.de)

Theme Parks and Adventure Tours

★★ **Abseiling:** The Olympiapark (Olympic Park) presents its tent-like roof with a special attraction on some days - abseiling from the roof of the Olympiastadium (Olympic Stadium). (https://www.olympiapark.de)

★★★ **Animal worlds:** In the evenings, the Munich Zoological Garden takes its guests through the area using night vision goggles. The Tierpark Hellabrunn also organises children's birthday parties and offers courses for photographers. Hobby painters can expand their technique in drawing courses. (http://www.hellabrunn.de)

★★ **The art of the ring:** The Trau-Dich Circus offers workshops and holiday programs for children. The daring can learn to juggle, walk on stilts or ride a unicycle. (https://zirus-trau-dich.com)

★ **Baking bread:** Every Saturday, the Hofbräuhaus-Kunstmühle shows how Bavaria makes pretzels. (https://www.hofbraeuhaus-kunstmuehle.de).

★★ **The world of tango:** The dance club Lo de Laura seduces with workshops and milongas to the passionate eroticism of Argentine tango (https://www.lodelaura.de). During the summer, when the weather allows, an open-air milonga takes place at the Königsplatz. (https://www.tango-am-koenigsplatz.de)

★★ **Salsa Munich:** Anyone who wants to swing to the rhythm of salsa can enjoy their passion at the Salsa Club München. (https://salsaclub-munich.de)

★★ **Buddhist meditation:** The Buddhistische Zentrum München (Buddhist Centre Munich) offers the opportunity to meditate. Courses and events lead to peace and enlightenment. (https://www.diamantweg-buddhismus.de)

Current Events

Current events can be found in the Stadtportal München and the city magazines.
Munich official website: www.muenchen.de
Event information: www.ganz-muenchen.de
https://prinz.de/muenchen https://www.in-muenchen.de

Travel Points at a Glance

Museums and Castles

★ **Spielzeugmuseum** (→ Travel Point ②)
In the Talburgtor, a collection shows the development of toys over four centuries. One can see dolls, trains, teddies, and barbies.
https://spielzeugmuseummuenchen.de

★ **Museum infopoint** (→ ⑧)
The interesting exhibition in the Alter Hof introduces the history of the Neuveste with audiovisual finesse.
https://www.museen-in-bayern.de/der-infopoint

★★ **Valentinmusäum** (→ ⑪)
The museum pokes fun at the society of the turn-of-the-century.
https://www.valentin-musaeum.de

★ **Bier- & Oktoberfestmuseum** (→ ⑪)
At the Isartor, the museum waters the palate with the tradition of Bavarian beer.
https://www.bier-und-oktoberfestmuseum.de

★★ **Münchner Stadtmuseum** (→ ⑯)
The city presents its history in its former armoury. The curators exhibit weapons, paintings, documents and statues of the Münchner Kindl.
https://www.muenchner-stadtmuseum.de

★★ **Jüdisches Museum** (→ ⑰)
The Jewish Museum shows cultural objects of Jewish life in Munich on three levels: ritual objects, pictures and documents.
https://www.juedisches-museum-muenchen.de

★★ **Jagd- und Fischereimuseum** (→ ㉒)
The Hunting and Fishing Museum presents the flora and fauna of Bavaria. The curators show hunting weapons, ceremonial sleighs and stuffed animals.
https://www.jagd-fischerei-museum.de

Travel Points at a Glance

★ **Bürgersaalkirche** (→ ㉔)
The museum at the Bürgersaalkirche introduces the life of Rupert Mayer SJ, who railed against the Nazi regime during the Third Reich.
https://www.mmkbuergersaal.de

★★ **Theatermuseum** (→ ㊱)
The German Theatre Museum at the Hofgartenarkaden presents the history of the theatre.
http://www.deutschestheatermuseum.de

★★★ **Münchner Residenz** (→ ㊲)
The residence was once the city palace of the Wittelsbacher dynasty. Its area extends over 25,000 square metres. The Residenzmuseum has over 130 furnished rooms. The Schatzkammer (treasury) displays jewels, crowns, sceptres and gold work. The Münzmuseum (Coin Museum) presents coins, and the Cuvilliés Theater is the most beautiful rococo theatre in the world.
https://www.residenz-muenchen.de

★ **Palaeontology** (→ ㊼)
The Bayerische Staatssammlung für Paläontologie presents an outline of Bavaria's prehistoric times. It includes dinosaurs, prehistoric elephants and saber-toothed tigers.
https://bspg.palmuc.org

★★ **NS-Doku'zentrum** (→ ㊽)
The NS-Dokumentationszentrum presents the rise of the Nazi regime in Munich on three levels. Temporary exhibitions delve deeper into specific topics.
https://www.ns-dokuzentrum-muenchen.de

★★ **Archeology** (→ ㊌)
The Archäologische Staatssammlung presents finds from the early history of Bavaria in five sections (Prehistory, Romans, Middle Ages, Mediterranean collection, Numismatics).
http://www.archaeologie-bayern.de

★★ **Völkerkundemuseum** (→ ㊾)
The Völkerkundemuseum Fünf Kontinente (Ethnological Museum) exhibits the art and culture of the peoples of the world. The collection covers Africa, North and South America, Asia, Oceania, and the Orient.
https://www.museum-fuenf-kontinente.de

★★ **Alpine Museum** (→ ㊴)
The Alpenverein introduces the world of the mountains. One can see photos, paintings and the equipment of the first pioneers.
https://www.alpenverein.de

★ **Kartoffelmuseum** (→ ㊽)
The Potato Museum deals with the art to grow potatoes, their cultivation and distribution.
http://kartoffelmuseum.de

★★ **Volkssternwarte** (→ ㊽)
The Munich Public Observatory at the Ostbahnhof introduces the (in)finite expansion of the cosmos. With their 80cm reflecting telescope, the astro-enthusiasts show planets, galaxies and galactic nebulae. A planetarium covers the starry sky, and seminars explain the latest results in astrophysics.
https://sternwarte-muenchen.de

Travel Points at a Glance

★★★ **Deutsches Museum** (→ 82)
The Deutsche Museum takes its visitors into the world of technology. The curators explain historical instruments on 5,000 square metres. Those instruments made the modernity possible. Interactive models invite participation. Along the guideline, many kilometres long, young and old can playfully immerse in the world of the sea and the air, mining and the infinite expanses of space.
https://www.deutsches-museum.de

★ **Sudeten' Museum** (→ 82)
The Sudetendeutsche Museum on Hochstraße sheds light on the culture of German emigrants in today's Czech Republic over 1,100 years - from their immigration in the Middle Ages to their expulsion after World War II.
https://www.sudetendeutsches-museum.de

★ **Feuerwehrmuseum** (→ 87)
The fire brigade museum shows firefighting equipment and uniforms from two centuries.

★★ **Tierpark Hellabrunn** (→ 90)
The Hellabrunn Zoo presents the flora of Europe, Africa, Asia and America on 40 hectares. The zoo has a polarium, a bird aviary, a monkey house and a polar bear slide. It is one of the largest zoos in Europe. Children's birthday parties and nightly adventures complement the program.
https://www.hellabrunn.de

★★ **Bavaria Filmstadt** (→ 91)
The exciting Bavaria Filmstadt in Geiselgasteig presents the history of the company: recording studios, original sets and 4-D cinema. The production of a feature film can be seen up close.
https://www.filmstadt.de

★★ **Burg Grünwald** (→ 92)
In Grünwald Castle, the curators present the history of fortresses in southern Germany: knight's castles, refugee castles, and princely castles.
http://www.archaeologie-bayern.de

★★ **Verkehrszentrum** (→ 96)
The branch museum of the Deutsche Museum shows exhibits from traffic and mobility. One can see bicycles, horse-drawn carriages, vintage cars, buses, cable cars and trams.
https://www.deutsches-museum.de

★★★ **Schloss Nymphenburg** (→ 101)
Schloss Nymphenburg was a summer residence of the Wittelsbacher dynasty. Kurfürst Ferdinand Maria built the central pavilion in 1664. Kurfürst Max Emanuel and his son Kurfürst Karl Albrecht expanded the complex. Friedrich Ludwig von Sckell designed the English landscape garden. Amalienburg, Badenburg and Pagodenburg are the highlights of the extensive landscape garden. During summer, the Nymphenburger Festspiele entice the senses with classical music.
https://www.schloss-nymphenburg.de
https://www.schloss-festspiele.de

Travel Points at a Glance

★★★ **Botanischer Garten** (→ 102)
Covering 22 hectares, the garden introduces the splendour of flowers, bushes and trees. The area ranges from orchids, water lilies, fruit trees to medicinal herbs. The Alpinum shows the flora of the mountains. https://www.botmuc.de

★★★ **Schloss Blutenburg** (→ 103)
The late Gothic Blutenburg was once a hunting lodge for the Wittelsbacher dynasty. The complex was built between 1430 and 1490. Jan Polack's panel paintings come from the heyday of the Bavarian Gothic. Management organises the Blutenburger Konzerte in the castle's ballroom.
https://www.blutenburg.de
https://schlosskonzerte-blutenburg.de

★ **Sea Life** (→ 104)
The complex Sea Life at the Olympiazentrum presents the water world of Bavarian rivers and lakes.
https://www.visitsealife.com/muenchen

★★ **Olympiaturm** (→ 104)
The Olympiaturm at the Olympiapark can be climbed using an elevator.
https://www.olympiapark.de

★ **BMW Museum** (→ 105)
At the Olympic Centre, BMW presents the company's history in a futuristic circular building.
https://www.bmw-welt.com

★★★ **Schloss Dachau** (→ 107)
Dachau Castle was the first summer residence of the Wittelsbacher Dynasty. Herzog Wilhelm IV and Herzog Albrecht V built the complex in the 16th century. The richly decorated ballroom is impressive. The fruit trees in the courtyard like garden tempt to minstrelsy during spring.
https://www.schloesser.bayern.de

Travel Points at a Glance

★★★ Gedenkstätte KZ Dachau (→ ⑩⑧)
The Gedenkstätte KZ Dachau (Dachau Concentration Camp Memorial) commemorates the more than 200,000 innocent people who were imprisoned, tortured and killed at the site by the Nazi regime. The tour passes the places of terror. Seminars make tangible what must never be forgotten.
https://www.kz-gedenkstaette-dachau.de

★★★ Schloss Schleißheim (→ ⑩⑨)
The baroque castle was a summer residence of the Wittelsbacher dynasty. Kurfürst Maximilian I built the rustic Alte Schloss in the late Renaissance style. By 1726, Enrico Zuccalli added the Neue Schloss in the Italian Baroque style. Joseph Effner and François Cuvilliés the Elder expanded the palace in the French Rococo style. Kurfürst Max Emanuel built Schloss Lustheim in the east of the complex in 1684.
https://www.schloesser-schleissheim.de

★★ Flugwerft (→ ⑩⑨)
The branch of the Deutsche Museum exhibits the world of aerospace at the former Flugplatz Schleißheim: helicopters, air planes, engines and a flight simulator.
https://www.deutsches-museum.de

★ FC Bayern Erlebniswelt (→ ⑬)
The masters of German football present the victorious history of the football club FC Bayern München.
https://fcbayern.com/museum

★★★ ESO Supernova (→ ⑬)
At the ESO Supernova visitor centre, the curators introduce the world of the cosmos in a futuristic building: the solar system, stars and galaxies. The latest cosmological models are explained.
https://supernova.eso.org

Travel Points at a Glance

Art Collections

★★ MUCA (→ ⑱)
The Museum of Urban and Contemporary Art in a former substation, a private initiative, presents temporary exhibitions by outstanding artists who transformed street and urban art. The focus of the permanent exhibition is on Bansky.
https://www.muca.eu

★★ Kunsthalle München (→ ㉝)
The Hypo-Kulturstiftung (a cultural foundation) shows two to four top-class temporary exhibitions every year. The topics range from early history to contemporary art and from the Orient to America.
https://www.kunsthalle-muc.de

★ Kunstpavillon (→ ㊷)
The art pavilion at the Alter Botanischer Garten offers local artists an exhibition space for their works.
http://www.kunstpavillon.org

★★★ Glyptothek (→ ㊺)
The Glyptothek is home to outstanding ancient statues, busts and reliefs. The works range from the Greek archaic period to the Roman period.
https://www.antike-am-koenigsplatz.mwn.de

★★ Antikensammlung (→ ㊻)
The collection of antiquities complements the exhibition in the Glyptothek with craftwork from the ancient period.
https://www.antike-am-koenigsplatz.mwn.de

★★★ Lenbachhaus (→ ㊼)
In the pompous villa of Italian style, the curators present paintings from the 19th and 20th centuries, especially Der Blaue Reiter (The Blue Rider): Paul Klee, Franz Marc and Wassily Kandinsky.
https://www.lenbachhaus.de

★ Amerikahaus (→ ㊾)
The Amerikahaus offers temporary exhibitions that introduce the culture of the United States.
https://www.amerikahaus.de

★★ Ägyptische Kunst (→ ㊿)
The exhibition in the Staatliche Museum Ägyptischer Kunst focuses on Egypt from the early times to Christianity. https://smaek.de

★★★ Alte Pinakothek (→ ㊾)
Munich's art collection is spread across three museums: Alte Pinakothek, Neue Pinakothek, and Pinakothek der Moderne. The collection of the Alte Pinakothek extends from the 14th to the 18th century. The curators show impressive paintings by Giotto, Altdorfer, Dürer, Tintoretto, Titian, François Boucher and El Greco.
https://www.pinakothek.de

★★★ Neue Pinakothek (→ ㊾)
The Neue Pinakothek presents works from the 19th and 20th centuries. Among the artists presented are Jacques-Louis David, Gainsborough, Delacroix, Cézanne, Manet, Monet, Gauguin, van Gogh, Rodin, Klimt, von Stuck and Picasso.
https://www.pinakothek.de

Travel Points at a Glance

★★★ Pinakothek der Moderne (→ 54)

The Pinakothek der Moderne presents art from the 20th century. The museum is divided into *Sammlung Moderne Kunst, Staatliche Graphische Sammlung, Neue Sammlung* and *Architekturmuseum.*

The Sammlung Brandhorst shows art from the post-war period.

https://www.pinakothek-der-moderne.de
https://www.museum-brandhorst.de

★ Schack-Galerie (→ 63)

The curators present works by the artists Feuerbach, Spitzweg, Rottmann, Böcklin, and others.

https://www.pinakothek.de

★★ Nationalmuseum (→ 64)

The Bayerische Nationalmuseum (Bavarian National Museum) presents works of art from the Gothic to Art Nouveau. The focus of the collection is on carvings from southern Germany. A folklore section introduces the country's customs.

The neighbouring Sammlung Bollert shows 128 wooden sculptures. They range from Tilman Riemenschneider to Jörg Lederer.

https://www.bayerisches-nationalmuseum.de

★★ Haus der Kunst (→ 65)

The Haus der Kunst was built in 1937 by the architect Paul Ludwig Troost in the spirit of the Nazi regime. The curators present temporary exhibitions depicting renowned artists.

https://hausderkunst.de

★ Monacensia (→ 69)

The exhibition in the public lending library of Bogenhausen shows private items of numerous writers. Readings by current authors complement the exhibition.

https://www.muenchner-stadtbibliothek.de/monacensia-im-hildebrandhaus

Travel Points at a Glance

★★★ Villa Stuck (→ 71)
The Villa Stuck on Prinzregentenstraße presents works by the pioneering painter Franz Ritter von Stuck in his house and studio. Among other paintings, the *Guardian of Paradise* and *The Kiss of the Sphinx* can be seen.
https://www.villastuck.de

Theatre & Concert Halls

★★ Cuvilliés Theater (→ 37)
The Cuvilliés Theater at the Münchner Residenz offers theatre and opera in a lively rococo ambience. Pieces by Wolfgang Amadeus Mozart, Carl Maria von Weber and Engelbert Humperdinck are staged in an enchanting setting. The plays performed in the Bavarian dialect are very popular.
https://www.muenchenticket.de

★★★ Nationaltheater (→ 39)
The Nationaltheater houses the Bayerische Staatsoper (Bavarian State Opera). The stage orchestrates opera and ballet. It offers space for around 2,100 visitors. The Münchner Opernfestspiele (Munich Opera Festival) in the summer is well attended.
https://www.staatsoper.de

★★ Residenztheater (→ 39)
The Residenztheater at Max-Joseph-Platz 1 is Munich's stage for spoken theatre. Plays by Goethe, Schiller and Brecht are performed. Avant-garde and experimental theatre are also staged at times. All plays are in German.
https://www.residenztheater.de

★★ Künstlerhaus (→ 41)
The Künstlerhaus presents a wide range of offerings: classical music, jazz, readings, youth programs, and dance performances.
https://www.kuenstlerhaus-muc.de

★★ Deutsches Theater (→ 43)
The Deutsche Theater (Feenpalast) on Schwanthalerstraße is dedicated to musicals, variety shows and revues: Jesus Christ Superstar, Dance of the Vampires, Rocky Horror Picture Show.
https://www.deutsches-theater.de

★★ Kammerspiele (→ 67)
On Maximilianstraße, Bavaria's most beautiful Art Nouveau building offers modern spoken theatre. Bertolt Brecht premiered his play *Trommeln in der Nacht* here.
https://www.muenchner-kammerspiele.de

★★★ Prinzregententheater (→ 70)
The representative opera temple awaits its 1,000 visitors in an auditorium shaped like an amphitheatre. In addition to classical concerts and opera, world music, ballet and spoken theatre are shown.
https://www.theaterakademie.de

★★★ Gasteig (→ 80)
The Gasteig in Haidhausen presents classical music. In the Philharmonie, 2,500 visitors can enjoy the top-class performances of the Münchner Philharmoniker. Due to refurbishments, the events will be staged at the Isarphilharmonie until about 2028.
https://www.gasteig.de

Travel Points at a Glance

★★★ Gärtnerplatztheater (→ 86)
The opera house on Gärtnerplatz was constructed by the architect Franz Michael Reiffenstuel in the Italian Neo-Renaissance style. It presents operetta, dance theatre and musicals.
https://www.gaertnerplatztheater.de

★★ Marionettentheater (→ 87)
On Blumenstraße in the Glockenbachviertel, a lovingly furnished puppet theatre welcomes children and those still young at heart to a magical dance of the puppets.
https://www.muema-theater.de

★★ Olympiapark (→ 104)
In addition to opera performances, the former Olympiahalle offers rock and pop concerts.
https://www.olympiapark.de

Places of Worship

★★★ St Peter (→ 3)
The so-called *Old Peter* is the oldest church in town. The temple dates back to the beginnings of Munich in the 12th century. The high altar is exceptional. The wooden figure shows Saint Peter. Erasmus Grasser carved the statue around the year 1517. The central fresco by Johann Baptist Zimmermann (1756) depicts the crucifixion of Saint Peter upside down.
https://alterpeter.de

★★ Heilig-Geist-Kirche (→ 12)
The Heilig-Geist-Kirche (Holy Spirit Church) was once the church of a hospice that Herzog Ludwig I founded in 1208. The ceiling fresco by Cosmas Damian Asam (around 1727) shows the beginnings of the institution. The *Hammerthaler Muttergottes* (Virgin Mary) still attracts pilgrims today. The cycle *Seven Gifts of the Holy Spirit* by Peter Jacob Horemans is impressive.
https://heilig-geist-muenchen.de

★★★ Asamkirche (→ 19)
The Asam brothers built an outstanding private chapel on Sendlinger Straße by 1748. The richly decorated interior is overwhelming. The church is considered the high point of Rococo in Bavaria.
https://www.muenchen.de

★★★ Frauenkirche (→ 21)
The Frauenkirche is a landmark in Munich. The master builder Jörg von Halspach constructed the brick building by 1494. Patricians donated the altars. The cenotaph of Emperor Ludwig der Bayer by Hans Krumpper is worth seeing. The southern tower can be climbed.
https://www.muenchner-dom.de

★★ St Michael (→ 23)
Herzog Wilhelm V commissioned the Jesuit church, which was finished in 1597. A bronze angel awaits visitors at the holy water font. The barrel vault is overwhelming. The high altar shows the Archangel Michael fighting the devil. King Ludwig II is buried in the princely crypt underneath the church.
https://www.st-michael-muenchen.de

Travel Points at a Glance

★ **Bürgersaalkirche** (→ 24)
The Bürgersaalkirche was completed in 1778. The cloister impressively recreates Jesus's suffering with life-sized figures. The museum describes the life of Rupert Mayer SJ, who died shortly after the end of World War II as a result of his imprisonment during the Nazi regime.
https://www.mmkbuergersaal.de

★ **Salvatorkirche** (→ 28)
The Salvatorkirche serves as a place of worship for the Greek Orthodox community. The irresistible charm is in keeping with the Greek Orthodox tradition. The cemetery of the Frauenkirche was once located at the Salvatorkirche.
https://www.salvatorkirche-münchen.de

★★ **Theatinerkirche** (→ 33)
The votive church for the birth of the heir to the throne, Kurfürst Max Emanuel, was built by Agostino Barelli and Enrico Zuccalli in 1675 on behalf of Kurfürst Ferdinand Maria and his wife Henriette Adelaide von Savoyen. The baroque temple impresses with its lively feeling of lightness. The church is home to an important royal crypt of the Wittelsbacher dynasty.
http://www.theatinerkirche.de

★★ **St Bonifaz** (→ 43)
The basilica-style church is part of a Benedictine monastery. The architect Georg Friedrich Ziebland completed it in 1850 on behalf of King Ludwig I. The patron of art found his final resting place at this location. Only the central square survived World War II, however. Allied air raids destroyed the other parts. The symbol of the New Jerusalem floats above the altar. The order's homeless assistance is exemplary and applauded by the whole city.
https://www.sankt-bonifaz.de
https://www.sankt-bonifaz.de/obdachlosenhilfe/dienste

Travel Points at a Glance

★★ Ludwigskirche (→ 56)

Leo von Klenze completed the magical Ludwigskirche in 1844. The three-aisled basilica impresses with its exotic-looking Byzantine style. The second largest monumental fresco in the world, created by the artist Peter Cornelius in record time, rises above the altar. It shows the Last Judgment.

https://www.st-ludwig-muenchen.de

★ St Anna im Lehel (→ 66)

At the St. Anna Platz, there is a picturesque monastery church called St Anna. It was built by the architect Johann Michael Fischer. The parish church opposite, also St Anna, was constructed by Gabriel Seidl. The baroque monastery church shows scenes from the life of Saint Anna, the parish church is dedicated to the apocalypse. Jesus rides on a horse above the entrance and saves the believers.

https://www.erzbistum-muenchen.de

★ St Lukas (→ 75)

The graceful Protestant church was built by Albert Schmidt in 1896. The decorated stained glass windows were created by Hermann Kaspar in 1946. Peter and Paul await the believers at the canopy.

https://www.sanktlukas.de

★ St Johann Baptist (→ 77)

The architect Matthias Berger completed the cathedral in 1874 in the neo-Gothic style. The painting of the Last Judgment was designed by the artist Johann Baptist Schmidt.

https://www.pfarrverband-haidhausen.de

★ St Johannes (→ 77)

The Evangelical Lutheran Church of St Johannes on Preysingplatz was completed in 1912. The architect Albert Schmidt designed it in the neo-Romanesque style.

https://www.stjohannes.de

Travel Points at a Glance

★ St Nikolai (→ 78)
During the Middle Ages, St Nikolai at the Gasteig was the church of Munich's lepers.
https://www.pfarrverband-haidhausen.de

★ Mariahilf (→ 83)
The architect Joseph Daniel Ohlmüller built the church in the neo-Gothic style in 1839. The Auer Dult takes place three times a year at the Mariahilfplatz. This is also where the Pride march gathers for Christopher Street Day in July.
https://www.erzbistum-muenchen.de

★★ St Maximilian (→ 88)
The neo-Romanesque church's high stone altar is modelled on a megalithic grave. On the side wall, David fights Goliath.
https://www.st-maximilian.de

★★ St Paul (→ 97)
The Church of St Paul was built by Georg von Hauberrisser in 1906. The Marian Altar by Gabriel Hackl and the Joseph Altar are worth seeing. A monstrance keeps a splinter from the cross of Christ.
http://www.pfarrverband-muenchen-westend.de

★★★ St Maria und St Korbinian (→ 111)
The spiritual stronghold of Munich was on the Domberg in Freising during the Middle Ages. The largest and most beautiful sacred house of worship in the region can be discovered to the north of Munich. The best artists of their time worked on the baroque complex such as Jörg von Halspach, Egid Quirin and Cosmas Damian Asam, Peter Candid and Johann Baptist Zimmermann. The crypt contains the bones of Saint Corbinian. The Bestiensäule (beast column) next to it impresses.
https://www.freisinger-dom.de

Culinary Delights

The area around Munich is surprisingly barren. The lush meadows are deceptive: pasture farming was the only form of cultivation for centuries before the invention of fertilisers. The layer of the soil is often only some 30cm thick. The region specialises in the breeding of pigs and cows. Dairy products, potatoes, meat and offal are the staple foods in Munich. The Isar also offered fish. Seasonal fruits and vegetables complement the menu. The potato was introduced north of the Alps only in the 17th century.

★ Pastries

Munich entices the pallet with a wide variety of pastries but in a different way than other regions of Germany. The hearty *Zwetschgendatschi* made of plums is very popular in autumn after the harvest. *Dampfnudeln* are also known. *Kiacheln* are offered deep-fried in clarified butter.

★ Schmalzbrot (lard-bread)

The bread in Munich is a delicacy that many enjoy with butter and parsley only. If the bread is made traditionally, it is baked from sourdough. Industrialised manufacturing has reduced selection, but smaller bakeries are experimenting with traditional recipes again and gradually enter the market. If one wants to add flavour and calories, one spreads lard from pigs or geese on top.

★ Leberkäse

The Münchner Leberkäse (literally: liver-cheese, see photo) is a popular delicacy for in between meals. A slice is placed in a roll and garnished with sweet mustard. The sausage meat made from pork and bacon, seasoned with curing salt, pepper, coriander and ginger, is baked in rectangular moulds in the oven. Only outside Bavaria does the Leberkäse have to contain liver.

★ Weißwürste

The saying goes that the Weißwurst (white sausage) must not survive the 11 am bell ringing. (In the past, the ingredients were leftovers from the day before.) The Weißwurst is said to have been created out of necessity on Carnival Sunday 1857 because the restaurant had run out of established sausages. The Munich white sausages consist of veal, bacon, cooked veal head and salt. One adds parsley, pepper and onions to this. Some skin the sausage with knife

Culinary Delights

and fork, others eat it with the skin on, and many enjoy cutting it out. Munich white sausage mustard is the condiment that is added by most.

★ Obatzter and Brezn

A ripe Camembert is stirred with butter until it becomes foamy. One adds finely chopped onions, salt, pepper and paprika, mix in caraway and Weißbier (wheat beer) and let the mixture steep for a few hours. For a stronger taste, Romadur or Limburger are suitable. White bread is generally preferred because the Obatzter already puts a lot of flavour on the palette and needs no further enhancers.

★ Fish

Bavaria's lakes and rivers are predominantly home to carp and trout. The Steckerlfisch - a whitefish or mackerel grilled slowly over charcoal - is most popular at traditional markets and folk festivals.

★ Schweinsbraten & Haxe

Pork dishes are the favourite dishes of many Munichers - and not just on Sundays. Every traditional Bavarian restaurant offers roast pork and pork knuckles (see photo). The staple food is served with dumplings - preferably potato dumplings, but bread dumplings are also popular. A thick layer of fat must surround a pork knuckle. (Watch your diet - a typical blue-collar dish.) It's the standard Sunday lunch of the lower and middle class. If the meat strips off easily from the bone, it has been simmered. One takes a piece of the neck or the back for roast pork. In Munich, the pork is fried in the oven in a brew of dark beer. Coleslaw with bacon is the side dish of choice.

★ Grillhähnchen

Oktoberfest has made spicy grilled chicken famous and popular all over the world. The crispy off-the-shelf chicken is served with potato salad and pretzels and eaten with the fingers. (No fork or knife allowed.) One accompanies it with a pint, and all is well.

★ Beer gardens

In many beer gardens, visitors can bring their food. One has to get the drinks at the counter, but the food can be bought at the supermarket. However, potato salad, radishes, Obatzter, giant pretzels and herb butter should never be missed at a *"beer garden picnic"*. A visit is best enjoyed with friends when everyone provides a home-cooked dish to the table.

Annual Calendar

Spring

★ **Frühlingsfest:** Every year after Easter (end of April), a folk festival on the Theresienwiese warms up the liver.
https://www.muenchen.de/veranstaltungen

★ **Maidult:** In the first week of May, the Mariahilfplatz offers a fair with stalls (household goods, textiles).
Internet: Auer Dult on Facebook

★ **Lange Nacht der Musik:** (Long Night of Music) At the beginning of May, a hundred venues join to present a musical spectacle. Munich is turned into a huge stage. Live concerts, dance and cabaret entertain the city.
https://www.muenchner.de/musiknacht

★ **Stadtgeburtstag:** Munich was first mentioned on June 14, 1158. The city celebrates the day between Marienplatz and Odeonsplatz.
https://www.muenchen.de/veranstaltungen

Summer

★ **Tollwood:** Mid-June, a summer festival offers snacks, beer and music events at the Olympiazentrum. The festival attracts thousands.
https://www.tollwood.de

★ **Münchner Filmfest:** The Munich Film Festival, held at the end of June, features top-class productions. Every year the festival has a different motto.
https://www.filmfest-muenchen.de

★ **Kocherlball:** In mid-July, the city organises the Kocherlball in the Englischer Garten, a dance event that was once aimed at maids and servants. https://www.muenchen.de/veranstaltungen

★ **Münchner Opernfestspiele:** From end of June onwards, the Bavarian State Opera offers special performances - a highlight of the summer.
https://www.staatsoper.de/festspiele

Annual Calendar

⭐ **Musik-Sommer:** In August, the Theatron in the Olympiapark is dedicated to music events: rock, pop, jazz. www.theatron.de

Autumn

⭐ **Oktoberfest:** The largest folk festival in the world takes place at the end of September on the Theresienwiese. The entrance of the Wiesenwirte opens the spectacle on the first Saturday. A parade welcomes the visitors on the first Sunday. https://www.oktoberfest.de

⭐ **Lange Nacht der Münchner Museen:** At the end of October, one hundred museums, galleries and exhibitions open until midnight. Shuttle buses run between the events.
http://www.muenchner.de see also Facebook

Winter

⭐ **Tollwood-Winterfestival:** From the end of November to the end of the year, Tollwood organises a winter festival on the Theresienwiese. Mulled wine, dance, music and cabaret offer an alternative to the quietness of Advent.
https://www.tollwood.de

⭐ **Christkindlmarkt:** During Advent, Munich presents an enchanting Christmas market from Marienplatz to Karlstor. Mulled wine, gingerbread and cookies bring the magic of the season to life.
https://www.muenchen.de/veranstaltungen

⭐ **Tanz der Marktweiber:** Carnival in Munich is quiet, but the Viktualienmarkt is raging on Shrove Tuesday. The highlight is the dance of the market women at lunchtime.
https://www.muenchen.de/veranstaltungen

⭐ **Starkbierzeit:** (Strong beer season) Before Easter, the strong beer festival begins with tapping the first barrel. Highlight: Politicians and celebrities are made fun of. https://paulaner-nockherberg.com/starkbierfest

Highlight Tour 1: The Beginnings of Munich

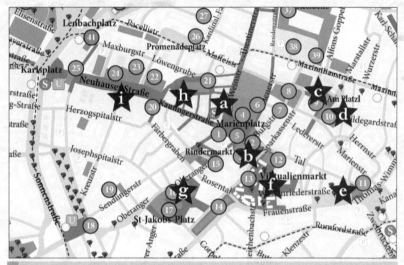

What to expect? Romanticism of the Middle Ages. Bavarian cosiness. Marian devotion. Fervent faith immortalised in carvings and frescoes.
Highlights: Figure decoration in St Peter and the Frauenkirche. The frescoes of St Peter and the Heilig-Geist-Kirche. The cellar vault at the Alter Hof. High altar in St Michael.
Duration: Full Day **Entrance:** Adults 9 €, Concession 5 €

The tour around the old town begins at the Marienplatz, the city's former market square, the heart of Bavaria's capital.

⭐ Marienplatz (→ ① ② ④ ⑤)

Herzog Heinrich der Löwe founded Munich in 1158. The first city wall stretched from the Augustinerstraße to the Talburgtor and from the Marienhof to the Rindermarkt. The area was called Heinrichsstadt. The Talburgtor dates from this time. The citizens held a market at Marienplatz. The Munichers added the Alte Rathaus in the late 15th century. The carillon at the Neue Rathaus (performances: 11 am, 12 pm and 5 pm) commemorates the wedding of Herzog Wilhelm V and Renata of Lorraine in 1568. The Mariensäule in the centre of the square is a symbol of the Thirty Years' War. Kurfürst Maximilian I erected the column in 1638.

⭐ St Peter (→ ③)

The church on the Petersbergl is dedicated to Saint Peter. It is the oldest place of worship in Munich. The tower of St Peter can be climbed via a steep staircase. Alternatively, an elevator leads to the platform of the tower at the Neue Rathaus where one catches the birds-eye view, too.

Highlight Tour 1: The Beginnings of Munich

A figure of Saint Peter carved by Erasmus Grasser in 1517 dominates the altar of St Peter. During a papal election, the congregation takes of its golden tiara. The ceiling fresco by Johann Baptist Zimmermann (1756) depicts the crucifixion of the Evangelist. Numerous donations were made by the patricians to decorate the side chapels. The Schrenk Altar shows Jesus as the judge of the world.

★ Alter Hof (→ ⑦ ⑧)

The Stadtschreiberhaus is located on Burgstraße. The alley connects the Marienplatz with the Alter Hof, the first residence of the Wittelsbacher dynasty. Herzog Ludwig II laid the founding stone in 1255. Emperor Ludwig der Bayer expanded the complex into an imperial castle in the 14th century. The Museum infopoint tells its story.

★ Am Platzl (→ ⑨ ⑩)

In the Middle Ages, the polluting industry was located at the Am Platzl. During absolutism, the employees of the Münchner Residenz settled there. In the 19th century, prominent student associations shook hands with the Hofbräuhaus. After World War II, the area turned into a red-light district. Today, gourmet restaurants serve traditional home-style cuisine.

★ Isartor (→ ⑪)

The salt carts from Bad Reichenhall once arrived along the trade routes from the Alps at the Isartor. They ensured the city prospered.

★ Heilig-Geist-Kirche (→ ⑫ ⑬)

During the Middle Ages, the Heilig-Geist-Kirche was part of a hospice that was founded in 1208. The ceiling fresco by Cosmas Damian Asam depicts its beginnings. The Hammerthaler Muttergottes is venerated by numerous pilgrims. The adjacent Viktualienmarkt was once part of the hospice. Today it offers delicacies and fresh produce.

★ Stadtmuseum (→ ⑯)

The city museum on St-Jakobs-Platz is located in the former Zeughaus (armoury). It shows the history of Munich from its beginnings to the present. The city model by Jakob Sandtner from 1570 is impressive. The curators present Moriscan Dancers (Erasmus Grasser), medieval weapons and the Münchner Kindl. (Currently, the museum is closed for refurbishment)

★ Frauenkirche (→ ㉑)

The Frauenkirche is Munich's landmark. Jörg von Halspach built the church from 1468 onwards. The cenotaph of Emperor Ludwig der Bayer was designed by Hans Krumpper in 1622. Patricians donated the altars in the side chapels, demonstrating their piety. The tower can be climbed.

★ St Michael (→ ㉓ ㉔)

The Jesuit Church was built in 1583 as a response to the Reformation. The high altar shows the Archangel Michael fighting the devil. Christoph Schwartz completed the work in 1587.

Highlight Tour 2: Absolutism

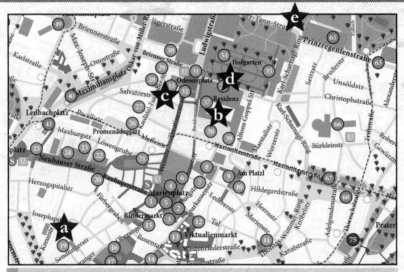

What to expect? Enjoyment of life. Exuberant Baroque. Art as a means of power. Utopian worlds. Sensuality and theatricality.
Highlights: The splendour of the Rococo (Asamkirche, Cuvilliés Theater). The Antiquarium of the Münchner Residenz. The gardens of Schloss Nymphenburg and Schloss Schleißheim.
Duration: One to three days **Entrance:** Adults 54 €, children 44 €.

After the Thirty Years' War and during the era of absolutism, the Wittelsbacher dynasty concentrated their efforts on the north of the old town and the surrounding castles.

⭐ Asamkirche (→ ⑲)
U-Bahn: Sendlinger Tor

The Asamkirche is a private church dedicated to Saint Nepomuk. The brothers Cosmas Damian and Egid Quirin Asam built the Rococo chapel between 1733 and 1746. In the early morning, the rising sun bathes the church in a mystical light. The rich gold decoration and stucco are overwhelming.

⭐ Münchner Residenz (→ ㊱ ㊲)
U-Bahn: Sendlinger Tor → Odeonsplatz

The Münchner Residenz is the city palace of the Bavarian regents. It developed from the Neuveste, a refuge castle that was founded in 1385. The palace was extensively expanded under Kurfürst Maximilian I, Kurfürst Max Emanuel and Emperor Karl Albrecht. King Ludwig I added the throne room (today Herkulessaal) and the royal wing.

The Residenzmuseum manages more than 130 rooms that convey the magic of the Renaissance and Baroque. When the residence was

Highlight Tour 2: Absolutism

built in 1568, the Antiquarium housed the duke's collection of antiquities and the library. The dignified Steinzimmer were reserved for the Emperor. Kurfürst Maximilian I set them up in the Kaiserhoftrakt (imperial wing). The complex has three chapels: the Hofkapelle (court chapel) was intended for the court, the Reiche Kapelle for the regent and the splendid Allerheiligen Hofkirche was added by King Ludwig I. In the Schatzkammer (treasury), the museum shows the jewels and goldsmiths' work of Bavaria: crowns, globes, crucifixes and clocks. The Cuvilliés Theater is the most beautiful rococo theatre in the world. In the evening, concerts are performed in the Herkulessaal.

⭐ Theatinerkirche (→ 33)

The church on Odeonsplatz is the visible sign of the end of the Thirty Years' War. Kurfürst Ferdinand Maria and his wife Henriette Adelaide von Savoyen built it in gratitude for the birth of Kurfürst Max Emanuel. The church disempowered the Jesuits in Bavaria. The huge single-nave and the barrel vault in the Italian Baroque style are overwhelming.

⭐ Hofgarten (→ 34)

Kurfürst Karl Theodor opened the joyful court garden with the lovely Hofgartentempel (court temple) in the centre to the Munichers in 1780. He wanted to avoid a revolution by willingly giving concessions to his citizens.

⭐ Englischer Garten (→ 61)

The extensive park, designed in the style of an English landscape garden, was created in the 18th century. At the Eisbach, windsurfers brave the waves; the Monopteros offers a good view, and at the Chinesischer Turm (Chinese Tower), a beer garden serves Bavarian cosiness. Pedal boats on the Kleinhesseloher See (a lake) tempt the playful to splash around.

⭐ Schloss Nymphenburg (→ 101)

S-Bahn: Marienplatz → Hauptbahnhof
Tram 17: Hauptbahnhof → Nymphenburg

Schloss Nympenburg was modelled after an Italian country villa. Kurfürst Ferdinand Maria gifted it to his wife. Under Kurfürst Max Emanuel and Emperor Karl Albrecht, the complex developed into a summer residence. King Maximilian I transformed the park into an English landscape garden during the 19th century. In the Schönheitengalerie (Beauty Gallery), a painting depicts Lola Montez. King Ludwig II was born in the Blauer Saal (Blue Hall). The park delights with numerous pavilions.

⭐ Schloss Schleißheim (→ 109)

S-Bahn S1: Marienplatz → Oberschleißheim

To the north of Munich, Kurfürst Max Emanuel built a second summer residence to reinforce his ambition - he craved imperial dignity. The complex is also called the Versailles of Munich. Schloss Lustheim was a gift to his wife. The castle impresses with its extensive baroque garden.

Highlight Tour 3: Kingdom of Bavaria

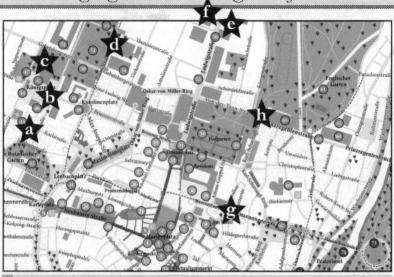

What to expect? Cosmopolitan spirit. Classicism. International art of the first order. With antiquity, King Ludwig I drove the Middle Ages out of Munich.
Highlights: Ancient treasures in the Glyptothek and the Antikensammlung. A well regarded collection of paintings in the Pinakotheken. Exotic-looking Ludwigskirche.
Duration: One to several days **Entrance**: Adults 41 €, Concession 29 €

When Bavaria was declared a kingdom in 1806, the country doubled in size, and Munich expanded to the north into the Maxvorstadt. It is named after King Maximilian I. The visionary King Ludwig I took the lead in designing the new neighbourhood until the mid-19th century when he had to step down.

⭐ St Bonifaz (→ 43)
U-Bahn: Königsplatz

Georg Friedrich Ziebland completed the Basilica of St Bonifaz in 1850. Only the central part survived World War II, however. The artists Peter Burkart, Friedrich Koller and Christine Stadler designed the interior - a reference to the New Jerusalem. King Ludwig I is buried in the church.

⭐ Königsplatz (→ 44)

The Königsplatz prompts the Munichers to heated discussions. The square was designed according to the principles of classical antiquity, but the Nazi regime used it for parades and propaganda. Books burned here in 1933. At construction, the Propyläen was supposed to be the new entrance gate into Munich, but the city grew so rapidly that houses soon surrounded the square.

Highlight Tour 3: Kingdom of Bavaria

★ Glyptothek (→ ㊺ ㊻ ㊿)

The Glyptothek and the Antikensammlung were created under King Ludwig I between 1830 and 1848. Leo von Klenze and Georg Friedrich Ziebland built the museums. They show statues and craftwork from the Mycenaean period to the Romans. The Aeginetes, the Munich Kouros and the Barberinian Faun are impressive. The Museum Ägyptischer Kunst opposite the Alte Pinakothek exhibits artefacts from the lands of the Nile.

★ Pinakotheken (→ ㊾ ㊼ ㊽)

King Ludwig I not only collected ancient art from the Mediterranean but he also encouraged his agents to auction paintings. He exhibited the collection in the Alte and Neue Pinakothek. In 2002, the city expanded the exhibition space by adding the Pinakothek der Moderne. The Alte Pinakothek shows works of art from the 14th to 18th centuries (Giotto to François Boucher). The Neue Pinakothek continues the collection up to Pablo Picasso.

★ Ludwigskirche (→ ㊽)

The exotic-looking Ludwigskirche on Ludwigstraße opposite the University was built on behalf of King Ludwig I by the architect Leo von Klenze in 1844. The monumental fresco by Peter Cornelius shows the Last Judgment; the Marienaltar depicts the Virgin of Mercy (1480, Ulm School).

★ Universities (→ ㊿ ㊼)

Munich's world-class universities opened in the 19th century. Luminaries such as Carl von Linde worked at the Technische Universität. His students included Rudolf Diesel, Willy Messerschmidt and Claude Dornier. The Ludwig Maximilians University offers all faculties. It is one of the best universities in the world.

★ Maximilianstraße (→ ㊼ ㊻)

In the second half of the 19th century, Munich expanded along the Maximilianstraße under King Maximilian II. This is where the unique Maximilian style emerged. The Bavarian state parliament holds meetings at the Maximilianeum (built in 1874 by Friedrich Bürklein).

★ Prinzregentenstraße (→ ㊼ ㊺)

The Prinzregentenstraße was created under Prince Regent Luitpold between 1891 and 1901. It is the last grand boulevard in Munich, which terminates in the neighbourhood Bogenhausen at the Prinzregententheater, built by Max Littmann in 1901.

★ Oktoberfest (→ ㊾ ㊾ ㊾)

The Oktoberfest at the Theresienwiese began with the wedding of Ludwig I and Therese von Saxony-Hildburghausen. The Lady Bavaria at the Ruhmeshalle has protected the country and its subjects since 1850. In the hall of fame, Bavaria's luminaries are honoured with busts.

Highlight Tour 4: Munich Boheme

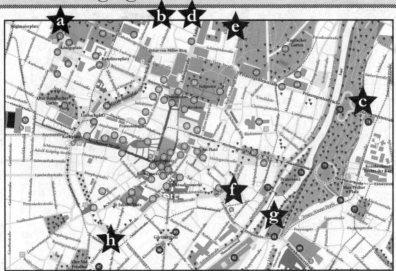

What to expect? Breaking with tradition and established values. Creativity. Humanity. Visions. Compensation and renewal. Challenging the norms.
Highlights: The works of the group *Der Blaue Reiter* in the Lenbachhaus; the paintings by Franz von Stuck in the Villa Stuck; the atmosphere in Schwabing and the Glockenbachviertel.
Duration: Day tour **Entrance:** Adults 22 €, children 11,50 €

At the turn of the century, freethinkers arrived in Munich, setting new trends and rebelling against traditional social norms. Among them were artists, scientists and entrepreneurs. They scattered throughout the city, but the neighbourhood Schwabing attracted them all.

⭐ Lenbachhaus (→ 47)
U-Bahn: Königsplatz

Franz von Lenbach was a portrait painter who knew how to please the influential and powerful of his time. He was born the son of a master bricklayer and successfully climbed the social ladder within the established system. The group *Der Blaue Reiter* (The Blue Rider) was different. It broke with conventions and traditions and renewed the art of painting. The curators at the Lenbachhaus present both styles.

⭐ Akademie der Bildenden Künste (→ 58)
U-Bahn: Giselastraße

Franz von Lenbach was a professor at the academy, and the founders of the group *Der Blaue Reiter* (Wassily Kandinsky, Paul Klee and Franz Marc) were his students. Today, the university inspires its new blood to

Highlight Tour 4: Munich Boheme

be creatively courageous. Student exhibitions sometimes present groundbreaking works of art.

⭐ Villa Stuck (→ 71)
U-Bahn: Prinzregentenplatz

Franz Ritter von Stuck was born into simple circumstances. He was the son of a miller. Paintings such as *The Sin, Guardians of Paradise* and *The Kiss of the Sphinx* catapulted him into the rank of luminaries. Prince Regent Luitpold knighted him in 1905. The curators introduce his extraordinary life and work to a broad audience in his home and studio.

⭐ Simplicissimus (→ 52 53)
U-Bahn: Universität

The Simplicissimus was a literary magazine that caricatured the power dynamic of the authorities. The best writers of the time contributed to the magazine: Hermann Hesse, Gustav Meyrink, Thomas Mann and many others. The editorial team met at Café Luitpold on the Wittelsbacher Platz and in the Alter Simpl (Türkenstraße 57).

⭐ Schwabing (→ 60)
U-Bahn: Universität

The proximity to the university predestined the neighbourhood Schwabing to become the centre of Munich's bohemian life. Left-wing progressive ideas and social experiments were cooked up in Schwabing until the 1960s. Hippie communes emerged, cabaret artists mocked society, and Vladimir Ilyich Lenin hid in Schwabing in the early 1900s. Today, the Münchner Lach- und Schießgesellschaft and the Rationaltheater entertain anyone who still dreams idealistic dreams.

⭐ Valentinmusäum (→ 11 84)
S-Bahn: Isartor

It's easier to make people laugh at the misfortunes of those in power than at their reflection. The cabaret artist Karl Valentin, a son of the Au, made the people smile at themselves. His museum at the Isartor presents his twisted humour (mainly in German).

⭐ Müllersches Volksbad (→ 81)
S-Bahn: Rosenheimer Platz

Philanthropists tried to alleviate the suffering of ordinary citizens. In the 1890s, the entrepreneur Karl von Müller built an Art Nouveau swimming pool at the Isar for the burghers of Haidhausen, but the bath was too expensive for Munich's day labourers, and they could not afford the pool. The style still convinces.

⭐ Glockenbachviertel (→ 87)
U-Bahn: Sendlinger Tor

Munich was once considered a vibrant capital of the homosexual scene. Their primary hunting ground was in the Gärtnerplatzviertel. Freddie Mercury, the lead singer of the group Queen, staged his 39th birthday at the club Mr Henderson. The alternative scene still sparkles along the Hans-Sachs-Straße, and during Christopher Street Day, the boys hang plump fruits on the rainbow.

Highlight Tour 5: Nazi Regime

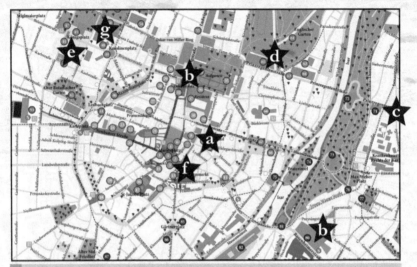

What to expect? Nationalism. Trembling shadows. Heroic resistance fighters. The power of ideology. Persecution and oppression. Blood and violence.
Highlights: Beer hall atmosphere. Consecration of the flag. Maxvorstadt, the centre of the Nazi regime. NS-Dokumentationszentrum. Gedenkstätte KZ Dachau.
Duration: Two days. **Entrance:** Without charge

Adolf Hitler named Munich *Hauptstadt der Bewegung* (capital of the movement). The many sites are spread across the city. The tour follows the timeline of historical events.

⭐ Hofbräuhaus (→ ⑩ ⑪)
S-Bahn: Marienplatz

After World War I, Adolf Hitler was a right-wing radical agitator who hung out in Munich beer halls. On February 24, 1920, he founded the National Socialist German Workers' Party at the Hofbräuhaus. Their 25-point program called for the revocation of German citizenship from Jews.

⭐ Hitler Putsch (→ ⑳ ㉜)
S-Bahn: Rosenheimer Platz
U-Bahn: Odeonsplatz

On November 8, 1923, in the now destroyed Bürgerbräukeller on Rosenheimer Straße, Adolf Hitler forced the then Bavarian Minister President Gustav von Kahr to resign. The day after, the Bavarian state police violently suppressed the march of Adolf Hitler's Kampftruppe (the nucleus of the SS) onto the Feldherrnhalle. Adolf Hitler was arrested. While incarcerated in Landsberg am Lech, 50 kilometres west of Munich, he dictated *Mein Kampf*, the manifesto of the Nazi regime.

Highlight Tour 5: Nazi Regime

The Odeonsplatz at the Feldherrnhalle was used by the SS (Schutzstaffel) to swear in their soldiers. A memorial commemorated the Hitler Putsch. Avoiding it meant sneaking through the Viscardigasse.

On November 8, 1939, Georg Elser carried out an assassination attempt on Adolf Hitler in the Bürgerbräukeller, which failed.

☆ Prinzregentenplatz (→ ㊆)
U-Bahn: Prinzregentenplatz

On October 1, 1929, Adolf Hitler moved into an apartment at Prinzregentenplatz 16. Today, a Police Station occupies the building.

☆ Haus der Kunst (→ ㉕)
U-Bahn: Odeonsplatz

The Haus der Kunst was built by the architect Paul Ludwig Troost in 1937. The Nazi regime staged the Große Deutsche Kunstausstellung there. The museum became a model for all other Nazi buildings.

☆ Munich Agreement (→ ㊻)
U-Bahn: Königsplatz

On September 30, 1938, the world avoided war by sacrificing Czechoslovakia. The agreement was signed in the Führerbau at the Königsplatz. This ended the Sudeten crisis. Today, the building houses the University of Music and Theatre.

☆ Kristallnacht (→ ② ⑯)
S-Bahn: Marienplatz

From the Alte Rathaus, the Nazi regime launched the Kristallnacht during an intimate evening of camaraderie in memory of the failed Hitler Putsch on November 9, 1938. Jewish synagogues and institutions such as the Uhlfelder department store were looted and set on fire on that day.

☆ NS-Doku'zentrum (→ ㊽)
U-Bahn: Königsplatz

The NS-Dokumentationszentrum between Königsplatz and Karolinenplatz on the site of the former Braune Haus explains the rise of fascism in Munich and Bavaria. Eyewitness reports and documents illustrate the first years of the Nazi regime.

☆ Gedenkstätte KZ Dachau (→ ⑩⑦)
S-Bahn: Dachau, then Bus 726

The Nazi regime opened its first concentration camp on March 22, 1933, in the former Königliche Pulver- und Munitionsfabrik Dachau (an ammunition factory). Theodor Eicke, commandant of the camp, later rose to become leader of the SS guards. He rolled out the statutes, which he meticulously developed in Dachau, to all concentration camps in the Reich. Dachau became the training camp for all guards. Around 200,000 innocent people were imprisoned in the Dachau concentration camp and around 40,000 prisoners lost their lives. The memorial warns the generations to come of the extraordinary cruelty the human species is capable of. A visit to the place of horror is highly recommended.

Walkabouts

The Munich of the Munichers

The coin has two sides, not just in Munich. Anyone who admires the neatness of the Isar will be disgusted by the cleanliness of the Dachau concentration camp, where order turned into torture. Long live the Dachau of those who sacrificed their future until the last day to throw a few crumbs of bread over the fence to a prisoner. Even success has a dark side if it is without ethics. Anyone who squints at the light-emitting diodes of the high-tech industry while on prowl at night will see the Janus head smiling confusingly: *pride motivates, national pride demolishes.*

At the midnight hour, when clammy-dark beer cellars squeeze greasy air into delicate lungs, the obfuscated halls intoxicate. When pounding brass bands stomp wild rhythms and the raging vibe escalates, the atmosphere may implode - just like then - during the Weimar period.

When the beer mugs swing and the tuba booms, when flirtatious ladies nibble at the radishes and bulging curves whip with joy, then the knee teeters, the elbow sways, then the individual, blinded by the crowd, degrades to a link in the chain, indistinguishable in the silhouette of the merrier. The mood may shift, at any time, when a ragtag delivers a speech about ... what one always knew but never dared to say. This is how right-wing propaganda feeds the masses: *The grumbling is seductive, intoxicating, just like Bavaria's sweet manna!*

And the one who closes his eyes will hear the putschists marching in, clanking their boots on wooden floors, the bellowing of burlier throats - a shot in the air! Another closes his eyes and smells the puddles of stale beer, the spittle under the table.

Eyes wide shut, a fellow to the left: "*Now we get started.*" Eyes wide shut, a fellow to the right: "*We rough them up.*" And then he arrives, the one everybody waited for. "*That's it, that's it!*" Applause across the hall. A croaking tongue, shrill like a cawing gramophone: "*My words, my words!*" And the crowd drums the finger: "*He tells the truth.*" And the crowd thrusts the finger: "*They are to blame!*" The rabble applauds, the house bawls out!

And then someone stands up with his eyes wide shut. His name was Georg Elser. He moved to Munich to stand up. He was a simple citizen but he moved to Munich to stand up. And he stood up! He did! We must not forget him.

◄ **At the Mariensäule, putti slay people's instincts.**

The Historical Centre

Insiders Know ...

Medieval Godliness with Gooseflesh
St Peter radiates mysticism carried on angelic wings! Munich's year of grace promised plenary indulgence, and *Old Peter* triumphed at the contest of the most ebullient altar. Anyone not moved does not understand.

Twisting like a Schäffler
Munich celebrates its festivals at the Marienplatz, and when the Schäffler turn, the carillon of the new town hall reenacts a traditional one - several times a day. Not to be missed!

Glancing Across Town with Eagle Eyes
The view across Munich and the Alps from the new town hall is breathtaking, especially when the föhn wind blows. An escalator at the thoroughfare speeds the staircase up - ready, get set, and go ...!

Scrambling like a Monkey
Bavaria's fairy-tale-treasure-box is magic. A monkey once hauled baby Emperor Ludwig der Bayer from his cradle to the top of the tower at the Alter Hof. Diapers out to face the monkey! The legend demands it!

Where Horsemeat and Dried Fruit Remain Forever Young
Germany's largest open-air market indulges the senses. The Viktualienmarkt offers delicatessen, sausages and maypole close to the Marienplatz. The Bavarian tradition even feasts on horsemeat and dried fruits!

The Devil on a Visit to Munich
When he spits flames, the devil is about, and in Munich, there is the proof: he branded his foot into the marble at the leading portal of the Frauenkirche - not to be missed.

Angels Struggling for Paradise
The Jesuit Church of St Michael shines stately at the Neuhauser Straße, consecrated to the fight of good against evil. Eyes wide open because the spirits of light triumph over the lord of darkness.

Baroque Insanity Without a Safety Net
They were the leading artists of the rococo - the brothers Asam. Their private chapel is overwhelming, bewildering, enticing, sensual and outdoing the Kings. Mirror, mirror on the wall, who rules the country after all?

◄ The Marienplatz is Munich's oldest part.

① Marienplatz 60
② Altes Rathaus & Talburgtor . 62
③ St Peter 64
④ Glockenspiel 68
⑤ Mariensäule 70
⑥ Neues Rathaus 72
⑦ Burgstraße 76
⑧ Alter Hof 78
⑨ Am Platzl 82
⑩ Hofbräuhaus 84
⑪ Isartor 86
⑫ Heilig-Geist-Kirche 88
⑬ Viktualienmarkt 92
⑭ Schrannenhalle 94
⑮ Rindermarkt 96
⑯ Münchner Stadtmuseum .. 98
⑰ Jüdisches Zentrum 100
⑱ Sendlinger Tor 102
⑲ Asamkirche 104
⑳ Kaufingerstraße 108
㉑ Frauenkirche 110
㉒ Jagd- & Fischereimuseum .. 114
㉓ St Michael 116
㉔ Bürgersaalkirche 120
㉕ Karlstor 122
㉖ Promenadeplatz 124
㉗ Kardinal Faulhaber Straße . 126
㉘ Salvatorkirche 128
㉙ Platz Nationalsozialismus .. 130
㉚ Wittelsbacher Platz 132
㉛ Odeonsplatz 134
㉜ Feldherrnhalle 136
㉝ Theatinerkirche St Kajetan . 138
㉞ Hofgarten 142
㉟ Bayerische Staatskanzlei ... 144
㊱ Herkulessaal 146
㊲ Münchner Residenz 148
㊳ Max-Joseph-Platz 154
㊴ Nationaltheater 156

A wild boar shows the way to the hunting museum. ▶

Munich's old town centre has retained its medieval character. At the spacious *Marienplatz*, the Munichers dance to all rhythms. The *Alte Rathaus* and the *Talburgtor* date from the city's beginnings. The *Old Peter* on Petersbergl was the first church in Munich. It is where the Bavarian capital hatched from the egg. The hospice at the *Heilig-Geist-Kirche* cared for the sick during the Middle Ages. Secularisation transformed the hospice into the *Viktualienmarkt* and the *Schrannenhalle*.

The carillon at the *Neue Rathaus* reenacts the wedding of Herzog Wilhelm V with Renata of Lorraine. The *Mariensäule* opposite celebrates the end of the Thirty Years' War. The *Burgstraße* leads to the medieval residence of the Wittelsbacher dynasty, the *Alter Hof*. The museum infopoint tells the story of the castle. The Middle Ages sawed and hammered at the *Am Platzl*. Today, the *Hofbräuhaus* offers traditional home cooking. At the *Isartor*, many bakeries and hostels settled because there, the carts from the Alps passed the city wall.

Shortly after the city was founded, the citizens set up another market at the *Rindermarkt*.

After the holocaust during the Nazi regime, Munich is proud to be home to a thriving *Jewish community* again. The former armoury is used by the *Münchner Stadtmuseum* (Munich City Museum) today. The exhibition takes its visitors through the metropolis's long history on two levels.

The *Sendlinger Tor* marks the southern border of the second city wall. There, the splendour of the *Asamkirche* is overwhelming.

The character of the city centre changes along the *Kaufingerstraße*. The former trading route was converted into a pedestrian zone in 1972. The imposing *Frauenkirche* is Munich's top landmark. It was built in the 15th century. The former Augustinian monastery is now home to the *Jagd- und Fischereimuseum* (a hunting and fishing museum). The Jesuit Church of *St Michael* was the spiritual centre of the Counter Reformation. Adjacent to it, the Bürgersaalkirche is dedicated to the Virgin Mary. The Karlstor marks the end of the old town.

Munich's nobility settled at the *Promenadeplatz* and along the *Kardinal Faulhaber Straße*. The *Salvatorkirche* is now home to the Greek Orthodox community. The *Platz der Opfer des Nationalsozialismus* commemorates the Holocaust of the Third Reich, and at the *Wittelsbacher Platz*, Kurfürst Maximilian I leads the way. The *Odeonsplatz* is the link from the old town to the *Maxvorstadt*. There, the *Theatinerkirche* soothes the mind. During absolutism, the dukes of Bavaria strolled in the *Hofgarten*, and their throne stood in the *Herkulessaal*. In the *Bayerische Staatskanzlei*, Bavarian politicians show the way. The *Münchner Residenz* was the city palace of the Wittelsbacher dynasty, and the *Nationaltheater* awaits opera enthusiasts at the *Max-Joseph-Platz*.

① Marienplatz

Facts & Figures

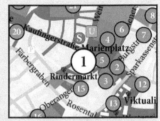

The Marienplatz once was the turntable of the city. The square was called *Schrannenplatz* until 1854. When the prayers of the townspeople to the Virgin Mary, launched at the Mariensäule, warded off a cholera epidemic, the magistrate renamed the piazza. The Middle Ages held a market at the city's pulsating heart, and the Munichers turned over any long-distance trade here. The barkers relocated their grain bags, fishing nets, apples and potatoes to the Viktualienmarkt during the 19th century. Merchants traded fine cloth and wine at the 100-metre-wide square until 1850, and local farmers offered meat, milk, cheese, poultry and eggs. The Marienplatz still resonates with chanting and processions, pageants and weddings. It also witnessed the execution of obstinate Protestants and witches. Today, the *FC Bayern München* celebrates its numerous football titles here and the Advent jingles with a Christmas fair.

Munich at the *Isar* owed its affluence to the *Salt Goddess* in the Middle Ages. The **Marienplatz**, the town's main square, distributed the white gold. It was excavated at the Alps and brought on carts to town. Salt was a commodity essential to preserve food. The transport, stamp duty, and the need for intermediaries made salt a luxury product, not the mining itself.

When Emperor Ludwig der Bayer granted Munich stacking rights in 1332, he brought prosperity to the city. The royal decree forced traders to cross the Isar at the Gasteig, and they had to put the white wheels down for sale at the central market for three days.

Munich's monopoly on salt turned into clinking coins. Trading relocated to the Promenadeplatz in the 15th century - the business had become industrious. The population grew fast, and the burghers enlarged their city in the 14th century to loosen the asphyxiating girdle. The second moat ran from the Isartor to the Sendlinger Tor, Karlstor and the Odeonsplatz.

The **Marienplatz** also merchandised fine cloth and wine besides salt, and the local farmers of the alpine foreland guaranteed staple food and supplies. They sold eggs and herbs outside the Alte Rathaus, and breeders offered fish at the central fountain, kept in nets for freshness.

▲ In the Medieval Ages, traders sold wriggling fish at the Fischbrunnen.

Munich's economic, political and social heart pulsated at the Marienplatz. Here, the city fathers proclaimed their wisdom and beheaded criminals. Protected by sturdy walls, the citizens chanted, prayed and rejoiced, and their rulers celebrated their weddings at the piazza.

The citizens paved the square around 1300, and in 1315, Emperor Ludwig der Bayer prohibited any building work that would obstruct the open space. A police force defied shady characters and detained offenders, imprisoning the culprits in the dungeon of the Alte Rathaus. The building at Marienplatz 1, corner of Weinstraße, displays a fresco depicting the sentry.

Location: Marienplatz **Entrance:** Without charge **Opening times:** Always accessible
Stadt München: https://www.muenchen.de
Stadtmagazin: https://www.in-muenchen.de // https://www.ganz-muenchen.de

The Basilisk at the Well

A basilisk soared through Munich's skies during the Middle Ages until the citizens fossilised the beast to bronze and glued it with prayers to the Mariensäule. The monster crowed like a rooster and wagged its tail like a lizard. The burghers hardly knew its image, though, because those who had glanced into its face were immediately petrified, unable to utter another word. Once upon a time, when the Middle Ages were still dark, the Medusa of Munich wove its nest at the well of the Marienplatz, and the maidens, drawing water at the fountain, died in the hundreds. Good advice was hard to find. Finally, a light of inspiration glimmered! Blindfolded, the Bavarian heroes in lederhosen covered the shaft with a mirror lashed on long sticks, and when the basilisk saw its ugly character, it turned into stone. Today, the serpent screams silently at the Mariensäule, coated in bronze.

(2) Altes Rathaus & Talburgtor

Facts & Figures

Munich's burghers built their town hall east of the Marienplatz in 1310. A storm demolished the wooden house in 1460; a tempest's lightning smouldered the timber to ashes. The master builder Jörg von Halspach reconstructed the Alte Rathaus 20 years later, this time in stone. Fashion changed the facade like a chameleon for 500 years, and only in 1861 did the Munichers reflect on their tradition and refurbished the complex in its original style. Finally, the magistrate cut thoroughfares through the building in 1877 and 1934 to redirect the traffic from the adjoining Talburgtor, the oldest part of the structure. Bricklayers had erected the watchtower in the 12th century. Today, it houses a small Spielzeugmuseum (toy museum), delighting the young at heart. World War II destroyed the Alte Rathaus, but the Munichers reconstructed it after the fighting had ended.

Shortly after Herzog Heinrich der Löwe (Henry the Lion) had founded Munich in 1158, the burghers constructed Munich's first town hall, the **Alte Rathaus**, adjacent to the **Talburgtor**, a watchtower. The two buildings conclude the eastern edge of the Marienplatz. The Munichers fortified the Heinrichsstadt and encircled it by a town wall.

Merchants travelling along the salt road entered the town at the Talburgtor during the Middle Ages, arriving at Munich's central market. Weavers offered fine cloth, freshly baked bread teased the noses, and the dungeons screamed with imprisoned swindlers caught at the Marienplatz. Law and order were imperative in medieval Munich.

The Munichers insisted on their right of self-government, however they had to subordinate to the Dukes of Bavaria. Two city councils have decided over the affairs since 1289, but only the patrician families held power; their Inner Council dominated the city. Most of the influential had attained prosperity through long-distance trade with salt, and they annually elected the burgomaster, the city's mayor. The Outer Council, recruited from the guilds, served as an advisory board.

With time, the town pressed for additional rights, enforcing the privilege of minting and the control of customs legislation.

The dance hall of the Alte Rathaus was well-known and very popular in the lands. Here, the patricians staged exuberant balls. The statue of a *Moriscan Dancer* at the thoroughfare testifies to the gaiety.

The Bavarian Parliament once resided in the town hall, and in 1848, Munich elected its delegation to the Frankfurt National Assembly in the festival hall.

In 1938, the Nazi regime ordered the Kristallnacht from the Alte Rathaus, setting loose the first stage of the Holocaust. The leaders had been gathering for a remembrance celebration of the Hitler Putsch (Beer Hall Putsch).

▲ Jörg von Halspach constructed the Alte Rathaus, Munich's old town hall, in 1480.

Location: Marienplatz **Entrance**: Only during the Stadtfest (Founding Day of Munich)
Spielzeugmuseum: https://spielzeugmuseummuenchen.de
Opening Times: daily 10.00 - 17.00. Entrance: Adults 6 €, Concession 2 €

The Spielzeugmuseum in the Talburgtor

The toy museum in the Talburgtor is a treasure trove. The steep stairs lead to magical dolls, steaming trains, humming bears, wooden toys, Barbies and sturdy robots made out of metals. Has children's play changed over time? The privately organised exhibition shows the development of toys over four centuries. The Czech-German cartoonist, author and film director Ivan Steiger founded the museum in 1983. He is also running a collection in Prague. Today, his daughter Helena Steiger manages the museum. The location is significant: in the Alte Rathaus opposite, the patricians enjoyed balls in a dance hall - at about the same level. The statue of a Moriscan Dancer in the thoroughfare reminds passers-by of the festivities. The Münchner Stadtmuseum presents the original figure carved by Erasmus Grasser.

(3) St Peter

Facts & Figures

The beginnings of St Peter stretch back to times before the founding of Munich: in the 11th century, monks from Schäftlarn had established a chapel at the Petersbergl, a small mound overlooking the river Isar. Today's baroque church rests its three aisles on late Gothic founding walls, some of which are still visible. Two rows of stifling side chapels sandwich a luminous nave. The cleverly designed lighting arrangement draws the faithful towards the central axis, the altar and the apse. Nikolaus Gottfried Stuber carved the main altar in 1739, framing a figurine of Saint Peter, carved in timber by Erasmus Grasser some two hundred years earlier. Four church fathers accompany God's fisherman. The ceiling fresco by Johann Baptist Zimmermann, delicately executed in 1756, shows the crucifixion of the first Bishop of Rome, the rock on which the church rests its faith.

The history of **St Peter**, Munich's *Alter Peter* (Old Peter), stretches back to the 11th century: a Romanesque chapel at a mound overlooking the Isar already invited the faithful around the year 1050. The burgess replaced the prayer house with a Gothic church some 250 years later, but the devastating fire of 1327 obliterated it. The Munichers rebuilt the temple, and sixty years later, a late Gothic sanctuary spread its glory again. It forms the basic structure of the contemporary church still today, although it has been altered and enlarged several times.

For centuries, twin towers flanked the entrance of St Peter until a lightning set their wooden roof on fire in 1607, causing the steeples to collapse. It was Satan harbouring a grudge against the Munichers: *"The burghers are too much loved by God"*, so his thought. The citizens combined the foundations of the two towers and replaced the turrets with a concentric one.

The clerics redesigned the church in baroque style during the Thirty Years' War, and in 1654, they added a barrel vaulting across the longhouse. In 1795, a cannonball hit St Peter: Austrian soldiers had set up camp at the nearby Gasteig and fired at Napoleon's advancing forces, but they missed the target and hit the church instead of the French troops.

In 1789, Kurfürst Karl Theodor sealed the graveyard, relocated all bones, and embedded the most precious memorial stone plates into the exterior wall.

During World War II, the walls of St Peter collapsed, hit by an Allied air raid. The city fathers surrendered to the idea of ablating the building. They wanted to replace the demolished walls with a modern structure, but the pastors Max Zistl and Max Stritter saved the building. Thanks to their tireless dedication, the Munichers rebuilt the church in medieval style. The pastors had stopped the blasters at the last minute, who had already installed the explosion to destroy the church.

▲ Only the courageous want to climb the 299 steps to the observation deck.

Location: Petersplatz 1 **Entrance:** Without charge **Opening Times:** 9.00 - 20.00
Internet: https://alterpeter.de
Ascent to the tower: daily 12.00 – 16.30. Entrance: Adults 5,00 €, Concession 3,00 €

Kindling a Fire

The 13 February 1327 was a cold winter day. At the Order of Poor Clares at St Jakob Anger, shivering nuns were about to kindle an open fire for their morning prayers when their clammy hands dropped a piece of scorching charcoal, igniting the timber of the stalls. When the flames reached the neighbouring candle manufacturing area, the conflagration was unstoppable. A stiff foehn wind scourged the devil's tongues across town for two days; the sparks inflamed most of the city's straw-roofed wooden houses. The chroniclers reported that the blaze wrecked about a third of the settlement, destroying the Heilig-Geist-Kirche and St Peter. Emperor Ludwig der Bayer mandated swiftly: *"From now on, buildings are to be constructed from brick stones only, and only fire wardens without eye patches are to be employed to guard the city."*

Highlights of St Peter

St Peter is the oldest church in Munich and an important landmark of the city, guiding the way to the centre of town. Shortly after the settlement was founded, the citizens built their first church next to the Marienplatz. It was only with the construction of the Frauenkirche in 1271 that the parish split in two.

Exterior: The gravestones on the outer wall originate from the church's adjacent cemetery, which Kurfürst Karl Theodor sealed from further use in 1789. The cross of the church tower is not oriented to the west as usual but is rotated by 90°: the devil is said to have kicked it out of anger because he could not bear the passionate purity of the Munichers. What is true, however, is that the architects want to offer less surface area for the wind so that the cross does not fall onto the central nave during one of the many storms. An Austrian cannonball that hit the church in 1796 is walled into the outer choir wall. It can be spotted with some patience from the Viktualienmarkt.

Interior: After entering the three-aisled church, the bright nave inevitably attracts the visitor's attention and draws the faithful to the central axis. The main fresco in the nave shows the crucifixion of Saint Peter. He is upside down; his head points to the ground. The German Baroque painter Johann Baptist Zimmermann created the scenes from his life between 1753 and 1756. Hermenegild Peiker sensitively reconstructed them after World War II.

The extraordinary baroque high altar by Nikolaus Gottfried Stuber and Johann Georg Greiff (1730-1734) encloses a figure of Saint Peter with a golden tiara, which Erasmus Grasser carved around 1517. Four church fathers flank the apostle. Egid Quirin Asam created them in 1732/33. Their eyes are fixed on Peter, and they hold closed books in their hands. During the sede vacante, Munich removes the tiara from the figure of Saint Peter until a new pope is elected.

In the presbytery, six impressive panel paintings from the former Gothic high altar show scenes from the life of Saint Peter. The Krakow painter Jan Polack created them between 1492 and 1495. Schloss Blutenburg presents other pieces of his work.

The Schrenk Altar in the first northern side chapel depicts Jesus as the judge of the world. In addition to the crucifixion, scenes of the

▲ The Juliet at the Alte Rathaus testifies to the town twinning with Verona.

last judgment illustrate the apocalyptic attitude of the Munichers, overshadowing the zest of life. The altar was created around 1400.

Opposite, the Pötschner Altar shows the Adoration of the Magi. The late Gothic painting was made around 1477. The donor family prays at the wings.

In the southern tower chapel (baptismal chapel), a work by Hans Krumpper (made around 1620) depicts Jesus as the Saviour of the world.

The main organ of St Peter was created in 2003 by the organ builder Klais. It has 58 registers on four manuals.

The 91-metre-tall church tower can be climbed. The steep staircase passes eight bells dangling in the tower. The oldest bell (Poor Sinner Bell) dates back to 1327. It once rang to announce an execution.

Herzog Heinrich der Löwe and the Dragon

Many legends trailed around Henry the Lion, the founder of Munich. When Emperor Friedrich I Barbarossa outlawed the vassal, then aged 49, by an imperial ban, the lands zealously forgot his tales, and only at the Isar, the people kept his memory alive! The duke, on a journey to the Occident, spinsters report, once witnessed a horrific spectacle: a lion was desperately warding off a fire-breathing dragon. Henry took to heart, drew his sword and rushed to fight the beast. The knight's searing lance pierced the dragon's heart, winning the day. In gratitude, the wounded lion kept at his saviour's side, and the duke became known as *Henry the Lion*. Henceforth, burning claws saved the courageous nobleman at times from danger and distress, *Hakuna Matata*, and his enemies were wary of his superhuman powers.

④ Glockenspiel

Facts & Figures

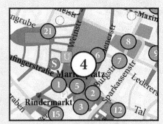

The harried visitor needs a little patience before the 32 solar-powered copper figures of Germany's largest carillon begin to rotate. Intoxicated by 43 bells, minstrels and knights dance at the wedding of Herzog Wilhelm V and Renata of Lorraine in 1568. Then, a tournament challenges the knights: two riders rush towards each other. To the chagrin of the French, the blue and white squire triumphs - always - three times a day. Last but not least, the Schäffler turn around themselves and around the circle - finally, the plague is banished - hurray! When the rooster crows from the gable roof, the bells fall silent, and the game is over. In the evening at 9 pm, the night watchman and the angel of peace put the Munichers to bed. The bells play music from Richard Wagner's *Die Meistersinger von Nuremberg* and the *Lullaby* composed by Johannes Brahms.

Several times a day, the **carillon at the Neue Rathaus** brings the 1568 wedding between Herzog Wilhelm V and Renata of Lorraine to life. The union was a political move: two important Catholic duchies united in marriage and demonstrated strength to an unsettled Europe that was crumbling under the pressure of the Reformation. Despite being heavily in debt, the bride and groom staged the truly biggest celebration of the century.

The nobility from all over Europe participated in the wedding. Five thousand knights were invited, and many more showed up. Even Erzherzog Ferdinand, the younger brother of Emperor Karl V, took part. He kept quarters at the Alter Hof. His entourage alone numbered 700 horses.

The chefs prepared more than four hundred dishes; 521 oxen were slaughtered and grilled. The burghers celebrated the marriage over 18 days with bowl stabbings, masked balls, concerts, hunts and a tournament of lances - the symbol of every marriage. Orlando di Lasso, the greatest musician of his time, provided the musical direction. The Belgian had lived in Munich since 1565. However, despite the opulent display of strength, the Thirty Years' War could not be avoided.

▲ The Glockenspiel shows the wedding of Herzog Wilhelm V and Renata of Lorraine.

The wedding took place on Sunday, February 22, 1568 in the Frauenkirche. Munich was covered in snow, but the sun was shining. The banquet in the Münchner Residenz ended with a cheerful dance. Finally, the bride and groom were accompanied to their bridal chamber. They drank a few more cups of wine and then retired to ... rest.

Two days later, the guests presented gifts: jewels, precious stones, necklaces, diamonds, rings, and much more.

The next few days, the party went hunting, enjoyed theatre and feasted at opulent banquets.

Knight games at the Marienplatz ended the celebrations on March 10.

Location: Marienplatz **Entrance:** Without charge **Times:** daily 11.00, 12.00 & 17.00 At 21.00, the night watch brings the Münchner Kindl to bed.
Internet: https://marienplatz.de/sehenswuerdigkeiten/glockenspiel

Ludwig the Strict & Maria von Brabant

Scribes wrote *1256* into the volumes of history when turmoil watered the soil with blood. Herzog Ludwig II waged war on the Rhenish Pfalz; he received a dispatch - *his consort longed to see him*. However, the foolish scoundrel of a messenger had confused the letters, and the Duke read, burning with gleaming eyes, lines that Maria von Brabant had directed to one of the knights. *Promises! Adultery!* The Duke spat with fire; he cursed the world; he rushed to Mangoldstein, and he executed his wife, her ladies and the castle guard. Only now, his blistering blood ran cold in his veins. Never had his wife been unfaithful to him. Overnight, his hair turned ash-white, and he retreated into seclusion. Day by day, the penitent crawled to the chapel at the Petersbergl, where, at last, the Lord granted forgiveness - amazing grace.

Mariensäule

Facts & Figures

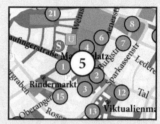

The Mariensäule in the centre of the Marienplatz was gifted by Kurfürst Maximilian I in 1638. The votive offering appreciates the Mother of God for her help during the turmoil of the Thirty Years' War. The Swedish occupation had left Munich unscathed, thanks to the prayers the Munichers had sent off to her. On a column of reddish marble, a gilded virgin triumphs over sin. She rests on a crescent moon, holding baby Jesus in her arm; he blesses the world. Her flowing, long hair resembles the apocalyptic woman. At the base of the column, four putties triumph over hunger (dragon), war (lion), disbelief (adder) and illness (basilisk). The statue of the Virgin Mary was cast for the grave of Herzog Wilhelm V and Renata of Lorraine but was never used. From 1606 to 1620, the figure flanked the altar of the Frauenkirche. The column also serves as a reference point for Bavaria's land surveying.

The **Glockenspiel** and the **Mariensäule** wrap Munich's main square into a blanket woven by history. Ideologically, they frame the period of the Thirty Years' War, setting the scene. Kurfürst Maximilian I had founded the Catholic League in Munich in 1609, taking over the leadership of the Counter Reformation. After the Catholic League under Johann Graf von Tilly devastated Magdeburg in 1631, Kurfürst Maximilian I feared a similar fate for Munich when the Protestant Swedish King Gustav II Adolf marched on Munich with three regiments a year later. He had already liberated Nürnberg and taken Augsburg by storm. Only financial bloodletting saved Munich from his cannons.

At the Gasteig, a delegation from Munich's Electoral War Council and the Inner Council kneeled to offer the Swedes the keys to the city and a payment if they would spare Munich and not plunder it. The demand was 300,000 Reichstaler - an incredible sum, but the only way to prevent rape, chaos and manslaughter.

Kurfürst Maximilian I had fled to Salzburg some weeks earlier and solemnly vowed to *"do a godly work if the lands [...] were to be saved from the enemy's destruction."*

▲ The Mariensäule is a reminder of the time of the Thirty Years' War.

Munich was spared, but the Swedish troops devastated the outskirts, such as the Au and Haidhausen. As security to enforce payments, King Gustav II Adolf took 42 hostages, among them priests, monks, councillors, innkeepers and craftsmen. They remained in his care for three years. A few weeks later, the Swedish army moved on.

After surviving the plague in 1634/36, Kurfürst Maximilian I donated a Mariensäule. The Virgin, cast by Hubert Gerhard in 1593, sits enthroned on a Trojan column with flowing hair, a crown on her head and a sceptre in her hand. Four putties at the foot of the pedestal triumph over unbelief, war, hunger and the plague.

Location: Marienplatz **Entrance:** Without charge **Opening Times:** Always accessible
Internet: https://www.muenchner-stadtmuseum.de
Literature: Michael Schattenhofer: Die Mariensäule in München

The Children of Israel had Poisoned the Wells!

Fate struck relentlessly when the great plague decimated Bavaria in 1349 - and of course, Europe blamed the cause for the Black Death on the assassins of Jesus Christ: *"The Jews had poisoned the wells!"* - the outcry across the continent. The Bavarian Herzog Ludwig and many burghers groaned under the debt they had accumulated by the usurers, and the Munichers promptly stormed the ghetto at the Marienhof, to the North of the Neue Rathaus, slaying men, women and infants alike, as ever incriminating the epidemic on the defenceless. In Strasbourg, too, the burgess killed two thousand, and in Bern, Stuttgart and Augsburg, every Jew had to die. In Frankfurt, Mainz and Köln, the innocent fared no better. Plague does not distinguish between religion, but persecution broke the rabbis' necks.

⑥ Neues Rathaus

Facts & Figures

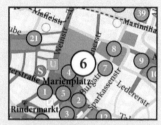

The young architect Georg von Hauberrisser, ambitious and intoxicated by his visions, harboured striking plans, and he realised them at Munich's neo-gothic town hall in 1865. Along the shell-lime façade, statues of Bavaria's regents presented their monarchic glory for the last time. Then, the 1918 revolution replaced them like flower petals blown away by the autumn wind. Little angels trumpet between their crowns, fiery goblins throw eery grimaces, and feral demons snarl with their tongues. Bourgeois' virtues remind of decency, and the personifications of tempers make fun of the commoner. Dragons add fire to Bavaria's turbulent history, and a staircase presents the stages of life at the Prunkhof, the inner courtyard. Wait - there is more! The observation deck, 50 metres aloft, offers a view over the city, a glance shrouded in legends. Bavaria is magical, and the Neue Rathaus presents its story!

The completion of the **Neue Rathaus** (new town hall) ended an architectural history patronised by the Wittelsbacher dynasty that had started with the construction of the Alter Hof some 700 years before.

With the arrival of democracy, Munich's vigour had petered out, falling into despair during the turmoil of the 20th century: World War I, the unsettling Weimar period, and the Nazi regime carved deep wounds into the flesh of society. When Adolf Hitler declared Munich to be Germany's *Capital of the Movement*, the city had reached its low point. Only by hosting the Games of the XX Summer Olympiads in 1972 had the town recovered a sense of its glorious past.

Construction shifted to the suburbs after World War II. The Neue Rathaus was the last grand building within the historical city centre, masoned at a time when the workers still fired the brick stones under the supervision of a monarch. But! The visionaries had already entered the stage: Munich was ready to mould the past into new ideologies. At last, the representative building mania of the Wittelsbacher dynasty had run dry.

The Neue Rathaus tells its story quickly: As Munich's population grew, the Alte Rathaus became too small, and by the middle of the

▲ The 80-metres tall tower titillates the clouds at the Neue Rathaus.

19th century, the magistrate had commissioned a new office building. The architect Georg von Hauberrisser, a 25-year-old youngster from Graz, won the tender in 1865, convincing the city fathers of his economical design.

In 1874, the bricklayers completed the offices facing the Dienerstraße. Space was tight on the day of the move, and a central building with a mighty 80-metre-tall tower followed in 1892. Masons laid the final brick to the west wing in 1909, shortly before the outbreak of World War I. Some 40 years later, *Bomber Harris* turned the building into rubble, and one wonders: Why do kids always need to demolish the sandcastles of other toddlers?

Location: Marienplatz 8 **Entrance:** Without charge **Opening Times:** 10.00 - 19.00
Ascent to the tower: Mon - Fri 10.00 - 19.00, Sat 10.00 - 16.30, Sun 10.00 - 14.30
Entrance: Adults 4 €, Concession 1 €

Benno, Patron Saint of Munich

A statue of Benno, patron saint of Munich, squints against the sun and observes the passers-by at the western facade of the Neue Rathaus. Legends twine around his charitable heart, which saved many souls. The Munichers worshipped his relics by about 1576. When the Swedes arrived at the gates during the Thirty Years' War, the burgess evacuated Benno's mortal remains to Salzburg. After prayers to the Virgin Mary had scared away the Protestants, his bones solemnly marched back. Saint Benno pulled off many miracles in his time, such as the birth of Kurfürst Maximilian I's two sons. The Elector, buttoned-up, begged Benno for masculinity, and the saint granted his plea. Relics promised eternal life. If the believer followed the example of a holy man, the saint connected him to the will of God and nudged him away from purgatory.

Highlights of the Neue Rathaus

The New Town Hall was built in the neo-Gothic style. It is the visible symbol of the rapid increase in population during the 19th century after Bavaria became a kingdom. Immigration from all over the country enforced a new building, which the architect Georg von Hauberrisser realised from 1865 onwards. To this day, the mayor of the state capital works at the Marienplatz with his 650 employees. His offices are at the corner of the Weinstraße.

Anyone who turns his attention to the decoration of the facade will be surprised: Rulers from the Wittelsbacher dynasty rub shoulders with civic virtues; frightening goblins make grim faces. The Münchner Kindl is also depicted. It can be seen at the top of the tower, corner of Dienerstraße. Next to it, Saint George is stabbing a dragon. At the Wurmeck (corner of Weinstraße) the monster emerges from obscurity and scares away the Munichers. There, cheerful Schäffler encourage citizens to leave behind the Black Death. With exuberant joy, they perform a traditional folk dance. Next to it, a Bavarian lion proudly watches over the citizens and defends the city.

The facade of the town hall presents all of Bavaria's rulers (dukes, electors and kings) before the turmoil of the 20th century deposed them from power. On the right side of the Königsloge (royal box) above the entrance to the courtyard, King Ludwig II shines. In the middle of the facade, Prince Regent Luitpold rides majestically. The town hall was completed during his reign.

The balcony on the right is dedicated to civic virtues (industry, domesticity, civic courage, charity). A knight watches over angels at the top of the tower that frame a city coat of arms.

Along the Weinstraße, the builders immortalised the character traits of the Munichers with self-irony. There, personifications of garrulousness (a woman with a coffee cup), thirst (a drunkard) and a swank make fun of the Munichers. A statue of Saint Benno commemorates Munich's patron saint.

At the entrance to the magnificent courtyard below the Königsloge is Munich's coat of arms. Inside the passage (left side), an elevator takes visitors to the tower's observation deck. On the right, a staircase leads to the publicly accessible administration rooms. The graceful inner

▲ King Ludwig II appears at the royal box of the New Town Hall.

courtyard stands out with its curved spiral staircase (left side). The so-called *staircase of ages* depicts the different stages of human life: childhood (boy with mother), youth, adult and old age. Animals symbolise the decades: bull and magpie represent the 30s, fox and hen the 50s, tomcat and owl the 80s.

Above the entrance to the ticket hall (north side), a greedy cashier with a bag of money awaits the citizens. In addition, the Ratstrinkstube caters to any appetite. A cheerful reveller greets them at the portal. The paintings of the restaurant are dedicated to drunken happiness.

The municipal canteen on the east side of the Prunkhof offers inexpensive alternatives. It is open to everyone, not only to the employees of the town hall. During summers, one can dine al fresco.

The Lindworm at the Wurmeck

A relief on the facade of the New Town Hall (corner of Weinstraße) shows a lindworm that unexpectedly emerges from the hellish underground. Munich was considered the epicentre of the Black Death in Europe during the Middle Ages. Epidemics broke out regularly in the city. The lindworm often circled above the roofs with wings like bats, polluting the air with its deadly breath. The citizens hid in their houses, but they still perished in large numbers - young and old, rich and poor. One day, the beast settled at the Marienplatz to weave its nest. In desperation, the Munichers gathered courage and aimed a cannon at the monster - fired - the shot hit the beast - the dragon was dead! As a reminder, a stonework on the corner of Weinstraße depicts the horrific struggle. From now on, the corner was called Wurmeck (corner of the lindworm).

⑦ Burgstraße

Facts & Figures

During the Middle Ages, the Burgstraße connected the patricians at the town hall to Bavaria's sovereigns at the Alter Hof. The axis of power was the first path that the Munichers paved. Here, local celebrities and some influential lived: Munich's 18th-century leading architect, François Cuvilliés the Elder, dwelled at Burgstraße 8; the falconer looked after the dukes' birds of prey at the *Falkeneck*, today Burgstraße 10. Diagonally opposite, at the *Löweneck* (lions-corner), formerly a kennel, the dukes held lions. Munich's town clerks worked at the upper floor of Burgstraße 5, the *Stadtschreiberhaus*, issuing regulations and decrees. At street-level, the dukes taxed the trade with wine, to everyone's dismay. Wolfgang Amadeus Mozart composed the opera Idomeneo from autumn 1780 to spring 1781 at Burgstraße 7, but to no avail - the court refused to hire him as a musician.

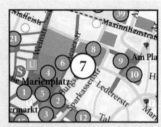

The **Stadtschreiberhaus** (house of the town clerk) at Burgstraße 5 is Munich's oldest late-Gothic townhouse that survived. A wooden house occupied the location already in the 13th century, but the city-fire of 1327 demolished it. The townspeople reconstructed the house in stone, as documents from 1525 show.

The Stadtschreiberhaus charms with its central bay window, framed by two half-sized lateral gables. Common parlance archly calls them *Ohrwaschel* (earlobes). The residents pulled goods to the upper floors using rope winches at the pediment. Frescoes decorated the facade, as was customary at that time. Most likely they had been executed by Munich's prolific decorator Hans Mielich. The cycle shows Roman Emperors, caryatids on painted Ionic columns, lion heads, and flowers. The Greek gods Hermes and Athena embellish the upper windowsills.

The entrance to the right leads along a steep *Himmelsleiter* to the upper floors (staircase to heaven: an arduous ladder-like flight of stairs). Munich's only remaining Gothic tower, the *Schneck* (snail tower), adorns the inner courtyard, where the Genießer-Brunnen (fountain of joy) splutters, buoyantly designed by Hans Mayer in 1952.

▲ The Stadtschreiberhaus at Burgstraße 5 is Munich's oldest townhouse.

Bavaria's cunning dukes controlled the town's wine trade from the hall on the ground floor. Any barrel imported had to be presented for duty to the officers at the town clerk's house. Later, innkeepers converted the premises into a wine bar, where the town's intellectuals caroused deep into the night, while at the upper tier, administrative staff bowed and scraped over important papers.

The office for river panning next door issued mining rights at the Isar. The yield in gold was low; however, the dukes encouraged their citizens to burrow for treasures in the riverbed as the country lacked the commodity. Hope only dies last in Munich, too.

Location: Burgstraße **Entrance**: Without charge **Opening times**: Always accessible
Stadtschreiberhaus: https://www.muenchen.tv/der-muenchner-weinstadl-140322
Mozart in Munich: https://musikspaziergang.de

Herzog Christoph and the Knight

Bavaria delights in the anecdotes of Herzog Christoph, telling the yarn of his impregnable physical strength. Once, a foreign knight challenged the Duke to a battle of the lances, a game of jousting. However, when the nobleman witnessed the Hercules of Bavaria wrestling two bears into submission and dragging them across the Burgstraße in chains, he admitted that the Duke enjoyed invincible powers, and the challenge was decided before the competition had begun. Hikers roaming the meadows of the Isar today forget that in Bavaria's forests, wolves and witches, bears and goblins dwelled during the Middle Ages. Living in the wilderness outside the protective town wall was dangerous, and only a few, like Herzog Christoph, had the stamina to survive wild beasts and fend off spinsters.

Alter Hof

Facts & Figures

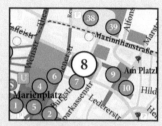

The Alter Hof was the home of the Wittelsbacher dynasty during the High Middle Ages. The dynasty had ruled over Bavaria since 1180. Munich's founder, Herzog Heinrich der Löwe, had already established a mansion at this location; in 1255, Herzog Ludwig II laid the founding stone of the fortress at today's southern edge of the complex. When the Bavarian Ludwig IV ascended to Germany's throne as Emperor Ludwig der Bayer, he nominated the Alter Hof to his predominant castle and expanded it to the east and west. He also added the chapel St Lorenz (demolished in 1816). The dukes stayed close to the north-eastern edge of the city when they relocated to today's Münchner Residenz in the 16th century. Allied air raids demolished the complex during World War II, but it was partly restored in the 1950s. The Museum infopoint tells the story of the castle in its basement.

Herzog Albrecht IV issued Bavaria's principle of primogeniture in 1506, which, from now on, determined the line of succession. The eldest son inherited the lands upon the sovereign's death and not - as previously - all siblings. Guarding against partition meant that power remained in one hand; the nation's unity was not weakened.

The dukes had stitched the tatters of the last partition together during the War of Succession of Landshut in 1504/05 after Herzog Georg der Reiche of Lower Bavaria had passed away without an heir. Upper Bavaria now controlled all lands of the alpine foothills, and Munich asserted its power against its competitor Landshut and its rival Regensburg. The city had turned into a residential town and ruled over vast stretches of land. By and by, Munich ripened to become Bavaria's princely metropolis: Munich had outgrown its medieval teething age.

The town at the Isar owes its dominant role within Bavaria to two incidents: Herzog Ludwig II elected Munich to his residence after the country's first partition in 1255. Secondly, Lower Bavaria lost the war of predominance when the Duke of Landshut died before he had fathered an heir, neglecting his duties in the marital bed.

▲ During the Middle Ages, the dukes of Bavaria resided at the Alter Hof.

A regional centre of power hardly ever enforced its dominance only by winning on the battlefield but mostly gained its supremacy by wise marriage. A fertile consort, who bestowed the sovereign with virile sons, was often more critical to the region's long-term success than a fierce army. A bride's infertility or a groom's impotence led to wars of succession, bloodshed, and the redrawing of the map.

Munich's history as a royal seat began in 1255 when Herzog Ludwig II laid the founding stone for the **Alter Hof** at the northeastern corner of the first enclosure. During his reign, the masons constructed the Burgstock, the building to the south of the compound.

Location: Alter Hof 1, 80331 München, Telephone: +49 89 21014050
Museum infopoint: Opening times: Mon - Sat 10.00 - 18.00 Entrance: Without charge
https://www.museen-in-bayern.de/der-infopoint/der-infopoint.html

Emperor Ludwig der Bayer and the Monkey

The dukes bred exotic animals at their fortress: bears, parrots, lions and many other species. Once, according to common parlance, a monkey stole baby Emperor Ludwig der Bayer from his cradle. When the nurse noticed the scoundrel, she screamed with horror, frightening the buffoon. The hobgoblin, with the baby in its arms, was terrified and hurried to safety. Quickly, the court rushed after the trickster, who fled to the attic, where he scrambled through an open hatch and climbed the turret - today called the *monkey tower*. The court, beyond the pale, scampered for cushions to spread at the courtyard, softening a potential fall. Finally, a cunning cook lured the monkey into the castle with sweets. There, the hairy beast returned the little suckling to his cradle, and all are glad that the story retells a farce only.

Like many of his contemporaries during the Middle Ages, Herzog Ludwig II struggled to nurture and rear an heir. Only his third wife, Mathilde von Hapsburg, delivered a healthy son, who one day became the Emperor of Germany - a *Bavarian by the Grace of God!* He was to fall in love with the Alter Hof and steadily expanded the ensemble, adding further wings and the chapel St Lorenz at the northern edge of the castle. Although medieval times condemned an Emperor to peregrination, Emperor Ludwig der Bayer nevertheless spent more than 2000 days at the Alter Hof, a record amongst the sovereigns of his time.

In 1314, Germany's devout countries elected Ludwig as their King, and in 1328, the Bavarian ruler became the Emperor of the *Holy Roman Empire of the Germanic Nation*. The Munichers kept his imperial insignia at the chapel St Lorenz, guarded by four Cistercian monks. The Bayerische Nationalmuseum presents the benefactor's relief and several figurines from the chapel, which King Maximilian I tore down in 1816 during the age of Bavaria's secularisation. An office building replaces the church today.

Munich benefited from Emperor Ludwig's dignities and experienced a golden age. He enriched the town by awarding his beloved Munich the staple right and the privilege of minting.

Ludwig decreed after a devastating fire in 1327 that the Munichers had to construct all new buildings in stone. The directive pressured the treasury, but Munich profited from the long-term investment by adding stability and avoiding disaster.

Munich's dual role started with Emperor Ludwig der Bayer; the conflict was tense at times but prosperous otherwise: on the one hand, Munich insisted on its right of self-administration as a free city. On the other hand, the city hosted the Bavarian dukes and was thus obliged to submit to the sovereign.

The dukes recognised the danger too, at the latest in 1385 when an uprising challenged their power. The Bavarian rulers forced the city to repent. They demanded the construction of a fortress, a refuge, the *Neuveste* outside the town moat (today Münchner Residenz), and a connecting arch to the Alter Hof. The centuries expanded the fortress to a stately residence, and the royal household finally relocated the Duke's treasures from the Alter Hof to the new premises in the 16th century. After the relocation, construction work moved to the Neuveste - a stroke of luck for historians because the Alter Hof thus preserved its Gothic character.

▲ Emperor Ludwig der Bayer rides at the Alter Hof in Munich to this day.

The Alter Hof was severely hit by the 70 Allied air raids on Munich during World War II, and the medieval walls collapsed under the heavy bombardment. Finally, the city administration had to demolish the Pfister- and the Brunnenstock in the 1950s and replace them with contemporary buildings. The magistrate, however, refurbished the historical Burgstock and the Zwingerstock.

The Burgstock's vaulted cellar hides a little-told surprise: here, the multimedia *Museum infopoint* narrates the story of the medieval fortress with audiovisual finesse. Additionally, visitors will find comprehensive informational material on all museums and castles in Bavaria at the neat counter on the ground floor. The advice is valuable before any trip across the lands.

The Alte Münze (Old Mint)

Opposite the Alter Hof is the Old Mint on the Pfisterstraße. The complex now houses the State Office for Monument Preservation. The pretty inner courtyard in the Renaissance style is a pioneer north of the Alps. The four-wing complex rises over three floors - each with an arcade. The building was constructed between 1563 and 1567 as a stable. The ruler cared for his horses and stored his carriages here. The Wittelsbacher dynasty kept their Wunderkammer (Chamber of Wonders) on the upper floor. When Kurfürst Maximilian I took office in 1598, he had an inventory drawn up: 6,000 objects were counted. In 1809, the Royal Mint moved in, and this is how the name came about. Until 1986, Bavaria printed coins at the Alte Münze. The medals for the 1972 Summer Olympics were also minted here.

(9) Am Platzl

Facts & Figures

The trapezoidal square *Am Platzl* changed its facade like a chameleon, moving with the fashion of the times. Today, gourmet restaurants like the *Orlandohaus* serve haute cuisine - in the traditional style of Bavaria. Orlando di Lasso, the most famous musician of his age, composed his masterpieces at a previous building. The humanist Herzog Albrecht V appointed him as a court musician in 1556. The late 19th century refurbished the houses in the style of the German Renaissance when student unions and duelling fraternities swaggered to the piazza: *Corps Macaria* unrolled its piste at Am Platzl 6, and *Corps Franconia München* opened its union at Am Platzl 7. Common parlance calls the sidewall of the house Am Platzl 2 *Ohrwaschel* (ear lobe). The oldest apartment buildings of Munich struggle for survival at the corner of Platzlgasse. Their founding stones date from the 16th century.

The wind blows from the west to the east north of the Alps, and thus, the patricians dispelled any craft polluting the air to the city's eastern periphery. Most of the rivers north of the Alps - like the Isar - flow from south to north, and thus, the magistrate forced any trade contaminating the waters to the northern edge of the enclosure.

Munich's **Am Platzl** is at the northeastern corner of the first city wall, where the city's founders banished the odour-intensive and foul industries - out of sight, smell and taste of the nobility. The Middle Ages allocated this area to tanners and coopers. Their water mills clattered at a tributary of the Isar.

After a devastating fire turned the wooden structures at Am Platzl to ashes in 1418, the Munichers replaced their clay and straw houses with stonewalled buildings. When the settlement hosted the Münchner Residenz - after unification during the War of Succession of Landshut - the royal household appreciated the vicinity of the trapezoid to the palace. Employees settled with their families at Am Platzl, among them the gentleman of the horse, the dukes' chef, the chief judge, the master butcher and the kingly cooper.

▲ Europe's most important musician, Orlando di Lasso, dwelled at the Orlandohaus.

Munich refurbished the square in the style of the German Renaissance at the turn of the 20th century; duelling fraternities opened - more than ten associations by 1900.

During the Weimar Republic, Adolf Hitler founded the National Socialist German Workers' Party (NSDAP) at the Hofbräuhaus. After World War II, the Am Platzl transformed into a red-light district; dubious bars brought revelry into the neighbourhood.

Recently, puritans insisted on tradition and moved the border of the restricted area to the suburbs - speculators delighted in the financial opportunity. Today, butlers in white serve gourmet delicatessen garnished with blessedness.

Location: Am Platzl **Entrance**: Without charge **Opening Times**: Always accessible
Internet: https://www.sueddeutsche.de (Wie Studentenverbindungen ticken)
Literature: Cornelia Oelwein: Das Münchner Platzl - Lebensfreude im Quadrat

The Platzl-King

The Am Platzl succumbed to shimmering light and fluorescent lamps between World War II and the 1970s when Abraham Albert Berger was the King of the night. The Czech was born in 1927, and he established four bars at the piazza, among them the Separeé XX and the Papagei Bar. Already their neon signs promised wickedness, and the door latches trickled off grease. On 16 May 1970, he suddenly disappeared, swallowed by a dragon. Two months later, a fisherman pulled him out of the Chiemsee with a shot in his neck. Bavaria's forces investigated but to no avail! Decades later, a new King with a white crown conquered the trapezoid: the renowned star cook Alfons Schuhbeck - later imprisoned for tax fraud. The nightclubs changed to gourmet restaurants, and Munich's conservative Puritans returned to the square, now accompanied by their wives.

(10) Hofbräuhaus

Facts & Figures

The Hofbräuhaus sells more than 10,000 steins daily; more than two million visitors boogie at the world's jolliest beer hall annually. Primaeval Bavarians rejoice at the traditional beer cellar, too, romantically enraptured. More than 5,000 regulars join forces at over one hundred wooden tables, taking delight in the grotto's intoxicating foam. The Hofbräuhaus was born out of a necessity: the noble household wanted golden manna, and Munich's virtuous sovereigns had to learn the art of the hops during the 16th century. Today, Bavaria's Treasury Department administers the brewery. The worldwide best-known tavern puts on the frills while pretending to be a cultural institution. The master of the beer still conjures the nectar from malt, hop and water only, and the chefs of the busy kitchen prepare the pigs using traditional recipes. *Oans - Zwoa - G'suffa!*

Alcohol kills off germs. Contaminated water regularly relinquished medieval towns to epidemics, and the answer to the attack of bacteria was wine and beer, by which the Dark Ages breastfed the children.

Vintners harvested grapevines in Bavaria until the 16th century. When the climate changed and the weather turned cold, hop production replaced Bavaria's wine heritage. Hop prefers it wet; thus, the plant thrives magnificently to the north of Munich, in the Hallertau.

Brewing was part of the lady's duty during the Middle Ages. Although the distilling machines were a thorn in the side of the sovereign, Herzog Stephan II allowed the splashing about for private consumption in 1372. At that time, the maidens stretched the aromatic tincture with all kinds of additives. Besides ox-gall, they mixed in henbane and belladonna should they wish for a divorce. The golden manna intoxicated the senses and refined any dirndl to satanic charms.

Herzog Albrecht IV finally put order in the market when he decreed Munich's first beer regulation in 1487. From now on, the devilish nectar was to be brewed from water, hop and malt only, and ever since, men's virility returned with a cleared vision.

▲ The Hofbräuhaus is the most famous beer-hall in the world.

In 1516, Herzog Wilhelm IV expanded the regulation to the rest of the lands, passing Bavaria's purity law.

For civil servants, beer was part of their regular pay. The court employed many servants, and the liquid bread was palatable. Finally, Herzog Wilhelm V drew up the cunning plan to have a go at brewing and founded a **Hofbräuhaus** in 1591 to supply his subjects.

Kurfürst Maximilian I inherited empty coffers; during his reign, the brewing rights for wheat beer returned to the sovereign. Maximilian I opened a second brewery at today's Hofbräuhaus, this time for the top-fermented - and the public house was born.

Location: Am Platzl 9 **Entrance**: Without charge **Opening times**: daily 11:00 - 22.00
Internet: https://www.hofbraeuhaus.de
Literature: Annette von Altenbockum: Das Münchner Hofbräuhaus

A Municher in Heaven

Aloisius Hingerl, *A Municher in Heaven*, was an infamous regular at the beer halls. In the satire by the local poet Ludwig Thoma, the commissionaire once executed an assignment with such haste that he suffered a heart attack and dropped dead! Two angels dragged him to paradise, where the Lord ordered him to harp and rejoice. However, Aloisius could not liven up to exult without snuff and a pint of lager, and the gracious Almighty admitted the chap was not made for his Garden of Eden. Finally, he appointed him as a heavenly messenger and released him to the Bavarian State Chancellery to deliver God's divine intervention. When Aloisius arrived with the Lord's proclamations in Munich, he alluded to his entrenched habit, caroused at the Hofbräuhaus, and the Bavarian State Government still longs in suspense for divine inspiration!

Isartor

Facts & Figures

The Isartor, Munich's only city gate that survived the ravages of time, was constructed in 1337 and remains robust - what an achievement! A 40-metre-tall watchtower at the back overlooks two flanking turrets and striking battlements, which enclose a trapezoidal courtyard. Merchants paid their road duty at the gate in peacetime, and during times of war, the Barbican protected the defenders against muskets. After the invention of cannons, the town's fortification became obsolete. At last, Kurfürst Karl Theodor demolished the city wall during the 18th century; King Ludwig I refurbished the Isartor some decades later, preserving its structure as a witness to Munich's medieval past. At the western tower, a fantastically comical museum entertains the grim: the Valentinmusäum. With wit, the satirist takes the mickey out of the Munichers of the turn of the century.

Life was dangerous during the Middle Ages. Highwaymen and gangs of ex-soldiers lurked along trading routes and behind bushes. Farmers slaved away to enrich their overlord and kept only little to themselves. Even nature allowed no time for idleness: thunderstorms and flooding frequently threatened the harvest, farmhouse, cattle and the wife's fertility.

Common parlance knew: the reeds close to the banks of the Isar and the marshy lands were haunted at night. Trolls, gremlins and demons dwelled in meadows, moors and swamplands. Bavaria's treasure box is filled with legends that vividly tell their misdeeds. Even today, those lost at New Moon report ghostly tales about their escape from bewitching maidens in the undergrowth.

One may imagine: ... *and then the medieval traveller arrived at fortified Munich where the citizens enjoyed freedom - where the guards locked the gates at night, and whereabouts the bears and wolves, the forest spirits and the sorceress never ventured.*

Strollers arriving late at the **Isartor** quickly apprehended the fortification, bolting them out. Inside, the community protected the individual. In the open fields, the lone wolf fended for himself. Many gladly accepted a six-penny fine for the security guard to reopen the gates.

▲ Carts from the Alps arrived at Munich's market through the Isartor.

Medieval towns were a living union, enclosed by a protective wall. The citizens separated the inside from its surroundings and thus permitted the development of a new system, carried by the human imagination and outgrowing the laws of evolution. The dynamic within, just like in a biological cell, is defined by the flow allowed through the guarded gates: salt trade, merchants, artists, robbers or the Black Death.

Nevertheless, a settlement cannot survive - then and now - without an ambit area feeding its belly. Yet! The peasants worked for breadcrumbs to facilitate the stockade but benefitted little during the Middle Ages.

Location: Tal 50 **Entrance**: Without charge **Opening times**: Always accessible
Valentinmusäum: Opening times daily 11:01-17:59, Wednesdays closed
Entrance: Adults 2,99 €, Concession 1,99 €   https://www.valentin-musaeum.de

King Armleder, the Robber Baron of the Isar

At the times of Emperor Ludwig der Bayer, travellers across the Bavarian uplands had to be wary of marauding knights and their brutal blades, like the battle-axe of *King Armleder*. The ex-soldier roamed with a gang of wild horsemen the meadows of the Isar, rampaging and plundering. His story was tragic: after the 1322 Battle of Mühldorf, the treasury's coffers were empty, and the Emperor refused to disburse the soldiers their pay. The squire now blackened his face, turned to robbery and slew the Jews. When the highwayman disrespected Christians and pricked the hearts of merchants, Ludwig sent his henchmen. Soon, Armleder was killed, and judgement day befell the villain, whom the sovereign had denied his fair wages - a story told many times across Europe: the end of a war was as dangerous as the times of raging battles.

(12) Heilig-Geist-Kirche

Facts & Figures

The Heilig-Geist-Kirche guarded the soul of a hospice until its closure in the 19th century. Today, the Viktualienmarkt offers delicacies where benevolent monks once looked after the aged and the sick. The infirmary also enclosed a bakery, an asylum, a foundling house and a graveyard. The Order of the Holy Ghost erected the first chapel for the home residents in 1208. By and by, the friars enlarged the prayer house, and in the year 1394, the order laid the founding stone for a hall church. Finally, the artists Johann Georg Ettenhofer, Cosmas Damian and Egid Quirin Asam redecorated the interior in Baroque style during the 1720s. The main altar, carved by Antonio Matteo, and the cycle *The Gifts of the Holy Spirit* by Peter Jacob Horemans root in alpine folk belief. The breathtaking ceiling by Cosmas Damian Asam depicts the founding of the hospice.

The Middle Ages knew of poverty. Confined living space provoked epidemics; hygiene standards were low. Philanthropists - members of the nobility and patricians with deep pockets - founded hospices: the Heilig-Geist-Spital was one of them. They intended by alleviating the suffering to make their case for eternal salvation.

The **Heilig-Geist-Kirche** was not a parish church but the spiritual home of the penniless - the reason the Munichers had built another temple within earshot of St Peter. Pope Innocent IV elevated the prayer house, built in 1250, to a Romanesque Catherine Chapel - an *Ecclesia Sancta*. Ecclesiastical law, henceforward, overtrumped civil law at the hospice, the *Heilig-Geist-Liberty*.

The chapel also succumbed to the devastating 1327 fire, but the monks, with zeal and caution, gleaming with godly passion, reconstructed the church until 1392. The brethren expanded it over the following centuries, and in 1729, the clerics consecrated the tower. Uncommon, God's pointing finger stretches its ashlar at the eastern edge.

Secularisation dissolved the Heilig-Geist-Spital in 1806 when Maximilian Graf von Montgelas demolished the hospice. A market for victuals

▲ The Heilig-Geist-Kirche once served as a chapel for the adjacent hospice.

replaced the hospice, formerly offering their products at the Marienplatz. In 1844, the Archdiocese of Munich & Freising converted the Heilig-Geist-Kirche to a parish church.

Forty years later, the architect Friedrich Löwel expanded the prayer house by three yokes, and in 1907, the congregation added a porch to the south.

Firebombs devastated the building on 25 April 1944. In peacetime, the prelate Konrad Miller, guided by the hand of God, rebuilt the house of the Lord, and the artist Karl Manninger reconstructed the frescoes with patience step by step. The tirade on the western side reminds of the Bavarian unity of the church, state and the city. ➡

Location: Prälat-Miller-Weg 1 **Entrance:** Without charge **Opening times:** daily 9.00 - 20.00
Internet: https://heilig-geist-muenchen.de
Literature: Elfi Zuber: Das Angerviertel

The Messenger of the Heilig-Geist-Kirche

Legend tells of a rouge baker who invented the pretzel in Bad Urach in 1160. Law and order had sentenced the swindler to death, but he saved his life when he promised to bake a bun through which the sun shines three times, the symbol of the Holy Trinity. Others recognise in the form of the pretzel a praying monk crossing his arms at the chest. The ceiling fresco of the Heilig-Geist-Kirche depicts the Bavarian delicacy, honouring a donation by the patrician family Wadler of the year 1318. The charity entertained the poor with the pleated breadsticks at the Heilig-Geist-Spital once a year. On 27 December, a messenger used to herald the feast, but in 1801, the monks discontinued the tradition because the alms fell short of demand, and the incensed crowd, still hungry, flogged the *pretzel's messenger* nearly to death.

Highlights of the Heilig-Geist-Kirche

Christian teaching projected the seven works of mercy onto the Holy Spirit, and so in the Middle Ages, the infirmaries for the sick were called Holy-Spirit-Hospitals. The order, which lived according to the rules of the Augustinians, was supported by Holy Spirit brotherhoods that were not subject to vows but supported a hospice through prayers, alms and active service. The iconography of these churches was often based on the life of the Virgin Mary and shows works of mercy - and this is also true for the Heilig-Geist-Kirche in Munich.

The **high altar** depicts the enlightenment of Mary and the Apostles by the Holy Spirit. The painter Ulrich Loth created the work in 1644. The altar was made based on a design by Nikolaus Gottfried Stuber. Archangels and putti decorate the panels. The symbol of the Trinity is the culmination in the vertical direction.

The **Hammerthaler Muttergottes** in the north aisle, a miraculous image, was carved at the Tegernsee around 1440. The figure came to Munich around 1600 through the family Hammerthal and worked her miracles in the Augustinian Church until 1802. After the order was dissolved in Munich, the miraculous image was transferred to the Heilig-Geist-Kirche, where it can be seen today. It is frequented by pilgrims and believers; the community asks for silence, please.

The **main frescoes** show the outpouring of the Holy Spirit above the high altar and the founding of the hospital in the nave, both works by Cosmas Damian Asam around 1727. The founder Herzog Ludwig I, pilgrims, burghers, the sick, the poor, orphans and the brothers of the order of the hospital can be spotted. The pretzel-rider appears at the edge of the painting.

The **Seven Gifts of the Holy Spirit** were made by the Antwerp artist Peter Jacob Horemans around 1753. They adorn the north and south walls of the church:

The Gift of Strength (Daniel overwhelms a lion.)
The Gift of Science (globe, compass and telescope.)
The Gift of Piety (burning love and devotion.)
The Gift of Fear of God (King David praises God.)
The Gift of Counsel (scales, justice, telescope.)
The Gift of Wisdom (obelisk, burning bush.)
The Gift of Understanding (dove, sceptre, trinity.)

▲ The Virgin Mary is enthroned on the facade above the entrance to the Heilig-Geist-Kirche.

The **Trinity Altar** next to the Hammerthaler Muttergottes shows the coronation of Mary. The group of figures comes from the Dreifaltigkeitskapelle at the Dreifaltigkeitsplatz, consecrated in 1681. It was transferred to the Heilig-Geist-Kirche in 1802.

In the Krieger-Gedächtnis-Kapelle (Warrior Memorial Chapel), a late Gothic cross is worth seeing; it was carved around 1510. Plaques commemorate the fallen of the parish.

The original twelve-stop organ by Franz Borgias Maerz was destroyed during World War II. Today's organ was once a house organ in a Roman villa. It was extensively renovated and expanded.

The Heilig-Geist-Glocke (a bell) was cast by Ignaz Bauer in 1860. It weighs around 935 kilograms.

The street Tal

In front of the Heilig-Geist-Kirche, a street called Tal stretches 500 metres from the Isartor to the Marienplatz. It once was part of the trading route from the Alps and the salt road from Bad Reichenhall to Landsberg am Lech. Numerous inns and hotels along the path offered accommodation for traders and other travellers during the Middle Ages. The Deutsche Arbeiterpartei (German Workers' Party), a forerunner of the NSDAP, met at the Sterneckerbräu (Tal 54) from 1919 onwards. Adolf Hitler frequented the tavern. The Fountain of Mercury halfway (Tal 13) is a copy of the statue of Giovanni da Bologna in Florence. Friedrich von Thiersch designed the God of merchants and thieves around 1911 (execution: Hugo Kaufmann). The Eselsbad (a bathhouse) was once located in Tal 71; a barber looked after the citizens there.

Viktualienmarkt

Facts & Figures

Even long-established Munichers are surprised: a 22,000 square metre farmer's market within walking distance of the town hall resisted speculators. *Tradition* is the only possible reason. When King Maximilian I dissolved the Heilig-Geist-Spital in 1807 during secularisation, the greengrocers migrated from the Marienplatz to the Viktualienmarkt. The 140 market stalls, some built with a cellar, offer bread, herbs, spices, vegetables, game, sausages, fish, flowers and everything, the palate desires. The quality of the products is high! Many gourmet restaurants patrol the square in search for delicatessen early in the morning. As a consequence, prices have skyrocketed. During the carnival season, jesters stage a colourful parade at the Viktualienmarkt, celebrating a pagan festival that terminates with the *Tanz der Marktweiber* (dance of the market women), a humorous pandemonium.

Feasting is a humanist's delight and - in contradiction to Sigmund Freud - more sensual than eroticism. Any anthropologist, who wants to understand the tribal dynamic of a society, must frequent the food markets and not the dim nightspots of the seedy red-light district.

Gourmands will encounter quality at the **Viktualienmarkt**, sprinkled with the holy waters of St Peter and the Heilig-Geist-Kirche. Here, the merchants seduce with healthy living: organically cultivated fruits and vegetables, herbs and dried berries, cream cheese and pickled olives. The stalls even host a horse butcher, a covered fish market, a poulterer and a flower girl. In 1972, on the occasion of the Olympic Summer Games, a small beer garden opened, delighting boozers and strollers.

Last but not least, the highlight: the *Zwölf-Metzger-Apostel* (twelve-butcher-apostles) underneath St Peter! They offer Bavarian sausages and meat. Already in 1315, the city fathers relocated Munich's meat market from the Marienplatz to the pathway below the prayer house. Once the butchers had moved their blades to the abattoir in Sendling, the architect Arnold Zenetti constructed the row of shops at the Viktualienmarkt. The neo-Gothic clinker style harmonises well with the parish church.

▲ The Viktualienmarkt offers traditional Bavarian cosiness at the maypole.

Permanent booths superseded temporary stalls in 1870. The city leases them for five years to credible contenders according to assortment, experience and quality. Even Argentinians have applied successfully.

Only the well-off Munichers can afford the Viktualienmarkt, however, and most only during the festive season. The majority will shop at supermarkets, which sell industrial agriculture, sealed in over-dimensioned plastic jackets. The blue-blooded, who regularly choose quality at the Viktualienmarkt, can be assured, no matter what, to be a part of a small, long-established and elitist bourgeois Bavarian upper class, which already had made something out of their lives by leaving their mother's womb.

Location: Viktualienmarkt **Entrance:** Without charge
Internet: http://biergarten-viktualienmarkt.com
Opening times: Mon - Fri 10.00 - 18.00, Sat 10.00 - 15.00, Sunday closed

When Bakers Plunge into Holy Waters

A stream once gurgled close to the Viktualienmarkt, the Rossschwemmbach. The tributary of the Isar meandered from the Alte Rathaus along to the Tal and the Alter Hof. At the back of the Marienplatz, the city maintained a bizarre tradition. One acknowledges - the bakers' guild had no easy life during the Middle Ages: the Dukes strictly regulated their income by dictating the weight and the price of the bread, and the flour of the mills was not free of charge. Many bakers tried to outsmart their honourable customers by secretly adding *roughage* to their mixture, but the deception never paid off. The Munichers jeeringly caged the calories-robber in a basket and immersed them into the Rossschwemmbach. Not everyone survived, though, and the purified never repeated the swindle.

(14) Schrannenhalle

Facts & Figures

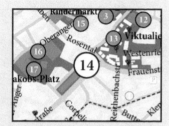

The grain merchants yelled at the Marienplatz - it was far too noisy for the taste of the King. The barkers stood cramped on the square - it was far too intolerable for the burghers, scraping between the stalls and whitening their gowns at the sacks of flour. At last, King Maximilian II came, saw, and commissioned a corn market - not any corn market, but a royal one - the Maximiliansgetreidehalle. Karl Muffat, architect, urban planner and entrepreneur - an enthusiast of Paris - designed the iron-cast building with eyes of glass in 1851. The merchants, however, abhorred the marvel for lacking a cart path, and they pouted to the city's periphery. And the hall? The cocoon in steel! It sulked and burnt away with rage on 8 April 1932. The Munichers bent the steel girders back in position and reopened the glass palace in 2005, now called *Schrannenhalle*, filled with delicatessen and champagne bars.

The cast-iron architecture took root in the 19th century, supporting structures without weight-bearing walls and filling the gaps with glass; birdlife was visible from the coffee table without nature's droppings.

The architectonic innovation saved cost: the Industrial Revolution hurled cast iron in the chord from the blast furnaces as a mass product, low-priced and standardised. However, the first buildings bent on summer days like Beckham because the science of differential expansion was yet unknown to the architects. When heated, the girders expanded, depending on extent and character, some more, some less, bringing the structures down. Without separating walls, harmless fires quickly hissed across the hall. Most glass palaces constructed in Europe during the 19th century burnt down within a few decades, or they collapsed, and the marvel of Munich fared no better.

The cast-iron architecture caused much excitement amongst the Munichers: the buildings floated without clayey tiles, like the Hanging Gardens of Babylon, suspended at the clouds, separated only by glass panels from the skies, guarding delicate roses at rippling fountains, kept in the warmth, yet looked after by the sun.

▲ The Schrannenhalle is high society's answer to the Viktualienmarkt.

The **Schrannenhalle** was the first of its kind in Bavaria, introducing the industrial style to Munich. When King Maximilian II opened the palace of commerce at the Viktualienmarkt in 1853 (burned down in 1932), the Munichers felt besotted. At one fell swoop followed the glass palace at the Alter Botanischer Garten in 1854 (burned 1931), the Großhesseloher Brücke (a bridge over the Isar, still standing) in 1857, and in 1860, King Ludwig II commissioned a conservatory at the rooftop of the residence (1944 destroyed by Allied air raids). The central train station marked the culmination of the style. World War II demolished that building, too.

Location: Blumenstraße 4 **Entrance:** Without charge **Opening Times:** Mon-Sat 10.00 - 20.00
Internet: https://www.viktualienmarkt-muenchen.de/schrannenhalle
Literature: Volker Hütsch: Der Münchner Glaspalast

Introducing Munich's Smart Set to a Dunkel

The Schrannenhalle was, for Munich's stylish game, a fountain of champagne. The in-crowd, however, avoids the area since the demise of Walter Sedlmayr. The dialect poet and comedian was a flagship-Bavarian, and he was the proprietor of the inn *Beim Sedlmayr* at the Viktualienmarkt. In July 1990, his private secretary discovered him not sleeping but dead in his room. The police investigated and stumbled upon a clandestine double life: Walter Sedlmayr was a well-known figure in Munich's homosexual-sadomasochistic underground scene. The detectives convicted his half-brother and a protégé as the perpetrators. The reason for the killing was fraud, totalling millions. And to this day, the Munichers cannot comprehend the close ties between traditional Bavarian savoir vivre and homosexual-sadomasochistic propensity.

(15) Rindermarkt

Facts & Figures

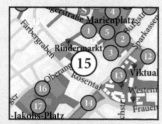

Farmers drove animals for sale to the Rindermarkt until 1369; the patricians complained about the noise of the cows and horses, and the magistrate relocated the cattle market to the Am Anger. The square near the town hall became a prime location; wealthy burghers moved in - among them the Duke's brother Ferdinand. He resided at the Rindermarkt during the late 16th century. The pious man was the Lord's warrior: he bashed the heads of Protestants during the Cologne War to secure the diocese to his younger brother Ernest of Bavaria. The cattle returned to the well in 1964 after World War II, now monsters in stone, designed by professor Josef Henselmann. Gabriel von Seidl constructed the richly ornamented Ruffini complex at the southwestern corner of the trapezoid in 1905. A Spanish fruit house sells dried apples, bananas and peaches on the ground floor.

Markets are a good indication of a community's economic success. During the 13th century, Munich was crammed inside the enclosing of its first city wall, exercising restraint and patience, but the burgess longed for glory. Finally, the city fathers drew up wide-ranging plans and relocated the cattle trading from the Marienplatz to the southern city gate in 1240, today's **Rindermarkt** (cattle market). There, butchers ended the creatures' roaring by swiftly cutting their throats.

A gate at the Rindermarkt once protected the city from intruders. It was located where the Rosenstraße passes into the Sendlinger Straße today. A fresco traces the medieval history at the Ruffini complex. In 1369, when the expansion of the settlement finally materialised under Emperor Ludwig der Bayer, the Munichers moved the cattle market to a square called *Am Anger*. Patricians now erected their townhouses in close proximity to the Marienplatz, banishing the craftsmen to the area outside the first but inside the second wall.

The Löwenturm (lion tower) stands at the southern edge of the Rindermarkt. Nobody is sure, but historians assume that the structure once served as a dynasty tower, detached from the city wall. The complex

▲ Workers fired the brick stones of the Löwenturm in the 15th century.

might as well have been a water tower to secure Munich's supply during a siege.

Since 1964, the Rindermarktbrunnen (cattle market well) bubbles sprinkling water across the stony cattle. Professor Josef Henselmann chiselled the idyllic scene into Labrador marble. A herd of sturdy animals draws nearer to refresh at a cooling trough. The hindmost throws its head. A stout herder is sunk in dreams at the effervescent basin, sustained by a crook. The rocky three-dimensional painting reminds of Ticino's river Maggia, where the professor had found his inspiration during holidays. However, the implementation in brutal concrete divides opinion - then and now.

Location: Rindermarkt **Entrance:** Without charge **Opening times:** Always accessible
Internet: https://www.muenchen.de/sehenswuerdigkeiten/orte/120333.html
Ruffini-complex: https://www.sueddeutsche.de

A Gang of Collusive Conspirators

As tradition prescribes, the Bavarians are lazy with their tongues, but not Peter the Rag-Rug from the Rindermarkt. Peter was a talkative man, spreading rumours without filtering whatever had captured his curious ear. Once, some burghers assembled at the Rindermarkt to deliberate about a fictive gang of conspirators. *"One may recognise the ringleader by a red patch on his jacket"*, a burgess susurrated, and another sewed a garish dot on Peter's jerkin, unperceived by the blabbermouth. The chatterbox, ears wide open, made haste to the Duke, fizzing with agitation. The sovereign privy to the spoof wondered whereby he could recognise the chieftain. *"By a red stain on his coat"*, Peter responded, and the Duke pointed his finger: *"One like this?"* Snarky was the laughter when the gossip straddled the pillory for several days.

⑯ Münchner Stadtmuseum

Facts & Figures

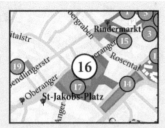

The city fathers constructed the late Gothic armoury at St-Jakobs-Platz 1 around the year 1500. The contorted building attracts attention by the inclination of its tent roof, pushing off the winter snow. The permanent exhibition *Typical Munich* presents the fickle history of the metropolis at the Isar. The basement floor culminates in the figurines of Moriscan Dancers, carved by Erasmus Grasser for the ballroom of the Alte Rathaus. Jakob Sandtner's wooden city model brings the Munich of 1570 to life and a collection of dolls - the *Münchner Kindl* - waters children's eyes. The originals of the cherubs at the Mariensäule battle against Satan next to weaponry of the 14th to the 18th century. Bavaria ascends to a kingdom on the upper floor. A brief outline of National Socialism and a summary of the post-war era completes the museum. (Currently, the museum is closed for refurbishment.)

Some buildings converse, just like old trees, and they tell a moving story about their history, a yarn hardly to be forgotten. The Munichers constructed a townhouse at **St-Jakobs-Platz** in 1401 and enlarged it to a Zeughaus (armoury) 90 years later. Its architect, Lukas Rottaler, was the successor of Jörg von Halspach, the mastermind of the Frauenkirche and the Alte Rathaus. Their similarity in style is undeniable.

The burgess stored weapons at the armoury's basement and filled the upper five floors with grain to survive Bavaria's harsh winters, years of crop failure or a besiegement. Horses and carriages were kept in the barn to the right.

Already in the 19th century, the burghers intended to convert the building into a museum, presenting their plans in 1858 but executing them only some thirty years later. Besides an extensive graphic collection of cityscapes inherited from the art dealer Josef Mailinger, the townspeople exhibited their historical collection of armoury, mostly from medieval times.

The Munichers discovered the futility of the old blades during the revolutionary year 1848: after the burgess had stormed the barricades

▲ The leaning of the Zeughaus shoves the winter snow from the roof.

and entered the Zeughaus on 4 March to seize the arms, the wannabe revolutionists had to accept that corroded sabres, halberds and long-dead rifles would not save their 19th-century-revolution, and thus the bolshy pranksters secretly returned the *borrowed* instruments to their rightful place - a place in history only.

Nevertheless, King Ludwig I silently crept down the massive stairs of his throne, put down the heavy crown, retired with acrimony, and sulked. Until his last breath, he never rose himself to pardon the Munichers for their incapacity to understand his wooing of the Irish dancer Lola Montez, the final nail that had sealed the sarcophagus of his reign.

Location: St.-Jakobs-Platz 1 **Opening Times**: Currently closed for refurbishment
Internet: https://www.muenchner-stadtmuseum.de
Literature: Florian Dering: Münchner Kindl

Uhlfelder Department Store

Taking a stroll from the Rindermarkt to the St.-Jakobs-Platz, one may notice the blue lettering: *Kaufhaus Uhlfelder*. Munich's most popular emporium brought a *joie de vivre* to the city. In 1931, the entrepreneur installed a sensation: Munich's first moving stairs, seducing customers to float like angels across three levels. The Jew Heinrich Uhlfelder had founded the department store in 1878. On 9 March 1933, the Nazi regime placed his son and successor, Max Uhlfelder, under preventive detention, and on Kristallnacht, the Munichers plundered and torched his shopping paradise. Towards the end of the year, the Nazis forced him to sell at less than fair value before authorising his departure from Germany. Finally, he arrived in the United States via India. Most of his family perished in concentration camps.

(17) Jüdisches Zentrum

Facts & Figures

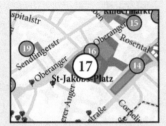

On 9 November 2006, 68 years after Kristallnacht, Munich's Jewish community celebrated the inauguration of its new synagogue. The architectural practice Wandel, Hoefer & Lorch from Saarbrücken designed the house of the Lord *Ohel Jakob* - God's tent. Today, the community embraces 10,000 believers; after Berlin, it is Germany's second-largest Jewish congregation. The brightly illuminated temple hosts 585 faithful. The worshippers modelled the 28-metres-tall exterior facade of travertine limestone after Jerusalem's Wailing Wall. At night, yellow-red lights break through the darkness like a velveteen carpet. At the main entrance, the initial letters of the Ten Commandments in Hebrew scriptures point to the way of the Lord. The adjoining museum presents the Jewish faith and aids by insight to embrace all peaceful religions as equals.

After seventy years of sorrow, the **Jewish community** had found a home in Munich again. As a symbol of resistance, they laid the founding stone of their synagogue on the day of Kristallnacht. Three years later, they consecrated the temple on 9 November.

Never in human history had oppression succeeded, and the persecution of the Jews failed during the Nazi regime too. Munich's newly erected main synagogue presents a visible sign to all tyrants - we water the delicate plant of hope with perseverance, and we will survive. The Jewish community celebrates its fellowship at the cultural centre on St.-Jakobs-Platz. An all-day school, a nursery, a well-stocked library and meeting rooms enrich the complex. Even a kosher-certified restaurant conjures Jewish delicatessen.

A round tour leads through a 32-metre-long underground corridor to the synagogue. Its walls remind of the more than 4500 heart-rendering victims of the Nazi regime. After deportation, many of the helpless met their deaths in concentration camps.

The Museum of Jewish History, extending over 900 square metres and three levels, shows cultural items, votive offerings, objects of ritual, photographs and historic documents. A diverse bookshop presents

▲ The synagogue Ohel Jakob radiates its spirit since 2006 across Munich.

literature about the life of the Jews in Munich and across the world. Inspiring changing exhibitions seduce the visitor to return and become a part of the community.

The main synagogue, Ohel Jakob, God's tent, teaches us: compassion and charity are the two shoulders upon which the peace of the world rests. The history of humanity delights in plenitude and plurality. The world is a pond filled with water lilies, where all roots are connected to a single source. The kind at heart will nurture the net of life to enjoy all the fragrances of God's colourful flowers, not break or cut any of them. *Shalom*: Shall our ever remembrance of the past lead the planet to a peaceful future.

Location: St.-Jakobs-Platz **Opening Times**: Only guided tours
Museum of Jewish History Opening Times Tues - Sun 10.00 - 18.00. Entrance: Adults 6 €
https://www.ikg-m.de/juedisches-zentrum // https://www.juedisches-museum-muenchen.de

The Red Light at the Fausttürmchen

The executioner once lurked at the Fausttürmchen thirty metres to the southeast of the Sendlinger Tor, a fortification tower. The night watchmen called the spot a urinal, and Munich's gravediggers buried the suicides at its wall. Its gable trapped clouds; crows danced with bones at the turret when the guard called out *midnight*; no warden ever served without a crucifix and a rosary at the Faustürmchen. When a corruptible alderman gave passage to a marauding knight, the Munichers immured the patrician at the Faustürmchen - without much ado. The tower was recognisable from afar: at its spire, a stony fist clenched. It glowed in red whenever the city had sentenced an innocent. Common parlance knows: *the turret's fist drummed three times at the hangman's door had he beheaded the wrong lad* - a bit tardy - is it not - for the delinquent. What sadism!

(18) Sendlinger Tor

Facts & Figures

Emperor Ludwig der Bayer completed the Sendlinger Tor in 1319, a part of the second enclosing. The barbican safeguarded Munich from the marauding Middle Ages, similar to the Isartor in the east. The masons complemented the gates with two flanking towers in 1420. Under a retractable bridge, a town moat fortified the city. When Kurfürst Karl Theodor decided to dismantle the city wall, the magistrate demolished the central tower in 1808, where a fresco of Altötting's Black Madonna once affirmed her auspices. At the turn of the century, humming gasoline cyclists demanded a passage as ample as their wing mirrors, and the city planners fused the three thoroughfares into one in 1906. They also filled up the moat and scooped out the flanks for pedestrians. At last, Ludwig von Sckell planted the forecourt in 1810, today a pitiful array of flower pots and half-dead trees.

The contrast of Munich's urban landscape is profound at the **Sendlinger Tor**: inside the torn-down medieval city wall, the old town shines; outside, foul-smelling exhaust insults the nostrils.

Towards the Marienplatz, exquisite fashion shops offer a sense of stylish living. During the Middle Ages, bustling inns and taverns settled along the arterial road, providing lodgings to merchants on their way to Italy. Johann Wolfgang von Goethe spent the night at the Sendlinger Tor in 1786 incognito on his journey to the oranges of the Mediterranean, hardly mentioning a word about Munich in his journal.

The city planners destroyed the meadows to the outside during the 19th century. Since World War II, the congested Altstadtring, Munich's inner bypass, meanders along the Sonnenstraße; the noisy corner had become a transport hub, where the underground and streetcars cross. The architect Ludwig von Sckell added bare trees and flower pots to pretend greenery, but most commuters pity the effort.

At the oldest movie theatre in town, the Filmtheater, cineasts celebrate premiers of local film productions. A blue stele at the sideline, styled like a wig of the 1970s, reminds of the AIDS epidemic: *To the dead, infected, their*

▲ The memorial commemorates those who died from the AIDS epidemic.

friends, their families, 1981 to date. 5000 Munichers had passed away since the outbreak.

At the Sonnenstraße, washed by traffic, Bavaria's Kings graciously permitted the construction of an evangelic church: St Matthäus. The Nazi regime had blasted the predecessor in 1938, however, probably because Munich's then protestant bishop Hans Meiser refused to profess to the Third Reich's ideology. The architect Gustav Gsaenger designed the current church with an arched roof in 1955, resembling a chain bridge into the future. Common parlance knows the structure, which looks like a water basin, as the *Bathtub of the Loving God* - cunning.

Location: Sendlinger-Tor-Platz **Entrance:** Without charge
Filmpalast: https://www.filmtheatersendlingertor.de   **MUCA:** https://www.muca.eu
Aids-Hilfe München: https://www.muenchner-aidshilfe.de

The Museum of Urban and Contemporary Art

Since its opening in 2016, the Museum of Urban and Contemporary Art (MUCA) in the former substation at Hotterstraße 12 shows the absurdity of contemporary urban life. Urban art is fought out on the streets - sometimes as a commissioned work, often beyond the grey area of legality. Artists like Richard Hambleton, Banksy and Shepard Fairey have made it into exhibition spaces. Their art is subversive, sarcastic and feeds the zeitgeist. The patrons, Stephanie and Christian Utz, founded the museum on three floors in Munich's Hackenviertel. The meeting place in the industrial building shows top-class artists in temporary exhibitions. The in-house permanent collection is one of the largest in Europe. Young talents are actively supported. The satire of their art challenges established norms and worldviews.

Asamkirche

Facts & Figures

The Asamkirche is consecrated to Saint Nepomuk. The lands recruited the pious man as their patron saint in 1728. The architects Cosmas Damian and Egid Quirin Asam created the private chapel to immortalise their genius. Egid Quirin purchased several townhouses in 1729 to use them for their project. 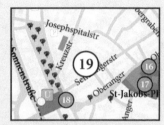 The jewel of the rococo stretches over three levels, on an area of eight by thirty metres. The house of prayer is sandwiched to the left by the private quarters of Egid Quirin and to the right by the priest's residence. Already the facade hints at the greatest stuccoer of his time: cheerful Greek Gods rub shoulders with Christian saints and the Holy Family. The brilliantly decorated interior overwhelms the senses like a psychedelic drug and enforces a mystical experience of God, voluntarily or by succumbing to the golden sledgehammer.

The Bavarians are prone to carry any ideology to the extreme. The Alpine people thus provoke a conclusion that is so final that they enforce a new beginning. The **Asamkirche** is an example: the brothers Asam toppled the baroque to the rococo in 1746 and terminated the style before it had seen the light. Indeed, the master builders still had to design the Cuvilliés Theater (finished in 1753), the Wieskirche (1754) and Augsburg's Schäzlerpalais (1770), but Munich had reached the point of culmination already before the style had hit the ground.

The fear of divine judgement drove the people to an attitude of pious godliness during the Middle Ages. During absolutism, Europe's aristocracy tied their subjects with sensual delights to the royal household. The Asamkirche is a child of this period, an era of courtly intrigue, a time when Madame de Pompadour and Madame Dubarry pulled strings in Paris, an epoch when Bavaria's Emperor Karl Albrecht desired predominance over the German-speaking territories, relying on the help of France.

The interest of King Louis XV of France was unequivocal: he sought an alliance partner in the Teutonic regions to push back the influence of the Austrian Hapsburg dynasty. Bavaria joined the roulette table of

▲ The rich stucco decoration of the Asamkirche catches the eye.

politics, played and lost. When the last of the Hapsburg dynasty had died without a male heir, and Frankfurt had squeezed the imperial crown onto Emperor Karl Albrecht's pate, the tempters of Paris withdrew. Maria Theresa forged an alliance with Prussia, invaded Munich and frightened Karl Albrecht away from his cosy eiderdowns.

Bavaria rid itself of Vienna's suffocating fist only with Napoleon's help after the French Revolution. The Asamkirche is a captivating witness to this turbulent period. It is a testimony to Munich's daring absolutism, which had hoped for supremacy on the continent, gambled and lost the game. ➡

Location: Sendlinger Straße 32 **Entrance:** Without charge **Opening Times:** 9.00 - 18.00
Internet: https://www.muenchen.de/sehenswuerdigkeiten/orte/130982.html
Literature: Peter B. Steiner: Die Asamkirche in München

How Saint Nepomuk Got to His Church

The Asamkirche is based on a solemn vow sworn by the brothers Asam amidst the Donau. Like all rivers, even the most peaceful one throws swaying waves on tempestuous days. It happened in 1729: the Asam brothers embarked on the Weltenburg Monastery in Kelheim close to Regensburg, wanting to deliver church decoration for the abbey, stowed in their luggage. A gale suddenly hit the heavily laden barge and rocked the crew up and down the torrents, spinning the pitiful around in circles. The boat nearly capsized! Finally, the distressed pledged to erect a church should they survive. Promptly, Saint Nepomuk appeased the winds. *A Church! Dedicated to whom? To ME?* He lifted the crew gently to the nearby bank with hails of *hey and ho*, and thus, the patron saint of bridges achieved his place of worship - dedicated to him and him only.

Highlights of the Asamkirche

The Asamkirche emerged from a private initiative. The Asams were a family of artists in Munich and indisputably the most creative spirits of the Rococo period. The Asam brothers financed and designed the church in a former townhouse between 1733 and 1746. Cosmas Damian Asam was a painter, and his brother Egid Quirin Asam was one of the most prolific plasterers of the century. They worked on the monastery church in Rohr, the monastery in Metten, the castles in Bruchsal, Ettlingen and Mannheim and the Weingarten monastery.

The **facade** already stands out with its rich stucco decoration. In addition to Saint Nepomuk above the entrance, one identifies Apollo with a harp, the winged horse Pegasus and the nine Muses. Below, Athena leads a young boy up the mountain of the muses.

In the **anteroom**, the ceiling with a sun symbol is overwhelming. The apostle Peter holds the keys to paradise into the room on the left. On the right is Saint Jerome with a Bible: *"Everything repressed will come to light, nothing will go unpunished."*

The **main room** is narrow and overloaded with gold. Wherever one looks, one is blinded by splendour and jubilation; no calming is ever possible. The senses are overwhelmed, the mind is overloaded, the heart opens to an experience of God. The interior is divided vertically into three parts: the gloomy lower section with the benches symbolises earthly suffering. The lighter middle section refers to the emperor, and the top third symbolises the kingdom of God.

Four pillars frame the **high altar**, modelled on the Bernini columns of Saint Peter's tomb in Rome. On the upper floor, God the Father appears with a triple tiara. The dove of the Holy Spirit hovers above him; below, the crucified Christ redeems the world. Side windows illuminate the ensemble. In the morning, the rising sun bathes the interior in a mystical light.

The impressive **ceiling painting** shows scenes from Saint Nepomuk's life and cruel martyrdom. Cosmas Damian Asam completed the frescoes in the year 1735. They depict the story of Saint Nepomuk: *Saint Nepomuk prevails against King Wenceslau. Nepomuk helps the poor and sick. Soldiers throw the saint off the bridge.*

The **confessionals** in the anteroom and the main room are richly decorated: skulls and putti scare the onlooker; a dead person stretches out of a coffin in despair; a monk bends over him.

The **fresco on the left side wall** shows the tomb of Saint Nepomuk, which is located in Prague Cathedral. Votive offerings are given.

The **fresco on the right side wall** depicts the Queen's confession.

Above the door to the sacristy are **portraits** of the artists Cosmas Damian Asam (left) and Egid Quirin Asam (right).

Silver reliefs with images from the saint's life decorate the interior. They show the stages from his birth to his death.

▲ The facade of the Asamkirche shows Greek mythology.

Wilhelm Stöberl built the **organ** above the entrance in 1982. It has 16 registers on two manuals and a pedal.

The Martyrdom of Saint Nepomuk

Johann Nepomuk had taken the Queen's confession. King Wenceslaus accused his wife of infidelity - he was raging with jealousy. The King insisted on knowing the confession, but the priest refused to reveal the secret. Not even under torture, said Nepomuk a single word. At last, King Wenceslaus had him thrown off a bridge in Prague, and the saint drowned in the river. The Viennese chronicler Thomas Ebendorfer reported the martyrdom of Saint Nepomuk in the Liber Augustalis in 1450. John of Pomuk, as the saint was also called, is said to have been born in Pomuk near Pilsen around 1350. Pope Benedict XIII canonized him in 1729. His martyrdom made him the saint of bridges and rivers. He is also the patron saint of Bavaria and Bohemia, keeps floods away from homesteads and farms, and guarantees discretion and secrecy.

20   Kaufingerstraße & Neuhauser Straße

Facts & Figures

Munich's buzzing shopping mile follows the axis Isartor - Marienplatz - Karlstor. Documents from 1239 already alluded to a transit, which shouldered the salt-carts from the Alps to Landsberg am Lech. In 1972, the magistrate transformed the commercial road into a pedestrian area for the Games of the XX Summer Olympiads. Many retailers settled at the shopping promenade, amongst them department stores and fashion houses. Nowhere in Munich is the church density as high as along the Kaufingerstraße. Within only a few metres, the Heilig-Geist-Kirche and the parish church St Peter, the Frauenkirche, the former Augustinian monastery (today the Jagd- und Fischereimuseum), the Jesuit Church of St Michael and the prayer house Bürgersaalkirche soothe the souls of the pious. Fountains provide invigorating refreshment - welcomed on sultry summer days.

The Schöner Turm, a fortification tower, once kept a watch where, at the Augustinerstraße, the **Kaufingerstraße** leads into the **Neuhauser Straße**. The entrance gate was Munich's western demarcation line during the 12th century, a part of the first city wall. A discreet marking on the pavement references its location; a bronze plaque at the adjacent shopping arcade displays the destroyed city gate. The tower continued to exist even after the Munichers had completed the second city wall in the 14th century. At the gate, the burghers passed from the inner city, the Heinrichsstadt, to the parts of the expansion.

The pedestrian zone narrows between Schöner Turm and Karlstor, close to the former Academy of the Jesuits. Here, the traffic artery followed an S-curve during the Middle Ages, a loop still reflected in the indentation some 700 years later. In the 12th century, the Munichers built a chapel at this location.

Today, the Richard Strauss Brunnen refreshes passers-by outside the Jesuit monastery. The artist Hans Wimmer designed the fountain in 1962. Scenes from the opera Salome embellish its slender shaft. Richard Strauss was a talented composer born in Munich in 1864.

The Munichers love fountains: shortly before the Karlstor, a satyr sprays water on a cheeky boy. When the Munichers unveiled the figure in 1895, the uproar was so great that Prince Regent Luitpold had to seek out the artist in his atelier to curb public anger. What had happened?

Well, the boy, how to say, the little boy, well, the boy was naked, and the Ladies feared for their innocence. Not even Prince Regent Luitpold could persuade the stubborn sculptor to glue a fig leaf over the small part of the boy or dress the statue in one of the three hundred swimming trunks that puritans from all over Bavaria had posted to resolve the conflict.

▲ The goldsmith carries the Schöner Turm at the Neuhauser Straße.

Location: Kaufingerstraße & Neuhauser Straße **Entrance:** Without charge
Internet: http://www.shops-muenchen.de // https://www.mux.de/Kaufingerstr
Opening Times shops: Mon - Sat 10.00 - 19.00, Sundays closed

The Goldsmith at the Schöner Turm

The city's goldsmith lived at the Schöner Turm during the Middle Ages. Once, a patrician commissioned a piece of jewellery. The sun squinted through the crevices of the roof on this happy summer day, and the goldsmith found delight in his creation, chaperoned by chirping birds. When he returned to his workshop from a repast, the jewellery had disappeared. The patrician was so enraged over the loss of the precious metal that he had the goldsmith sentenced to death. Long since the innocent had decomposed in his grave, workers found a bird's nest at the projecting alcove, sheltering the glittering splendour. A thievish magpie had maliciously stolen it in its beak. For the goldsmith, Solomon's wisdom arrived too late, and therefore, to this day, he hunches at the corner of Liebfrauenstraße, nearly crushed from the weight of the tower.

(21) Frauenkirche

Facts & Figures

The Frauenkirche (Church of Our Lady) is Munich's most prestigious landmark. The master builder Jörg von Halspach constructed the late-Gothic brick building in less than twenty years, enclosing an abundance of space that overwhelms. Patricians and Munich's hard-working guilds donated the side chapels during the 15th century. Today, they provide art historians insight into the life of the city during the late Middle Ages. The dukes redesigned the cathedral in the 17th century to spiritually prepare the Bavarians for the forthcoming Thirty Years' War. At that time, the artist Peter Candid added a cycle of paintings depicting the Glory of the Virgin Mary. In 1622, Hans Krumpper designed the cenotaph of Emperor Ludwig der Bayer. Many Wittelsbacher sovereigns of the Middle Ages rest in the crypt. To this day, no building in the old town may exceed the 99-metre-tall towers of the Frauenkirche.

When the city was founded in the 12th century, Munich competed with Freising's episcopal see for the country's resources. The two rivals even strove for the souls, and thus, the burgess replaced a three-aisled Romanesque building with a late Gothic hall church in 1468. The new construction offered more prayer benches than the city counted inhabitants. Why? The Munichers planned to move the episcopal see from Freising to Munich, but the Popes refused. The King achieved the relocation only in 1821.

Herzog Sigismund laid the founding stone for the **Frauenkirche** in 1468. Already in 1477, Master Heinrich von Straubing finished the roof. The foresters had shipped 1400 rafts with 15 tree trunks each from the Alps along the Isar to Munich. In 1488, the Cardinal placed the keystone, but the Munichers continued to potter about at their cathedral for centuries, rebuiling, modifying and enlarging the complex.

Herzog Albrecht IV changed the collegiate church into a Frauenkirche, a cathedral. As a spiritual preliminary to the Thirty Years' War, Herzog Wilhelm V and later Kurfürst Maximilian I, the hero of the Battle of White Mountain, introduced the Renaissance, installed a Virgin Mary to

▲ The towers of the Frauenkirche rise 99 meters into Bavaria's blue sky.

each wall, and Hans Krumpper added the Cenotaph of Emperor Ludwig der Bayer.

The Wittelsbacher wanted to secure their claim to the throne, and thus, they moved their pawns along the checkerboard of politics; they became the masterminds of the Counter Reformation.

Allied air raids destroyed the Frauenkirche during World War II, but the Munichers rebuilt their landmark in 1953.

Even popes celebrated holy mass under its dome. In 1977, Kardinal Ratzinger, the later Pope Benedict XVI, started his ecclesiastical journey at the Frauenkirche. A commemorative plaque honours his contribution at the entrance.

Location: Frauenplatz 12 **Entrance:** Without charge **Opening Times:** daily 8.00 - 20.00
Internet: https://www.muenchner-dom.de
Ascending the Tower: daily 9.30 - 20.00 (not during service)

The Devil's Footprint at the Frauenkirche

The devil snarled with saltpetre: the Munichers were building a new cathedral, mightier than he had ever seen. On the night before the consecration, he decided to pay the new building a visit when it was still safe for demons to enter. Riding on the wind, his horse, the devil slipped into the house of the Lord and gingerly poked around. *"Ha! What a joy! The Munichers, these mules, they forgot the windows!"* Satan rejoiced, and he stomped his foot into the marble, leaving a mark which is still visible at the west portal - and any sceptic may investigate to be convinced: at the spot where the devil has left his footprint, no window can be seen, and thus - quod erat demonstrandum - it must be the imprint of the prince of hell. For joy and rejoicing, Satan forgot his windhorse when he left the church, and ever since, a terrible breeze whiffs around the Frauenkirche.

Highlights of the Frauenkirche

The Frauenkirche is the most prestigious landmark of Munich. During secularisation, King Maximilian I moved the archdiocese from Freising to Munich in 1821, and the church ascended to a cathedral. The building is impressive from the **outside**, with a length of 109 metres and a width of 40 metres. The two brick towers rise 99 metres above ground. They are visible from afar. Visitors can climb the southern tower. It offers a stunning view of Munich and its surrounding area.

At the **main entrance**, a footprint with a spur at the heel is imprinted on the floor - the devil's step. Satan stomped it into the ground the day before the consecration: the people of Munich had forgotten the windows - and indeed, the windows cannot be seen from this location.

The rear part hosts the **cenotaph** of Emperor Ludwig der Bayer, who died in 1347. Hans Krumpper carried out the work in 1622. Inside the show grave lies a late Gothic memorial plaque, but no body. Four kneeling standard bearers accompany Herzog Wilhelm IV (west side) and Herzog Albrecht V (east side).

Since its renovation in 1990, the **nave** has shone in dazzling white colour. The abundance of light defines the atmosphere of the temple - the Munich Cathedral is friendly and inviting.

Roman Anton Boos designed the gilded statue of Mary Immaculata in the chancel in 1776. The busts show, among other characters, prophets and apostles. Erasmus Grasser carved them in 1502.

The main **choir chapel** at the eastern end of the ambulatory shows behind a wrought iron grille with roses the *Miraculous Image of the Archbrotherhood of Our Lady of Altötting*. The brotherhood was founded by Herzog Wilhelm V in 1579.

The enchanting **automaton clock** in the choir ambulatory in front of the eastern wall was probably made around 1500. Two lions hold a clock in their paws. The moving characters in the automated puppet theatre show God the Father, Jesus and Mary. Erasmus Grasser probably carved the figures. The dial below predicts the movement of the sun, the planets and the signs of the zodiac. The moon ball represents the phases of the moon.

The **sacrament chapel** is reserved for prayers. An eternal light and coloured windows give the room a meditative atmosphere.

The **high altarpiece** above the sacristy portal shows the *Assumption of the Virgin Mary into heaven*. The artist Peter Candid created the work in 1620.

The Munich Frauenkirche is home to four **organs**. They had been made by the workshop of Georg Jann from Regensburg. The main organ has 95 registers. It accompanies the celebrations during services and concerts. The music of Munich's cathedral can also be enjoyed virtually.

Next to the chancel, a steep double staircase leads into the **crypt** of the Frauenkirche. Many members of the Wittelsbacher dynasty are buried here, including Emperor Ludwig der Bayer. He was joined by the last Wittelsbacher king, Ludwig III, who had to step down in 1918 and died in exile in Hungary in 1921.

▲ A city model at the Frauenkirche shows Munich's old town.

Tales from the Frauenkirche

Due to a lack of money, the towers of the Frauenkirche only received their French domes around 1525. Sketches from the 15th century show the tops with crenellations. "My dear two asparagus," Kurfürst Max III Joseph called the tops. The left tower of the Frauenkirche remains closed because horrifying ghosts haunt it - no one dares to risk an encounter. Heimeran von Straubing built the enormous roof structure of the Frauenkirche. However, one beam remained loose. After completion, the master pulled it out and asked the upcoming centuries to identify the place where in the roof he removed it. Unfortunately, to this day, no one can spot the location. Last but not least: According to legend, the mortar of the Frauenkirche was not mixed with water, but - with wine, of course!

㉒ Jagd- und Fischereimuseum

Facts & Figures

Since 1966, the former Augustinian monastery has housed the Museum of Hunting and Fishing, the wildest of its kind. During his life, Graf Arco-Zinnenberg had compiled an extensive array of trophies, which provided the foundations of the exhibition. Christian Weber, SS-Brigadeführer, inaugurated the museum at Schloss Nymphenburg during the Nazi regime. The collection moved to the Kaufingerstraße after World War II, and in 2003, the museum became a member of an organisation that confronts right-wing extremism, anti-Semitism and racism. The curators present hunting weapons, antlers, sleighs and animal skeletons; a replica illustrates the Isar-wetlands, and more than 1000 stuffed animals display Bavaria's wildlife. A petting corner and dioramas depicting scenes from the Stone Age to the present times visualise Bavaria's passion for hunting.

Until the dissolution of the monasteries in 1803, the building where today the **Museum of Hunting and Fishing** introduces Bavaria's wildlife was the home of the Order of Augustinians. The founding statement issued by Herzog Rudolf shows that the mendicant order took up its mission at the Haberfeld in 1294, immediately outside of the first city enclosure. The monastery was located along a trading route to Landsberg am Lech. Most importantly, the order's beer enjoyed widespread popularity.

The brethren expanded the complex during the 14th century. Martin Luther was a member of the Augustinian Order; historians believe he lectured at the monastery when he passed Munich on his way to Rome in 1510/11. The artist Veit Schmidt converted the Gothic chapel into Munich's first baroque prayer house in 1621, following a design by Hans Krumpper. During the Counter Reformation, the Augustinian Order guarded the Hammerthaler Muttergottes, a pilgrims-altar worshipped for many miracle cures. After the abbey had been dissolved, the figurine relocated to the Heilig-Geist-Kirche.

The north wing housed the living quarters of the monks and a brewery. Today, Munich's police headquarters is based at the former brewing

▲ Bronze-figures attract attention outside the museum: a boar and a catfish.

kettles between Ettstraße and Augustinerstraße.

During the 19th century, the cloister was used as a customs house, and since 1911, the Weißer Saal (white saloon) has staged classical concerts.

World War II destroyed the sacred walls, but the architect Erwin Schleich could reconstruct the building. Since 1966, it houses the Jagd- und Fischereimuseum.

A visit to the exhibition also offers a glimpse of the former monastery, which is enjoyable by itself. Besides the remarkable stucco works of the longhouse, the monstrous flight of stairs attracts attention. At the upper floor, the steps pass Gothic glass windows, reminiscent of the Lutheran order.

Location: Neuhauser Straße 2 **Entrance:** Adults 5 €, Concession 3 €
Opening Times: Thur - Sun 09.30 - 17.00
Internet: https://www.jagd-fischerei-museum.de

The Bavarian Wolpertinger

The Bavarian Wolpertinger, known by science as *Crisensus Bavaricus*, is a fabulous hybrid creature comprising body parts from different animals. The magical creature resembles the body of a small mammal, such as a fox, squirrel or rabbit. Horns, antlers, claws and pinions sprout from its skin, depending on the kind. Many fables weave their tendrils around the Wolpertinger: common parlance knows that only a virgin attended by a snazzy youngling, and only during twilight and fifteen days before the next thunderstorm, will catch sight of the beast. Its preferred diet is Prussian skulls. The Wolpertinger must be chased with a candle during the harvest moon! Legend says the creature will go lame when the maiden scatters salt on its bushy tail. The Bayerischer Alpenverein recommends always keeping an Anti-Wolpertinger-Box handy when touring the Alps.

St Michael

Facts & Figures

The Order of Jesuits concocted the theological foundation of the Counter Reformation at the Church of St Michael in Munich during the Thirty Years' War; the Archangel Michael was their rightful warrior. At the facade, cast in bronze by Hubert Gerhard in 1588, he shovels the incredulous protestant Satan into the cauldron, surrounded by those sovereigns who contributed to Bavaria's conversion to Christianity. A twenty-metre wide cupola, at that time only superseded by St Peter in Rome, straddles the magnificent interior. At the entrance, an angel awaits the faithful at the holy water. He was a part of the never-completed sepulchre for Herzog Wilhelm V. The high altar repeats the War in Heaven, this time including the apocalyptic woman. Christoph Schwartz painted the fresco in 1587. Theologians equate the damsel in distress with the Virgin Mary.

Bavaria's Jesuits dominated the Counter Reformation. Ignatius Loyola, a Basque aristocrat, established the *Order of the Society of Jesus* on 15 August 1534. It was hierarchically structured and loyal to the Pope in Rome. Due to their pragmatism, their ideas spread fast across Europe!

The order had led the way not only liturgically but also ran the country's educational system. Cleverly, Loyola's statutes demanded a concomitant academy. The Jesuit's mission to schooling endeared them to all classes. Any head teacher wielding the wand feeds his students with his ideology, and the Jesuits recruited their disciples from peerage and patricians. At their gymnasium, the country's leaders were memorizing their ideas.

What is more, Bavaria's sovereigns made their confessions to the order, and thus, the Jesuits etched their power onto the conscience of the rulers. Their pragmatic approach also convinced the lesser people. In Bohemia, the preachers had guided many lost souls back into the bosom of the Catholic Church during the 16th century. In Bavaria, the rulers relied on the Jesuits to drive reforms from the inside, hoping to avoid a schism.

Herzog Wilhelm IV had invited the order to Ingolstadt in 1549; he wanted to establish a Catholic University there. Ten years later, at the request of

▲ Herzog Wilhelm V was born on the day of the Archangel Michael

Herzog Albrecht V, their ideas arrived in Munich. Over time, the Jesuits established the spiritual centre of the Counter Reformation at the Isar. Herzog Wilhelm V faithfully commissioned the construction of the Jesuit Church of **St Michael** and added the Jesuit academy in 1583.

The tower collapsed during the hastily advanced building works, and the Duke interpreted the accident as a cue from God: "I *must enlarge the complex.*" The Jesuits added a choir and a transept, and after the completion in 1597, Bavaria was in debt for 300,000 guilders, an enormous sum of money. When the masons had finished the church, Herzog Wilhelm V stepped down. ➤

Location: Neuhauser Straße 6 **Entrance:** Without charge **Opening Times:** 08.00 - 19.00
Internet: https://www.st-michael-muenchen.de
Literature: Bernhard Paal SJ: Die St. Michaelskirche in München

The Alte Akademie (Old Academy)

Once Herzog Albrecht V had appointed the *Order of Jesus* to Munich, the streets echoed with Jesuit education; a college was always part of their monastery. Friedrich Sustris based the design of the Alte Akademie on the Spanish Escorial. In 1549, the Jesuits arrived in Ingolstadt, a town some 70 kilometres north of Munich; they introduced schooling to Bavaria following the principles of the Florentine *Academica Platonica*. Ever since, Bavarian rulers swotted under the index finger of the order: Herzog Wilhelm V, Kurfürst Maximilian I and the Austrian Emperor Ferdinand II warmed the benches in Munich. The order equally protruded the simple people: the schoolmasters re-enacted pieces from the bible, and the holy performances won the masses over to their interpretation of the sacred text.

Highlights of St Michael

Herzog Wilhelm V, the patron of the Jesuit church, was born on September 29, 1548, the day of the Archangel Michael, hence the church's name. The temple, finished in 1597, was built in the Renaissance style. Its facade follows the Neuhauser Straße, the nave faces north - an exception.

The **facade** reflects the political ambition of the Counter Reformation, which Bavaria established to confront the ideas of Martin Luther: the three-story facade presents the rulers who had made outstanding contributions to the Catholic faith in Bavaria. Christ Salvator is enthroned on the gable of the roof. On the ground floor, the Archangel Michael fights evil in the form of a Protestant devil. The Dutch Renaissance sculptor Hubert Gerhard executed the work. Herzog Wilhelm V embraces a model of the church; his initiative made the Bavarians fund the construction.

The **cycle of images** in the bright interior meditates on the victory of Catholicism as the true religion. The choir is reminiscent of an ancient triumphal arch. When completed, the barrel vault, which spans twenty metres, was the largest after St Peter in Rome. The monumental windows flood the interior with light, and the magnificent white stucco reinforces that impression.

The monumental **nave** is 28 metres high and 80 metres long. It depicts the life of Jesus from birth to resurrection and redemption. At the entrance, a bronze angel welcomes the believers with holy water. He directs the eye along the central axis to the high altar. Hubert Gerhard cast the figure in 1595.

The climax is reached at the steps of the **choir**: the crucifixion. Mary Magdalene kneels movingly at the feet of her beloved King of Kings - a symbol of those who dedicate their lives to Jesus Christ. The path to the high altar illustrates the resurrection of Jesus. Finally, the Saviour returns to redeem the world.

King Ludwig II is buried in the **crypt** next to Herzog Wilhelm V and Kurfürst Maximilian I.

The **high altar** shows a painting by Christoph Schwartz from 1587: the Archangel Michael fights the devil. In the run-up to the Thirty Years' War, the Apocalypse, along with depictions of the Virgin Mary, was the main symbol of the Counter Reformation's fight against Protestantism's new ideas.

The baroque **pulpit** shows the Archangels Michael, Raphael and Gabriel. The circular painting in the **western transept** commemorates the martyrdom of 30 Christians in Nagasaki in 1597 under Emperor Taikosama. The Leuchtenberg monument next to it is dedicated to Herzog von Leuchtenberg, who died in 1824. The monument was created based on a design by Leo von Klenze.

The Dreifaltigkeitsaltar in the transept refers to the sacrifice of the Old Covenant. Anton Maria Viani created the painting. The circular painting next to it depicts Saint Aloysius of Gonzaga. The Spaniard died in 1591 during an epidemic in Rome.

▲ Herzog Wilhelm V commissioned the Jesuit Church of St Michael on Neuhauser Straße.

The **organ** was created by the organ builder Sandtner from Dillingen in the 1980s. It has 64 registers on four manuals and a pedal.

King Ludwig II: Thundering Mourning

The fairytale King Ludwig II found his final rest in the crypt of the Church of St Michael. He drowned in the Starnberger See (Lake Starnberg) on June 13, 1886, and nobody knows how. Six days later, the Munichers buried him. The hearse drove from the Münchner Residenz onto Neuhauser Straße, passing thousands of mourners. The king was dressed in the regalia of the Grand Master of the Order of St Hubert; he held a sword in his left hand. Eight black horses pulled the carriage; Prince Regent Luitpold led the funeral procession. At the Church of St Michael, the deceased was carried to the crypt and the king was placed in a sarcophagus. Nobody wanted to give an eulogy; the country had fallen into silence. Then - a thunderstorm came up - the clouds darkened - electrified air sizzled - lightning struck the church - the king's last word.

(24) Bürgersaalkirche

Facts & Figures

Johann Georg Ettenhofer designed the Bürgersaalkirche as a prayer house for the German Marian Congregation in 1710; the faithful consecrated the church some sixty-five years later. The Allied air raids during World War II only scratched the building, and thus, until 1947, it became the replacement church for the destroyed Frauenkirche. A statue of the Madonna embellishes the red-white facade; a papal cross at the pediment tops the building. On the ground floor, the lower church reenacts the stations of the cross with four life-sized figures each. A museum tells the history of the congregation and the story of Rupert Mayer SJ, who died from the late effects of his detention in a concentration camp. The single nave prayer house above is the primary meeting space of the congregation. Last but not least, the high altar depicts the Annunciation.

The **Bürgersaalkirche** was built on the suffering of people caused by people. Not only the moving display of the stations of the cross at the lower church is a testimony of humanity's cruel atrocities, but also the repeated arrest of Munich's apostle Rupert Mayer SJ. The Jesuit died from an apoplectic stroke on 1 November 1945 during mass - a late sequela to his solitary confinement in the concentration camp Oranienburg.

Father Rupert Mayer SJ embodies the antithesis to Kardinal Faulhaber, who directed the Archdiocese of Munich & Freising through the testing times of the Nazi regime. The conflict, which tore the Catholic Church apart, manifested in the controversy of these two God-fearing men.

The Church was anxious about communism because Karl Marx and his disciples considered religion an *"opium of the people"*. Moreover, Kardinal Faulhaber had to ensure the congregation would survive, defending it against the threats from fascism, offering hope by encouraging faith.

Rupert Mayer SJ went a different path. He preached that Christian values cannot be reconciled with Nazi ideology. The regime had no choice! It silenced the pious man by confining him and classifying him as an enemy of the state.

▲ The Bürgersaalkirche survived World War II without much damage.

The NS leadership was worried about the Jesuit's power and influence. *"Father Rupert Mayer SJ must not become a martyr"*, so the instructions and the Nazi regime detained the preacher at nearby Kloster Ettal and not in Dachau. He nevertheless became a victim of the Nazis, a priestly indulgence - because the Church had kept too close diplomatic ties with the regime.

When the Order of Jesuits repatriated Father Rupert Mayer SJ to the Bürgersaalkirche in 1948 after his death, the benevolent missionary enjoyed a level of reverence that impelled Pope John Paul II to beatify the priest on a visit to Munich's Olympiastadion in 1987.

Location: Kapellenstraße 1 **Entrance:** Without charge **Opening Times:** daily 9.00 - 19.00
Internet: https://www.mmkbuergersaal.de/buergersaalkirche.html
Literature: Anton Koerbling SJ: Pater Rupert Mayer

The German Marian Congregation

The Marian Congregation seeks God: the spiritual exercises of Ignatius Loyola, the founder of the Order of the Society of Jesus, escort the faithful along the soul's hidden paths; one will arrive in the arms of God by circumnavigating the devil. The Sodales commit in marriage to the Virgin Mary, and their prayers to the Madonna open the gates to paradise. Three decades after the founding of the Jesuits, the Marian Congregation, a lay movement, was established in Rome, where a Jesuit pastoral worker spearheads a Bible study group. Many Bavarian towns felt inspired and established Marian Congregations during the 16th century, including Dillingen, Koblenz and Augsburg. Munich followed in 1578; the Bürgersaalkirche is their cultural centre, a prayer house dearly loved by God.

(25) Karlstor

Facts & Figures

The Karlstor, mentioned in 1302 for the first time, protected the western part of the enclosure during the Middle Ages when the commercial road shouldered the trade to Landsberg am Lech. In 1791, Munich was at a bursting point, and Kurfürst Karl Theodor had the moat filled, the fortification demolished, and the bridge removed to make space. An explosion destroyed the central tower in 1857; the architect Arnold Zenetti reconstructed the complex four years later. In 1902, Claudius von Seidl designed the buildings at the forecourt. After World War II, the magistrate refurbished the entrance in neo-Gothic style. The three musicians at the central thoroughfare once embellished the Fischbrunnen at the Marienplatz. Alongside, four local characters grin devilishly, among them *Finessensepperl*, the Bavarian messenger of love, and the jester *Georg Prangl*.

The Munichers loved to hide geometric relationships in the city's morphology: the distance from the Marienplatz to the **Karlstor** coincides with that from the Marienplatz to the Sendlinger Tor. Equally, the segment from the Marienplatz to the Isartor corresponds to that from the Marienplatz to the Odeonsplatz. In short, Munich's east-west and north-south elongations are congruent.

The first city enclosure harboured alchemical relationships in its structure. At the historical centre, the Heinrichsstadt, the ratio of distances from the city gates to the Marienplatz measured seven to five: it was 700 feet from the Marienplatz to the Schöner Turm and 700 feet from the Marienplatz to the Schwabinger Tor but only 500 to the Talburgtor and the Rindermarkt. The inner city thus stretched across a width of 1200 feet from end to end. The diameter of the second enclosing measured 1200 metres, three times the size - the Trinity. The burgess constructed a chapel 500 feet from the Schöner Turm, outside the first city wall and close to today's Jesuit church where the Neuhauser Straße bends.

The science of the mysticism of numbers helps to understand many details of Munich's historical urban planning. However, historians still

▲ A pedestrian zone covers the area around the Karlstor since 1972.

wonder why the first enclosure had five and not four entrance gates - perhaps a hint to the four nails and the piercing of the lance of Jesus at the cross?

The Munichers love to dig in their heels; they surrender to authority only ostensibly. Common parlance knows the Karlstor by the code word *Stachus* despite Kurfürst Karl Theodor sacrificing his name to the plaza. The Munichers never liked Karl Theodor; the dispute escalated to nasty games: when the sovereign renamed the *Obere Tor* to *Karlstor*, the townspeople met at the *Stachusgarten*, a coffeehouse close by because they would not want to utter the name of the mischievous Elector - never ever ever.

Location: pedestrian area **Entrance:** Without charge **Opening Times:** Always accessible
Internet: https://www.muenchen.de/sehenswuerdigkeiten/orte/120458.html
Literature: Freimut Scholz: Die Gründung der Stadt München

When the Karlstor Exploded

It was the 16 September 1857, eleven o'clock in the evening. The law-abiding citizens snored under their eiderdowns when a deafening blast cut through the silence of the night. Dancing tongues of flames lightened up the night sky; wooden beams and pieces of brickwork whooshed through the air. What had happened? The gunpowder stored at the central tower of the Karlstor had caught fire, exploded, and the blast shattered the gate. An investigation found that the ironmonger Rosenlehner, who occupied the neighbouring building, entrusted by the city council with the storing of saltpetre for defence, stockpiled such an amount that Munich had to ablate the central tower after the explosion. Five burghers lost their lives, and ever since, anxious Rosenlehner, the scoundrel, was deaf and dumb.

(26) Promenadeplatz

Facts & Figures

Aristocratic palaces, built during the 18th century, string together at both sides of the Promenadeplatz, an elongated piazza. In the 19th and 20th centuries, banks and insurance companies moved into the buildings. Only the sculpture of a Madonna at the Gunetzrhainerhaus (Promenadeplatz 15), constructed in 1730, survived the recent transformation. Four bronze statues embellish the bushy grass strip: Orlando di Lasso (Renaissance musician), Christoph Willibald Ritter von Gluck (composer), Lorenz von Westenrieder (historian) and Kurfürst Max Emanuel (absolutist). The reformer Maximilian Graf von Montgelas stands tall at the western edge, cast in aluminium. He is known as the father of modern Bavaria. At his house (Promenadeplatz 2), built by Emanuel Joseph von Herigoyen in 1811, the hotel *Bayerischer Hof* rocks exhausted guests to sleep.

Munich rerouted its salt trade from the Marienplatz to the **Promenadeplatz** in 1406. Henceforth, merchants marketed the white gold in barns to the north of the Heinrichsstadt. During boom years, over 150,000 hundredweights exchanged hands, which was the source of the city's wealth.

During Absolutism, Munich's nobility wanted to settle within earshot of the Münchner Residenz. Soon, the messieurs felt disturbed by the barkers' yelling, and they forced the salt traders to a site next to today's Hauptbahnhof (Central Station).

Ladies were seen taking a stroll once the world sauntered with elegance across the Promenadeplatz. Even Bavaria's state reformer Maximilian Graf von Montgelas discovered the plaza in 1811, where he dictated his projects onto paper at the corner to Kardinal Faulhaber Straße. The statesman was so fascinated by Immanuel Kant and the French Revolution that he exorcised the Middle Ages from Bavaria's soul within a few decades. He presided as the First Minister over the country's fate for twenty years (from 1799 to 1817); he introduced such a profound reform package that Munich still termers from the aftershock.

▲ The statesman Graf von Metternich reformed Bavaria in the early 19th century.

The Count's secret pact with Napoleon made the country a kingdom. He introduced compulsory education, decreed vaccination against smallpox, offered a state pension, and supported widows and orphans. The reformer passed a new criminal code and interdicted penitentiary torture in 1813. He even drafted a constitution, which Bavaria introduced later.

His fiscal legislation terminated feudal prerogatives. He combated corruption by enforcing exams, and remunerated the administration according to performance. He expedited the dissolution of monasteries and financed his reforms by selling church property.

Lage: Promenadeplatz **Eintritt:** Kostenlos **Öffnungszeiten:** Jederzeit zugänglich
Internet: https://www.muenchen.de/sehenswuerdigkeiten/orte/120336.html
Literatur: Oliver Braun et al.: Revolution in München

Lola Montez, an Irish affair

King Ludwig I had just celebrated his 60th birthday and lamented the loss of his youth when he dutifully inspected the new dancers of the royal theatre on 7 October 1846. Among them gloated an Irish beauty, masquerading as a Spaniard. Her name was Lola Montez (Lunfardo for *Breasts like Mountains*) - her eyes ignited forests - the King's heart was burning with desire. Witnesses report that Ludwig I had questioned the authenticity of Lola's boobies, on which she cut her bodice open and invited the philanderer to investigate her splendour. Little Ludwig bestirred itself, and the King promoted the pair of breasts to a countess. He bestowed a mansion on the dancer and immortalised her image in his *Gallery of Beauties*. The infatuation lasted for two years, then it went too far for the taste of the Munichers, and they forced the King to abdicate.

(27) Kardinal Faulhaber Straße

Facts & Figures

Bavaria's nobility settled along the Kardinal Faulhaber Straße and the Prannerstraße during the 17th and 18th centuries, enjoying the vicinity of the Münchner Residenz. Today, white-collar workers employed by banks and insurance companies operate in the buildings. The architect Enrico Zuccalli constructed the Palais Porcia in the style of the Italian Baroque on behalf of the Fuggers in 1693 (Kardinal Faulhaber Straße 12). The Palais Holnstein, 1737 designed by François de Cuvilliés in rococo style, turned into the archbishop's palace of the Diocese München-Freising. The Palais Sensheim (Prannerstraße 7) was built in 1764 and refurbished in neo-baroque style in 1900. Bavaria's federal state parliament once was in session at Prannerstraße 8. However, the Allied air raids of World War II destroyed the complex, and the post-war period failed to reconstruct the building.

1918! Demoralising hunger put Germany on its knees. The soldiers returned from the trenches bleeding and traumatised. Disorientation and political uproar overwhelmed the lands. The people were weary of World War I. Munich had its belly full of the Prussian authoritarian state, which pulled the strings of Bavaria's puppet King Ludwig III.

Finally, exasperation festered the city into action. Left-wing radicals demanded the King's abdication and aspired to replace the monarchy with a parliamentary democracy. A pacifistic group under the leadership of Kurt Eisner had separated from the social democratic party SPD in 1917 and called for immediate peace. When hardship pressured the impoverished, the splinter party USDP organised a demonstration at the Theresienwiese on 7 November 1918. Towards the evening, a revolutionary hardcore formed comprising soldiers, workers and farmers; jointly, they marched to the Münchner Residenz, chanting to depose the King. Even the royal guards forsake the last of the Wittelsbacher monarchs; King Ludwig III hastily fled the country.

In the darkness of the night, Kurt Eisner declared the Wittelsbacher dynasty as discharged and proclaimed the Free State of Bavaria. A

▲ Bavaria's aristocracy erected their palaces along the Kardinal Faulhaber Straße.

soldiers' and workers' council nominated the pacifist as the first-ever First Minister of Bavaria; Kurt Eisner directed the country's fortunes for one hundred days. He introduced general suffrage and organised a parliamentary election, but the USDP only wrestled 2.5% of the seats.

On his way to the constituent assembly, where Kurt Eisner intended to resign, the right-wing radical Anton Graf von Arco assassinated the politician on 21 February 1919 at the corner of **Kardinal Faulhaber Straße**. The revolution had shed its first blood and drawn the sword of terror. A sense of calmness, dubious and dangerous, only returned when Adolf Hitler seized power.

Location: Kardinal Faulhaber Straße **Entrance**: Without charge **Opening Times**: Always accessible **Internet**: https://www.br.de/nachricht/franz-graf-pocci100.html
Literature: Sigrid von Moisy: Franz Graf Pocci 1807-1876

Franz Graf von Pocci, Count Punch of Munich

The Biedermeier was dispassionate and reserved! The collective repression of human instincts caused Sigmund Freud to call the period neurotic. Only a few succeeded, like Franz Graf von Pocci, in balancing the bottomed-up era by finding creative release in artistic expression. The *Count Punch of Munich* descended from a family of Italian nobility. The royal court in Munich appointed him as its chamberlain and master of ceremony. However, his passion was to care for the (moral) education of Bavaria's children. When his friend *Father Schmid* opened a marionette theatre in 1858, Franz Graf von Pocci composed the plays. The literary adventurer penned over forty puppet shows, enchanting Bavaria's youth. His plays immortalised the philanthropist, at least in the hearts of the children - then and now.

(28) Salvatorkirche

Facts & Figures

The Salvatorkirche enjoys a long history. The master builder Lukas Rottaler erected the Gothic church in 1480. During the Middle Ages, the Frauenkirche buried its dead at the graveyard. Kurfürst Karl Theodor dissolved the cemetery and relocated the bodies to the Südfriedhof
during the 18th century. Since 1828, the church serves the Greeks as a prayer house. Most of them had fled their country during the liberation fight against Turkish occupying troops. The single-nave with five bays delights with its late-Gothic interior, vaulted by a star-shaped ribbed roof. The furnishing of the church with icon paintings, tapestry and tribune reflects Greek Orthodox tradition. An image of Jesus Christ embellishes the left; to the right, the Virgin Mary radiates with splendour. Paintings of the Holy Communion and the Holy Trinity decorate the entrance.

The centuries meet at the **Salvatorplatz,** where the Frauenkirche buried the deceased during the 15th century. Two hundred years later, Munich's first opera house delighted visitors. The Jungfernturm to the back once protected the northern city wall, and the Archbishop's Palace is home to the Diocese München-Freising. Kardinal Faulhaber, the son of a farmer, held the office during the Nazi regime.

The role Kardinal Faulhaber had to play under the Nazi regime led to much criticism during the second half of the 20th century, but the conflict was insoluble. Unlike the ideology of Russian Bolshevism, which regarded religion as the *opium of the people,* fascism respected Catholic liturgy as a part of the country's heritage. Furthermore, the Nazi regime availed to Catholicism, seeking to justify the systematic persecution of the Jews, scapegoating them as the assassins of Jesus Christ. Nevertheless, the Nazis never observed reluctance to silence any dignitary or high church official should he raise his voice against the regime. The clerics trod through a dangerous minefield.

The church fathers feared that Bolshevism could suffocate religion, and they sought to curtail the Communist's influence on the people. What is more, the clerics had to defend the institution against the Nazi regime to avoid expropriation - to keep alive.

Kardinal Faulhaber criticised Adolf Hitler at times, yet he collaborated with the regime willingly. The limit of ecclesiastical courage was reached when the cardinals preached Pope Pius XI's encyclical *With Burning Anxiety* on Palm Sunday 1937, which took an unequivocal stand against the Nazi regime. The deportation of a few clerics sufficed to silence Germany's State Church, however. One seriously wonders: Did the times allow for the facilitation of hope by faith only behind closed doors, just like during the Apostolic Age?

▲ The Frauenkirche once buried its dead at the Salvatorkirche.

Location: Salvatorstraße 17 **Entrance:** Without charge **Opening Times:** during the day
Internet: https://www.salvatorkirche-münchen.de
Literature: Heinz Hürten: Akten Kardinal Michael von Faulhabers 1917 - 1945

Munich's Iron Maiden

The second city wall once passed to the north of the Salvatorkirche. Remains of a brick tower have survived at the Jungfernturmstraße. The Munichers erected the building in 1493; in 1804, the structure was partly demolished. A gruesome history haunts the Jungfernturm (tower of the virgin). Here, the authorities executed dreadful court hearings during the Middle Ages. If the patricians wanted a corrupt judgement, they forced the delinquent to the tower, where he had to "kiss" the swords of an iron maiden in penance. The expression of love opened a trapdoor, and the convicted tumbled into a dungeon. Rumour has it that the iron maiden was spiked, embracing the sentenced with her arms to endow the sinner with a quick death. The Mittelalterliche Kriminalmuseum in Rothenburg ob der Tauber shows such an instrument.

(29) Platz der Opfer des Nationalsozialismus

Facts & Figures

Ten months after the end of World War II, Karl Scharnagl, Munich's first post-war mayor, renamed the square at the Brienner Straße to *Platz der Opfer des Nationalsozialismus*. The historical reappraisal of the Nazi holocaust will never finish, but he took the first step. On 8 November 1985, the magistrate ignited the eternal flame at the six-metre tall granite pillar designed by the mindful sculptor Andreas Sobeck. A blazing torch burns inside an iron-grilled cage, an image of humanity incarcerated behind bars, longing for freedom from ideological fanaticism. At the nearby green, a memorial embedded in the pavement commemorates the deported Roma & Sinti, a monument designed by the artist Toni Preis. It reminds everyone that the Nazi regime murdered not only Jews but many minority groups, including homosexuals and the political opposition.

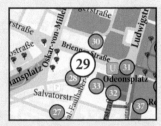

Munich's last transport of Jews - mostly children - headed to the concentration camp Theresienstadt on 23 February 1945, fifty days before the end of World War II. Right to the last minute, Bavaria's civil servants loyally surrendered their allegiance to Adolf Hitler, defiantly shouldering the ideology of the Third Reich. The Munichers displaced, deported and assassinated about 12,000 Jews; many had contributed with their sharp mind to the cultural and economic prosperity of the city.

In Munich, the systematic **deportation** and extermination of the Jews started in October 1941; the city was Germany's forerunner in the holocaust. In his political hometown, Adolf Hitler could test his racist ideas before opening the gates to hell to the remaining parts of Germany. During the following four years, more than forty trains left the collecting stations in the suburbs Berg am Laim and Milbertshofen, where the Nazi regime quartered the Jews; whosoever had not escaped by that time could only seek to hide.

The tension, the incertitude, the trepidation, the jittering and the suffering is unimaginable; day by day, they foresaw their deportation. Like outcasts, they carried the sign of death on their forehead, arduously

▲ The eternal flame commemorates the victims of World War II.

dragging themselves from hour to hour.

Munich's Gestapo headquarters, the Secret State Police, was based at the Wittelsbacher Palais, overlooking the Brienner Straße. Where today the Bayerische Landesbank issues mortgages, the Gestapo once composed the death list of those who were destined for concentration camps. The list included not only Jews but also opposition leaders, homosexuals, ecclesial dignitaries, Sinti & Roma and all those who were unfit to serve the Aryan race. None could hide from the meticulously working German civil servants eagerly following orders; the Nazi regime would have been impossible without them.

Location: Platz der Opfer **Entrance**: Without charge **Opening Times**: Always accessible
Internet: https://www.muenchen.de/sehenswuerdigkeiten/orte/120316.html
Literature: Angelika Baumann et al.: München arisiert

Rama Dama

Munich was a heap of rubble after World War II; the city was exposed to the elements; the people were starving; debris towered everywhere - a haven for mice and rats. Mayor Thomas Wimmer, a former prisoner of the Dachau concentration camp, showed his courage. Leadership means taking action, and *Rama Dama* (*cleaning up the mess*) was his philosophy. On 29 October 1949, a sunny autumn day, the mayor rolled up his sleeves and loaded the rubble of the Marienplatz onto US-American trucks; more than 7500 Munichers followed his example. The time had come to hand the past over to historians, to dare a new beginning, to focus on reconstructing the city. At last, the social democrat cleaned up the devastation that was left behind by the Nazi regime; he planted a tree amidst the ashes - thank you.

Wittelsbacher Platz

Facts & Figures

Leo von Klenze designed the classicistic Palais Arco-Zinneberg at the western edge of the Wittelsbacher Platz; the Allied air raids of World War II destroyed the building; the complex was reconstructed in 1960. A concert hall, the Odeon, once excited its audience at the eastern border, but the war had wrecked the building beyond repair. Today, Bavaria's Ministry of the Interior is housed at that location. To the north lies the Palais Ludwig Ferdinand, constructed by Leo von Klenze in 1826, his home and studio for more than twenty-five years; there, he worked on the blueprints of the Maxvorstadt. Today, the Siemens headquarters is developing a strategy for the planet's future at the Wittelsbacher Platz. An equestrian statue, which depicts Kurfürst Maximilian I, dominates the square. The artist Bertel Thorvaldsen cast the figure in 1839.

During the Tehran Conference in 1943, the Allied Forces discussed separating Bavaria from Germany and establishing an Alpine federation. They intended to deindustrialise the country and convert the lands into a rural state. When the 7th US Army marched into Munich on 30 April 1945, the plans were forgotten, and Bavaria appreciated its occupational force.

After the war, the conciliatory Bavarian-American relationship encouraged the economic upswing of the southern federal provinces. Until its fall in 1989, Munich benefitted from the Berlin Wall, a symbol of the divide of post-war Germany. Most Prussian large corporations, which had settled in Berlin, scouted for a new base; many chose Germany's southernmost city to establish their headquarters. Undoubtedly, various factors have entered into the decision-making process - the beautiful countryside, the air quality of the Alps, Munich's central location within Europe - but being occupied by American and not by French or British troops may have tipped the scales. As one example among many, the Allianz Versicherung, the world's most successful primary insurer, moved its head office to the Leopoldstraße in 1949.

▲ Kurfürst Maximilian I leads Bavaria into the future.

The Bayerische Motorenwerke BMW had manufactured their automobiles in Eisenach during World War II. After the Berlin Wall was erected, they moved their production sites to Munich, and by 1952, the first car left the assembly line at the Isar.

The Prussian large corporation Siemens also moved its headquarters from Berlin to Munich. The renowned technology company relocated its head office to the Palais Ludwig Ferdinand at the **Wittelsbacher Platz** in 1957. An administration building followed in 1999, designed by Richard Meier. There, the Siemens Forum, a museum of technology, explains the workings of the world.

Location: Wittelsbacher Platz **Entrance**: Without charge **Opening Times**: Always accessible
Goethe-Institut: Oskar-von-Miller-Ring 20, https://www.goethe.de/de/index.html
Café Luitpold: Brienner Straße 11, https://www.cafe-luitpold.de

The Café Luitpold

München is running behind Wien - at least in terms of coffee culture. The Bavarians may have freed Austria from the Turks during the Battle of Vienna in 1693, but the coffee remained glued to Austria's capital. The culture of the brown broth invaded Munich only with the opening of the Café Luitpold on 1 January 1888, where the Munichers sipped the dark gold under a twelve-metre tall glass dome. Palm trees and a water fountain accentuate the cosy atmosphere. Today, the café offers poetry readings, panel debates and dance performances. While cruising the floor with Tango steps, visitors may remember that the Café Luitpold witnessed the founding of the group *Der Blaue Reiter* by Wassily Kandinsky and Paul Klee. At times, the coffeehouse also hosted the editorial of the *Simplicissimus*.

(31) Odeonsplatz

Facts & Figures

The Odeonsplatz connects the old town to the Maxvorstadt. Until 1816, the Schwabinger Tor, once the town's northern entrance, protected the city at today's intersection of the Brienner Straße with the Ludwigstraße. After the Munichers had ground down the old city walls, Leo von Klenze transformed the Odeonsplatz into an Italian piazza. A concert hall, the Odeon, destroyed during World War II, gave the square its name. Today, the open space is sandwiched to the south by the Feldherrnhalle, to the west by the Theatinerkirche and to the east by the Münchner Residenz. At the north-eastern corner, an equestrian statue shows King Ludwig I. The adjoining classicistic buildings, today the *Bavarian State Ministry of the Interior* and the *Bavarian State Ministry of Finance*, were the first ones completed; they defined the style of the boulevard.

By appointing Bavaria to a Kingdom in 1806, Napoleon, the new Master over Europe, gained a devoted ally in the German-speaking lands. Paris wanted to strengthen the dukedom, and thus, France dovetailed parts of Swabia and Franconia to the Kingdom. Geographic expansion required a sophisticated administration, which the Alpine country centralised in Munich, following the example of its new paragon.

After Kurfürst Karl Theodor had demolished the city walls in the late 18th century, the settlement stretched out to the meadows in the north, outside of the former gates. Had the city's population been 40,000 in 1800, one hundred years later and after a wave of immigration, more than half a million citizens dwelled in the state capital; the tenfold increase forced the settlement to accept the role of a metropolis.

In 1808, King Maximilian I elevated the Münchner Residenz, the royal winter palace, to Munich's new geographic centre when he designed the Maxvorstadt towards the north and not to the south. Consequently, he transformed the **Odeonsplatz** into a hub that joins the town's medieval and modern parts.

The sovereigns also added an avenue to the east, the Brienner Straße,

▲ The impressive statue of King Ludwig I was inaugurated in 1862.

to connect the Münchner Residenz with the summer palace Schloss Nymphenburg, Munich's Versaille. At the Propyläen, the arterial road left the Maxvorstadt. Munich increased so rapidly during the 19th century that the area around the Königsplatz soon flooded with residential buildings. Even the spacious private gardens surrendered to the eager builders. Green spaces only survived around the neighbouring Karolinenplatz.

Finally, at the turn of the 19th century, the city also expanded to the south, where residential areas for the middle class emerged, and the old town marked again the geographic centre of Munich.

Location: Odeonsplatz **Entrance:** Without charge **Opening Times:** Always accessible
Café Tambosi: https://tambosi-odeonsplatz.de
Literaturhaus München: https://www.literaturhaus-muenchen.de

Death by Elephant

In 1888, Munich celebrated the one-hundredth birthday of the 1868 deceased King Ludwig I; a tinny-tooting parade closed the festivities. Horsemen, knights, maidens and music corps passed the royal box at the Odeonsplatz, gracefully welcomed by Prince Regent Luitpold. In the parade marched eight elephants from Hagenbeck's circus; at the Odeonsplatz, everyone had to turn - they too. The elephants, confused by the roundabout and returning onto the Ludwigstraße in the opposite direction, now faced the noisy stovepipe of an oncoming steam engine, part of the team *Profession Modern Industry*. Who whooshed, who snorted first? We do not know! The annals only report that the elephants broke loose, stomped through the crowd and crushed four panicking onlookers to death.

(32) Feldherrnhalle

Facts & Figures

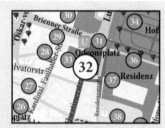

The architect Friedrich von Gärtner designed the Feldherrnhalle in 1844, a true-to-original copy of the Loggia dei Lanzi in Florence. Three round arches straddle an elevated pedestal. In 1906, the city fathers added two lions at the flight of steps, guarding the complex. Along the arcades, the statues of Johann Graf von Tilly and Carl Philipp Fürst von Wrede ready their troops to battle; Johann Graf von Tilly served the Bavarian army as a general during the Thirty Years' War and Carl Phillip Fürst von Wrede during the Napoleonic Wars. A five-metre-high bronze figure pays homage to Bavaria's army in the middle. In 1892, Prince Regent Luitpold inaugurated the warrior carrying a round shield and a helmet. He lifts a banner, accompanied by a lion and a personification of Bavaria's femininity; palm leaves and a laurel wreath embellish her- two symbols of peace.

In the 19th century, the German duchies, carried by a wave of national pride, united to form the German Empire. The confederation won the 1870/71 German-French war, and the Munichers welcomed their returning heroes at the Siegestor. A torchlight procession at the Odeonsplatz concluded the festivities. Ever since right-wing populists have smelled the opportunity: *the Odeonsplatz is the perfect stomping ground for parades.*

After World War I, Munich became a fertile ground for nationalistic ideologies, attracting many right-wing radical groups from all over Germany. By 1920, the smouldering antidemocratic and antisemitic sentiment in the Bavarian capital escalated.

At that time, Adolf Hitler, an Austrian-born private raised near Linz, founded the National Socialist Workers Party - one among many political organisations in Munich. Different fascist groups wrestled for power at that time. When Bavaria declared a state of emergency in September 1923, electing the nationalist Gustav von Kahr as their general commissioner, Adolf Hitler saw his opportunity and staged a coup.

On 8 November 1923, Gustav von Kahr delivered a programmatic speech, and Adolf Hitler marched his servile Kampftruppe into the

▲ Bavarian generals embellish the Feldherrnhalle at the Odeonsplatz.

Bürgerbräukeller, a traditional Bavarian beer hall - a single shot sufficed to declare the regional government as discharged and proclaim a national revolution. The next day, the right-wing extremists paraded to the **Feldherrnhalle**, seeking the support of the people. Adolf Hitler expected no resistance, yet the federal police barred his way - again, a gun fired. During the shoot-out, sixteen fascists lost their lives, *martyrs* according to Nazi propaganda. The police detained Adolf Hitler and sentenced him to five years of imprisonment, but exemplary conduct set him free after eight months. The attempted coup had failed but gave birth to the myth of the blood-trenched standard.

Location: Odeonsplatz **Entrance:** Without charges **Opening Times:** Always accessible
Internet: https://www.schloesser.bayern.de/deutsch/schloss/objekte/mu_feldh.htm
Literature: Klaus Gietinger: Hitler vor Gericht. Der Prozess nach dem Putsch von 1923

The Shirkers' Alleyway

At the Residenzstraße, between the Feldherrnhalle and the Münchner Residenz, a memorial burlesqued during the Nazi regime. It commemorated the revolutionaries who stumbled into their deaths during the 1923 failed Hitler Putsch. Four stormtroopers sentinelled the devilish *place of honour*; passers-by from the Residenzstraße to the Odeonsplatz had to greet the guards with a Hitler salute, which many a Municher wanted to avoid. Alternatively, some sneaked through the Viscardigasse to the other side of the Feldherrnhalle and arrived at the Odeonsplatz by the Theatinerstraße. Common parlance knew the pathway as the *Drückebergergasse*, the shirkers' alleyway. Today, a bronze trace burnt into the pavement by the artist Bruno Wank remembers this silent act of resistance.

㉝ Theatinerkirche St Kajetan

Facts & Figures

Kurfürst Ferdinand Maria and his wife Henriette Adelaide von Savoyen gave birth to a son in 1659, the later Kurfürst Max Emanuel. In gratitude, they donated *"the most magnificent church Munich had ever seen."* The architect Agostino Barelli from Bologna laid the founding stone; Enrico Zuccalli placed the keystone in 1690. Since François Cuvilliés the Elder had the prayer house refurbished in 1768, the facade dresses in Rococo style. Stuccoed figurines embellish the enormous single-nave interior which is covered by a spacious barrel vault, constructed in Italian Baroque style. The altar shows the *Blessed Virgin Mary with Child*, a work by the artist Gaspar de Crayer, a student of Rubens. Many members of the Wittelsbacher dynasty found their resting place in the vault. The tomb of King Maximilian II and his wife Marie Friederike von Preußen is in a side chapel on the ground floor.

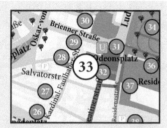

The lean decades of the Thirty Years' War fired their last shot in 1648. The resolution of the war tasted bitter in Southern Germany: abandoned were the fields, and black ravens were flying over rotting corpses; hunger and epidemics had disfigured many a beautiful maiden; the country had fallen into dismay.

Then, the Italian Henriette Adaleide von Savoyen—the wife of Kurfürst Ferdinand Maria—entered the stage, and the sun rose over Bavaria. Within a short time, the laughter of the vivacious maiden dispelled the shadows hanging over the lands. Her curly hair, dancing in the wind, scared any melancholy away; vibrancy had returned to the city of the praying virgins.

Adelaide had no easy life when she arrived for her wedding in Munich at the age of sixteen. Eight summers Bavaria had to wait for the happy announcement, and in the end, only a solemn promise gave a supporting hand. When the heir scrimmaged on the mother's arm, southern beauty had prevailed. Musicians, vocalists, painters and sculptors entered Munich; they inveigled the city to a sense of Italy's joie de vivre. Doves of peace had swallowed the dark clouds hanging over the city; Munich now danced to the rhythm of the Baroque.

▲ The Theatinerkirche celebrates the birth of Kurfürst Max Emanuel, heir to the throne.

Many historians belligerently describe Kurfürst Ferdinand Maria as melancholic, but Bavaria had luck when the Elector ascended to the throne. He was offered the imperial crown but declined. Tired or wise, he allowed his people a much-needed breathing time, and Bavaria recovered from the turmoil of the Thirty Years' War.

The **Theatinerkirche**, a votive offering, expresses this spirit. Finally, Henriette Adelaide von Savoyen turned the temple into a royal church, depriving the Jesuits of power. The docile Theatines now had a say, not shouting but whispering the word of God - compassionately and without the finger-pointing.

Location: Odeonsplatz **Entrance:** Without charge **Opening Times:** daily 7.00 - 20.00
Internet: http://www.theatinerkirche.de
Kunsthalle München: https://www.kunsthalle-muc.de

The Hunger Bell at the Theatinerkirche

The Theatines were committed to poverty; their order forbade them to beg for alms. They could only ring a hunger bell when they hadn't eaten for three days. In Munich, the monks were integrated into the structure of the residence and lacked nothing. However, on Saint Peter's Day (February 22), 1727, a bell suddenly rang at the Odeonsplatz that no one had ever heard before, and no one knew its purpose or meaning. The citizens were amazed - the bell did not stop ringing. Finally, as the sound grew fainter, someone remembered: *This is the hunger bell*! The Munichers rushed to bring chicken, cheese, fruit and fish - so much they loved the Theatines! The monks were saved, and the order survived. Last but not least, the saying is that if the tower clock of the Theatinerkirche stops ringing, a Wittelsbacher dies.

Highlights of the Theatinerkirche

The Theatinerkirche St Kajetan is the first significant church constructed in Munich after the Thirty Years' War. The architects Agostino Barelli and Enrico Zuccalli erected the temple in Baroque style between 1663 and 1675. Kurfürst Ferdinand Maria and his wife, Henriette Adelaide von Savoyen, had taken a solemn vow *to build the most beautiful and valuable church* if they gave birth to an heir. In 1765, François Cuvilliés the Elder completed the **facade** in Rococo style. The triangular gable of the roof, the base and the attic emphasise the width of the church. Doric and Ionic pilasters give order to the structure; they visually connect the two towers. The gable shows the alliance coat of arms of Kurfürst Max III Joseph and his wife, Maria Anna von Sachsen.

Whoever walks along the **nave** inside will be struck by the bright stucco, which, thanks to the sunlight shining through the windows, directs the view upwards and into the 29-metre-high space of the vault and the towering dome.

The **high altar** by Gaspar de Crayer from 1646 shows *Mary on the throne with saints at her feet*. The Flemish painter created the painting for the Augustinian Church in Brussels. It replaces the former high altar, which was destroyed during World War II.

The monumental **dome** is reminiscent of the vault of heaven. In the lantern, God the Father, creator of the world, sits. The dome has a diameter of almost 18 metres and stretches 70 metres high. W. Leuthner created the allegories of the eight Beatitudes.

In the **north transept**, the altarpiece *The Holy Family* by the artist C. Cignani from 1676 is impressive. Mary and Jesus are framed by her parents Joseph and Anna. John the Baptist duplicates this particular Trinity with his parents, Elizabeth and Zechariah. King David pays homage to the saviour.

In addition to the Frauenkirche and the Jesuit Church of St Michael, St Kajetan is home to a burial place of the Wittelsbacher dynasty. Kurfürst Ferdinand Maria and Prince Regent Luitpold of Bavaria rest here. Access to the **crypt** is at the Marian altar in the north transept. On the ground floor, King Maximilian II and his wife Marie Friederike von Preußen sleep the eternal dream in a side chapel. Flowers point towards their monumental sarcophagi.

▲ The coat of arms of Kurfürst Max III Joseph adorns the facade of the Theatinerkirche.

The **Kajetan altar** in the south transept shows the Saint's intercession during the plague in Naples in dark colours. The renowned German artist Joachim von Sandrart painted the scene between 1667 and 1671.

A. Feistenberger designed the **pulpit** in the crossing. It is made of dark oak; the work was executed between 1685 and 1689. The Theatines Kajetan and Andreas Avellinus can be seen at the pulpit.

At the **main portal** above the entrance, an inscription reminds visitors of the motivation for the construction of the church: *"In the year of salvation 1675, Kurfürst Ferdinand Maria and Henriette Adelaide von Savoyen dedicated this temple to St Kajetan [...] based on a vow [...] Max Emanuel, the hereditary prince, was given to them."*

The Kunsthalle München

In 1985, at Theatinerstraße 8 between Fünf-Höfe and Theatinerkirche, the Hypo-Kulturstiftung (Hypo Cultural Foundation) established one of Munich's most renowned galleries. The temporary exhibitions range from archaeology to the Old Masters and modern art. So far, the curators have presented art from Egypt, works from the Orient, impressionists and the world of Walt Disney. On display were paintings by Dürer, Holbein, Rembrandt, Titian, Gauguin, van Gogh, Auguste Rodin, Pablo Picasso, Marc Chagall and many others. The museum holds between two to four exhibitions annually. They are among the highlights of the Munich cultural calendar - almost half a million enthusiastic visitors pilgrimage to the gallery annually. Guided tours and lectures accompany the program.

(34) Hofgarten

Facts & Figures

The splendid square-shaped garden, designed in the style of the Italian Renaissance, is a joyful place of calm. Kurfürst Maximilian I commissioned *the Haven of Sweet Temper* in 1613, expanding a former arboretum. Arcades embrace the playground of the muses on two sides; the monumental Bayerische Staatskanzlei towers at the eastern corner; towards the south, the Herkulessaal delights with classical and world music. The Hofgartentempel, 1616 constructed, rests in the centre. The star-shaped pathways quarter the lush vegetation. Fountains in the form of seashells made of Trento marble invite Munich's sparrows to splash around. Alley trees provide shadow to blotting flowerbeds, plonking chestnuts onto the pebbles in the autumn. In the east, the Loreley writhes sylphlike, timidly spraying her waters to welcome all visitors.

When the Bavarian regents relocated their residency from the Alte Hof to the Neuveste, they planted an arboretum at today's Marstallplatz, watering the garden by tapping into a brook. In 1518, Herzog Wilhelm IV scattered pebbles on the green to traipse across a pleasure garden designed in the style of the Italian Renaissance. From 1560 onwards, Herzog Albrecht V laid out the Albrechtinische Gärten, which Kurfürst Maximilian I enlarged to the **Hofgarten**.

Kurfürst Max III Joseph craved fresh fruit and vegetables, and so he buried seeds in the princely garden and plugged the apples sweet in the autumn. Lime and chestnut trees provided an umbrella for his joy to swagger. After Kurfürst Karl Theodor had demolished the medieval city wall in 1780, he opened the garden to his people to make them forget about revolutionising and stroll like royals instead.

During the first half of the 19th century, King Ludwig I constructed the partition to the Odeonsplatz, the Hofgartenarkaden, and embellished them with frescoes depicting scenes from the Wittelsbacher dynasty. The sixteen paintings by the artist Peter Cornelius, unveiled in 1829, tell of the heroic deeds of the Bavarian sovereigns.

At the Hofgarten, court architect Leo von Klenze stood his test when, at a young age, he designed the entrance in 1817, thus laying the foundation for his decades-long collaboration with King Ludwig I.

The Hofbrunnenwerk at the arcades of the northern closure feeds the fountains with water. It floods the splattering at the temple of the Goddess Diana and bestows the waterworks at the four sea-shell fountains with much vigour, releasing an air of freshness.

During World War II, the Hofgarten was shedding tears, being ploughed by the Allied air raids. As the earth was dug up and over, the soil blossomed again with lush green in the 1950s.

▲ Leo von Klenze designed the entrance to the Hofgarten.

Location: Hofgarten **Entrance:** Without charge **Opening Times:** Always accessible
Internet: https://www.muenchen.de/sehenswuerdigkeiten/orte/120231.html
https://www.schloesser.bayern.de/deutsch/garten/objekte/mu_hofg.htm

The Tellus Bavarica at the Hofgartentempel

At the rooftop of the dodecagonal Hofgartentempel in the centre of the garden, a bronze figure watches over Munich's climate - the so-called *Tellus Bavarica*. The symbol of the flourishing Bavarian landscape gracefully glances at the musicians summoning in her temple. She covers her head in oak leaves, symbolizing Bavaria's forests. A deerskin swathes her right arm, referring to the game of the Alpine woodlands. She clasps grain fruits in her left hand like once the Greek Goddess Demeter. At her feet wheels a wine barrel, the sap of Franconia. A salt disc leans next to her graceful body, the white gold of the Alps. Hubert Gerhard cast the Bavarian Diana, Goddess of the woods, in 1594, and in the year 1613, the artist Hans Krumpper raised her to the status of a *Tellus Bavarica*.

(35) Bayerische Staatskanzlei

Facts & Figures

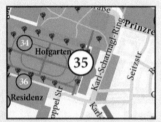

The Bayerische Staatskanzlei at the east of the Hofgarten, home to the Bavarian federal state government, houses the offices of the region's decision-makers since 1993. The politicians and civil servants are located in a building constructed by Diethard Siegert and Reto Gansser. Behind the 200-metre-long steel construction, 300 employees concoct the destiny of the Free State. A 32-metre tall central cupola, designed in the style of the Italian Renaissance, towers over the glass wings. The dome was a part of the Royal Bavarian Army Museum, constructed in 1905 and destroyed during World War II. The extensions to the side traverse an area as large as the White House in Washington. Common parlance calls the building the *Bavarian Kremlin*, out of awe, lovingly benevolent and not derogatorily. The Staatskanzlei, a hotbed of politics, is the landmark of Bavarian interests in a federal German state.

Since the end of World War II, Bavaria has been governed by the CSU, the Christian Socialist Union, a descendant of the BVP, the Bavarian People's Party. The success of the conservative right-wing party rests on the shoulders of rural core voters bound to tradition; faithfully, they carve their cross at the conservative spectrum. Only in scurrying towns, where social disparity fertilises poverty, can Germany's Socialist Democratic Party nominate the mayor, like in Munich, where nearly always the red warriors rule.

At the initiative of the US-American occupation force, the people cast their vote for the delegates of the Bavarian federal state parliament on 30 June 1946, one year after the unconditional surrender of Germany. The CSU achieved an absolute majority, and Hans Erhard presided over the fate of the lands as the first Bavarian state premier, steering Bavaria into the future.

After World War II, Europe was on the move. History forced ethnic Germans in the Sudetenland, Bohemia and Donauschwaben to leave home. In Bavaria, about two million displaced people settled, more than in any other federal state; the new Bavarians accelerated the economic and cultural upswing of the region.

▲ The Staatskanzlei was initiated by Franz Joseph Strauß and completed in 1993.

Germany's federal structure grants the provinces many freedoms. The politician Franz Joseph Strauß, state premier of Bavaria from 1978 to 1988, utilised the liberal system and opened the rural lands to the world. At his initiative, Bavaria moved the **Bayerische Staatskanzlei** from the Prinzregentenstraße to the Hofgarten.

Germany's focus on regions demands premises fit for representation, and the conservative party wanted a building as large as their *hands*. They also constructed the hub airport at the Erdinger Moos, and thus, the regional politicians left a legacy that environmental groups still dispute.

Location: Franz-Josef-Strauß-Ring 1 **Opening Times:** Not accessible
Landesportal: https://www.bayern.de // https://www.freistaat.bayern
Literature: Manfred Treml: Geschichte des modernen Bayern

The Dead Soldier at the Staatskanzlei

About 13,000 Munichers died on the Western Front during World War I. Meaningless was the death of the all too-young heroes. A monument at the base of the Staatskanzlei remembers the soldiers. The artists Wechs & Finsterwalder designed the crypt in 1926; Karl Kreppe cast the bronze statue of the *Dead Soldier*. The unknown warrior had lost his identity in the hail of bullets. During World War I, he had bled to death - anonymously, bland, cannon fodder, deprived of humanity. Twenty years later, history repeated itself, and in 1950, the Munichers added a second inscription - for those who were killed in action during World War II. Cynics remark: "*There is sufficient space for another engraving.*" Close to the arcades of the Staatskanzlei rests a black cube. The installation honours all resistance fighters who withstood the Third Reich.

(36) Herkulessaal

Facts & Figures

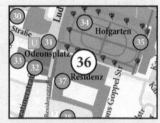

A King requires a throne room, and thus, Ludwig I pushed a gilded chair to the southern edge of the Hofgarten and masoned a classicistic building around it, the Herkulessaal. Today, the festival hall, a cavity for sound, amplifies the vibrations of violins, pianos and bandoneons. When, during World War II, Allied air raids destroyed the concert hall Odeon at the close-by Odeonsplatz, the Munichers converted the Herkulessaal into a concert hall. Until the opening of the auditorium at the Gasteig in Haidhausen, Munich's enthusiastic music fans flocked to the Münchner Residenz. Still today, music gourmands applaud the Munich Symphony Orchestra and other luminaries from around the world in the former royal hall. Tapestry depicting the deeds of the Greek hero Hercules served as the namesake. Herzog Albrecht V commissioned the cycle in Antwerp for Schloss Dachau in 1565.

Not only do Munich's art collections enjoy an excellent reputation, but the **concert halls** impress with artistic perfection, too. Bavaria experienced its first musical highlight during the 16th century when the Renaissance musician Orlando di Lasso arrived at the Isar in 1556. He followed an invitation by Herzog Albrecht V, and out of Munich, he continued to define the fashion of his time.

When Wolfgang Amadeus Mozart travelled across Europe for an appointment, he auditioned at the court of Munich, too. At Burgstraße 5, he composed the opera *Idomeneo* in 1781, but unfortunately, no position was vacant. The 25-year-old stepped again into his carriage and headed to Wien and Salzburg.

King Ludwig II, the fairy tale monarch, loved to get lost in the musical dramas of Richard Wagner, and he financed many of the master's premieres, staging them at Munich's Nationaltheater, amongst them *Tristan & Isolde*, the *Ring Cycle*, and *Die Meistersinger von Nürnberg*.

Gustav Mahler also enjoyed visiting the Alps, and he donated his 4th and 8th symphonies to Munich.

Last but not least, Munich honoured Richard Strauss, a son of the

▲ The Herkulessaal served under King Ludwig I as Bavaria's throne room.

city, with a fountain at the Neuhauser Straße. His opera *Die Frau Ohne Schatten* reopened the Nationaltheater after World War II.

Munich proudly hosts three symphony orchestras: the *Bavarian Radio State Orchestra*, the *Munich Symphony Orchestra* and the *Bavarian State Orchestra*. Since the inauguration of the new philharmonic hall in 1985, music fans met at the Gasteig in Haidhausen. Chamber orchestras present their art at the **Herkulessaal** or in the Münchner Residenz. At times, concerts are staged at Schloss Nymphenburg, Schloss Schleißheim, Schloss Blutenburg, Schloss Dachau and the Allerheiligen Hofkirche.

Location: Hofgartenstraße **Entrance and Opening Times:** Depending on performance
Internet: https://www.muenchenmusik.de/konzertsaele/herkulessaal
Deutsches Theatermuseum: http://www.deutschestheatermuseum.de

The Deutsche Theatermuseum (German Museum of Theatre)

Munich's enchanting Hofgartenarkaden houses the German Museum of Theatre, initiated by the Royal Bavarian Court Actress Clara Ziegler. In her villa at the Englischer Garten (English Garden), the artist showcased requisites and costumes from Munich's stage productions until 1944. Finally, the city commissioned a museum at the Hofgarten, and the gallery opened in 1979. The curators present an overview of the history of the theatre; they exhibit blueprints of buildings, costume and stage designs, documents and requisites. Professionals across the world highly regard the collection's extensive reference library. The vast archive administers more than 50,000 costume sketches, 400,000 role portrayals, 250,000 graphic sheets and 120,000 books about acting and the world of the stage.

(37) Münchner Residenz

Facts & Figures

Ever since Herzog Albrecht IV had moved the Alter Hof to the Neuveste in the 15th century, the Bavarian electors, emperors and kings resided at the Münchner Residenz to the north of the old town, Munich's royal winter palace. Over 500 years, the master builders enlarged the palace to 25,000 square metres. Today, the complex is home to various museums, which exhibit Bavaria's treasures: the Residenzmuseum guides the visitors along 130 furnished rooms; the Schatzkammer presents the state's jewellery (crowns, sceptres and gold works); the Münzmuseum shows a selection of coins from antiquity to modern times, and the fascinating Cuvilliés Theater enthrals with gilded stucco in Rococo style. The Allerheiligen Hofkirche, accessible as a part of the Residenzmuseum, stages classical music and other concerts in the evening.

The **Münchner Residenz** evolved into a city within the city. Munich's historical impetus relied on those rulers who eternalised their ideas into marble: Herzog Albrecht V, Kurfürst Maximilian I, Emperor Karl Albrecht and King Ludwig I. They envisioned the biggest dreams and projected their endeavours onto the royal winter palace.

Herzog Friedrich, Herzog Johann II and Herzog Stephan III founded the compound as a refuge in 1385, calling the fortress *Neuveste*.

In the 16th century, Herzog Albrecht V converted the fortress into a princely residence. He commissioned the Antiquarium, where he exhibited his collection of statues, marble busts, reliefs and coins. The Duke had enjoyed a humanistic education; with the building, he wanted to affirm the Wittelsbacher's right to power.

Herzog Wilhelm V and Kurfürst Maximilian I, the masterminds of the Counter Reformation, enlarged the palace by adding a representative wing at the Kaiserhof. Under their reign, the adoration of the Virgin Mary climaxed.

During absolutism, Bavaria's desire for honour and glory was augmented, and the electors added further wings to the compound. It was

▲ The Münchner Residenz once served as Bavaria's splendid Royal Palace.

a political necessity at that time that aspiring emperors must dwell in a stately residence and maintain an imperial court to show their capability to rule like a superior. The Wittelsbacher dynasty desired to play a role in Europe's machinations, and thus, Munich's princely seat turned ever more ostentatious. At last, success arrived in 1742 when the assembly in Frankfurt chose Karl Albrecht as the new emperor. However, his luck had run out within a few days, and the heavy crown was handed over to the House of Lorraine.

King Ludwig I added finishing touches to the palace in the 19th century, expanding it by the Königsbau and adding the Herkulessaal.

Location: Residenzstraße 1 **Opening Times:** daily 9.00 - 18.00
Entrance: Adults 23 € Concession 20 €
Internet: https://www.residenz-muenchen.de

The Impler-Uprising

Emperor Ludwig der Bayer had passed away, and his four sons jointly ruled over Bavaria. However, the treasury reeled close to bankruptcy, and high taxes burdened the country. At last, the people revolted; they marched against Munich, attacked the patricians, stormed the house of the cloth merchant Johann Impler, a member of the Inner Council, and accused him of being the mastermind of the relentless levies. Enraged, the burgess beheaded the manipulator and barred the dukes from town. Bavaria's rulers besieged the city and resolved the conflict by force. As a punishment, they demanded the construction of the *Neuveste*, today's *Royal Winter Palace*, and the castle was to be financed by the burgess out of their pocket. The dukes also insisted on a southern keep because conflicts may threaten their power from the inside - thus the rebellion's wisdom!

Cuvilliés Theater

During the Baroque, French absolutism blossomed in Bavaria; the ideology sprouted during the 17th century under Kurfürst Ferdinand Maria, and at long last, the monarchy withered when King Ludwig III had to step down at the end of World War I. With the rise of absolutism, the pristine singing game evolved into an elaborate mise-en-scène called opera. Like no other, the genre expressed the ruler's power and affirmed his direct descent from the Gods.

Commentators measured an ensemble's success by the splendour of the ambience; it defined the ranking of Europe's aristocracy. According to the opinion of the time, a dynasty wealthy enough to genuinely afford a grand theatre must be mighty. Art perfected the opera as a vehicle to spread propaganda, and the **Cuvilliés Theatre** evolved into a *simulacrum* of the social hierarchy.

The theatre's seating arrangement reflected the position of the individual within society, God-given by the colour of his blood. It were the regents and not, as today, the actors, singers or musicians who were at the focal point. All eyes were on the sovereign; the performance was not played out on stage but in the audience. The architects oriented all lines of sight towards the ruler, the vanishing point and the target of all attention. Even the stage design had to focus the set along the central axis; only the regent was to perceive all actors and all action on stage; only he was omniscient; only members of the royal family had the right to a proscenium box at the sides of the stage. Red stuccoed draperies connected them to the royal box along the dress circle.

The city nobility counted their blessings at the ground-floor boxes, depending on their status closer or further away from the sovereign. At the dress circle, the high nobility blew their noses into silken cloths. The landed gentry attended the performances at the upper circle, which was unembellished. Last but not least, the theatre dispelled civil servants to the sparsely decorated second balcony. Anyone not regarded as presentable twiddled their thumbs outside.

More than one thousand candles enchanted a performance, a spell of magic. Candles were expensive; a worker had to labour for a week to purchase a waxed wick. Only the regent could afford the flood of photons, the dance of the flames, the play with fire, the throw of shadows.

▲ The Kronprinz-Rupprecht-Brunnen sprays its waters at the eastern side of the Residenz.

The master builders covered the elector's box with mirrors, and the reflectors exponentiated the symbolism of his almighty power. The regent, a thousand times reverberated, blurred in the stream of sensation. Each mirror was cut individually by the artisans, grounded by hand; each reflector had its unique charm. At the elector's box, the sum of mirrors elevated the regent's glory to absolute power by multiplying his image manifold: the monarch was almighty, omnipresent, unattainable.

Finally, the coquettish game of the court had found its master in the opera; its rituals replicated the structure of society. Where the individual powdered his nose at the theatre, there the wig stuffed his place in society. Opera and absolutism were a pair made for each other.   ➡

Heavy is the Rock at the Münchner Residenz

A massive rock, 182 kg in weight, is chained to a winch next to the Münzmuseum at the Kapellenhof. During the Middle Ages, Herzog Christoph swirled the colossus through the air with ease. Above the stone, at a height of ten feet, three nails pierce the wall. Herzog Christopher jumped off the cuff so high he could hit the top nail with his foot. Munich's strongman was the younger brother of Herzog Albrecht IV. He was eligible by law to partake in the ruling of the country, but he had renounced his rights. Albrecht, however, mistrusted his brother and incarcerated the Bavarian Hercules. Historians suspect the legends about Christopher's vibrant virility wanted to justify the Duke's suspicion. Whosoever heaved and leapt was dangerous and had to curve the bars from the inside.

Residenzmuseum

Across 130 rooms, the **Residenzmuseum** provides insight into the life and work of the Bavarian regents, from the founding of the palace during the 15th century to the day when the 1918 revolution overthrew the monarchy. The vast ensemble dressed up for representation intended to affirm Bavaria's claim to power within the German-speaking countries and the Wittelsbacher's strive for supremacy amongst the European dynasties.

The compound grew to its current size in three stages: during the 16th and 17th centuries, Herzog Wilhelm V and his son, Kurfürst Maximilian I, extended the palace to become Bavaria's secular and spiritual centre. Their construction work wanted to justify Bavaria's demand for the leadership of the Counter Reformation. During Absolutism, Emperor Karl Albrecht leveraged the palace to an elegant ambience, following the example of King Louis XIV of France, the Sun King. When Bavaria had risen to a kingdom in the 19th century, King Ludwig I began the construction of the Königsbau.

The court subdivided the flight of rooms into royal apartments, guest rooms and staterooms. The Antiquarium, the imperial hall and the portrait gallery sold Bavaria's grandeur to diplomats. The structure of the royal wing follows the ideal of France: two antechambers shield the regent's private rooms, consisting of a bedroom, an assembly hall and a study. The Prince Regent's rooms were similarly organised to prepare the successor to his role as a king. Munich unlocked the splendid Steinzimmer only for the Emperor, shall he sojourn in town. Some guest rooms carry the names of those who visited frequently. For example, the *Trierer Zimmer* refer to the archbishop of Trier, who visited Munich often. The design of the rooms, their furnishing, sculptures, stuccos and wall frescoes follow the respective fashion of the time.

The palace bombarded heaven with prayers launched from three chapels. At the Hofkapelle, the court attended mass daily. At the Reiche Kapelle, the regent received the Lord's instructions. Finally, King Ludwig I added the Allerheiligen Hofkirche to command new walls as canvases for his frescoes.

Honours and riches are both a privilege and a burden. The regent may have specified the ceremony, but he had to submit to the ritual, too. Privacy at court was unknown. Only the quaint cabinets adjoining

▲ Rubbing all four lions' noses brings luck for the rest of the day.

the bedrooms offered integrity from the ears and eyes of ever-scraping servants.

King Ludwig II's blue veins bled under the burden of attention, and the royal rituals subjugated his soul. Introvert, highly intuitive and probably homosexual, but without any love that satisfied his heart, the Bavarian Fairy-Tale-King escaped into a dream world and none was allowed to accompany him. When he visited the Cuvilliés Theater to enjoy the latest opera, he insisted on solitude - no audience, no applause, only empty seats, silence. He withdrew to Turkish Pavilions, magic grottoes and the rooftop of the Herkulessaal, where he enjoyed the tranquillity of a conservatory. When he drowned at the Starnberger See on 13 June 1886, Bavaria's coldness had embraced him.

A Poodle Haunts the Castle

When the Austrians marched into Munich, they searched in vain for the hiding place of the treasure chamber, and only the betrayal of a greedy traitor opened the coffers. Although he was richly rewarded, the treacherous was troubled by guilt and never found peace. Shortly after, the townspeople struck him to death - they hanged him at the gallows. Not even amongst the dead, he freed himself from his fault - God's angels must have pounded him into the realm of the shadow. As witnesses report, he had to swallow the gold that the Austrians paid him for his vile treachery. As a punishment, he was condemned to haunt the palace in the shape of a poodle at midnight. Be aware! He is an evil spirit: his mouth spits devilish flames, and his eyes blaze up with sweltering fire. Never stay too close to the Münchner Residenz at night. Danger to life!

38 Max-Joseph-Platz

Facts & Figures

The Max-Joseph-Platz presents classicism at its best. On the southern side, the Königsbau of the Münchner Residenz braves the harsh weather north of the Alps. King Ludwig I, the Bavarian Greek, commissioned the extension, modelled after the Palazzo Pitti in Florence. The National-
theater occupies the eastern side of the square and the Palais Törring-Jettenbach the southern edge. Townhouses line up along the Residenzstraße to the west. A statue of King Maximilian I beckons his subjects, holding a sceptre in his lap. King Ludwig I uncovered the monument on the tenth anniversary of his father's death. Maximilian aspired to become a scientist, not a politician; his humanistic heart won the Munichers over when he initiated far-reaching reforms. During his reign, the country received royal dignities from Napoleon in return for Bavaria strengthening French troops.

When **Max IV Joseph** accepted the offer to become Bavaria's Elector in 1799, he had no idea about the task ahead: the rallying cry *Equality, Freedom, Fraternity* of the French Revolution, which had fired its first shot on 14 July 1789, resonated in Bavaria too. Kurfürst Karl Theodor, his predecessor, had suppressed the Jacobites by force; Munich's nobility was nervous. Many citizens sympathised with the revolution and demanded to break with Austria.

The French Revolution crossed the Rhine on 1 March 1799, and Vienna stationed 100,000 soldiers in Bavaria, who devoured the lands. The country had two choices: to endure the annexation by the Hapsburg dynasty or to join the revolution. At last, French troops arrived at the gates of Munich on 18 June 1800, displacing the Austrians. Kurfürst Max IV Joseph fled; the townspeople opened the gates and welcomed the French with a kiss as their redeemer. No! The Bavarians never acclaimed the voracious Austrians; the tongue preferred to lisp the French way - Austria never was accepted as a friend - too severe was the competition for power.

Munich's Jacobines dreamed of an independent South German Republic based on democratic order. They sought to free the people

▲ Bavaria ascended to the rank of a kingdom under Max IV Joseph.

from tyranny and absolutism. However, the French supreme commander General Moreau had no ear for their aspirations: *"I have come to defeat an enemy, not to support a citizen's uprise."*, was his response.

The elector had fled, for sure, but Francophile Max IV Joseph negotiated well with the diplomats from Paris. While in exile, he signed a secret pact with Napoleon, engineered by his Minister Maximilian Graf von Montgelas, and he gained his freedom. The country became a kingdom, Graf von Montgelas reformed the lands, the blankets changed their name to duvet, the sidewalks to trottoir, and the Jacobite's desperate scream for democracy faded.

Location: Max-Joseph-Platz **Entrance:** Without charge **Opening Times:** Always accessible
Internet: https://www.muenchen.de/sehenswuerdigkeiten/orte/120307.html
Literature: Ernst Fischer, Hans Kratzer: Unter der Krone. 1806 bis 1918

An Explosion at the Königliche Erzgießerei

Munich was proud to have mastered the art of casting statues in bronze, and in 1826, the *Königliche Erzgießerei* (Royal Metal Foundry) was about to pass its first test. The columns for Schloss Gaibach had tempered successfully, and the iron caster Stiglmaier faced a new challenge: *the deceased King Maximilian I must be eternalised.* The workers rasped and sculptured the mould for eighteen months, and in 1852, the time had come: the metallurgists audaciously filled the design with liquid ore. The metal fumed and steamed, it hissed and swished, it bubbled and simmered, and the cast, it upheld, it upheld ... then ... a thunder! An explosion! The blazing ore skidded the plaster across the hall and injured Leo von Klenze. Three years later, Christian Daniel Rauch from Berlin assumed the process, this time successfully.

(39) Nationaltheater

Facts & Figures

The architect Karl von Fischer designed the Nationaltheater in a classicistic style. Bavaria's National Opera House, commissioned by King Maximilian I, is world-renowned for its excellent acoustics. When a fire destroyed the building in 1823, Leo von Klenze renovated the temple of music in less than two years, following the original blueprints. The Théatre de l'Odéon in Paris served the architects as an inspiration. The Greek God Apollo and nine muses watch over the artistic success of the ensemble at the portico; Ludwig von Schwanthaler sketched the Pegasus-Mosaic at the gable. The building's auditorium, gilded with blue and red, holds an audience of 2100 listeners, spread over five levels and centred around the king's box; the opera's spectacular 2500 square-metre stage allows for the production of demanding performances with elaborate stage design.

Munich's patricians had acquired a taste for musical dramas when the first opera house opened at the Salvatorplatz, but the ravages of time dilapidated the building, and it closed in 1795. The Cuvilliés Theater at the Münchner Residenz still performed the singing game, but its gates only opened to members of the nobility. During the late 18th century, the burgess longed for a new opera house, and their demand was heard. The twenty-one-year-old Karl Fischer won the tender, and after ten years of construction, the musical comedy *Die Weihe* by Ferdinand Fränzl opened the **Royal Opera House** on 12 October 1818.

Five years later, on a cold winter's night, a relentless fire destroyed the Nationaltheater, and not even the King could command the blaze with his tears. Maximilian I spurred his court architect Leo von Klenze to rebuild the temple of the muses in record time, utilising the original blueprints.

World War II did not spare the opera house; donations by the Munichers paid for the temple of art to be rebuilt. On 21 November 1963, Richard Strauss's opera *The Woman without a Shadow* reopened the stage - Munich had returned to sit with the angels.

Today, the Bavarian Government subsidises the Nationaltheater with

▲ Bavaria's Nationaltheater presents high-class opera.

roughly 100 Euros per seat and performance, allowing the producers to engage renowned musicians. Many famous artistic directors have made an impression on the theatre, including August Eberding and Sir Peter Jonas. And conductors such as Bruno Walter, Hans Knappertsbusch, and Zubin Mehta have flailed their batons at the opera house.

Munich hosted many premiers, such as Richard Wagner's *Tristan und Isolde* in 1865, *Die Meistersinger von Nürnberg* three years later, and *Die Walküre* in 1870. Richard Strauss enchanted the audience with his opera *Die Feuersnot*, and Gustav Mahler performed his 8th Symphony with bravura in the house.

Location: Max-Joseph-Platz 2 **Entrance:** Depending on performance
Guided tours: 14.00, Entrance: Adults 10 €
Opernshop: Marstallplatz 5   **Internet:** https://www.staatsoper.de

The Drunken Nationaltheater

The 21 January 1823 was a cold winter's night. The Nationaltheater performed a ballad opera by Étienne-Nicolas Mehul when the decoration caught fire, spreading to the drape; minutes later, the blaze blasted across the auditorium. The musicians bagged their instruments and ran, tumbling into the chilly night. The Munichers rushed to extinguish the flames, but the pipes were frozen, and the firefighters could watch only powerlessly. At last, the king commanded to seize the barrels at the Hofbräuhaus: *"Beer must stop the fire - it must!"* Pointless! *"God's punishment!"* whispered the puritans, *"The King had constructed the zestful place on the site of the Franciscan monastery!"* The monarch ignored the detractors, introduced a beer tax, and Leo von Klenze restored the theatre in less than two years.

Maxvorstadt, Schwabing and Lehel

Insiders Know ...

The Mandala-Church St Bonifaz
Only the church's square-shaped carcass survived World War II, so the monks moved the altar to the centre and called the mandala *New Jerusalem* - the Kingdom of Heaven on earth.

The Barberini Faun Infatuates the Ladies
The youth spreads his legs, and self-assured, he presents his genitals, the Barberini Faun. At the Glyptothek, the Greek statues take off their clothes and feel not a scrap ashamed.

Was Mary an Egyptian?
A statue of the Nile-Goddess Isis with her son Horus made the Bavarians wonder: *A pre-Christian Egyptian cult of the Virgin Mary?* The Museum of Egyptian Art knows the answer!

The Battle of all Battles, the Mother of all Combats
Visited Alexander the Great Munich? Yes, but only some 2000 years after his death when Albrecht Altdorfer immortalised him in 1529; the Alte Pinakothek exhibits his painting *The Battle of Alexander at Issus*.

The Frescoes that were to Eclipse Michelangelo
King Ludwig I was the embodiment of a patron of the arts; he aspired to outstrip Florence and Rome. The frescoes at the Ludwigskirche eclipse Michelangelo? Nevertheless, they are worth a visit.

The Day it Rained Leaflets
It was pelting down with leaflets at the auditorium of the university: Students called for resistance against the Nazi regime! It was the last campaign of the group *Die Weiße Rose*. A memorial commemorates the heroes.

Strolling nobly
The French Revolution made its mark in Munich, too. However, it were not the sharp blades of the guillotine that silenced the people but the opening of the Englischer Garten to strollers.

A Sense of Godliness at the Bayerische Nationalmuseum
Depictions of the Virgin Mary excited the burgess during the Middle Ages. The Bayerische Nationalmuseum exhibits this fervent piety by presenting Bavaria's soul carved in wood!

◄ The Maxvorstadt presents art from two millennia.

(40) Wittelsbacher Brunnen 162
(41) Künstlerhaus 164
(42) Alter Botanischer Garten . . . 166
(43) St Bonifaz 168
(44) Königsplatz & Propyläen . . . 170
(45) Glyptothek 174
(46) Antikensammlung 176
(47) Lenbachhaus 178
(48) NS-Doku'zentrum 180
(49) Karolinenplatz 182
(50) Ägyptische Kunst 184
(51) TU München 186
(52) Alte Pinakothek 188
(53) Neue Pinakothek 192
(54) Pinakothek der Moderne . . . 194
(55) Ludwigstraße 196
(56) Ludwigskirche 198
(57) LMU 200
(58) Bildende Künste 202
(59) Siegestor 204
(60) Schwabing 206
(61) Englischer Garten 208
(62) Archäologische Sammlung . 212
(63) Prinzregentenstraße 214
(64) Bayerisches Nat'museum . . . 216
(65) Haus der Kunst 218
(66) St Anna im Lehel 220
(67) Maximilianstraße 222
(68) Völkerkundemuseum 224

At LMU, the Alma Mater welcomes her students. ►

The *Maxvorstadt* north of the old town was designed during the 19th century; it saved Munich from its medieval lethargy.

The *Wittelsbacher Brunnen* commemorates the cholera epidemic of 1854. The fountain was created to celebrate the new water pipe from the Mangfalltal. At the turn of the century, the bourgeoisie shook hands with artists at the *Künstlerhaus*. King Maximilian II discovered his passion for science at the *Alter Botanischer Garten*. King Ludwig I commissioned the Church of *St Bonifaz*; the patron is buried there.

The *Glyptothek* at the *Königsplatz* houses an important collection of ancient statues. Opposite, the *Antikensammlung* exhibits the corresponding craftwork, and the *Lenbachhaus* introduces the Munich artist scene of the late 19th century.

At the *NS-Dokumentationszentrum*, the curators explain Munich's role during the Nazi regime, and the *Karolinenplatz* commemorates Napoleon's Russian campaign. Bavaria's participation was the price of becoming a kingdom.

In addition to the *Museum Ägyptischer Kunst*, Munich is home to three galleries: The *Alte Pinakothek* shows works of art until the end of the 18th century. The *Neue Pinakothek* continues the collection until the turn of the century, and the *Pinakothek der Moderne* presents contemporary art.

The north of the Maxvorstadt is docile. Students sweat over experiments at the *Technische Universität München*. Creative minds paint and model at the *Akademie der Bildenden Künste*, and the future of the country studies the books of all faculties at the *Ludwig-Maximilians-Universität*.

Like the backbone of a skeleton, the *Ludwigstraße* connects the *Siegestor* in the north with the *Feldherrnhalle* in the south. King Ludwig I designed the boulevard in a classicist style, and with the *Ludwigskirche*, he set a monument to himself.

West of the Englischer Garten stretches *Schwabing*, the students' and artists' district. The timeless temporary exhibitions at the *Haus der Kunst* on *Prinzregentenstraße* rebel - sometimes. In addition, the *Archäologische Staatssammlung* presents the beginnings of Bavaria from the Bronze Age to the Romans. The *Englischer Garten* is the green lung of Munich. It was the elector's response to the French Revolution at the end of the 18th century. The *Bayerische Nationalmuseum* presents the culture of Bavaria. Its highlights are carvings from the Alpine region. The heart of Lehel beats at the Church of *St Anna;* designers set up shop along the *Maximilianstraße*. Last but not least, the *Völkerkundemuseum Fünf Kontinente*, an ethnological museum, invites everyone to the cultures of the world.

(40) Wittelsbacher Brunnen

Facts & Figures

The city fathers commemorate the 1883 completed aqueduct from the Mangfalltal to Munich at the Wittelsbacher Brunnen. The new water system sloshed drinkable water around town, freshly tapped at the Alps. By 1895, the 25-metre-long monumental fountain spluttered with joy in recognition of the effort; the architect Adolf Hildebrand designed it. The hero to the left refers to the destructive power of water. He rides a horse with the fin of a dragon and dashes a boulder. A personification of femininity to the right gracefully symbolises her fertility; she rides a bull and waggles a captivating carapace. Exuberant crustaceans and seashells embellish the rim of the basin, lovingly chiselled into the marble. At the centre, an effervescing water cloche climaxes into the pool. During the summer, blinding photons romantically flood the fountain at night.

In 1854, a **cholera epidemic** splashed around the ditches of the town; more than 3000 Munichers surrendered their lives to the gluttonous bacteria. Only the prayers chanted at the Mariensäule obviated greater calamity, thus the opinion of the 19th century.

When the burgess had weathered the epidemic, the magistrate decreed: *"We must show our gratitude to the Blessed Mother for her support. The Schrannenplatz shall be called Marienplatz from now on."* Covertly to not upset Catholicism, the city fathers appointed a commission led by the 36-year-old scientist Max von Pettenkofer; his team was to study the course of the epidemic.

And the researcher discovered: the epidemic had spread along Haidhausen's sewages. Max von Pettenkofer concluded - the world learnt about bacteria only after Robert Koch's discovery some twenty years later - that cholera claws its evil to the raunchy puddles of town.

After having chanted many Ave Marias, the city council decided prayers alone would not suffice; the learned men replaced the worn-out pipes; rangers cleared the forests for an aqueduct across southern Bavaria, and since 1884, a conduit has carried water from Alpine sources to Munich.

The professor for sanitation effectuated with the mountain water that

▲ The Wittelsbacher Brunnen honours the aqueduct from the Alps to Munich.

Munich evolved into one of the most pristine cities within thirty years.

To honour the scientific success, the city fathers built a lasting monument to the aqueduct. The inscription reads *Wittelsbacher Brunnen, 1895. In remembrance of the completion of the civic water supply from the Mangfalltal.*

Since immemorial times, as described by Greek Mythology, water is the domain of the god Poseidon and his cousins. Water may destroy, like the stumblebum slinging rocks at the fountain. Water may fructify when the dirndl has a good wallow in the mud. Merely, who of the two is righteous, and who is the evil one?

Location: Lenbachplatz **Entrance**: Without charge **Opening Times**: Always accessible
Drinking Water: https://www.swm.de/wasser/trinkwassergewinnung
Waste Water: https://www.wwa-m.bayern.de/abwasser/index.htm

The Wilhelminische Veste

Herzog Wilhelm V lived at the Wilhelminische Veste during the 16th century, opposite today's Wittelsbacher Brunnen: he wanted intimacy with the Jesuits, seeking their protection. There, Kurfürst Maximilian I rested his head on the bosom of his wife, too, Maria Anna von Österreich, to steady himself during the Thirty Years' War. After the Electress had passed away, a ghost spooked at the building. It was the femininity of the times that could not find peace; the deceased First Lady liked to make appearances during frosty winter nights - so the guards at the gates told. Once, a guard fainted, overwhelmed by her white gown and about to freeze to death. His comrades discovered him just in time before he perished. As he awoke, he recounted the ghost, and thus the legend must be truthfully true.

Künstlerhaus

Facts & Figures

The architect Gabriel von Seidl erected the Künstlerhaus at the southern end of the Lenbachplatz from 1887 to 1900, a masterpiece of historicism. There, Munich's painters rubbed shoulders with Bavaria's bourgeoisie, the new patrons of the arts at the turn of the century. The house staged many masked balls on its premises, in saloons designed in the style of the Italian Renaissance, like the Venetian hall, which the artist Julius Mössel had decorated with scenes from the Commedia dell Àrte. Even Franz von Lenbach had left his mark. World War II turned the Künstlerhaus into rubble, but Munich resurrected the building in 1961. Today, the event space organises concerts, book readings, theatre and cabaret performances. The not-for-profit organisation subsidises its running expenses by letting its halls to enterprises for conventions and congresses.

Adolf Hitler inspected the **Künstlerhaus** in search of a private mansion in 1938. He strode through the premises and discovered with dismay that one of the windows glanced at Munich's main synagogue - Germany's third-largest. He squealed with indignation: *"The Synagogue must be demolished."*

Karl Fiehler, once an assiduous abetter, now Munich's Lord Mayor, routed like a well-functioning machine the eviction order to the Jewish community on 9 June 1938. *"We grant the congregation twenty-four hours to evacuate."* Six days later, he blasted the walls and levelled the underpinnings to a parking spot.

Karl Fiehler had made a living by distributing ration cards when he met the Führer. It were those lower civil servants who enabled the regime. Now in power, he zealously executed every instruction barked by his esteemed leader.

After the pillage of the synagogue, the organisation *German Art & Painting* moved into the Künstlerhaus, and Adolf Hitler stretched out his legs at the Prinzregentenstraße, reflecting: *the Munichers had remained silent. None protested. Perhaps* - thus he observed - *Perhaps ... the time had come to crank up the Final Solution to the Jewish Question.*

▲ The Künstlerhaus introduced patrons to impoverished artists.

Five months later, on 9 November 1938, the long-awaited call rang out from the Alte Rathaus: *"All Jewish facilities are to be destroyed and their owners arrested."* And the people of Munich rampaged; they burnt down the synagogue at the Herzog-Rudolf-Straße and plundered the department store Uhlfelder at the Rindermarkt.

After the war, the American occupation force classified the servile Karl Fiehler as an activist; they sentenced him to two years in a labour camp, and Germany's jurisdiction happily dismissed his legal proceedings, which cheekily wanted to claim a retirement pension from his time as mayor during the Third Reich.

Location: Lenbachplatz 8 **Entrance:** Without charge
Opening Times: Dependent on Performance
Internet: https://www.kuenstlerhaus-muc.de

The Fat Man from the Lenbachplatz

The 19th century bred ghosts. When the burgess tottered home from the taverns at night, a stranger followed, broad and tall in appearance, enqueued amongst the carousing. Many night revellers saw him and essayed to cast the shadow off, but always in vain: *the creature was stuck to their toes*. Anguish infused the night, the darker the clouds, the more terrifying the shade. Many a brave man ran for shelter to the sentry on Lenbachplatz where the drunkards holed up into the small hours until the crack of dawn. With time, the ghost became so well known that the townspeople baptised him *"Fat Man"*. He resembled the shadow of the epoch - the alter ego of the bourgeoisie, the dark side of the Biedermeier. The political lethargy retaliated when National Socialism led the world into a devastating war in the 20th century.

Alter Botanischer Garten

Facts & Figures

The spirit of science finally conquered Munich during the 19th century when King Maximilian I inaugurated the downtown botanical garden in 1812. One hundred years later, the scholars relocated the plants to an extended field near Schloss Nymphenburg. Only the east portal, constructed by Emanuel Joseph von Herigoyen, survived the gnawing of time. In 1937, Josef Wackerle added a Neptune Fountain, which Friedrich Ludwig von Sckell had designed. The Kunstpavillon welcomes local artists to present their creativity at the garden's northern border. Towards the west, the Park Café serves traditional Bavarian delicacies, much loved by students during the summer term. Opposite, at the Elisenstraße, the Court of Justice sits; next to it, in a red brick building, the Münchner Oberlandesgericht sentences victims; it is Munich's Higher Regional Court.

King Maximilian I, enthusiastic about nature, dispatched the young botanist Carl Friedrich Phillip Martius and the zoologist Johann Baptist Spix on a research expedition to Brazil in 1817. They returned three years later, richly laden with the treasures of the New World, dragging flora and fauna to Munich. The seeds in their bulky suitcases served as the bedrock for Munich's **Botanical Garden**.

To their surprise, the scholars of nature observed that Munich's climate was compatible with the exotics as long as the botanicals could hide in a greenhouse during winter. Shortly after, the landscape architect Friedrich Ludwig von Sckell constructed a 150-metre-long conservatory in the style of an orangery, comparable to the Iron House at Schloss Nymphenburg.

The vibrant green multiplied exuberantly at Munich's Botanical Garden. Had the horticulturists registered a mere 3500 plants in 1819, the population had grown to 7000 by 1830, and in 1851, the number hit the ten-thousand mark.

Then, the unexpected stabbed Munich's enthusiasm in the back! While Munich's botanists counted plants, entrepreneurs in England had opened the first World Expo, filled to the rim with industrial genius. And the

▲ The architect Josef Wackerle constructed the Neptunbrunnen in 1937.

Bavarians discovered that their pastoral lands were not competitive.

By that time, the race for markets, products and brands had reached an international dimension, and in rural Bavaria, the unemployed mounted. The sovereigns could not defend the country against the manufacturing industry of the north by trading in primary products, like the salt from the Alps.

King Maximilian II realised: *"The Bavarians have to embrace the industrial age!"* In the year of the cholera epidemic, the King organised Germany's first industrial exhibition. Its success was moderate, and Bavaria continued to consign its future to hop and barley for another 100 years.

Location: Sophienstraße 7 **Entrance:** Without charge **Opening Times:** Always accessible
Kunstpavillon: http://www.kunstpavillon.org
Park Café: https://www.parkcafe089.de

Munich's Glass Palace

Until the end of World War II, Bavaria was an agricultural country. After the completion of the Berlin Wall, however, Prussian industrial enterprises relocated to the Alps and thus leveraged Germany's South to success. Only then did the economy experience an upsurge. While England industrialised during the 19th century, Bavaria's unemployed suffered. King Maximilian II had to take action should he want to embrace the new times, and he decided to proceed the London way. Finally, August Voit constructed a 234-metre-long glass palace at the Botanical Garden to stage an industrial fair. The exhibition opened on 17 July 1854, but the Munichers hardly applauded, and the country muddled along as a land of pigs and chickens. Just like the Crystal Palace in London, Munich's glass palace burnt down as well - in the year 1931.

St Bonifaz

Facts & Figures

King Ludwig I laid the founding stone of the Benedictine Monastery St Bonifaz on the day of his silver wedding in 1835. World War II destroyed the basilica a century later, and modern times reconstructed the church, but only in parts. Georg Friedrich Ziebland had completed the former five-aisled neo-Romanesque church in 1850, modelled after the early Christian basilicas Sant' Apollinare in Ravenna and St Paul in Rome. The Allied air raids only spared a 32-metre-wide torso, however, about one-third of the original building. In 1995, the artists Peter Burkart, Friedrich Koller and Christine Stadler redesigned the interior. The squared-shaped ground plan invited the order to centre the main altar and curve the benches into a mandala. A holy tent fitted with a chain of lights wafts above, referencing the New Jerusalem. King Ludwig I, Bavaria's most prolific patron of the arts, rests buried in the church.

From 1802 onwards, at King Maximilian I's behest, Maximilian Graf von Montgelas enforced the expropriation of Church property, an economic and political necessity even in pious Bavaria.

Parishes and monasteries had reclaimed the lands during the Middle Ages, and the padres multiplied their fortunes by skilful diplomacy, granting indulgences and as the beneficiary of inheritances. According to historians, the holy cross owned about one-quarter of Munich's buildings in the late 18th century. Once enlightenment had infiltrated society, the sovereign transferred ecclesiastical property to the state. As an example, the Viktualienmarkt took over the Heilig-Geist-Spital.

King Ludwig I exercised a kinder attitude towards the Church as he required the cleric's walls as canvases for his frescoes, to teach his subordinates a sense of culture, while aspiring to unify the Church, arts and sciences. Driven by humanism, he attempted to heal the damage caused by the dissolution of the monasteries. Already in 1810, the crown prince demanded the resignation of Graf von Montgelas; in 1817, he enforced his downfall.

After Ludwig had ascended to the throne in 1825, the new sovereign

▲ The architect Georg Friedrich Ziebland designed the basilica St Bonifaz.

wisely returned some church property to the sulking clerics. Under his rule, the architect Friedrich Ziebland designed the Benedictine Monastery **St Bonifaz**.

In 1819, Ludwig, still a prince, commissioned the architect Leo von Klenze to construct a basilica in the style of Italy opposite of the Glyptothek at the Königsplatz, but the Munichers resisted: *"We faithful must not face the heathenish Gods of Antiquity waving from the pediments of their modern Greek temples when we leave our pious Christian church having attended service".* The future King avoided the conflict with his pontifical burgess and constructed the monastery at the Karlstraße decades later.

Location: Karlstraße 34 **Entrance:** Without charge **Opening Times:** 9.00 - 18.00
https://www.sankt-bonifaz.de   **Deutsches Theater:** https://www.deutsches-theater.de
Homeless Support: https://www.sankt-bonifaz.de/obdachlosenhilfe/dienste

The Deutsche Theater

A neo-baroque stage opened in 1896 at Schwanthalerstraße 13 between the Hauptbahnhof (main train station) and Sendlinger Tor; it was dedicated to dance, musicals and operetta. With 1,500 visitors, it is one of the largest venues in Munich. When it opened, the Palace of Music specialised in vaudeville, revue and comedy. Karl Valentin and Josephine Baker performed in the theatre during the 1920s. The damage from World War II was repaired by 1961; at re-opening, the house won the hearts of the Munichers with the West Side Story. After an extensive renovation in 2014, the theatre dedicates itself to musicals: Chicago, Jesus Christ Superstar, Mandela, Dance of the Vampires, Rocky Horror Picture Show - to name just a few. The auditorium in red gives the stage a fiery, passionate feel that is irresistible.

Königsplatz & Propyläen

Facts & Figures

The rich heritage of Greek antiquity inspired the Königsplatz. King Ludwig I had commissioned the architect Leo von Klenze to construct the Propyläen in Doric style, modelled after the Athenian Acropolis; the masons completed the marvel in 1862. Its reliefs show events from recent Greek history: their struggle for freedom against the Turks and the reign of the Wittelsbacher King Otto I, who ruled over the islands from 1832 onwards. Later, the Nazi regime staged their propaganda at the Königsplatz. Torchlight processions swore in the soldiers, the men promising to shed their blood for the Führer; the place of humanistic education echoed the ideology of felony during those cruel years. Books were burnt at the Königsplatz on 10 May 1933 - the intellectual cleansing was a smack in the face of ancient philosophers who once assisted the birth of democracy.

When Kurfürst Max III Joseph died without an heir in 1777, the imperial orb rolled to Karl Theodor, a Wittelsbacher of the Palatinate line. He paid for the honours with tears, however, not only because he had to relocate his retinue from Mannheim to Munich.

It was the times of storm and stress when Karl Theodor climbed the stairs to the chambers in Munich: In the spirit of the German enlightenment, Johann Wolfgang von Goethe had released *The Sorrows of Young Werther* in 1774; Gotthold Ephraim Lessing had published the stage play *Nathan the Wise*. When Karl Theodor marched his household into the Münchner Residenz, he encountered a *"race of beer-bellies"* - in the words of King Maximilian I described the Bavarians later. Dismayed, the ruler essayed to trade the Alps with the Netherlands, but his attempts foundered, shipwrecked by the Prussian King Friedrich II - and Karl Theodor's relationship with his subjects broke - for good. Three years later, the Elector wanted to return his residency to Mannheim, but his fantasy miscarried. The sovereign had lost contact with his underlings; to rule by authority remained the only option.

The absolutist announced on 2 June 1795 - at the dawn of the French

The Propyläen at the Königsplatz are modelled after the Acropolis in Athens.

Revolution - that the medieval walls beard no military meaning: *"We must demolish the fortifications. They suffocate the city."* And the burgess? They did not relish the idea.

Meanwhile, Goethe had returned from his Italian journey and founded a new literary movement in concert with Wieland, Herder & Schiller - the Weimar Classicism.

In contrast, the beer bellies at the Isar sulked. The grouches opened their feeble minds to the Elector only when they had learned to seek pleasure in a stroll at the Englischer Garten.

The rapprochement owes its success to Sir Benjamin Thompson, known in Munich as Graf von Rumford.

Location: Königsplatz **Entrance:** Without charge **Opening Times:** Always accessible
Wlan-Hotspots: https://www.muenchen.de/leben/wlan-hotspot.html
Summer in the City: https://www.muenchen.de/freizeit/sommer-in-der-stadt.html

Otto I, the Bavarian King of the Greeks

Greece surrendered to the Ottoman Empire from the 14th to the 19th century. At last, the Greeks defeated the Turkish fleet during the Battle of Navarino in 1827 and thus freed the country from Turkish occupation. The Munichers commemorated the event with bronze plates embellishing the Obelisk at the Karolinenplatz, cast from melted-down canons of the sunken Turkish battleships. The restructuring of the Mediterranean, however, proceeded at a snail's pace until the Greeks filled the power vacuum with a member of the European aristocracy. The people chose the Bavarian Otto I, the second son of King Ludwig I, as their new sovereign. Aged only 17, the young man became the ruler of Greece in 1832; with him, the political and cultural axis of Athens-Munich consolidated.

Kurfürst Karl Theodor demonstrated skill in choosing his adjutant. The North American from Massachusetts was a pragmatic man who strove to improve the lives of the simple people through social reforms, charitable institutions, and inventiveness.

Kurfürst Karl Theodor passed away without an heir, and the Mannheimer Max Joseph IV followed in his footsteps. The canny diplomacy of his minister Maximilian Graf von Montgelas succeeded in forging a secret pact with France to push back Austria's political influence. Finally, tears of joy and laughter bubbled along the riverbanks. On 1 January 1806, Bavaria's fairy tale dream became a reality. By the grace of Napoleon, the lands rose to become a *Kingdom* - Hallelujah.

The spell over the onerous medieval enclosing was broken; Munich was eager to expand towards the fields in the north. The city screamed for air, avenues the French way, for piazzas flooded by sunlight; lush gardens and parks were to sweeten life.

The city planners assiduously drew the many lines following the principle of rational urban planning. The King desired a chessboard pattern, and the Maxvorstadt emerged in 1805. The neighbourhood stretches from the University at the Ludwigstraße to the Odeonsplatz and loops back along the **Königsplatz**. Westwards, the district encloses many museums, amongst them Munich's Pinakotheken; southwards, St Bonifaz launches prayers to heaven. An avenue once interlinked Munich's old town with Schloss Nymphenburg in the outskirts. Along the boulevard, the King arranged for open piazzas, like the Karolinenplatz. At the time of construction, the promenade left the city at the Königsplatz, and from there, the road meandered across Munich's open fields, terminating at the Wittelsbacher summer residence, Bavaria's Versailles.

As a prince royal, the later King Ludwig I assumed the aegis over the design of the Maxvorstadt in 1815. His architect Leo von Klenze reworked the first draft by Karl von Fischer and Friedrich Ludwig von Sckell. The liaison between Ludwig I and his lifelong architect Leo von Klenze was so successful that marketing departments call Munich the *Athens at the Isar*.

The alpine masters mapped the Königsplatz in the fashion of the Mediterranean, and they encircled the square-shaped open space with the three styles of antiquity: the Glyptothek to the north, constructed in 1830, surrenders to the Ionic style. The Antikensammlung to the south, finished in 1848, borrows from the Corinthian style, and the Propyläen, completed in 1862, follows the example of the Dorian Acropolis in Athens.

▲ The humanist King Ludwig I inaugurated the Propyläen in 1862.

Conjoined with the Alte and the Neue Pinakothek, the Königsplatz embodies the Museumsquarter. Along the Ludwigstraße, the University spreads its wings at the Maxvorstadt, too.

However, the new Hellenes in town were too much foreign blood for the taste of the burgess, and in 1848, the Bavarians reasoned the King to resign, using his love affair with the Irish dancer Lola Montez as an excuse to act, pretending moral high-ground.

Although deprived of the throne, Ludwig I still completed the Propyläen by digging into his private purse. Last but not least, the spurned celebrated Munich's liberation from its medieval lethargy by embellishing the Propyläen with scenes from the Greeks' struggle for freedom, in the hope, that his former subjects would understand one day.

The Temple of (Little) Honour at the Königsplatz

After the Nazis had seized power, the NS leadership became interested in the Königsplatz: *"The square is perfect for parades."* They erected two temples of (little) honour at its eastern edge, next to the Braune Haus (today NS-Dokumentationszentrum), to render homage to their sixteen companions who had lost their lives during the failed Hitler Putsch. A guard of honour saluted passersby around the clock. Next door, the Nazi regime constructed the Führerbau (the Führer's building, today Munich's Conservatory of Music); southwards mushroomed the NSDAP's administrative offices. In 1935, the Nazis covered the square with 20,000 granite plates to echo the rhythm of the goose-stepping. The US-American occupation force blew the temples of (little) honour up in 1947; only their foundations survived.

㊺ Glyptothek

Facts & Figures

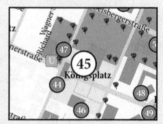

The Glyptothek, constructed by Leo von Klenze in 1830, presents antique sculptures, busts and reliefs. The museum houses Munich's oldest public art collection. From a young age, Ludwig I collected Greek and Roman statues. *"Olden clutter"*, according to his father. Upon this *"jumble"*, the gallery bases its outstanding exhibition. The figures from the *Aphaea temple* on the Greek island Aegina, the *Munich Kouros*, a depiction of the *Goddess Eirene*, the *Apollo of Tenea,* and a figurine called *The Old Drunkard* delight among the many precious objects. The chronologically ordered exhibition stretches from Archaic Greece (around BC 650) to the late Roman times (AD 550). Special exhibitions and guided tours consolidate our understanding of Mediterranean life and cultures. Theatre companies enact plays of ancient writers in the inner courtyard during summer.

In 1804/05, the crown prince Ludwig I encountered an elixir of life during a journey to Italy when he gazed at the rosy cheeks of Hebes. The sculpture of the Goddess of Youth, created by the artist Antonio Cenova at the end of the 18th century, ignited the King's sense of sensuality: the heart of Ludwig I flared up and rightly so.

Art kindled the passion of the eighteen-year-old humanist and baptised his soul to a life-long marriage with Hellenism. His agents acquired statues, sculptural groups, archaeological finds, porcelains and vases from Greece and Italy. The collection grew faster than Munich's masons provided exhibition space. At last, the King cooped up his marble friends at the **Glyptothek**. The architect Leo von Klenze constructed the building in the Ionic style from 1816 to 1830.

King Ludwig I believed that art would turn his people into philosophers. He obviated to corral his treasures and exhibited them in museums. The Glyptothek was the first gallery he opened to the public. His father, King Maximilian I, got to the heart of it when he described his son's collecting mania as an attempt to convert the Bavarians to Greeks and Romans, but *"This venture rests on bleak prospects."*, so his counsel.

▲ The Glyptothek presents Munich's vast collection of ancient art.

King Ludwig I clogged his ears, remained undisturbed and continued to collect - an entire life. Even when the Munichers forced him to abdicate in 1848, he could not relinquish of his compulsive passion for the countries around the Mediterranean.

The restless amorist died in 1868 at the age of 81 while overwintering in the South of France, at a mansion in Nice. Munich's Glyptothek exhibits his legacy. At the Basilica St Bonifaz, the Bavarian Greek rests in peace, and his heart, preserved and separated, is kept at the Gnadenkapelle von Altötting (chapel of grace). It is due to him, and him alone, that Munich may glance at the Greeks eye-to-eye.

Location: Königsplatz 3 **Entrance:** Adults 6 € **Opening Times:** Tues - Sun 10.00 - 17.00
Internet: https://www.antike-am-koenigsplatz.mwn.de
Theaterspiele Glyptothek: https://www.theaterspieleglyptothek.de

Wall Frescoes Lost & Found

Frescoes by the painter Peter Cornelius embellished the premises of the Glyptothek at their opening, depicting scenes from Greek mythology. To the Munichers, the world of mythology remained a riddle guarded by seven seals; however, rainwater was for no reason allowed to corrode the finery after World War II; moisture severely damaged the Glyptothek. At the time of reconstruction in 1972, mould had swallowed the paint. Today, the curators present the ancient sculptures against a milky-naked brick wall as background. One may argue that the heroes of bygone times stand out more brightly now. Perhaps the frescoed walls would have distracted from the ancient works, and maybe that's why the Munichers had to leave the pigments out in the rain - yet, one wonders about priorities.

Antikensammlung

Facts & Figures

Opposite to the Glyptothek, the Antikensammlung presents art from Greek and Roman antiquity. The collector's mania of King Ludwig I provided the foundation for this museum, too. A rift between the King and his leading architect Leo von Klenze provided Georg Friedrich Ziebland with the opportunity to construct the building in 1848. An image of Lady Bavaria adorns the Corinthian tympanum. The patroness of the arts and female personification of the country is the twin sister of Athene, who is watching as the Goddess of Wisdom over the Glyptothek. The collection stretches from the Mycenaean (around 1300 BC) to the Hellenistic Era and terminates with the ascent of the Etruscans & Romans. The compilation of Greek vases enjoys a worldwide reputation. Guided tours deepen our understanding of antiquity, upon which the Western hemisphere rests its culture and democracy.

Due to their tridimensionality, the statues exhibited at the Glyptothek are a direct bodily experience. The **Antikensammlung**, on the other hand, opens a rich treasure box of Greek mythology, the Gods of Antiquity and Greco-Roman culture. The terracottas, supplemented by glasswork and jewellery, allow the experience of the Mediterranean way eye-to-eye. A diorama of Delphi's sanctuary encourages the imagination to wander across the Greek world. The collection climaxes in the belly amphora by Andokides, depicting the hero Hercules resting on a klinē, flanked by the Goddess Athene and the God Hermes - splendid!

The terracotta of an upright woman attracts attention with its vibrant colouring. As reflection-spectral analysis demonstrates, the ancient world vividly ornamented its buildings, sculptures, and statues. Vermilion was the most popular paint, resulting in a red tone; it often provided the background colour. The artists mixed ochre from limonite clay; they derived ultramarine from the mineral azurite; the colour yellow, they manufactured from a blend of limestone and crystalline quartz.

The reconstruction of the paint may not correspond to in detail. Nevertheless, a learned group from Bochum arrived at an impressive

▲ The architect Georg Friedrich Ziebland completed the Antikensammlung in 1848.

approximation of the original scheme by scientific methods. Many museums rely on their investigations to exhibit coloured replicas beside the original artworks, demonstrating the antique's mastery of paint.

The curators arranged the exhibits according to topics of everyday life and the Gods of Olympus; pictorial representations of the Trojan War supplement the pieces. The museum covers themes like leisure in antiquity and sports to reassure our contemporary society that *Mens Sana in Corpore Sano* - a healthy mind only dwells in a healthy body - is a pearl of universal wisdom acknowledged today and 2000 years ago.

Location: Königsplatz 1 **Entrance:** Adults 6 € **Opening Times:** Tues - Sun 10.00 - 17.00
Internet: https://www.antike-am-koenigsplatz.mwn.de
Literature: Peter Köpf: Der Königsplatz in München

The Munich Agreement

In 1938, the world intended to avoid a war. On 30 September 1938, the Prime Ministers of Great Britain, France and Italy arrived at the Führerbau in Munich, close to the Königsplatz, to discuss a peaceful solution to the Sudeten crisis. On this day, the world bowed to Adolf Hitler and allowed the Third Reich to annex the Sudetenland. Czechoslovakia had turned into a pawn that was to be sacrificed by international politics. On 1 October, the Nazi regime occupied the country, but Adolf Hitler was disappointed: *No War!* One year later, the Führer avoided his mistakes, and diplomacy failed to resolve the tensions over Poland. On 1 September 1939, the Wehrmacht crossed the border, and World War II began amid great jubilation of the people. Great jubilation? Everybody was terrified!

Lenbachhaus

Facts & Figures

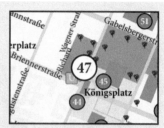

Gabriel von Seidl constructed the gilded mansion at the Königsplatz in 1891. The ostentatious country house took inspiration from the Italian Renaissance. Here lived and worked the portrait painter Franz von Lenbach. After the artist had died in 1904, the city council acquired the bourgeois castle and transformed it into a museum. Sir Norman Foster, a British star architect, designed the extension in 2013. The exhibition stretches in the master's restored private quarters from the late 19th to the early 20th century. Besides the paintings by Franz von Lenbach, the museum shows the work of the group *Der Blaue Reiter* (Blue Rider), including Paul Klee, Franz Marc, August Macke and Wassily Kandinsky. The 19th century presents Karl Spitzweg, Wilhelm Leibl and Lovis Corinth. The artists Joseph Beuys, Anselm Kiefer and Andy Warhol represent the 20th century.

Art historians argue whether **Franz von Lenbach** was an outstanding painter or a sound craftsman who splendidly mastered the brush. Without any doubt, his portraits of politicians, scientists, and the aristocracy achieved their desired impact: the canvases radiate power and greatness; his depictions are sublime; none will overlook them.

Franz von Lenbach was born in Schrobenhausen in 1836, the son of a master bricklayer. Like no other, he knew how to set the scene for the powerful of his time. In return, the 4000 portraits he painted filled his coffers with ducats - what an achievement!

Those he depicted craved more; Otto von Bismarck commissioned more than eighty portraits. When Franz von Lenbach arrived at his style, he refused to experiment: *never nothing new* was his slogan. The times were not fast-moving; they still galloped on horses, and the pressure to reinvent composition techniques was bearable. What is more, von Lenbach's clients knew what to expect. As long as tastes remained glued to the past, the impact on the audience was predictable, and Lenbach's patrons ensured that the fashion stuck unchanged - a win-win situation for painter and models!

▲ The Lenbachhaus exhibits the world's largest collection of the Blue Rider.

In contrast, *Der Blaue Reiter* (Blue Rider) attempted to reconcile the inner world with the outer; subjective experience must not surrender to collective norms.

The colour blue wielded the group into one voice. In 1903, Wassily Kandinsky wrote: *"The more intense the blue ... the deeper is the longing for purity, the higher the transcendental experience."* During World War I, the Blue Rider perished in the trenches.

Franz von Lenbach was at odds with any innovation. He died in 1904, ten years before the outbreak of World War I. The deceased would probably be horrified if he knew that his manor exhibits more than 200 paintings by the group Der Blaue Reiter.

Location: Luisenstraße 33 **Opening Times**: Tues - Sun 10.00 - 18.00
Internet: https://www.lenbachhaus.de **Entrance:** Adults 10 €, Concession 5 €
Bayerische Staatssammlung für Paläontologie: https://bspg.palmuc.org

The Archaeopteryx Bavaria

One hundred fifty million years ago, the Archaeopteryx Bavarica evolved a skin with feathers, not intended for flying but as thermal insulation. The Bayerische Staatssammlung für Paläontologie presents the fossilisation of the primaeval bird to the public, within hailing distance to the Lenbachhaus and the Königsplatz. The museum also exhibits the dinosaurs of Bavaria, the skeleton of an elephant excavated in Mühldorf, a sabre-toothed tiger, a mammoth and a giant deer. The scientists discovered most of the finds around Solnhofen. The Late Jurassic had formed lagoons along today's Donau (Danube), wetted by the sea, leading to a high level of salinity, where the deceased animals not decomposed but petrified; the incredible wildlife turned to stone and survived the beating of the time.

NS-Dokumentationszentrum

Facts & Figures
Munich opened the informative NS-Dokumentationszentrum (Nazi Documentation Centre) in 2015 on the site of the former Braune Haus (Brown House). On three levels, it describes the violence and crimes of the Nazi regime; the focus of the exhibition is on the rise of fascism after World War I. The curators use documents, images, and eyewitness reports to illustrate the instability during the Weimar period. The shocking permanent exhibition discusses the origins and rise of National Socialism in Munich as well as its role in society. It gives an overview of Bavaria during the war in an attempt to come to terms with the past. Temporary exhibitions deepen individual topics. Biographies of Munichers make the upheavals tangible. One must recognise that the past is still alive; the psychic energy cannot be denied - history must not repeat itself.

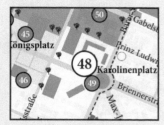

Munich was the birthplace of the National Socialist German Workers' Party (NSDAP). General Eisenhower called Munich the "*cradle of the Nazi beast*" after he had captured the city. Munich is linked to the rise of the Nazi regime like no other city; the Nazi Documentation Centre is located on the site of the Brown House, which once housed the headquarters of the NSDAP. Here, the movement perfected its ideology and turned it into a totalitarian regime. Munich was the hub of fascism until the Machtergreifung (seizure of power) in 1933. Only then did the political focus shift to Berlin.

On February 24, 1920, two years after World War I, Adolf Hitler founded the NSDAP in the Hofbräuhaus. Already at that time, his party program called for a German Empire, the repeal of the Treaty of Versailles and rejected German citizenship for Jews.

The Nazi regime attempted to seize power through a coup staged in the Bürgerbräukeller on November 8, 1923; they intended to install a dictatorship. However, the Bavarian state police thwarted the march onto the Feldherrnhalle and imprisoned Adolf Hitler in a correctional facility in Landsberg am Lech, where he wrote his book *Mein Kampf*.

▲ The NS-Dokumentationszentrum explains the rise of the Nazi regime in Munich..

After the Machtergreifung (seizure of power), the leadership initiated the Kristallnacht from Munich's Alte Rathaus (Old Town Hall) during an evening of comradeship on November 9, 1938; the world had taken the first step into the Holocaust.

A year later, Georg Elser detonated an explosive device in Munich's Bürgerbräukeller. The Führer was lucky - he escaped the assassination attempt; unexpectedly, he had left the building early.

During World War II, the Allied forces carried out 74 air raids on Munich; the bombs destroyed most of the old town - the city was bleeding. Much of it, the Munichers rebuilt after the war.

Location: Max-Mannheimer-Platz 1 **Entrance**: Without charge
Opening Times: Tues - Sun 10.00 - 19.00
Internet: https://www.ns-dokuzentrum-muenchen.de

Mayor Karl Fiehler

Karl Fiehler was a mid-level municipal administrative officer and a loyal supporter of the NSDAP. When Adolf Hitler seized power in 1933, he became mayor of Munich. He was an anti-democrat, an anti-Semite and an ardent admirer of the Führer. His obedience was anticipatory. In 1923, as part of Hitler's Stoßtruppe (the nucleus of the SS), he actively supported the Hitler Putsch staged in the Bürgerbräukeller. He entered the city council in 1924 and was a founding member of the party when it regrouped in 1925. His speeches were inflammatory; he was the backbone of the movement. When under pressure from the NSDAP, Mayor Karl Scharnagl had to resign from office on March 9, 1933, Karl Fiehler was appointed to Mayor of Munich by Interior Minister Adolf Wagner.

Karolinenplatz

Facts & Figures

The architect Karl von Fischer took the first step in constructing the Maxvorstadt at the star-shaped Karolinenplatz in 1809. He modelled the square after the Place d´Étoile in Paris. Only here, the widely spaced housing survived how the urban planners had designed the district at the drawing board. A stupendous obelisk rises at the centre of the roundabout. The phallus is 29 metres tall, resting on a marble plate that commemorates the 30,000 Bavarian soldiers who lost their lives during Napoleon's Russian campaign - a death toll Bavaria had to pay for receiving a crown. The masons cast the bronze plates from the cannons of those Turkish ships, which had sunk during the Battle of Navarino in 1827. World War II cut deep wounds into the Maxvorstadt; only a few buildings survived. The adjacent NS-Dokumentationszentrum remembers the damage with documents and eyewitness reports.

On 26 May 1930, the English industrialist Willy Barlow marketed his manor at the Brienner Straße 45. The purchaser was a minor political party founded at the Hofbräuhaus, still insignificant but rapidly growing: the National Socialist Workers' Party. Entrepreneurs had financed the acquisition of the *Palais Barlow*, now called Braune Haus.

At the NSDAP headquarters overlooking the **Karolinenplatz**, the Führer kept the blood standard. The revolutionaries had carried the banner during the failed Hitler Putsch in 1923. Under the Nazi regime, the Maxvorstadt changed its style dramatically: not philosophers toddled across the plazas as during the reign of King Ludwig I, but brown shirts goose-stepped through the streets. No new Athens glowed at the Isar no more, but the *Capital of the Movement* darted the flames of right-wing nationalism. And the berserks of the God Wotan opened the ground for the fires of hell, their torches igniting the world.

The Nazi regime partly purchased and partly expropriated a further fifty buildings in the Maxvorstadt. Adolf Hitler's Führerbau occupied the location next to the Braune Haus. Close by, the party meticulously administered its membership list in an administration building. The Nazi

▲ The obelisk commemorates the Bavarian soldiers, who lost their lives under Napoleon.

regime added two *Ehrentempel* at the eastern edge of the Königsplatz, rendering homage to those sixteen fascists whom the Bavarian police had shot during the Hitler Putsch.

The Allied air raids strategically targeted the Maxvorstadt because of its many NS buildings; Allied aircraft flew, raid after raid, across the neighbourhood and demolished 80% of the buildings.

The 7th United States Army marched into Munich on 30 April 1945 and first occupied the Maxvorstadt; the people surrendered without a fight - they were exhausted. The dust of the destruction had suffocated their will to put up resistance.

Location: Karolinenplatz **Entrance:** Without charge **Opening Timnes:** Always accessible
Amerikahaus (Karolinenplatz 3): https://www.amerikahaus.de
Börse München (Karolinenplatz 6): https://www.boerse-muenchen.de

The German San Francisco

During the 1970s, Munich turned into a party city. The metropolis at the Isar was once called the *German San Francisco*. At the Karolinenplatz, the *Eve Bar* and the bar *Pretty Woman* seduced wealthy gentlemen with table dancing. The dancers came from Romania and Bulgaria; on the blue sofa in the back room, they were to spy on drunken guests; the owners still faced court proceedings in 2018. The Y*ellow Submarine* in Schwabylon rose over three floors. Thirty sharks were swimming in a vast aquarium. In the *Crash* on Lindwurmstraße, the "election of the ugliest Municher" took place. The "topless sauerkraut meal" was also very trendy. The *Piper Club* on Kurfürstenplatz was Munich's meeting place for stoners, and the *Tiffany* at Leopoldstraße 69 was the bar the Rolling Stones frequented.

Museum Ägyptischer Kunst

Facts & Figures

Munich inaugurated its Museum for Egyptian Art in 2009; the collection of King Ludwig I forms its foundation. The chronologically ordered showrooms present the mystery of the Nile from the Neolithic to the rise of Christianity. The museum also displays Coptic, Nubian and Meroitic art. Assyrian monumental reliefs introduce the founding of the first cities in the Middle East. The jewellery of Queen Amanishakheto from Sudan, a larger-than-life statue of Ramses II, a sphinx-like figurine of Senusret II and the gilded sarcophagus lid of Queen Sitdjehuti are just a few of the museum's highlights. The building fascinates, too! The architect Peter Böhm lowered the entrance beneath the street level, suggesting an Egyptian temple. Light floods through the atrium into the building, and the bright courtyard adds to a journey in time that reaches back more than 5000 years.

In the 15th century, the humanist Herzog Albrecht V pondered the meaning of a statue depicting the Egyptian Goddess Isis. Like the Virgin Mary, she tenderly embraces her son (Horus in her case), who romps about on her lap. The resemblance is not accidental but archetypal. The lifelike emotionality of symbolic representation invited Christianity to assimilate pagan Gods into its rich mythological treasure box. The dissemination of the new teaching into other cultures was thereby facilitated, partly leading to the success of its preaching. Especially the civilisations of the Nile have left many traces in the Western World, and the chronologically organised collection of Munich's **Staatliches Museum Ägyptischer Kunst**, which covers the time from Prehistory to the rise of Christendom, allows to relive the evolution of God's depiction both in image and word.

In the late 16th century, Herzog Albrecht V acquired the first piece from Egypt for his Cabinet of Rarities. The Baroque awoke interest in the exotic, and during the reign of Kurfürst Karl Theodor, further historical artefacts forged their way to Munich.

In the 19th century, King Ludwig I brought many Egyptian statues to the Isar, where he housed them at the Glyptothek next to Greek and

▲ Munich's Museum Ägyptischer Kunst resembles a temple complex.

Roman busts.

When the Wittelsbacher patron of art purchased the golden treasures of Queen Amanishakheto, some of humankind's most valuable works of art found their way to Munich.

Even his court architect Leo von Klenze caught sight of many a treasure on his journeys to the Mediterranean. By and by, Munich's collection grew, and today, it is only superseded by the museums of London, Paris and Turin in Europe.

After World War II, the Museum Ägyptischer Kunst in Munich has expanded mostly through private donations. The curators buy at auction only a few objects and only those of high grade.

Location: Gabelsbergerstraße 35 **Entrance:** Adults 7 €, Concession 5 €, Sundays 1 €
Opening Times: Tues - Sun 10.00 - 18.00 **Internet:** https://smaek.de
Hochschule für Fernsehen und Film: https://www.hff-muenchen.de

The University of Television and Film Munich

Since opening the *University of Television and Film Munich* in 2011, the city has enjoyed an elite school where students embrace different careers in the creative industry. The architect Peter Böhm designed the inspiring complex opposite the Alte Pinakothek, a modern mirror image of the 19th-century building. On six floors, the 150-metre-long institute for film hosts a cinema auditorium, studios, lecture halls and a comprehensive media library. Fifteen lecturers take 350 aspirants under their wings, supporting them on their way to stardom. The line of ancestors delights autograph hunters. Renowned creatives like Doris Dörre, Bernd Eichinger and Wim Wenders graduated from the college; Hollywood honoured the alumna Caroline Link with an Oscar for her feature film *Nowhere in Africa*.

(51) Technische Universität München

Facts & Figures

Munich founded its polytechnic school in 1827; since 1970, the institute is called Technische Universität. Germany's elite University for Science and Technology is among the leading research centres in the country. Nearly 40,000 young adults study across more than 150 degree programs at the lecture halls in the Maxvorstadt and Garching-Hochbrück. Since 1922, the agricultural sciences have cultivated their seeds under the umbrella of the TU; their research ensures tomorrow's bread is on the table. Germany's first nuclear reactor was inaugurated in Garching-Hochbrück in 1957, dashing neutrons in service to science. Gottfried von Neureuther designed the central building at the Arcisstraße in neo-Renaissance style, modelled after the ETH Zürich in Switzerland. In 1992, German Bestelmeyer extended the premises with a machinery hall and lecture rooms.

Not institutions, but people research; King Ludwig I attracted many a luminary from the natural sciences to Munich by offering them a platform to ruminate and contemplate. Enlightenment's silent heroes were to investigate and lecture at Bavaria's universities and to ensure the country's technological future.

The King was a visionary. By founding universities, he wanted to fuse the arts with science. In Germany, the Industrial Revolution started late but forcefully. The steam engine has powered England's manufacturing industry since the 18th century. In Bavaria, the flywheels spun once the country had joined the German confederation after the 1870/71 war against France.

Bavaria showed wisdom in its appointments to the **Technische Universität**. Carl von Linde lectured at the university since 1875, invented an ammonia ice maker, and established an empire; Rudolf Diesel constructed the compression ignition engine, and Willy Messerschmidt studied at the Technische Universität, too - just like Claude Dornier, Hans-Maier Leibnitz, and Oskar von Miller. Together, they industrialised Bavaria and seduced the Bavarians to embrace the spirit of science.

▲ The 1916 erected Thiersch-Turm is an icon of the Technische Universität.

Under the protective wing of the polytechnic college, Bavaria's large enterprises saw the light of the day, focusing on mechanical engineering. The Linde AG was the first to open; the Maschinenfabrik Augsburg-Nürnberg (MAN) followed in 1898, and the BASF in Ludwigshafen gained a worldwide reputation for the ammonia fertiliser. Last but not least, the Messerschmitt-werke conquered the skies with their aeroplanes.

The Technische Universität led Bavaria into the industrial age. Still today, the world honours the university with Nobel Prize winners, including Rudolf Mößbauer, who discovered a novel way to perform nuclear spectroscopy.

Location: Maxvorstadt **Entrance:** Without charge **Opening Times:** Accessible during the day
Internet: https://www.tum.de
Studentenwerk München (student union): https://www.studentenwerk-muenchen.de

The Nuclear Research Reactor in Garching

The Allies prohibited post-war Germany from investigating hydrodynamics and atomic sciences because knowledge in those fields could be applied to the arms industry. Nevertheless, the first nuclear research reactor opened its gates in Garching-Hochbrück some ten years after the war, and in the year 2000, the physicists replaced the egg-shaped pile with the neutron source Hans Maier-Leibnitz. At the high-tech laboratory, the scientists ponder the fundamental laws of Physics, Chemistry and Biology. A neutron-spectrum analysis unveils the structure of organic compounds, the grid pattern of solid-state bodies and the dynamics of complex organic molecules. The reactor sells about 30% of its capacity to commercial users, and thereby, the institute subsidises its pioneering research.

㊸ Alte Pinakothek

Facts & Figures

Munich's treasure box of art extends over three galleries: the Alte Pinakothek, the Neue Pinakothek and the Pinakothek der Moderne. Together, they house an impressive selection of art. The Alte Pinakothek exhibits more than 700 paintings from the 14th to the 18th century, from Giotto to François Bouchier. The knowledgeable curators present the artists Altendorfer, Dürer, Bruegel, Dyck, Tintoretto, Raphael, Titian, El Greco and many more. King Ludwig I wanted his comprehensive collection to be accessible to the public, and thus, he commissioned his court architect Leo von Klenze to design a gallery where he could showcase his canvases stored in many castles. The massive brick building in the style of the Italian Renaissance opened its gates in 1836. The first of its kind was a model for many other European cities.

The Bavarians passionately collect art, but since their Gothic masters, they created little to be remembered for. Munich enjoyed another creative impulse towards the end of the 19th century, carried by Franz von Lenbach, Franz von Stuck and Der Blaue Reiter.

The Wittelsbacher became patrons of art with Herzog Albrecht V, who collected paintings and sculptures in his curiosity cabinet, pushing the country to the brink of ruin. In 1563, he arranged for an **art chamber** at today's Alte Münze, institutionalising Bavaria's collecting mania, the foundation of Munich's Pinakotheken.

Kurfürst Maximilian I expanded Munich's treasure box, too; he purchased art from German masters, such as the work *The Four Apostles* by Albrecht Dürer. The patron also commissioned a four-part cycle of hunting scenes, but only *The Hippopotamus* still pastures in Munich.

When Kurfürst Max Emanuel shipped 101 Flemish and Dutch paintings to Munich during the 18th century, the passion for collecting art kindled de novo. And the palatine Kurfürst Karl Theodor carried 800 masterpieces from Mannheim to the Isar when he accepted Munich's offer to the throne.

▲ The Alte Pinakothek carries its wounds of the past with dignity.

King Maximilian I enlarged the collection with 2000 canvases of German and Dutch masters, initially housed in the gallery Zweibrücken. Another 1500 paintings fell into the state's clutches during the dissolution of the monasteries.

Under King Ludwig I, Munich's art collection multiplied. He purchased 219 paintings of German and Dutch masters from the art dealer Boisserée.

During World War II, Allied air raids destroyed the Alte Pinakothek. Hans Döllgast renovated the building during the 1950s, consciously leaving the wounds visible: the brighter tint of the brick stones used for the repair indicates the extent of the damage.

Location: Barer Str. 27 **Entrance**: Adults 7,00 €, Concession 5,00 €, Sundays 1,00 €
Opening Times: Tues, Wed 10.00 - 20.30, Thur - Sun 10.00 - 18.00
Internet: https://www.pinakothek.de/besuch/alte-pinakothek

The Wounds of the Past

By the turn of the millennia, Munich had repaired, overbuilt and replaced most wounds of World War II. Nevertheless, the impact of an aerial bomb on the Alte Pinakothek is discernible. The architect Hans Döllgast had patched up the damage with brighter stones to indicate the location and the degree of the destruction. He wanted the future to remember the shoulders it stands on, forcing the post-war period to learn from the shadows of the past. Recently, Andreas von Weizsäcker and Beate Passow started the European-wide initiative *Wounds of the Past*: the project highlights the war damage still identifiable in the urban landscape. Glass panes safeguard bullet holes of machine guns to preserve their memory. Such an installation adorns the sculpture *Der Rossbändiger* (the horse tamer) close to the Alte Pinakothek.

Highlights of the Alte Pinakothek

The Alte Pinakothek is the first of three galleries where the Munichers present their fine arts collection. Its paintings span from the 14th century to the present. Leo von Klenze designed the Alte Pinakothek in 1836 on behalf of Ludwig I, the king who wanted to give his people access to the paintings.

The collection opens its exhibition on the upper floor with **early Dutch paintings**. The curators show works by Rogier van der Weyden, Joos van Cleve and Hans Memling. The section **Old German painting** includes Hans Holbein, Matthias Grünewald and Albrecht Dürer, and the section **Cologne painting** is dominated by Stefan Lochner.

The collection of **Italian paintings of the Renaissance** includes Filippo Lippi, Sandro Botticelli and Leonardo da Vinci. The golden age of **Venetian painting** draws on Titian, Jacopo Tintoretto and Paolo Veronese.

Flemish painting of the 17th century focuses on works by Anthony van Dyck. Paul Rubens is the pulsating heart of the Alte Pinakothek. **17th-century Dutch painting** prides itself on Frans Hals and Rembrandt van Rijn.

French painting is represented by Nicolas Lancret and Claude Joseph Vernet; **Italian Baroque** by Federico Barocci, Giovanni Battista Tiepolo and Guido Reni. **Spanish painting** shows the works of El Greco and Diego Velázquez. The gallery on the ground floor presents **Flemish paintings** (Jan Brueghel the Elder, Pieter Brueghel the Elder). The Alte Pinakothek website provides a comprehensive overview.

Artists from Bavaria can be studied in rooms II and IIb. Among the masters on display are Hans Holbein the Elder (*1465, Augsburg), Matthias Grünewald (*1480, Würzburg), Albrecht Altdorfer (*1480, Regensburg), Albrecht Dürer (*1471, Nürnberg) and Lucas Cranach the Elder (*1472, Kronach).

The battle of Alexander (Battle of Issos) is a highlight of the exhibition. Albrecht Altdorfer created the painting in 1528/9 for Herzog Wilhelm IV. It shows the fight between Alexander the Great and the Persian king Darius in 333 BC. A fantastic blue landscape rises in the background. The sun is leaning towards the horizon. The battlefield turns red. Thousands of knights march towards each other with lances. The warriors are

▲ At the Alte Pinakothek, Munich shows paintings from the 14th to the 18th century.

meticulously depicted in contemporary armour. The chariot of the Persian King Darius can be seen in the middle of the picture. Alexander pursues him.

The *Self-Portrait in a Fur Coat*, which Albrecht Dürer painted in 1500, represents the transition to modern times. The artist unmistakably states that he is following Jesus. The Imitatio Christi demonstrates his understanding that artists mediate between the secular and the sacred world. The way he presents himself resembles the Judge of the World. His right-hand rests delicately on the fur. Albrecht Dürer created the individual hairs with fine brushstrokes. Marten fur was only permitted to patricians of the Inner Council; Albrecht Dürer reached the honour only in 1509; by then, he had already finished the painting.

Simplicissimus

The picaresque novel *Der abenteuerliche Simplicissimus* (The Adventurous Simplicissimus) by Hans von Grimmelshausen was the inspiration when Albert Langen founded the literary review Simplicissimus in 1896. Munich had overtaken Vienna as a city of arts. The best writers of the time published in the magazine: Hermann Hesse, Gustav Meyrink, Arthur Schnitzler, and Thomas Mann. The illustrations of the literary texts gradually turned into political caricatures, and the authorities took action. They imposed fines and prison sentences. "Muzzle!" shouted Frank Wedekind, but the censorship helped the magazine to become famous, although the political powers threw it from one extreme to another. During the Nazi regime, it fell into a conversational tone. The last edition came out in 1944.

(53) Neue Pinakothek

Facts & Figures

The Neue Pinakothek presents paintings of the 19th and early 20th century, extending the Alte Pinakothek. The curators exhibit 50 sculptures and 550 canvases, stretching from Jacques-Louis David to Pablo Picasso. The gallery also hosts works by Goya, Gainsborough, Delacroix, von Kaulbach, Cézanne, Manet, Monet, Gauguin, van Gogh, Rodin, Klimt and von Stuck. Leo von Klenze had provided the basis of the gallery. After Ludwig I had purchased Klenze's collection in 1841, the King exhibited the paintings in a building opposite the Alte Pinakothek. The Allied air raids of World War II destroyed the Neue Pinakothek to such an extent that the city fathers had to clear the remains away in 1949. Critics praise the new complex, built by the architect Alexander von Brancas in 1981, because its unique construction allows only scattered light to illuminate the canvases. (The gallery is closed until 2029 for refurbishment.)

To collect is a passion and an addiction at the same time. When the masons still dried the mortar at the Alte Pinakothek, its exhibition space was already too limited for the growing collection of contemporary art compiled by Ludwig I. The King never tamed his propensity to purchase, but he rose to the challenge as a building contractor.

As a crown prince, he purchased paintings from Roman artists and commissioned Carl Rottmann to create a cycle of Greek landscapes. When Ludwig I acquired 58 pictures of his court architect Leo von Klenze in 1841, the Alte Pinakothek burst at the seams, and the King decided to add a second complex. Ten years after the opening of the Alte Pinakothek, Ludwig I laid the founding stone to the **Neue Pinakothek**, financing the gallery from his private purse. The architect Friedrich von Gärtner rushed to the drawing board, and the extension opened its gates on 23 October 1853. When King Ludwig I passed away in 1868, the gallery counted 400 canvases. French impressionists entered the collection under Hugo von Tschudi, who was appointed director-general in 1909.

The many Allied air raids on Munich during World War II destroyed the Neue Pinakothek, and the magistrate had to clear the building away

▲ Munich's Neue Pinakothek presents one of the largest art collections in the world.

in 1949. The Nazi regime had the paintings safeguarded in the Alps, and Munich now exhibited them at the Haus der Kunst, Prinzregentenstraße 1.

Alexander von Brancas designed the new Neue Pinakothek, which opened on 28 March 1981; it was an architectonic novelty: the pioneering pent roof windows diffused sunlight by scattering it in a way that the interior is evenly illuminated, without casting a shadow by exposing the paintings to a single light beam - genius. Since the 1980s, the masterpieces present their artistic power again at the Neue Pinakothek, just as in olden times, but now in a modern environment. Until 2029, the rooms undergo refurbishment.

Location: Barer Str. 29 **Opening Times**: Closed for refurbishment until 2029. A selection is shown in the Alte Pinakothek and in the Sammlung Schack.
Internet: https://www.pinakothek.de/besuch/neue-pinakothek

The Alter Simpl at the Türkenstraße 57

Every town needs a hideout where intellectuals can meet. The innkeeper Kathi Kobus founded such a place at Türkenstraße 57 when she took over the coffeehouse Kronprinz Rudolf and renamed it *Alter Simpl*. The satirical magazine *Simplicissimus* served as the namesake for the smoky bar. It was here that the editorial staff met at and under a table. The tavern promptly enticed Munich's art scene, and here, novelists like Oskar Maria Graf, Ludwig Thoma and Joachim Ringelnatz slurped their coffee. Could a writer or painter not stem the bill, Kathi Kobus invited him to leave a poem or a sketch to embellish the walls. The infamous dinner and dance parties, the cabarets and shows turned the Alter Simple into a jolly music hall, especially when Karl Valentin entertained the guests.

㊴ Pinakothek der Moderne

Facts & Figures

The Pinakothek der Moderne is the latest addition to the trilogy of Munich's art galleries. The creative architect Stephan Braunfels designed the architecturally exhilarating building, which opened its doors to the public on 16 September 2002. The museum presents works of art from the 20th and 21st centuries across 22,000 square metres; the exhibits continue the collection of the Neue Pinakothek in chronological order. The museum comprises four sections: the *Collection of Modern Art*, the *National Graphic Arts Collection*, the *New Collection* and the *Museum of Architecture*. The neighbouring *Palais Pinakothek* at Türkenstraße 4, inaugurated in 2006, focuses on education. The Sammlung Brandhorst, recognisable by its 36,000 ceramic bars, houses the treasures of Anette and Udo Brandhorst, the heirs of the Henkel imperium. Its emphasis is on the post-war period.

As the Alte Pinakothek called for an extension in the 19th century, Munich's collection of contemporary art demanded a building of its own at the turn of the millennium. An appeal to the public for donations yielded more than ten million Euros, which encouraged Bavaria's government to tender a building at the premises of the former *Türkenkaserne* in the Maxvorstadt, once home to military barracks. The architect Stephan Braunfels won the competition, and after six years of construction, Munich inaugurated its new museum on 16 September 2002.

The Munichers quickly embraced the gallery: in less than a year, one million enthusiasts visited the temple of art - the gaping vacuum in the cultural landscape was filled.

The works of art exhibited at the gallery convince, but the building's design tops them all. The architect merged various vanishing lines at the central dome, providing order to a confusing interior. The rotunda measures an impressive one hundred metres in circumference. The glass facade feels unobtrusive, yet it encloses a surface of 22,000 square metres.

An extensive programme of well-structured events accompanies the permanent exhibition. They educate and entertain at the same time.

Modern art has to break with traditions and will thus always be incomprehensible at first glance. Well-organised discussions and inspiring guided tours bridge the divide between established and **contemporary art**; they encourage discovering the new worlds created by the artists' visions.

Munich's corporate enterprises vastly contributed to the museum's success, in deed and funding. Many entrepreneurs continue to support the museum in securing Munich's place as an attractive location for top executives. A city must be entertaining and inspiring to remain attractive to world citizens - and the competition is fierce.

▲ The Pinakothek der Moderne houses international contemporary art.

Location: Barer Str. 27 **Entrance**: Adults 10,00 €, Concession 7,00 €, Sundays 1,00 €
Opening Times: Tues - Sun 10.00 - 18.00, Thur 10.00-20.00
Internet: https://www.pinakothek-der-moderne.de

The Lost Waterway of the Maxvorstadt

In the year 1700, Kurfürst Max Emanuel wanted to sail from the Münchner Residenz, his winter palace, to Schloss Schleißheim in the outskirts. Thus, he commissioned the Bavarian infantry to excavate a canal along today's Türkenstraße. The soldiers never finished the waterway, though, and the magistrate filled in the burrow during the 19th century. Common parlance claims that Turkish prisoners of war had to construct the canal, but historians dismiss this rumour. Kurfürst Max Emanuel had freed Vienna from the second siege by the Ottoman Empire in 1683; he victoriously returned to Munich with Turkish captives as a booty. Besides coffee, the Muslims introduced janissary music and brass instruments to the Alps. Little known, the roots of the traditional Bavarian brass bands are Islamic.

(55) Ludwigstraße

Facts & Figures

Administrative buildings of the Bavarian State Government sandwich the Ludwigstraße, an arterial road to the north commissioned by King Ludwig I in the 19th century. The crossings which intersect the Ludwigstraße are hardly visible, thus preserving the avenue's harmonious overall design - a stroke of genius by its mastermind Leo von Klenze. To the north, the Bayerische Staatsbibliothek (Bavarian state library), constructed by Friedrich von Gärtner in 1827, follows the style of the Palazzo Strozzi in Florence. It stores more than 7 million books of wisdom on its shelves. Its facade stretches over 155 metres and has 25 windows. Statues of Homer, Thucydides, Aristotle and Hippocrates embellish the long-drawn ramp of stairs. Inside, a breathtaking staircase leads to the reading room. World War II demolished the building, but post-war Munich reconstructed it in 1965.

Ludwig I commissioned the 1200-metre-long **Ludwigstraße**, an avenue to the north named after the King by the King. The promenade stretches from the Feldherrnhalle in the south to the Siegestor in the north. At the time of its construction, sheep grazed the meadows close to the Isar. The King paved the arterial road during the first half of the 19th century, opening the medieval town to the possibility of becoming a modern metropolis.

Leo von Klenze designed the master plan in 1815 and continued constructing the monumental buildings close to the Odeonsplatz in the style of the Italian Renaissance. In 1827, the architect Friedrich von Gärtner replaced him, drafting the premises from the Theresienstraße to the Siegestor. The new kid on the block broke up the strictness of the classicistic style and replaced its sharp corners with rounded ones. The Bavarian State Library (Ludwigstraße 16), constructed by Gärtner, and the Bavarian War Department (Ludwigstraße 14), built by Klenze, allow for a comparison of the styles.

The architects designed the buildings for residential use, but Munich's winter does not favour high ceilings; the tall rooms are impossible to keep

▲ The Bavarian state library guards 7 million books and 40,000 magazines.

warm during the dark season. Consequently, no tenant was willing to invest in the heating, and the buildings turned into administrative offices.

The harmonious overall concept is reflected in the buildings' standardised eaves height. Even the Siegestor to the north and the Feldherrnhalle to the south are of equal height.

The Leopoldstraße extends the arterial road to the north, following the former *Schwabinger Bach* (a stream).

Munich's nightlife rages until dawn at its many nightclubs. Not to be overlooked is the 17-metre-tall steel sculpture *The Walking Man* outside the office building of the reinsurance company Munich Re.

Location: Ludwigstraße **Entrance**: Without charge **Opening Times**: Always accessible
Bayerische Staatsbibliothek: https://www.bsb-muenchen.de
Cadu Cafe: https://www.cadu.de (Ludwigstraße 24)

The 1960s Student Protests

The 1960s student protests turned violent when Josef Bachmann, affiliated with a neo-Nazi group, attempted to assassinate the left-wing radical Rudi Dutschke on 11 April 1968. During the Easter demonstrations, the photojournalist Klaus Frings was killed. The movement's ultra left-wing now turned radical and created the terror group *Rote Armee Fraktion RAF* (Red Army Faction); the protests went underground. In the footsteps of South America's freedom fighters, the radicals Andreas Baader, Gudrun Ensslin and Ulrike Meinhof attempted to fracture the pillars of capitalism, igniting a bomb at the *Axel-Springer Verlag*, a German media group. In 1972, the police apprehended the group. During the Olympic Summer Games, the terror cell *Black September* took members of the Israeli Olympic team hostage to free them (and others) from prison.

(56) Ludwigskirche

Facts & Figures

The architect Leo von Klenze built the Ludwigskirche in 1844. The twin towers, 71 metres tall, pitch a double exclamation mark into the Ludwigstraße, breaking up the uniform eaves height of the arterial road. Jesus Christ welcomes believers at the facade. The four evangelists surround him. Ludwig von Schwanthaler designed the statues. The three-aisle basilica captivates the senses with its exotic Byzantine style. The accentuated transepts form with the nave a tau cross. The second-largest monumental fresco in the world, created by Peter Cornelius, radiates its splendour above the altar, depicting the Last Judgement. At the transept, a shrine to Our Lady shows the Virgin of Mercy, carved by the Ulmer Schule in 1480. The Allied air raids of World War II destroyed the church; architect Erwin Schleich reconstructed the temple in the 1950s. After the war, it served the US-American occupation force as a garrison church.

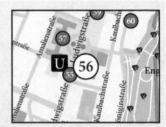

King Ludwig I believed that art betters people. His buildings along the Ludwigstraße brought an air of the Italian Renaissance to Munich. The King visited the land of the lemons seventy-seven times, always with an entourage of painters, sculptures and architects. In Rome, he kissed the muses, in Florence, he felt at home.

Art is expensive, then and now, and Bavaria's peasants had little patience for taxes in the name of culture. The **Ludwigskirche** ruined the city's treasury, and the magistrate refused to finance the temple: *"At the meadows in Schwabing, one preaches to sheep and cows,"* thus the opinion of the city fathers. When King Ludwig I threatened to relocate the university from Munich to Nürnberg, the bursar emptied his coffers.

The burghers lost their temper in 1848, however, and forced the King to step down. Only when Ludwig I had passed away in Nizza in 1868, did the people recognise, how little gratitude they demonstrated; in compensation, the funeral procession attracted a vast crowd; many wept salty tears.

The King's building frenzy had bestowed an economic upswing on Munich. For more than thirty years, his building projects had secured

▲ The Ludwigskirche is the highlight of the arterial road to the North of Munich.

the income of day labourers, masonries and artisans, and all the more with equitable wages.

When Ludwig I stepped down, the artists left. And when the Industrial Revolution gripped Europe, the workers and day labourers in Bavaria starved. In the suburbs, the toilers went to rack and ruin; working-class districts, like the Au, the Lehel and Haidhausen impoverished. The social tension slowly fermented to a brown broth, which sloshed its stench over beer-halls.

When the key to the last royal building was handed over to the magistrate, Munich's Golden Age ended. As so often in history, the people recognised the time of plenty only when it ended.

Location: Ludwigstraße 22 **Entrance:** Without charge **Opening Times:** 9.00 - 19.00
Internet: https://www.st-ludwig-muenchen.de
See also: https://www.muenchen.de/sehenswuerdigkeiten/orte/120382.html

The Kaulbachvilla at the Englischer Garten

Friedrich August von Kaulbach was a Municher and a painter at the turn of the century. Along with Franz von Lenbach and Franz von Stuck, he was one of Munich's creative luminaries at the turn of the century. He maintained an artists' villa at Kaulbachstraße 15, facing the English Garden. It was built between 1887 and 1889 according to his designs. Friedrich August von Kaulbach was a sought-after portrait painter. While Franz von Lenbach focused on the powerful in politics, von Kaulbach specialised in portraits of seductive women. Beautiful Ladies came and went in his studio: princesses, ladies of high society, dollar queens and lustres dancers. His photographic naturalism is convincing. His portraits are decorative and enthusiastic. The Neue Pinakothek shows some of his works.

(57) Ludwig-Maximilians-Universität

Facts & Figures

The magnificent buildings of the humanistic Ludwig-Maximilians-Universität circle the Geschwister-Scholl-Platz, a square cut in two by the Ludwigstraße. The architect Friedrich von Gärtner designed the neo-Romanesque complex in 1849. The three wings of the main building stand tall to the west of the avenue. Here, Munich's largest auditorium, designed by German Bestelmeyer in 1909, educates students. The theological college had settled east of the arterial road where the law faculty feeds its apprentices with paragraphs and legal constructs. About 1000 knowledge-hungry studied at the opening of the university in the 19th century; today, 50,000 interested students from all over the world, supported by 700 professors, have enrolled in more than 150 subjects across 18 departments. By now, the LMU has turned into Munich's third-largest employer.

Munich's **Ludwig-Maximilians-Universität** is arguably Germany's most prestigious educational institution. In 1472, Herzog Ludwig der Reiche founded an academy in Ingolstadt, and in 1800, King Maximilian I moved it to Landshut. Some twenty-five years later, King Ludwig I relocated the university first to the Alte Akademie in the Neuhauser Straße and then to the Ludwigstraße, where to this day, the professors educate their students at the magnificent building constructed by Friedrich von Gärtner. At last, the Munichers had a university to call their own.

King Ludwig I harboured big dreams when he designed the Maxvorstadt. He wanted to mould Munich into an alchemical amalgam of religion, art and science - a heroic endeavour because his Bavarian schoolboys rebelled against the Age of Enlightenment. To be sure, the Jesuits' academy was an intellectual epicentre during the 17th century. Their endeavours, however, led not to a spirit of enlightenment but the adoration of the Virgin Mary. Only when the sovereigns appointed scientists, the agriculturally minded Bavarians were prepared to consider the Industrial Revolution.

Like elsewhere, Munich opened its gates to female students late, only in 1903, and racism tarnished the halls for another 40 years. After the burning of books at the Königsplatz on 10 May 1933, the Nazi regime cleansed the university's technical staff of Jews. Any refusal to teach the ideology of National Socialism equalled emigration; to flee the country was an act of survival.

The Allied air raids of World War II destroyed the buildings of the LMU, but the city reconstructed them, and in 1962, the extension building at the Adalbertstraße was finished.

LMU's line of ancestors is long and high-ranking. Among the high ranking notabilities are federal chancellors, noble prize winners, state presidents and Olympic warriors. The future is built on the LMU, and the LMU leads into the future.

▲ The architect Friedrich von Gärtner designed Munich's humanistic university.

Location: Geschwister-Scholl-Platz 1 **Entrance**: Without charge
Opening Times: During the day **Internet**: https://www.lmu.de
Studentenwerk München (student union): https://www.studentenwerk-muenchen.de

Die Weiße Rose, a Resistance Group

The 18 February 1943 was blood-stained: leaflets hailed down the atrium of the university in Munich - students called to resistance. The janitor Jakob Schmid identified the delinquents, blocked the entrances and phoned the Gestapo; the sixth flyer of the *Weiße Rose* (White Rose) was the last. Since July 1942, the students smeared watchwords on walls, like *"Down with Hitler"* or *"Freedom from the Nazi regime"*; the tyrants became nervous: *"We must crush any opposition before the people are infected."* The leadership in Berlin presaged their weakness, sensed the fault of any authoritarian system, and assassinated the courageous students Hans and Sophie Scholl in a fast-track procedure. In death, their seeds blossomed: *"Not everyone in the Third Reich is committed to Nazi ideology."*

⑤⑧ Akademie der Bildenden Künste

Facts & Figures

The building at the Akademiestraße 2, constructed in neo-Renaissance style, is home to Munich's Academy of Visual Arts. The complex attracts attention because of its accentuated central architecture, lateral oriels, and open staircase. The architect partnership Coop Himmelb(l)au designed the extension in 2005. The academy educates about 700 aspiring students across 26 departments, Munich's artists of tomorrow. Besides the vocational training, the academy is well-known for its engaging public relations department. Numerous exhibitions showcase the academy's brilliant creative community; the curriculum supports the artists' professional careers. As the university works closely with the public, an artist is given an opportunity to be discovered early in life and thus mature to glory after his studies at the university. Art is a profession that pays for the bills of everyday life.

The Bavarian regents enjoyed whiling away their time with art. Already in the late 15th century, Herzog Albrecht V institutionalised the Wittelsbacher's passion for collecting art, and ever since, artists devoured a significant fraction of the country's annual national budget - the desire to be regarded as humanists pushed Bavaria several times to the brink of ruin.

The founding of the **Bavarian Academy of Visual Arts** was long in the making. Kurfürst Max III Joseph had established a drawing academy in 1770, which he relocated to the Alte Akademie at the Neuhauser Straße some ten years later. In 1803, the institution changed into Munich's *Royal Academy of Art*, and in 1813, the university allowed female students to enrol. Reparation payments by Paris after the 1870/71 war against France financed the building on the Akademiestraße. The architect Gottfried von Neureuther finished the neo-Renaissance ensemble in 1886; Prince Regent Luitpold inaugurated the halls. The academy trained Wassily Kandinsky, Paul Klee and Franz Marc. At that time, the conservative portrait painter Franz von Lenbach ranked amongst the institute's notable professors, to the dismay of the students, who rebelled by establishing the group *Der Blaue Reiter*.

▲ Gottfried von Neureuther constructed the neo-renaissance building in 1886.

During the Third Reich, the academy suffered terribly from the regime's ideological cleansing; the Gestapo imprisoned next to political opponents and the Jews many artists. Artists are dangerous, and Adolf Hitler had an account to settle with the establishment, which had disdained his paintings as worthless doodles; the Führer cleansed the country from degenerate art - in a manner of speaking - of any painting that was not to his liking.

After the 7th United States Army had freed Munich from Nazi oppression on 30 April 1945, creativity returned to the academy, but the institution never regained the glory it once enjoyed.

Location: Akademiestraße 2-4 **Entrance**: Without charge **Opening Times**: Only for exhibitions **Internet**: https://www.adbk.de see also: https://www.badsk.de **Students in Bavaria**: https://www.study-in-bavaria.de

The Group Der Blaue Reiter

Art must break with tradition to discover new forms of expression that may challenge collective norms. When Munich's expressionists, notably Wassily Kandinsky and Franz Marc, felt unrepresented by Bavaria's conservative artist association, they established a brotherhood called *Der Blaue Reiter (The Blue Rider)*. Paul Klee, August Macke and Alexej von Jawlensky joined the group, and at their peril, they organised an exhibition in 1911, which was well-received. The *Almanack* recorded their ideas in word and image, and time moulded the group's manifesto into the bible of modern art. Munich's *art scene* flirted with avant-gardism and even challenged Paris and Vienna. Adolf Hitler put an end to the creative spirit, however, and Munich never recovered from the bloodletting imposed on the academy by National Socialism.

Siegestor

Facts & Figures

The Siegestor, constructed in 1850, concludes the Ludwigstraße to the north. Its eaves height measures 20 metres, equal to the Feldherrnhalle in the south. Rome's Arch of Constantine served the architect Friedrich von Gärtner as an inspiration for his telling design. The monument with three thoroughfares glorifies Bavaria's military strength, symbolising power and readiness to combat. Munich's Arc de Triomphe, made of grey Kelheimer limestone, measures a width of 24 metres and a depth of 12 metres. The four Corinthian columns lead to a quadriga on the rooftop - four lions draw the carriage; Lady Bavaria Victorinox on a war-chariot, a 22-ton heavy and 5 ½ metres tall statue by the artist Friedrich Brunner, welcomes her triumphant troops returning to Munich. Last but not least, Johann Martin von Wagner created the friezes below.

What are the options for a humanistically educated King who craves to demonstrate strength but has neither military victories to boast about nor wants to run afoul with his neighbours and potential allies? In 1806, Bavaria had risen to a kingdom under Napoleon, but the country was politically too small to defy Austria, France, Russia or Prussia. Yet, a King without an Arc de Triomphe is not a King - not even when he is called Ludwig I.

Lacking military achievement, Ludwig I could not emulate the Roman Arch of Constantine, as the Tiber had paid homage to a victory in battle: Emperor Constantine triumphed over Maxentius. No enemy was in sight, whom to conquer promised glory, and thus, Johann von Wagner chiselled archetypal combat scenes without referring to a specific battle. The King loved the Mediterranean - so - Roman soldiers battle it out at the reliefs of the **Siegestor**. In-between float statues in white marble, designed by Ludwig von Schwanthaler - and the scene bellows with a lion roar: propaganda. Bavarians muddle along at the sides: the cycle of cute medallions symbolises the Bavarian administrative districts. Lower Bavaria excels in Alpine cattle breeding, and Swabia in weaving.

At last, a Bavarian army triumphantly marched through the gate of victory in 1871. Bismarck had won the war against France, and the lederhosen-heroes danced the Schuhplattler. Then, history steered the country through the turning loop. During World War I, the arc shed tears, and in 1944, Allied air raids flattened the monument. *"Courage! Courage!"*, the Munichers whistled and restored their archetypal victories in 1958, hoping for a better future.

A weighty Bavaria Victorix has throned on top of the arc since 1972. Knowing of war, she urges peace: "*Being the mastermind of the Counter Reformation and fascism is enough, dear Bavarian Gemütlichkeit.*"

▲ Friedrich von Gärtner modelled the Siegestor after Rome's Arch of Constantine.

Location: Between Ludwigstraße and Leopoldstraße **Entrance:** Without charge
Opening Times: Always accessible
Internet: https://www.muenchen.de/sehenswuerdigkeiten/orte/120454.html

The March of History

Royal photographer Josef Albert stood on the roof of the Feldherrnhalle and glanced along the Ludwigstraße. The Bavarian army marched from the Siegestor (Gate of Victory) to the old town under the leadership of the Prussian Kronprinz Friedrich. He waited - waited - then, he took a photo. It was July 16, 1871. The war against France was over - won! King Ludwig II was one of the riders. On January 18, 1871, Bismarck proclaimed the Prussian King Wilhelm I the first emperor of a new Germany - in Versailles. When the soldiers marched triumphantly through Munich's Siegestor, Bavaria's independence was lost. King Ludwig II had suggested that the imperial crown should pass alternately between Prussia and Bavaria, but the decision was made - no chance to interfere. Bavaria's sovereignty was lost: "*Hip-hip-hurray!*"

Schwabing

Facts & Figures

Schwabing is a neighbourhood north of Munich's medieval centre. It extends along Ludwigstraße and Leopoldstraße. The proximity to the university defined the character of the bohemian district next to the Englischer Garten at the turn of the century. Art Nouveau houses line the streets. The Münchner Lach- und Schießgesellschaft was founded in Schwabing in 1952. The theatre is located on Ursulastraße. The enterprise Utopia now runs the Reithalle München (Munich riding hall, Heßstraße 132); the city organises children's and youth theatre at the Schauburg (Franz-Joseph-Straße 47). Munich's funniest artists perform at the cabaret Rationaltheater (Hesseloherstraße 18). Not to be missed is the 17-metre-tall steel sculpture *The Walking Man* by the American Jonathan Borofsky; the figure marches into the future outside the Munich Reinsurance Company.

Schwabing is Munich's busiest district. The suburb was incorporated as a neighbourhood into Munich's administration in 1891. In the year 782, long before Munich was founded, a farmstead called Swapinga cultivated the fields. The name probably derives from a Swabian (Swapo). Grave finds provide evidence of people living in the region during the Bronze Age.

During the early Middle Ages, the region was administered by the Lords of Schwabing, vassals of the bishops in Freising. Their Schwabinger Burg (a fortress) was located on today's Occamstraße close to the Münchner Freiheit. It later passed to the patrician Gollier.

When the Maxvorstadt was built north of Munich in the 19th century, the rural character was built over, and the neighbourhood developed into an artists' stronghold. Revolutionaries also went hiding in Schwabing. Vladimir Ilyich Lenin lived illegally at Kaiserstraße 53 from 1900 onwards, working on the magazine *Morgenröte*. The district was also called *Munich's most beautiful daughter*, home to the artists Wassily Kandinsky, Lovis Corinth and Paul Klee. Gottfried Keller described Schwabing's parties in his novel *Der grüne Heinrich*. The author lived here during his student days. At that

▲ The Walking Man from Jonathan Borofsky marches at the Leopoldstraße since 1995.

time, Munich's bohemian atmosphere competed with Berlin and Vienna.

In the 1960s, riots exploded repeatedly along the Ludwigstraße. In Schwabing, alternative communities emerged, resisting bourgeois morality.

Today, Schwabing shines with its varied nightlife, cafes and happenings. Numerous restaurants and taverns offer live music until the early hours. During the *Corso Leopold* in May and September, the district is transformed into a street festival: stages and artisans entertain Schwabing and its many guests with cheerful music, theatre and dance; local bars provide traditional sausages and beer.

Location: District between the Ludwigstraße/Leopoldstraße and the Englischer Garten
Corso Leopold: https://www.corso-leopold.de
Literature: KulturGeschichtsPfad 12: Schwabing-Freimann (Landeshauptstadt München)

The Schwabing Riots of the Year 1962

In June 1962, unprecedented street riots threw Munich into chaos - stones were thrown, rubber truncheons waved, heads were bleeding! Then it rained, and the nightmare ended. Fifty years later, commentators still ponder the incident. What had happened? Witnesses report that a resident of the Leopoldstraße felt disturbed by a group of students with a guitar - they were singing - and he alerted the police. The long-haired good-for-nothings were to be walked off in handcuffs. The public, however, prevented the arrest and deflated the tyres of the police car; the officers called for reinforcements! Fourteen patrol cars arrived at the scene within minutes; truncheons flared up; passers-by rushed to the defence; additional police cars whistled in; more bystanders intervened - and then, it rained, and the rain ended the barricades.

Englischer Garten

Facts & Figures

Kurfürst Karl Theodor opened his hunting grounds to the public in 1789 and permitted his subjects to snoop around in the undergrowth. The English landscape garden stretches from the Hofgarten to the Hirschau; the five-kilometre-long grassland with an old tree population offers a perfect recreation zone. The Munichers enjoy nude bathing at the Schönfeldwiese close to the Schwabinger Bach. Surfers ride the waves at the Eisbach, and a Japanese Teahouse meditates *Oms* behind the Haus der Kunst. In 1836, the architect Leo von Klenze designed the Monopteros on an artificial elevation. The Steinerne Bank, a dreamy bench made of stone, hides in a magical forest. A grove at the Chinesischer Turm quenches the thirst with golden nectar and entertains its visitors with a brass band. For the romantically inclined, rowing boats and canoes splash around at the Kleinhesseloher See.

Europe's aristocracy was in a panic - despairing and frightened. The news had spread like wildfire: *The French had stormed the Bastille in Paris.* Kurfürst Karl Theodor, Elector of Bavaria since 1777, lowered his head and rested his chin on his fist: *"I have to keep my subjects at bay! They will revolt."*

One month later, Karl Theodor appointed Friedrich Ludwig von Sckell his court gardener. The landscape artist was to redesign the Wittelsbacher hunting grounds to the north of the palace into parkland - the terrain to the east of Schwabing must become the **Englischer Garten**.

So far, the meadows at the Schwabinger Tor had delighted only the sovereign and his noble guests. Hunting parties had entered the area on two sides, from the winter palace in the south and Schloss Schleißheim in the north. Alders, hazels, willows, birches and subalpine flora grew on the pastures along the Isar, where the river washed seeds from the Alps ashore during the spring. The rugged landscape was a paradise for birds and deer, hunting grounds of the Bavarian regents during the Middle Ages. When a nobleman visited Munich, like Emperor Leopold II in 1690, the court staged a great chase, and the burgess played the extras, crouching behind bushes and trees, hoping to avoid being shot by an accidental bullet.

Nevertheless, day in and day out, the townspeople lived trapped in a sad reality, confined behind the city wall. Taking a stroll was the privilege of the upper class, a pleasure that the people watched with a raised eyebrow and from a distance only, crooking the corners of their mouths to a smile and pretending to approve.

When Kurfürst Karl Theodor opened the Wittelsbacher hunting grounds to his subjects, the people felt ennobled, and the plan yielded fruits; the townspeople sniffed at fancy air and deferred the revolution to the next century, hosting a picnic in the park

▲ The English Garden is a landscape garden popular amongst nudists and romantics.

Location: Englischer Garten **Entrance:** Without charge **Opening times:** Always accessible
Englischer Garten: https://www.englischer-garten-muenchen-infos.de
Beergarden at the Chinesischer Turm: https://www.chinaturm.de

An American in Bavaria

A statue greets the visitor at the exit of the Englischer Garten close to the Prinzregentenstraße; Jakob Schwanthaler created it in 1796. It depicts the US-American Graf Rumford, born in Massachusetts. The strategist served at Bavaria's court since 1788. The memorial tells of the *philanthropist with a bright mind and a sincere heart*. Graf Rumford had fought in the American War of Independence, siding with the British. When the tides turned, he fled and arrived at Munich's court in 1791, where he modernised the Bavarian Army. The Count noted that *the troops were poorly paid and malnourished*, and he ordered the soldiers to till the fields at the Englischer Garten for private consumption. None remembers Graf Rumford for his heroism on the battlefield but for his pragmatic approach to social reforms.

instead; the cunning plan had saved Bavaria's absolutistic order until World War I.

In 1790, the engineer Adrian von Riedl plodded the first step in the transformation of Munich's green lung. At the order of Kurfürst Karl Theodor, he constructed a two-kilometres-long dam at the lower part of the Isar to protect the meadows from flooding. The tributaries usually gushed the landscape during the thawing period in spring; the new barrier along the Isar drained the swamplands. The landscape artist expanded the kitchen gardens cultivated by the Bavarian army to a spacious park. In the spring of 1792, the first part of the anti-revolution project opened its gates to the people under the public's applause.

After the refurbishment of the southern area, the landscape architects leapt to the terrain around today's Chinesischer Turm. The Elector strove to ensure the park's economic success by subjoining a model farm. By 1790, the agricultural initiative had taught the regent's army the tilling of the fields. Today, the administration of the Englischer Garten analyses customer relationships at the building. The Elector converted an ancillary two-story timber house attached to the farm into a dance hall and a bowling alley, rebuilt in stone in 1912. Later, the Chinesischer Turm joined the complex, surrounded by a beer garden, a children's playground, and a Biedermeier merry-go-round. The Chinese Pagoda at Kew Gardens in London stood as a model for its brother in Munich. At its opening, the trees reached the tower's second floor. Today, they form a concentric barricade, promising protection and cosiness. The townspeople amused themselves under the leaves, dancing to the sound of a military band. None in Bavaria remembered wanting to revolt while the dirndl spun their dresses, turning and turning and turning around their heels.

During the 19th century, the Englischer Garten expanded northwards; two farmhouses in Dutch style invited day-trippers. Since 1811, the rangers provided dairy products, refreshments and beer to the park workers. Later, they established a tavern and served light dishes to the public. At the eastern banks of the Kleinhesseloher See (a lake created by artificial flooding in 1812), the Bavarian Kings constructed a two-storey boathouse with bar and restaurant built by the architect Gabriel von Seidl in 1882. Fifty years later, the administration rebuilt the house in stone and added a terrace. Today, it is home to a large beer garden, Munich's most romantic.

After World War II, the US-American occupation force impounded the buildings; they returned them to the magistrate in the 1950s. Run

▲ The reinsurer Munich Re established its headquarters close to the Englischer Garten.

down and eaten by worms, the city had to demolish the construction in the 1970s and replace the rotten beams with freshly cut trunks.

The enchanting Werneckerwiese to the south of the lake had a particular function during the Age of Absolutism. Here, the nobility ignited fireworks, visible from across the city. The aristocracy gawked at the firecrackers from the Hofgarten, keeping a safe distance yet still delighting in the spectacle.

To the north, the Englischer Garten extends its trails into the Hirschau. The hiking path leads along the river's floodplains to Garching's centre of science and its research reactor. The tracks connect the English landscape garden to the Isar's recreation area, which meanders across Bavaria.

The Kocherlball - Sundays 6 am

Maidservants had no comfortable life at the turn of the century. The gentlemen demanded their presence around the clock and frowned upon idle leisure. However! Clever businesspeople invented the so-called *Kocherlball* in the year 1880, a vibrant dance at the Chinesischer Turm for Munich's domestic servants. Every third Sunday of the month, the rooster invited the townspeople to swing at 6 am before the dominions woke up. Brass bands in traditional Bavarian costumes played cheerful tunes and rocked the place. Out of anger, puritans infiltrated the magistrate to prohibit the ball in 1904 on the grounds of maintaining public order and morality. The dirndl returned in 1989 for a two-hundred-year celebration, whirling in their dresses to waltz, polka, the *Zwiefacher* and the Munich Française.

Archäologische Staatssammlung

Facts & Figures

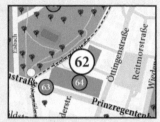

The Archäologische Staatssammlung presents archaeological finds from Bavaria's soils, ranging from the Stone Age to the Early Middle Ages. The Bavarian government opened the contorted cubical building in 1975. The exhibitions present in five departments - Prehistory, Romans, Middle Ages, Mediterranean, and Numismatics - the life of early nomads who had settled north of the Alps. The gallery illustrates the social, religious and economic endeavour of the people before their conversion to Christianity. Archaeology achieved its independent status as a faculty within the Bavarian Academy of Science in 1885. The museum specialises in collecting and archiving archaeological finds; its team collaborates with all Universities in Bavaria to further scientific research into the evolution of the human race. Its public outreach is well respected throughout the country.

Archaeologists date the most ancient traces of the alpine Neanderthal to 70,000 BC. In Regensburg, a city northeast of Munich, the scientists unearthed tools of the Cro Magnon man, an early human, who inhabited our planet during the Upper Paleolithic some 40,000 years ago. He modelled Goddess figurines; the widely acclaimed *Venus of Mauern* is an example.

The early inhabitants settled first along the Danube, where the climate was beneficial and natural caves offered protection. The bones unearthed reach back to the late Mesolithic.

The scientists discovered a nest of 33 skulls at the Ofnet Cave close to Nördlingen; they date from 7700 BC. Burial grounds and longhouses emerged during the Neolithic period.

From 5000 BC onwards, the people enjoyed a sedentary lifestyle; they constructed cult sites and created works of art. By about 3800 BC, the megalithic cultures constructed mounds and lake dwellings on stilts, trusting the protection of dolmen goddesses and sun gods. By 2200 BC, the Alpine people mined ores for bronze; richly ornamented graves entombed warriors and queens.

Archaeologists unearthed the grave of a woman in Weihenstephan, which dates from the 14th century BC. Respect and adoration had buried her with precious jewellery. Depositing burial objects with the dead became the new normal.

Scientists discovered the largest city complex in Heunischenburg close to Kronach. A massive stone wall surrounded the settlement, dating from 900 BC.

Society changed again during the Hallstatt period (800 - 450 BC). The people had settled at farmsteads and developed a sophisticated social structure. Ironmaking leveraged Celtic tribes to regional power. The Oppidum Manching is the most famous example.

▲ The Archäologische Staatssammlung presents Bavaria's early history.

Location: Lerchenfeldstraße 2, Entrance: Adults 7 €, Concession 5 €, Sundays 1 €
Opening Times: Tues/Wed/Fri/Sat 10.00-17.00, Thur/Sun 10.00-19.00
Internet: http://www.archaeologie-bayern.de

Herzog Tassilo III, the Last of a Dynasty

The Agilolfinger dynasty ruled Bavaria during the 8th century at the time of Charlemagne. The woods were sparsely populated and cumbersome to pass. The Agilolfingers reached the end of their aristocratic line with Tassilo III, the last of the so-called *Altbayern* (Old Bavarians). The Duke, only seven years old, had ascended to the throne in 749 after the death of his father Odilo. Until his sixteenth birthday, his mother ruled on his behalf; then, he freed himself from his custodian. Tassilo founded monasteries, travelled many times to Italy and sought to expand his influence towards the East. An alliance with the Langobards, however, sealed his fate. When Charlemagne besieged Padua, Tassilo III had to make way. The Frankish King degraded him to the rank of a liegeman in 787, and some ten years later, the Emperor banished him to a monastery, where he died.

⑥³ Prinzregentenstraße

Facts & Figures

The Prinzregentenstraße is the last arterial road in Munich. It begins at the Prinz-Carl-Palais near the Hofgarten and leads along the Friedensengel to the Prinzregentenplatz. Prince Regent Luitpold commissioned the boulevard in 1890 (finished in 1901). Unlike the Ludwigstraße, which Leo von Klenze designed with classicist rigour, the city planners allowed along the Prinzregentenstraße for a looser, more spacious development: the house fronts are not in line, and open squares interrupt the line of sight. The concept symbolises the emerging era. It was no longer kings but the bourgeoisie that defined the style. The starting point was not a monument like the Feldherrnhalle but a garden. Monumental buildings such as the Bayerische Nationalmuseum (Bavarian National Museum) were interrupted by piazzas. And townhouses, not a victory gate, finish the avenue.

The **Prince Regent period** derives its name from Prince Regent Luitpold. It was a contemplative time for Munich, a time of calm before the chaos of the 20th century reduced Europe to rubble twice. The Prince Regent period was a time of the upper middle class and a time of the Art Nouveau.

Prince Regent Luitpold was the fifth child of King Ludwig I, the younger brother of King Maximilian II and a sibling of King Otto I of Greece. When the Bavarians found King Ludwig II dead in the Starnberger See on June 13, 1886, Luitpold had to take over the affairs of the state; King Otto of Bavaria, the legal heir, was unfortunately incapacitated due to mental illness.

Luitpold never called himself king, so historians refer to the era as the Prince Regent period. During peace after the Franco-Prussian War of 1870/71, the Munichers built the Prinzregentenstraße; they finished it in 1901. It was Munich's last arterial road. Unlike the Ludwigstraße, open spaces break up the line of the buildings, and green oases delight the senses.

At the turn of the century, carriages trotted along the promenade from

▲ The Prinz-Carl-Palais is next to the Hofgarten.

the Hofgarten to the Friedensengel and the upper-class villas in Bogenhausen. After World War II, the Prinzregentenstraße degenerated into a highway.

When Prince Regent Luitpold died in 1912, the Munichers suspected that the time of idle pleasure had passed away for good with him. How popular the regent was in Bavarian testify the multitude of names that refer to him: Prinzregententorte, Café Luitpold, Luitpoldpark, Prinzregentenstraße, Prinzregententheater, Luitpoldbrücke and many more. They speak of the love of those who admired and adored a ruler who never wanted to become king and never wanted to rule but go hunting in the woods.

Location: Prinzregentenstraße **Entrance:** Without charge **Opening Times:** Always accessible
Schack-Galerie: Prinzregentenstraße 9, Opening Times: Wed - Sun 10.00 - 18.00
Entrance: Adults 4 €, Concession 3 €. https://www.pinakothek.de/besuch/sammlung-schack

The Schack-Galerie

At Prinzregentenstraße 9, the Bayerische Staatsgemäldesammlung (Bavarian State Painting Collection) shows the private collection of Graf Adolf Friedrich von Schack in the former Prussian Embassy. The building came into the possession of the Free State of Bavaria in 1939. Adolf Friedrich von Schack was interested in contemporary paintings and collected 267 works of art during his eventful life. They can be admired in the exhibition. The displayed artists include Anselm Feuerbach, Carl Spitzweg, Carl Rottmann, Arnold Böcklin and Moritz von Schwind. The patron primarily collected landscape and historical paintings. Franz von Lenbach's *Shepherd Boy*, Moritz von Schwind's *Des Knaben Wunderhorn* and Arnold Böcklin's *Triton and Nereid* are among the most admired works in the collection.

Bayerisches Nationalmuseum

Facts & Figures

The Bayerisches Nationalmuseum at the Prinzregentenstraße was inaugurated in 1900. It presents art from the Alpine region, covering the time from the Gothic to Art Nouveau. The collection focuses on wood-carvings from Southern Germany. The Wittelsbacher dynasty collected the pieces over centuries: statues, works of ivory, porcelain, textiles, gold and silver items. King Maximilian I had confided the treasures to the Bavarian Government. A folkloristic department and a crib collection unveil the spiritualistic soul of the people. The building, constructed by Gabriel von Seidl, architecturally combines all styles in Bavaria. The showrooms mirror the respective period of the exhibits. For example, works from the Gothic dwell in exhibition rooms covered by a barrel vault. With attention to detail, the architect decorated the facade with elements from the German Renaissance, the Baroque and the Rococo.

The idea of the Bayerische Nationalmuseum (Bavarian National Museum) was born when King Maximilian II visited the museums in London's South Kensington during the 1851 World Exhibition. Four years later and after the Germanische Nationalmuseum was founded in Nürnberg in 1852, the plans for a new museum in Munich became a reality. The first exhibition opened in 1867. Since 1901, the exhibits have been showcased in a building designed by the architect Gabriel von Seidl.

The curators present sculptures, paintings, ivory carvings and goldsmiths' works from all over Europe. The focus of the collection is on southern Germany. Porcelain, textiles, furniture, weapons and musical instruments are also displayed. They give an impression of everyday life and culture over the last 700 years.

The life-size figure *Entrückung der heiligen Maria Magdalena* by Master Tilman Riemenschneider (around 1490/92) is outstanding: When the former prostitute paid for her sins naked in the desert, her hair grew to cover and hide her femininity. The master of lime wood accentuates her curly strands with attention to detail and deliberately leaves some parts of her body uncovered.

▲ Gabriel von Seidl constructed the Bayerische Nationalmuseum in 1900.

The sculpture *Der Tod auf dem Löwen* was carved for the Heilsbronn monastery. It shows a personification of Death riding on a lion. The message is simple: Even the king of the beasts must submit to the course of nature - and so must you.

A *golden table lamp* created by François Raoul Larche in 1900 depicts a veil dance. The model is the American Loïe Fuller. The Art Nouveau art impresses with its dynamic rhythm of movement.

A late antique ivory tablet from the year 400 depicts the Church of the Holy Sepulchre in Jerusalem. It is one of the oldest known depictions of the resurrection and ascension of Jesus Christ.

Location: Prinzregentenstraße 3 **Entrance:** Adults 7,00 €, Concession 6,00 €, Sundays 1,00 €
Opening Times: Tues - Sun 10.00 - 18.00, Thur until 20.00
Internet: https://www.bayerisches-nationalmuseum.de

The Sammlung Bollert

The Bayerische Nationalmuseum presents the Sammlung Bollert (Collection Bollert) in an extension building since 2005. The barrister Gerhart Bollert had lived in Berlin, where he was a member of the German Reichstag. He purchased the artworks during the first half of the 20th century, including 128 wooden sculptures and many paintings from the Gothic to the Renaissance. The exhibition culminates in the woodcarving *Mary Magdalene anoints the feet of Jesus in the House of Simon* by Tilman Riemenschneider. The Meister der Biberacher Schule show their skill with the figurines *Saint Anna* and *The Coronation of the Virgin*, both carved in lime. The *Lüsterweibchen*, a woman indulging lustfully, was cut by the artist Veit Stoss. Last, Jörg Lederer, a craftsman from Kaufbeuren, whittled the *Adoration of the Magi*.

Haus der Kunst

Facts & Figures

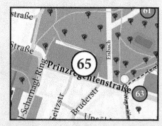

Munich was the *Capital of the National Socialist Movement* during the Nazi regime and a pioneer in architecture. When Paul Ludwig Troost constructed the Haus der Kunst in 1937, he created the blueprint for the fascists' taste; the design is based on a mishmash of an antique temple, an overdimensioned Art dèco and the classical style. Diagonally opposite, the Prinz-Carl-Palais, as a comparison, radiates classicism untainted. The complex at the Prinzregentenstraße became the model structure for Germany's style of architecture during the 1930s and early 1940s. Twenty-one Doric columns carry a 160-metres-long roof. Inside, the regime staged an annual exhibition called the *Große Deutsche Kunstausstellung*, which bored its applauding audience to death. After World War II, the US Army seized the building. It again opened as a museum in 1949 when the gallery presented the works of *Der Blaue Reiter* - a moving exhibition.

"When nations experience times of greatness, they will shape those periods extrinsically. The word in stone is more convincing than the spoken word." - Thus, Adolf Hitler during the opening of the *Erste Deutsche Kunstausstellung* on 22 January 1938 at the **Haus der Kunst**. Based on their *stone, blood and soil ideology*, the fascists organised an exhibition of degenerate art at today's Theatermuseum in the Hofgarten. There, the regime compared the works of expressionism, surrealism and dadaism with drawings done by disabled people. The Nazis intended to create a Pavlovian conditioning with mental illness and achieved only the opposite: They unveiled the process of projection of the extreme right-wing's psyche. Contemplating modern art should have triggered revulsion. However, many ignored the association and delighted in the artists' humanism instead; the soul had found a counterbalance to the ideology of the bleeding soil.

Fascism demands grand designs, bastions of stone, and megalomanic idolatry of the Aryan race; the National Socialist movement mutated from a political party to a pseudo-religion. And the Catholic Church remained silent even when the regime replaced processions and devotions with military parades, the consecration of the flag and the Hitler oath.

▲ The entrance to the Haus der Kunst hides behind the pillar file.

As so often in the history of the Germanic people, repressed instincts had overwhelmed the thin cognitive layer of consciousness. Not the tender emotions of the poet's imagination but raw crudeness dominated the behaviour. The Nazi's architectural design shook hands with the idea of a master race. The delusion of grandeur invited megalomania to sit at the dinner table, relentlessly sacrificing the individual at the fascists' temple. Column by column, the Haus der Kunst stomps uniformity into the ground, degenerating the victim and the perpetrator alike to the level of wild animals. The individual has no meaning, only the ideology they carry.

Location: Prinzregentenstraße 1 **Entrance:** Adults 14 €, Concession 10 €
Opening Times: Mon, Wed, Sun 10.00 - 18.00, Thur 10.00 - 22.00
Internet: https://hausderkunst.de

The Art of National Socialism

The Haus der Kunst on Prinzregentenstraße presented the Große Deutsche Kunstausstellung (Great German Art Exhibition) eight times between 1937 and 1944. It was one of the most important cultural events of the Nazi regime. At the same time, Adolf Hitler waged a relentless war against degenerate art, which he found undermining his authority. Instead, works by Werner Peiner, Friedrich Stahl and Karl Leipold were shown in a special exhibition. Society has forgotten the painters; their works have largely disappeared from the galleries. Their style of Romantic Realism glorified the working people, pregnancy, the tradition of the homelands, the sacrifice of soldiers, obedience and racial purity. They depicted the people embedded in nature; the models were young, physical, heroic and often naked.

(66) St Anna im Lehel

Facts & Figures

The heart of the upscale neighbourhood Lehel beats at the St Anna Platz. The convent Church of St Anna accentuates Bavaria's *joie de vivre* at the eastern edge of the open square. The architect Johann Michael Fischer constructed the House of Prayer in 1737; the Asam brothers designed the interior in Rococo style, depicting scenes from the life of Saint Anna, the mother of the Virgin Mary and the grandmother of Jesus Christ. Gabriel von Seidl designed the Parish Church of St Anna on the western side in the style of Historicism in 1892. The monumental three-aisled basilica stands out by its frescoes at the high altar. The artist Rudolf von Seitz painted the centre-piece *Trinity with Apostles, Mary and Anna*. The adjacent wing-frescoes *Marriage at Cana* and *The Communion of the Apostles* by Carl Becker-Gundahl flank the main scene.

The two prayer houses, the **St Anna convent church** (to the west of the St Anna Platz, constructed in 1728) and the **St Anna parish church** (at the eastern side of the square), invite visitors to study Munich's artistic development from the 18th-century Rococo to the neo-Romanesque Historicism of the 20th century.

The Bavarian architect Gabriel von Seidl deliberately drafted the parish church in contrast to the unpretentious, twin-towered Franciscan convent church when he chose a one-towered design with sculptural ornamentation. The apocalyptic equestrian statue of the redeemer Jesus solemnly rises from the cornice to confront the devil and his army. The portal is shaped like a triumphal arch, enclosing a tympanum with a rich figurine decoration.

The bright interior of the convent church avoids right angles and replaces the edges with floating lightness, remaining unintrusive; by contrast, the parish church seeks attention. The convent church surprises with a stretched oval and an altar facing to the west. In contrast, the architect of the parish church chose the layout of a three-aisled basilica.

The Asam brothers depicted the life story of Saint Anna with Baroque

▲ The apocalyptic Christ lifts off into the sky at the St Anna parish church.

lightness. Opposite, the interior of the parish church sobers the mind with a linear design.

An enchanting painting of Saint Anna smiles from the high altar of the convent church while she introduces her curious daughter to the scriptures.

At the parish church St Anna, Jesus Christ in Mandorla frightens the onlooker in his role as the world judge, a fresco painted by Rudolf von Seitz in 1898. At his feet, the Archangel Michael weighs the souls of the risen. To the left, the Greek and to the right, the Latin church fathers pray; the works were executed by the Nymphenburger Porzellanmanufaktur; they urge the believer to a life of proper conduct.

Location: St.-Anna-Straße **Entrance:** Without charge **Opening Times:** during the day
Klosterkirche: https://www.erzbistum-muenchen.de/pfarrei/st-anna-muenchen/cont/64346
Pfarrkirche: https://www.erzbistum-muenchen.de/pfarrei/st-anna-muenchen/cont/64345

Master Eder, his Pumuckl and the Lehel

The Lehel is Munich's oldest suburbia, upscale today but once a slum. Day labourers who were unworthy of the keep had to dwell outside the city walls during the Middle Ages. When Munich constructed the adjoining boulevards to the east during the 19th century, the neighbourhood flourished, and the affluent middle class refurbished the district in the style of Historicism. Today, the Lehel is a sought-after borough, and it hides an unacknowledged secret: trolls haunt the idyllic quarter. *Pumuckl*, a character invented by Ellis Kraut, an author of children's books, spooks in the backyard of the Widenmayerstraße 2 inside the workshop of *Master Eder*. The 60 episodes of the TV series and the feature films catapulted the red-haired goblin and the Bavarian dialect actor Gustl Bayrhammer to international fame.

67 Maximilianstraße

Facts & Figures

The once idyllic, 1½ kilometre long Maximilianstraße, commissioned by King Maximilian II, leads from the busy Max-Joseph-Platz to the Maximilianeum in the east, close to the Isar banks. The architect Friedrich Bürklein constructed the grand boulevard in 1874. Post-war Munich transformed the sublime royal avenue into a congested road, cut in half by the Altstadtring. Merely here, the innovative Maximilianstil enchants - an architectural style which only asserted itself in Munich. Open squares and rows of houses alternate along the promenade. Opposite the regional government building, the Museum of Ethnology *Fünf Kontinente* introduces the many cultures of the world. Designers, boutiques, jewellers, and luxury hotels offer a touch of nobility at the Maximilianstraße that is only suited for those affluent with a platinum credit card.

After the Munichers had forced King Ludwig I to step down in 1848, the stage was set for his son Maximilian II to ascend to the throne. The intellectual loved the sciences and preferred to become a researcher, but his fate was politics. When he took office, Bavaria still marched at the rear end of the Industrial Revolution; the focus had to shift from the arts to technology.

Domestically, the newly crowned King reformed the administration and cut the civil servants' insider relationships with the judiciary to guard against corruption. In foreign affairs, he stood for an empowered Bavaria within the German Confederation and successfully defended the country's independence.

During his reign, Munich embraced the outskirts. King Maximilian II connected the Münchner Residenz with the Isar by an avenue but never surpassed the masterly performance of his architecturally inspiring father Ludwig I, however much the son endeavoured. To break new grounds was his maxim, but the time had not yet come for a novel style. His reign still lacked the experience of the social and economic revolutions to come, which embraced capitalism and high-rise buildings.

▲ Kaspar von Zumbusch designed the monument of King Maximilian II.

Nevertheless, the King invented a new style, the **Maximilianstil**, following in the footsteps of London's Victorian period. The building of the Regierung von Oberbayern at Maximilianstraße 39 is the prime example, a design that only exists at the Isar because nobody was interested in a Gothic on steel girders, in a jumble of English neo-Gothic and Italian Renaissance.

The style focuses on vertical lines, mimicking the structure of a cathedral. Critics dismiss the composition that defines the character of the boulevard. Finally, Caspar von Zumbusch added a monument to the King in 1857, which rests on a traffic island flooded by humming cars.

Location: Maximilianstraße **Entrance:** Without charge **Opening Times:** Always accessible
Internet: https://www.sueddeutsche.de (Mehr als Prunk und Glamour)
Münchner Kammerspiele: https://www.muenchner-kammerspiele.de

The Münchner Kammerspiele

The *Münchner Kammerspiele,* Bavaria's enchanting Art Nouveau Theatre, hides at Maximilianstraße 26. The innovative house, founded by Eugen Robert in 1912, evolved into one of the most renowned stages in German-speaking countries. Well-known authors walked their works to the premiere at the dinky hall. Bertolt Brecht, for example, directed his play *Trommeln in der Nacht* (Drums in the Night) at the Kammerspiele in 1922. The theatre also engaged comedians like Karl Valentin and Lisl Karlstadt to entertain the audience. The architects Max Littmann and Richard Riemerschmid drafted the blueprint of the building in the year 1900. At times, the performances extend into the oval auditorium, and the audience becomes a part of the stage. Munich's directors enjoy blurring the boundary between reality and fiction.

Völkerkundemuseum Fünf Kontinente

Facts & Figures

At Maximilianstraße 42, the Museum of Ethnology *Fünf Kontinente* is a masterpiece of anthropology; it exhibits folk art from around the globe. The excellent collection, didactically well-presented, stretches from Africa and Latin America to Asia, Oceania and the Middle East. The museum  captivates anthropologists by mandating an outstanding selection of historical documents. The curators display a Greenland kayak from 1577, the oldest one in the world. The impressive works of ivory from East Asia enchant visitors. The museum shows terrifying weapons, masks and carvings from Africa, divine figurines of the Incas, and enchanting charms and shields from North America. Lovingly presented dioramas convey the impression of walking on-site; the passionately arranged displays overwhelm the imagination. The replica of a temple to Shiva and an oriental garden pavilion is experienced by all senses.

Munich enjoyed three phases of economic upswing during its 800-year history; each correlate with an increase in population by immigration.

Herzog Ludwig II nominated Munich as a residence city, which led to the settlement's first blossoming during the Middle Ages, and the town grew in size due to immigration.

When King Maximilian I negotiated royal dignities for Bavaria in 1806, Munich's geographical extent doubled, and equally, the national revenue prospered. Munich could finance its expansion to the north and construct the Maxvorstadt. After a century of deep sleep, the city welcomed a golden century; many immigrants settled - they arrived in Munich from the new areas incorporated into the kingdom.

The city experienced its last economic upswing after World War II. When the Berlin Wall sliced Prussian companies into two, many relocated their headquarters to the foothills of the Alps. The incipient construction boom resulted in an economic upswing. Italian, Spanish and Portuguese workers flocked to the Isar; Turkish and Eastern European industrious workers followed.

In the year 2000, a 25% cultural diversity and a share of 15% Germans

▲ The Museum Fünf Kontinente guards a well-respected ethnological collection.

with a migrant background enthused Munich. Unlike France and England, Germany hardly ever commanded colonies; Munich grew by immigration from European countries instead.

Nevertheless, any influx of people carries tension and conflicts. Conservative Bavarians rightly question the significance of their traditional values when forced to live in a globally operating international community.

It is the task of the 21st century to raze barriers, confront racism, and tear down walls. The first step is to replace divisions with understanding, and Munich's **Völkerkundemuseum Fünf Kontinente** leads the way.

Location: Maximilianstraße 42 **Entrance:** Adults 5 €, Concession 4 €, Sundays 1 €
Opening Times: Tues - Sun 9.30 - 17.30
Internet: https://www.museum-fuenf-kontinente.de

The Princess of Wanderlust

The daughter of Prince Regent Luitpold, a Bavarian princess born into a golden cage, could have enjoyed a tranquil life, but she decided otherwise. The adventures broke free, travelled across Europe at the humble age of twenty-one and discovered her passion for the peoples of the world. Wanderlust became her passion. Expeditions to the West Indies, Latin America and Africa followed. The well-read scientist spoke twelve languages, authored sixteen books and collected whatever fell into her clutches: plants, animals, objects of art, ethnological curiosities and much more. Her collection provided the foundation of Munich's Museum of Ethnology. In 1903, Prince Regent Luitpold, impressed by his daughter's achievements, finally opened women the path to study at Bavaria's Universities.

Along the Isar

Insiders Know ...

Art or Artist - that is the Question
The paintings by Franz von Stuck scream introverted extroversion to the world. The creator and his work fuse to a glamorous amalgam at the Villa Stuck - the atmosphere is refreshingly neoteric but not well-behaved.

Swimming in a Sea of Senses
The Müllersche Volksbad presents a thermal spa while dipping its head into art nouveau: the sauna and whirlpools are coated with stunning designs. Life flourishes most enchantingly.

About Engineers and Scientists
The leading line of the Deutsche Museum stretches over 16 kilometres; switches and buttons trigger dioramas at the pits and across the universe. Experiment without end! The world is your oyster.

Watching the Rainbow at the Glockenbachviertel
Munich was once the capital of the gay liberation movement. The starlets of the olden days glitter no more, but scintillas still whistle along the Hans-Sachs-Straße in the Glockenbachviertel.

When the Marionettes Enter Stage
Charming, enchanting, magical - that's how the puppet theatre presents its marvels to the old and young. The repertoire of the mannequins includes Goethe, Shakespeare and Schiller!

Celts in Christian Robes
The altar resembles a megalithic tomb! Christian teachings and nature worship chant united at St Maximilian's. Unbelievers want to be convinced firsthand - during a sermon, of course!

Where the Isar-Mermaids Paddle
Environmentalists naturalised the Isar: spectacularly beautiful gravel banks, flowers, bushes and birds - Munich's urban lifestyle shakes hands with ducks between the Praterinsel and the Flaucher.

Yes, that's it, Olden Knights
Karl Valentin sang about the fortress in Grünwald; today, the Archäologische Staatssammlung presents an exhibition about the castles of Bavaria. And the Bavaria Filmstadt inspires all cinephiles.

◄ An Amazone rides at the Villa Stuck.

- ⑥⑨ Bogenhausen 230
- ⑦⓪ Prinzregententheater 232
- ⑦① Villa Stuck 234
- ⑦② Friedensengel 236
- ⑦③ Praterinsel 238
- ⑦④ St Lukas 240
- ⑦⑤ Maximilianeum 242
- ⑦⑥ Wiener Platz 244
- ⑦⑦ St Johann Baptist 246
- ⑦⑧ Haidhausen 248
- ⑦⑨ Ostbahnhof 250
- ⑧⓪ Gasteig 252
- ⑧① Müllersches Volksbad ... 254
- ⑧② Deutsches Museum 256
- ⑧③ Mariahilfplatz 260
- ⑧④ Nockherberg 262
- ⑧⑤ Gärtnerplatz 264
- ⑧⑥ Gärtnerplatztheater 266
- ⑧⑦ Glockenbachviertel 268
- ⑧⑧ St Maximilian 270
- ⑧⑨ Flaucher 272
- ⑨⓪ Tierpark Hellabrunn 274
- ⑨① Bavaria Filmstadt 276
- ⑨② Burg Grünwald 278

The Friedensengel urges the world to maintain peace. ▶

The *Isar* is a mountain river that has always determined the lives of the Munichers. Numerous villages were founded along the river; Munich has swallowed many of them, but some still enchant their visitors with love and charm.

Bogenhausen

The origin of the district *Bogenhausen* dates back to the 8th century. Here, the *Prinzregententheater* presents world music and modern classical music; the Bayreuther Festspielhaus (Bayreuth Festival Hall) inspired the design. The *Villa Stuck* introduces the life and work of the painter Franz Ritter von Stuck. In vain, the *Friedensengel* (angel of peace) urges the world to peace. On the *Praterinsel*, an Alpine Museum introduces the world of the mountains. The Church of *St Luke* is Munich's most beautiful Protestant church, and the Bavarian State Parliament meets at the *Maximilianeum*.

Haidhausen & Au

Munich's day labourers once lived in the former working-class districts of *Haidhausen* and Au. At the Johanniskirchen and the *Wiener Platz,* Haidhausen still embraces the bourgeois romanticism of bygone times. At the *Ostbahnhof,* a party area was created for night owls. There, the *Volkssternwarte München* (a public observatory) guides its visitors through the wonders of the starry sky.

The *Deutsche Museum* presents technology of the last five millennia.

The cultural centre *Gasteig* is home to the Munich Philharmonic Orchestra. Above the idyllic *Auer Mühlbach*, the Hochstraße leads to the *Nockherberg,* where monks brewed a strong beer during the Middle Ages. Three times a year, Munich celebrates a folk festival at the *Mariahilfplatz* - the Auer Dult.

Gärtnerplatzviertel

At the end of the 19th century, investors designed the *Gärtnerplatzviertel* for members of the Jewish community. At the *Gärtnerplatz*, the *Gärtnerplatztheater* stages operetta and classical ballet. It is Munich's second opera house.

The *Glockenbachviertel* is the epicentre of the rainbow scene. In this neighbourhood, a puppet theatre delights children and all young at heart. The monumental Church of *St Maximilian* testifies how the bourgeoisie increasingly gained influence during the 19th century.

From the Flaucher to Grünwald

Recently, Munich naturalised the Isar. And the result is ...? The emerging coexistence of nature and culture has become a role model for Europe! The success is best spotted at the *Flaucher*. Close by, the *Tierpark Hellabrunn* is one of the most extensive zoological gardens in the world. The fortress *Burg Grünwald* introduces the history of Bavaria's castles. And! The *Bavaria Filmstadt* presents sets and props from past recordings and leads through the company's history.

⑲ Bogenhausen

Facts & Figures

Bogenhausen is a residential neighbourhood that was largely spared from the Allied air raids of World War II. Strolling through the district is a journey through the noble world of the upper class. Here, the Universitäts-Sternwarte München (Astrophysics department of the LMU) explores the cosmos (Scheinerstraße 1). As part of the Münchner Stadtbibliothek (City Library), the Monacensia in the Hildebrandhaus (Maria-Theresia-Straße 23) watches over numerous literary estates; it presents the items in a permanent exhibition. Munich offers swimming pools and sauna at the Prinzregentenbad (Prinzregentenstraße 80) and the Cosima Wellenbad (Cosimastraße 5). At the Cadillac & Veranda (Rosenkavalierplatz 12), cineastes enjoy the retro-world of the 1950s; a red Cadillac awaits visitors in the foyer. The cinema enchants with the world of Marilyn Monroe and James Dean.

Perhaps founding Munich on the eastern high bank of the Isar would have been advantageous, but a settlement already existed: **Bogenhausen**. Documents mention the farmsteads for the first time in 768. They were subordinate to the monastery in Schäftlarn and thus to Freising's bishops, the clergy with whom Herzog Heinrich der Löwe competed for resources. As an example, Heinrich redirected the former salt road, which ran past the village, to the Gasteig.

The first settlement dates back to the Bronze Age. Archaeologists also excavated a Roman estate from the 1st century and the remains of a Bavarian village.

In the 17th and 18th centuries, the nobility moved their summer residences to the high banks of the Isar. The rural character of the suburb was lost, and the area enjoyed a social and economic upswing. August Graf von Törring-Jettenbach built Schloss Neuburghausen, and in 1803, Maximilian Graf von Montgelas acquired Schloss Steppburg. Two years later, he concluded the Bogenhausener Vertrag (a treaty) with France there.

In 1816, the Royal Observatory moved into the area. As part of the LMU, the astronomers reach for the stars.

▲ The University Observatory at the Galileiplatz was founded in 1816.

From 1900 onwards, Friedrich Ludwig von Sckell designed the Herzogpark. In succession, artists, entrepreneurs and scientists discovered the posh area.

In the 1930s, party officials from the NSDAP, including Adolf Hitler and Heinrich Himmler, moved into the upper-class neighbourhood.

After World War II, the Nazis had to go, but their villas and extensive gardens remained. The Prinzregententheater and the parish Church of St George on the Montgelasstraße also survived. The founding walls of the chapel date back to Romanesque times. Its picturesque cemetery is a popular resting place for Munich's luminaries.

Location: Bogenhausen **Entrance:** Without charge **Opening Times:** Always accessible
Monacensia: https://www.muenchner-stadtbibliothek.de/monacensia-im-hildebrandhaus
Universitäts-Sternwarte: https://www.usm.uni-muenchen.de

The Thomas Mann Villa

Thomas Mann, a celebrated writer at the beginning of the 20th century, once lived at Thomas-Mann-Allee 10 near the Herzogpark. He was involved in the editing of the Simplicissimus. In Munich, he wrote the novel *Die Buddenbrooks* and the novella *Der Tod in Venedig* (Death in Venice). In 1929, the Academy in Stockholm awarded him the Nobel Prize for Literature. Thomas Mann actively confronted right-wing extremism. His *Appell an die Vernunft (appeal to reason*, October 1930) in the Beethoven Halle in Berlin called the growing National Socialism a *"primitive, blood-pure, simple in heart and mind, clobbering, blue-eyed, obedient and staunch uprightness."* In 1938, Thomas Mann emigrated to the USA. His German citizenship had been revoked. He died in Zurich in 1955 after he had returned to Europe. His remains are buried in Kilchberg.

Prinzregententheater

Facts & Figures

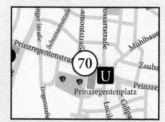

In 1901, Max Littmann constructed Munich's third opera house in sublime classicism and Art Nouveau styles. The architect modelled the theatre after the Bayreuther Festspielhaus, dedicated to the plays of the composer Richard Wagner. A statue depicts the genius at the adjacent green; Heinrich Waderé created it in 1903. The Prinzregententheater survived World War II with only minor damage. From 1944 to 1963, Munich used the stage as a replacement opera house for the destroyed Nationaltheater. Dilapidated, the halls closed in 1964, and the renovation dragged on for thirty years. The audience forms a semicircle around the stage, resulting in an arena; the view and acoustics are exceptional from all vantage points. Last, Julius Mössel designed the atmospheric garden hall, delightfully covered with floral ornamentation.

Munich has a love-hate relationship with the composer Richard Wagner. A statue shows him next to the **Prinzregententheater**. King Ludwig II admired the genius ever since he first met him at the age of 19 in the Münchner Residenz on May 4, 1864. Ludwig was fascinated by the world of Richard Wagner's operas, and he generously financed his work. Could the *Meistersinger*, the *Ring* or *Parsifal* ever have been created without the enthusiastic Wittelsbacher dynasty? Some doubt it.

King Ludwig II planned to build a splendid festival hall for the master on the high banks of the Isar near the Friedensengel. The architect Gottfried Semper had already drawn up the plans, but the ministers refused to finance the romantic-mystical project. *"No second Valhalla!"* was the unanimous opinion. Ludwig II turned away indignantly, and Bayreuth quickly jumped into the breach.

The house was built anyway, but only 40 years later, and it was not on the high banks of the Isar but at the Prinzregentenstraße. Ernst von Possart, general director of the Hoftheater (Royal Court Theatre) since 1893, took up the idea, and Prince Regent Luitpold gave his blessing.

The end of Munich's third opera house came in the 1960s: it had

▲ The Prinzregententheater combines Art Nouveau and classicism.

become dilapidated and had to be closed for safety reasons. Thanks to August Everding, however, the stage was saved. Today, in addition to the theatre, the building also houses the Bayerische Theaterakademie (Bavarian Theatre Academy). Acting, opera, directing, dramaturgy, lighting design and the art of theatre criticism are taught.

The theatre's program is diverse and refreshingly modern. It stages opera, concerts, readings, and contemporary dance, including Tango. The Akademietheater (Academy Theatre) in the Gartensaal (Garden Hall) serves as a stage for the university; it is mainly dedicated to experimental theatre.

Location: Prinzregentenplatz 12 **Entrance:** Depending on the performance
Theaterakademie: https://www.theaterakademie.de
Theatergemeinde München: https://www.theage-muenchen.de

Adolf Hitler's Private Apartment in Munich

Adolf Hitler paraded on 1 October 1929 from his shack in Haidhausen to a 400 square metre apartment at the Prinzregentenstraße, financed by the NSDAP. The right-wing party purchased the building in 1936 and transformed it into an informal headquarters. Stormtroopers guarded the house and secured the entrance. Five years later, the myrmidons constructed an air-raid shelter in the cellar, embellished with oak wood panels. Adolf Hitler resided on the second floor, where he met Mussolini in 1937 and Neville Chamberlain one year later. And the Führer had the interior designed in rustic-country style. A bust of Richard Wagner and a painting depicting Frederick the Great embellished the halls. An oak flooring underpinned the atmosphere, and the novels by Karl May shot Indians dead at Adolf's private library.

Villa Stuck

Facts & Figures

The Villa Stuck, the Lenbachhaus and the Kaulbachvilla are the three artists' mansions in Munich which emerged at the turn of the century. Franz von Stuck, the son of a diligent miller, grew up in an impoverished family, and Prince Regent Luitpold ennobled the successful painter to a knight in 1905. Franz von Stuck designed the representative mansion and the atelier at the Prinzregentenstraße close to the Friedensengel, his home. Today, the urban villa houses a museum, which joyfully presents the painter's Art Nouveau style. His living space hints at the personality of the magnificent artist; his creations cannot be separated from his character. After all, Franz Ritter von Stuck had pointed modernity onto a new path into the future. By the turn of the century, his paintings had catapulted Munich into the centre of European attention.

At the turn of the century, a new kind of artist emerged. He was charming, ingenious, witty, extraverted, and - above all - impression-managing. The **artist's villa** became his architectonic testimony. The esprit of the *new painter* sharply contrasted with the *poor poet* demanded by society. The Biedermeier wanted an artist, who was free of earthly delights, who lived impoverished in a shabby Karl-Spitzweg-Dwelling, who submitted to the elusive muse, and who was out of bread.

Franz Ritter von Stuck, however, despised his unpriviledged upbringing and stage-managed his genius. His art depicted his way of life, and he sprayed his lifestyle across the canvas. His flamboyant character was never distinguished from his work, and the image he portrayed was the most significant part of his artistic creation. The patrons, who purchased his imaginations, also bought a piece of his identity, and thus they partook in a world that otherwise remained sealed to the dabbler.

The atelier of Franz von Stuck was as dark as his paintings. He adored the mythological. His mansion was an incarnation of the symbolic. The artist painted his archetypal works *The Guardian of Paradise*, *The Sin* and *The Kiss of the Sphinx* many times. One version, he kept as a template.

▲ Franz von Stuck designed the classicistic villa where he lived and worked.

Franz von Stuck furnished his home in the style of his paintings, always with an eye on representation. He celebrated his life with style, mastering the presentation of himself.

The painter and his US-American wife idolised the ancient world. They staged their *joie de vivre* not only in paintings but celebrated the Mediterranean. At a masquerade, Franz dressed as a Roman Emperor, and Mary as Venus. For his 50th birthday, his friends staged a torchlight procession, immortalised in a painting.

Franz von Stuck's art and character were indistinguishable; they melted into an amalgam: his life was his work, and his work was his vocation.

Location: Prinzregentenstraße 60 **Entrance:** Adults 9 €, Concession 4,50 €
Opening Times: Tues - Sun 11.00 – 18.00
Internet: https://www.villastuck.de

Bank Robbery with Abduction

On 4 August 1971, Germany's first televised bank robbery targeted the Deutsche Bank on Prinzregentenstraße 70, and it captivated the Munichers. Two hooded men stormed the building shortly before 4 pm. When the police arrived at the scene, the bank robbery turned into an abduction, and for the first time, cameras feasted on the clash of state authority versus villains. Surprisingly, the 5000 curious onlookers sympathised with the purloiners. When one of the two filchers climbed into a getaway car shortly before midnight, booty and hostage secured under his arm and applauded by the masses, a sniper wounded the Bavarian cowboy. Before he crossed the river into the never-never-land, he shot his captive. The police detained the second culprit at the bank branch; a judge sentenced him to twenty-two years in prison.

(72) Friedensengel

Facts & Figures

The magistrate commissioned a peace monument at the Prinzregentenstraße to celebrate the 25th anniversary of the *Treaty of Frankfurt*; the architect Josef Bühlmann implemented the design. Nike flapped her wings on 16 July 1899 when the Greek Goddess of Victory floated onto the column. She wags a branch of the olive tree in her stretched-out left hand, and her right fist gracefully lifts a globe, where a figurine of the Goddess Athena rests. A square-shaped pedestal at the foot of the column shows gilded allegories depicting competition, victory, peace and culture. The cornerstones tell of the twelve Herculean deeds. Portraits of German regents grin in between, and caryatides carry the monument on their heads. A flight of steps leads to water spouting dolphins embellished with four cherubs. A grotto halfway adds some wanted magic to the ensemble.

The stroller along the Prinzregentenstraße from the city centre eastwards will find a lane branching off shortly after the Friedensengel: the **Möhlstraße** where Germany's most significant black market semi-legally traded merchandise under the counter after World War II.

The Möhlstraße crosses the neighbourhood *Bogenhausen*, incorporated into Munich's administration in 1892. Affluent Jews lived at the villas during Germany's rapid industrial expansion. The Nazi regime, however, confiscated their bourgeoise dwellings after Kristallnacht and passed them on to officials and party members while herding the Jews into overcrowded living quarters, the *Judenhäuser*. The Möhlstraße housed two of those shared accommodations. From there, under the watchful eye of the Gestapo, Adolf Hitler's myrmidons transported the captured victims to the concentration camp in Dachau.

The US-American occupation force seized the stately homes after World War II to set up reception camps for refugees. Among the beneficiaries were detainees of the Nazis and former prisoners of the extermination camps.

The allied forces classified those arriving at relief organisation as

▲ Nike, the goddess of victory, thrones on a 23-metres-tall column.

displaced people. They were distressed victims who could not return to their homelands. The status freed them from German jurisdiction, and they enjoyed many privileges. Among other things, they could receive bestowments as a compensation for their endured suffering. This right quickly turned into a blossoming black market.

Wooden stalls sprung up along the Möhlstraße, which offered anything unavailable on coupons. Historians have estimated that the black market at the Möhlstraße turned over one-third of Germany's coffee trade.

Today, consulari settled along the street, as well as a nursery school run by the Jewish community.

Location: Prinzregentenstraße **Entrance:** Without charge **Opening Times:** Always accessible
Internet: https://www.muenchen.de/sehenswuerdigkeiten/orte/120451.html
Friedensengel Sommerfest (July): https://www.stadtmagazin-muenchen24.de

The First Noble Prize for Physics

In 1901, the Department of Physics in Stockholm honoured Wilhelm Conrad Röntgen with the first Noble Prize ever. The committee acknowledged the scientist's discovery of short-wave radiation, which today carries his name - *Röntgenstrahlung*. Medical professionals now studied the workings of the human body without reaching for a scalpel. Röntgen, the son of a cloth manufacturer, was born in Remscheid, graduated in Zurich and moved to Strasbourg, later to Giesen and finally to Würzburg. In the year 1900, he settled in Munich, where he lived at Prinzregentenstraße 61 until 1919. He was a vibrant teacher; many students followed in his footsteps. Finally, the master received the highest scientific honour. Among Munich's laureates are Max Planck, Albert Einstein, Werner Heisenberg, Wolfgang Pauli and Klaus von Klitzing.

(73) Maximilianeum

Facts & Figures

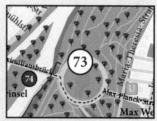

At the Isar's eastern slope, the Maximilianeum unfolds its wings leisurely to mark the vanishing point of the Maximilianstraße. The inspiring architect Friedrich Bürklein erected the building in 1874, creating the Maximilianstil. Since 1949, the Landtag of Bavaria sits at the terracotta complex in session. Initially, an elite association opened the way for students from all walks of life to success. Its stipendiary enabled the impoverished to study carefree at Munich's universities. The athenaeum attracts attention by its vibrant mosaics at the eastern facade; the side galleries disembogue into impressive towers; the middle part bends to the front, and pin-like statues embellish the eave. On the western side, the Berlin architectural group Léon Wohlhage Wernik built an extension cube in 2009 where the delegates pencil their directives.

Sheep pastured at the banks of the Isar until the 19th century. Once the city had embanked the rapid torrents in 1806, which were threatening to erode the elevation, King Maximilian II transformed the mound into a parkland and called it **Maximiliansanlagen**.

In 1856, Maximilian II commissioned landscape gardener Carl von Effner to design the thirty-hectare riverbank from the Ludwigsbrücke to the Friedensengel in the fashion of the time. After completion, he opened the enchanting marshlands to the Munichers as a nearby recreation area. Carl von Effner designed the terraces, pathways and meadows, adding bushes and flower beds to the old trees. To conclude, he scattered monuments and statues across the landscape. Wilhelm Zimmermann crowned the banks with canals and barrages as a finishing touch.

In the 20th century, the park expanded north- and southwards, tenderly transforming the rugged hills to a green pelt: the fertile lands now stretched along the floodplains from the Englischer Garten to the Flaucher.

In the second half of the 19th century, King Ludwig II planned a Richard-Wagner-Festival-Theatre between the Maximilianeum and the Gasteig, but the magistrate rejected financing the project. Empty coffers

▲ The Bavarian government sits at the Maximilianeum in session.

and discord with the composer axed the opera house. Only a statue of King Ludwig II reminds of his aspirations.

Where the romantic Auer Mühlbach enters the Isar below the Maximiliansbrücke, a delightful building hides, hardly visible. And the little castle asks: *"Who am I?"* No beauty queen of bygone times or a femme fatale rests her head within the sensually trundling walls, but Bavaria's first run-of-the-river power station brings electricity to the neighbourhood. Engineers fitted the plant with a wreathing turboprop in 1953, and since 1895, the power station supplies the energy for 250 households, shouldering its part to preserve the world's climate.

Location: Max-Planck-Straße 1 **Opening Times:** Not accessible
Stiftung Maximilianeum: https://www.stiftung-maximilianeum.com
Bayerischer Landtag: https://www.bayern.landtag.de

The Stiftung Maximilianeum (Foundation Maximilianeum)

King Maximilian II longed to live not as a King but as a professor of history. To no one's surprise, the learned initiated a graduate scholarship program in 1852. Still today, the foundation supports high-flying students who passed their exams at a Bavarian grammar school. Annually, the bursary blazes the trail for six to eight collegians. The selection follows strict criteria: only those who achieved the highest mark in their exams and were recommended by their school's principal may apply. The aspirants must demonstrate proficiency in general education and show social competence and a sense of responsibility. Based on written and oral exams, a commission decides over the admissions. The Maximilianeum's grant supports about 50 young adults in their endeavours to further the nation's well-being.

Praterinsel

Facts & Figures

The enchanted Praterinsel, 3.6 hectares slim, weathers the waves of the gelid Isar in fraternity with the adjacent Museumsinsel. The pebbled banks carry the Alpine Museum on the 500-by-100 metres wide elevation. The Stadtwerke München generate energy for the neighbourhood at the Praterwerk and Maximilianswerk. Floating footbridges join the timid island with the banks of the torrential river. A 170-metre-long footpath, the Regulierungswehr, leads to the Museumsinsel. It divides the rapids into the *Small Isar* to the east and the *Large Isar* to the west. The Auer Mühlbach flows into the river at the eastern banks - romantically wild, yet urban modern. Once, the factory Riemerschmid extracted vinegar and liqueur here, and since its relocation in 1988, a dance hall of the *Aktionsforum Praterinsel* seduces the youth to frolicking and dancing.

A river is a city's lifeline and its doom. The whirls quench the thirst, drive mills and machines and cleanse the streets from waste and filth. On the other hand, floods threaten the livelihood, and swamp formation jeopardises health. The **Praterinsel** demonstrates this ambivalence perfectly.

The Isar is a mountain river: pristine, untouched and a pleasurable recreation area. Her name derives from the Indo-European family of languages signifying *flowing water* - a sober name, straightforward and without frills. Nevertheless, during the thawing period in spring, its rhythm changes. Raging floods burst the banks, undermine the soil, and drown the wildlife.

Ever since its founding, Munich has been desperate to tame the Isar's passionate outbreaks. Finally, the burgess embanked the river during the 19th century, forcing the water into canals; the trembling whirls roll through the city in a concrete bed, moving straight but fast.

Since its embankment, the river has dug five metres into its pebbles and eroded the foundations of the escarpment. Ingenious engineers tamed the annual fluctuations by constructing the Sylvensteinspeicher in

▲ The Alpine Museum introduces the magic of the mountains at the Praterinsel.

the 1950s - a levee at the upper course of the Isar.

Since 2010, admirable nature conservationists naturalise the Isar and Alpine wildlife has returned. At the Praterinsel, the conflict between the need for protection and the desire for nature is evident. The canals regulate the flow of the river, yet the city maintains the sandbanks.

The raging river inspires as the island's history testifies. Until the dissolution of the monasteries, the Franciscans tilled the earth on the Praterinsel. Later, an amusement park invited the Munichers to party; then, heavy industry pounded at the weir, and now, the speakers of a nightclub roar.

Location: Praterinsel **Entrance**: Without charge **Opening Times**: Always accessible
Alpine Museum: https://www.alpenverein.de/Kultur/Museum
Aktionsforum Praterinsel: https://www.praterinsel.de/home.html

The Alpine Museum

Munich is a yodel distance from the mountains, and thus, nature worshippers feel morally obliged to run a museum that introduces the Alpine realms to urban dwellers. In 1911, the *German-Austrian Alpine Club* opened the magical worlds of the mountains at the Praterinsel, at the tavern *Café & Restaurant Isarlust*. After World War II, the Alpine Museum reopened in 1996, presenting a historical overview of the conquest of the Alps from the 18th century to now. Photos, topographic maps and idyllic paintings illustrate the precarious balance of the ecological system. The curators accentuate the craggy mountain equipment of the first adventurers; two hundred watercolour paintings describe the Tibet-Expedition of the brothers Schlagintweit, which the mountaineers organised in 1854.

St Lukas

Facts & Figures

The neo-Romanesque Church of St Lukas, constructed by Albert Schmidt in 1896, is Munich's largest Protestant church. The 63-metre-tall octagonal dome and the two flanking towers are visible from afar. Four freestanding columns carry the weight of the roof. Above the central portal, Peter and Paul welcome believers. The relief at the tympanum depicts *Jesus Christ, Lord of the World*. The layout of the interior follows a Greek cross in the style of the Rhenish early Gothic. The high altar depicts the *Descent from the Cross*, a painting by Gustav Goldberg. Laterally, under canopies, Peter and Paul calmly radiate a sense of tranquillity. Hermann Kaspar welded the richly decorated glass windows. The turret to the south is remarkable for its delicate style. The Church of St Lukas survived World War II without damage; it was one of the few buildings in Munich that was not devastated.

After the Thirty Years' War, the Bavarians continued to pray with a Catholic tongue. For more than 150 years, no **Protestant** dared to immigrate in fear of life. Then, for political reasons and not out of love, King Maximilian I married Princess Caroline of Baden, and she was - God forbid - a Protestant. Now, a flock of Lutherans marched under her wedding gown to Munich's princely court in 1797.

When Bavaria became a kingdom in 1806 and expanded its territory, Protestant Franconia and the free cities Nürnberg, Rothenburg ob der Tauber and Weißenburg were among the annexed areas.

The nobility was hung by the thread of Napoleon, and the Zeitgeist had to concede, willingly or by force. Maximilian Graf von Montgelas, Bavaria's first minister, swung the pen and solemnly passed a new Constitution in 1808: the freedom of religion was to become a fundamental right. Until then, an underground Protestant congregation had prayed covertly, but their numbers grew. Grudgingly, the Catholics condoned the evil faith and permitted the Protestants to erect a church.

The Bavarian government approved the financial resources for a prayer house on 6 September 1825, and eight years later, the Church

▲ Monumental domes complete the neo-Romanesque facade of St Lukas.

of St Matthäus shepherded its sheep to the west of the Sendlinger Tor.

St Markus to the east of the Wittelsbacher Platz followed in 1876. When St Lukas stood tall twenty years later, the third Protestant temple blossomed. With the construction of St Johannes in Haidhausen in 1916, all four Evangelists had humbly found a home in Munich.

Today, about 12% of all Munichers share the Protestant faith. The opening of the Evangelische Akademie in Tutzing in 1947, the Protestants' academic training facility at the Starnberger See, brought a level of freedom to the Lutherans never experienced before.

Location: Thierschstraße 28 **Entrance**: Without charge **Opening Times**: daily 10.00 - 17.00
Internet: https://www.sanktlukas.de // https://www.ev-akademie-tutzing.de
See also: https://www.bayern-evangelisch.de

Caroline of Baden, Queen of Bavaria

Princess Caroline of Baden, Queen of Bavaria, the second wife of King Maximilian I, passed away in 1841. She was a Protestant. Upon her arrival in Munich in 1797, her carriage brought the damn teachings of Martin Luther to the Isar yet again. Caroline insisted on exercising her faith, and pastor Ludwig Schmidt cared for the small congregation. The parson was Munich's first Protestant priest since the Thirty Years' War. The death of Queen Caroline revealed her travail: on orders of the Catholic archbishop Lothar von Gebsattel, the clerics dressed casually for her funeral. The Protestants carried the coffin to the entrance of the Theatinerkirche, where they whispered their prayers outdoors. Once they had finished, the Catholics silently dragged the corpse to the crypt, and the funeral procession dispersed. What a scandal!

Wiener Platz

Facts & Figures

Where Munich once welcomed travellers from Vienna along the arterial road, the Wiener Platz has offered a market with stalls since 1889. *Haidhausen's Belly* supplies residents with fresh sausages, meat, milk, cheese, fruit, and vegetables daily. On the corner of Innere Wiener Straße, the Hofbräukeller awaits the hungry with traditional dishes; it is one of the few remaining authentic beer cellars in the neighbourhood. In the centre of the Wiener Platz, the Fischerbuberl sprays water at a fountain. Ignatius Taschner created the statue in 1910. From 1882 onwards, a horse-drawn tram galloped along the Innere Wiener Straße - formerly the dividing line to the Burgfrieden, the inner keep. In 1889, the horses were replaced with an electric one. Several townhouses survived on the Krempe, where the day labourers once eked out a living, cramped, impoverished and without hope.

Warm beer ferments to vinegar. Regulations permitted brewers to create their beer only during the winter months. An innkeeper who kept the barley juice cooled into spring - an art by itself - provided the Munichers with the liquid manna for longer, and thus he reaped good profits.

Breweries at the foothill of the Alps kept their barrels in glacier caves and shipped them on rafts to Munich. In the regional capital, the brewers chopped the ice of the frozen Isar during the winter and stacked the slabs in halls and cellars, like here, at the *Wiener Platz*. The effort rewarded the entrepreneurs with the Bavarian Gold, the sympathy of the people and a profitable income.

Towards the end of the 18th century, Munich utilised the eastern **slopes of the Isar**; they were ideal for storing the intoxicating elixir to consume later in the year. In 1775, the Hofbräu at the Hochstraße was the first to establish a subterranean cellar. The word of their success quickly made the rounds. Within a short time, miners drove galleries into the rocky high banks, turning Haidhausen into a pimpled landscape.

Beer gardens and taverns added tables to the cellars, which blue-collar workers frequented. The drunken atmosphere ignited cracker-barrel-politics, stimulated by dark lager. Haidhausen had dug into the mud, literally and symbolically a hidden underground-cellar-town.

After World War I, the regulars' tables turned into political parties, seeking reception by the people. Adolf Hitler was one among many who wandered across Haidhausen like a ghost, infecting the mood, croaking speeches and selling his party program to drunkards.

It was merely a matter of time until the different splinter groups united under one right-wing extremist flag. Strengthened by numbers and with golden yeast in their veins, their slogans drove the world into disaster.

▲ Munich's most traditional market is trading at the Wiener Platz.

Location: Wiener Platz **Entrance:** Without charge **Opening Times:** Always accessible **Internet:** https://www.muenchen.de/sehenswuerdigkeiten/orte/120348.html
Café Wiener Platz: http://www.cafewienerplatz.de

The Volunteer Corps Lützow

After World War I, the ghost of chaos reeled Munich's streets and played with the fuse of explosives; rioting right-wing and left-wing extremists clashed in street fights. One of those self-important militant groups was the Volunteer Corps Lützow, which pitched its headquarters at the Hofbräukeller close to the Wiener Platz. From here, the hooligans fanned out for punitive action against innocent civilians. On 5 May 1919, the right-wing extremists shot twelve citizens from Perlach, a Munich suburb. Why? Because the parish priest had denounced them as communists. The bloodbath was not an isolated case. Historians believe that the *White Guards* executed more than 600 Munichers in total. Adolf Hitler was a child of this time, certainly a debaucher, but also a consequence of the turmoil.

77 St Johann Baptist

Facts & Figures

Haidhausen is proudly the home of two churches dedicated to Saint John the Evangelist. The one is Catholic, the other Protestant. The architect Matthias Berger designed the lean neo-Gothic parish Church of St Johannis at the Johannisplatz in 1874, the so-called *Dome of Haidhausen*.

The 97-metre-tall red brick tower, inspired by the Maximilianstil, catches the eye from afar. Joseph Knabel designed the marble altar in 1860; the artist Johann Baptist Schmidt created the painting of the Last Supper, and August Pacher soldered the glass windows in 1918. The renowned organist Max Reger played the church-pipes from 1901 to 1907. Around the corner of the Gasteig, the Protestant Church of St Johannis added to the diversity of the neighbourhood at the tranquil Preysingplatz. The architect Albert Schmidt constructed the church in neo-Romanesque style.

A chapel was established on the hills of Haidhausen during the Middle Ages. A document mentioned the prayer house for the first time in 1315, a part of the parish Bogenhausen. The *Alte Haidhauser Kirche* at Kirchenstraße 37, surrounded by a graveyard, is most likely her successor. Kurfürst Maximilian I donated a **St John relic** in 1619, and the Bavarians went on a pilgrimage to the cross, which became a popular spiritual foothold. From now on, the neighbourhood was married to the biblical evangelist Saint John.

The eastern elevation of the Isar was a military deployment area for hostile troops. It was the ideal stronghold to lay siege on Munich and fire at the lederhosen from above. What the foreign forces had not plundered, they burnt at withdrew. The Haidhauser may have survived the assault while hiding inside the city wall, but returning to their homes, they found their meagre belongings scorched. It happened during an invasion of the Austrians; it happened during the incursion of the French. During the Thirty Years' War, the Swede King Gustav II Adolf erected his camp at the hills in 1632, and he returned in 1647. When the foe failed to take the city, he avenged his defeat by pillaging Haidhausen, ravaging the village.

▲ The burghers lovingly call St Johannis the *Dome of Haidhausen*.

Austrian troops visited Munich several times, too, not on a sightseeing tour but with rifles in position, and they devastated the suburb: once under Oberstleutnant Menzel in 1741 and again in 1744, when the troops returned. During the Napoleonic Wars, Haidhausen went up in flames several times.

The *Goddess of Fate* always smiled harshly on Haidhausen; its people lived defenceless, too penurious to be protected by the keep; they supplied Munich with brick stones for the fortifications and, in times of political unrest, attacking armies plundered and burnt their dwellings. Haidhausen was the victim who footed the bill.

Location: Haidhausen **Entrance:** Without charge **Opening Times:** during the day
St Johann Baptist (cath.): https://www.pfarrverband-haidhausen.de (Johannisplatz)
St Johannes München (ev.): https://www.stjohannes.de (Preysingstraße 17)

Haidhausen's Brickyards

Munich lacks natural stone as a construction material. When Emperor Ludwig der Bayer decreed that all houses were to be built in stone, the Munichers diligently investigated any suitable rock and found the solution in the loamy soil to the east of Munich. Brickyards emerged in Haidhausen, and the city utilised the bricks for its fortifications, the Frauenkirche and the townhouses. The workers slaved away twelve hours a day, even children. Their daily life was of simple pleasures and hardship: digging out the mud, forming it into cuboids, burning the wobbly mass in shaft furnaces, eating, sleeping crammed between twenty other humpbacks at the factory's attic - and repeat. During the 18th century, it was Italian migrant workers who dirtied their hands in the name of Munich.

(78) Haidhausen

Facts & Figures
The densely populated Haidhausen stretches from the Gasteig to the Ostbahnhof. It was Munich's slum outside the keep, suburbanised in 1854 when investors designed the area anew at the turn of the century. Parisian streets and the style of rapid industrial expansion  stood as models. Common parlance knows the district as the *Franzosenviertel* (Frenchmen's quarter). Multistorey townhouses populate the neighbourhood from the Weißenburger Platz to the Pariser Platz. Roundabouts disperse streets in a star-like formation. The lovingly looked after Haidhausen-Museum witnesses this transformation from old to new. Open-air theatres, summer festivals and a Christmas fair enliven the piazzas. And at the Ostbahnhof, the Volkssternwarte München, Munich's amateur observatory, squints with glazed stove pipes at the foggy night sky.

Adolf Hitler forged big plans for **Haidhausen**. He demanded housing estates with standardised furnishing along the Rosenheimer Straße. The Nazi regime drafted a blueprint for twenty thousand residential units; the sameness of the design entombed individualism.

Like the railroad bed to the west, the Rosenheimer Straße was to turn into a goose-stepping route. Parades were to carry the torch of fascism along monumental boulevards to the centre. The regime planned to conclude the eastern end of the Rosenheimer Straße with a building dedicated to the Hitler Youth. Towards the west, the fascists designed yet another monumental structure: the Gau Munich - Upper Bavaria headquarters. The Führer demanded six tenement cities around Munich; his vision was to be rolled out over Germany, squeezing the people into a grid of uniformity - each citizen a number without hope to escape. The Nazi leaders sought to sacrifice individuality on the altar of ideology. Unity creates strength in numbers, but unity lacks flexibility. The downfall is apocalyptic when a crisis hits the system.

Haidhausen defended its charm, and the historically grown neighbourhood survived the onslaught. The vast piazzas remained, and the

▲ The chapel St Nikolai at the Gasteig was home to Munich's leprosarium.

townhouses too. Some harborages successfully hid from land jobbers. Today, the dwellings turned into luxury apartments.

When the Ostbahnhof was connected to the train network in 1871, medium-sized enterprises moved into the district. After a wave of industrialisation, factory workers migrated to Haidhausen; within a few decades, they transformed the neighbourhood into a vibrant community.

Munich's housing shortage after World War II lasted until the 1970s. Then, new satellite towns mushroomed in the outskirts, and some critics mock that real estate speculators had turned Adolf Hitler's inhuman vision of tenement cities into reality.

Location: Haidhausen **Entrance:** Without charge **Opening Times:** Always accessible
Internet: https://www.muenchen.de/stadtteile/haidhausen.html
Kultureinrichtung Lothringer 13: https://www.lothringer13.com

The Battle of Haidhausen

On 24 February 1530, Pope Clemens VII crowned the Hapsburg Karl V as Emperor; the brunt of the crown weighed heavily on his shoulders. The Reformation threatened to pull his empire apart, separating his lands into two irreconcilable camps. The Emperor hoped for appeasement, his eyes in tears about the consequences of a fracture. On his route to Augsburg, he passed Munich, where Kurfürst Wilhelm IV warmly welcomed him. At the elevation in Haidhausen, the burgess had timbered a wooden castle, and the militia demonstrated its combat readiness by simulating an attack: 1500 soldiers and 650 horsemen participated in the spectacle; eight volunteers died during the exercise. At last, the Emperor realised how voraciously the *Goddess of Harmony* was chased by the impending religious dispute.

Ostbahnhof

Facts & Figures

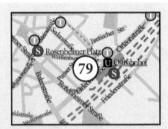

The workers connected the Ostbahnhof to the tracks of Bavaria's railway network in 1871. The hub linked Munich with Rosenheim and Simbach. The architect Friedrich Bürklein designed the reception hall, but World War II destroyed the building. A new hub was constructed in the 1950s. Next to it is the Rangierbahnhof München Ost (a marshalling yard). Travellers to Italy can load their cars here. The area around the Ostbahnhof is a party zone for young people. The night fever was set up along the Friedensstraße at the former Pfanni-Werke. The organisers offer young adults entertainment, concerts and gastronomy. On weekends, the Umadum Ferris Wheel allows a view of Munich from above. Just around the corner, the Volkssternwarte München guides through the mesmerising world of the universe with an 80 cm reflecting telescope.

Every child in Germany knows the products of a brand that went down in post-war history as **Pfanni**: potato puree, potato dumplings, mini potatoes, potato snacks, gnocchi, and fried potatoes. The company built its success on a plant that came to Europe from the Andes via the Canary Islands in the 16th century: the potato. It originally grew from Venezuela to Argentina.

The first potato dumplings came onto the market in the 1950s. Werner Eckart had founded the company the previous year. The production facilities were located along the Friedensstraße near Munich's Ostbahnhof. The local farmers carted the potatoes with tractors to the production lines and unloaded the tubers at the main entrance.

The factory determined the prices. After unification, Munich's farmers complained about market pressure. Their competitors in Eastern Germany produced more cost-effectively, and in 1996, the company moved to Mecklenburg-Western Pomerania. "What now?" asked the magistrate. The city meditated for a long while; meanwhile the factory transformed into a party area. The Kunstpark Ost was born, later the Kultfabrik, then the Werksviertel Mitte.

▲ The Ferris Wheel Umadum turns at the Ostbahnhof.

In Plant 3, the company produced dumplings and packaged the finished products. Today, Valais blacknose sheep graze on the roof.

At the Container Collective, 39 discarded shipping containers provide a home for bars, pubs and artisans - next, the NachtKantine booms with live music and comedy. The Technikum, formerly the development laboratory where new products were researched, was turned into an event location, too.

However, the pride of the company retained a bit of its post-war history. The Kartoffelmuseum (Potato Museum) at Grafinger Straße 2 deals with ephemeral art made from potatoes - interesting.

Location: Orleansplatz 11 **Entrance:** Without charge **Opening Times:** Always accessible
Werksviertel Mitte: https://werksviertel-mitte.de **Umadum:** https://umadum.info
Volkssternwarte München: https://sternwarte-muenchen.de

The Volkssternwarte München (Munich Public Observatory)

How far is it to the end of the world? When did the universe explode? Why does the moon show phases? How did our sun form? Are there other suns? Is there life on other planets? What was before the beginning? The Bayerische Volkssternwarte (Bavarian Public Observatory) at Rosenheimer Straße 145H answers these and other questions. With their 80 cm reflecting telescope, the astro enthusiasts show distant galaxies, galactic nebulae and the remains of stellar explosions. A planetarium explains the starry sky, and seminars introduce the latest results of astrophysics. The non-profit organisation has almost 600 members. The Astro Youth is trained to build telescopes, spend the night under the sky, count shooting stars and organise parties. "We are stardust! Let's dance through the night. Who counts the thalers?"

Gasteig

Facts & Figures

Munich's cultural epicentre, the Gasteig, celebrated its opening with a gala concert conducted by Sergiu Celibidache on 10 November 1995. After a lengthy building phase, the red brick building finally opened to the public. The Stadtbibliothek (Municipal Library) and the Richard Strauss Conservatory moved in, and Munich's Adult Education Centre offers training courses. Several concert halls chirp with classical music: in the philharmonic hall, more than 2000 visitors enjoy the performances of the Munich Philharmonic Orchestra, and at the Karl Orff Saal, an audience of 550 perks up their ears. The Black Box presents world music, discussion forums and other presentations. The Gasteig organises the annual Münchner Bücherschau, the ARD Music Contest and the Filmfest München. (Currently, the Gasteig is closed for refurbishment; its performances are staged at HP8.)

The steep climb - known in Bavarian slang as *garcher Steig*, or **Gasteig** for short - has a rich history. During the Thirty Years' War, Haidhausen had a pivotal role because from here, guns could rain down with ease onto Munich, striking the city from above. Thus, the strongly fortified hilltop at the eastern banks of the Isar was under the protection of the keep.

During the Middle Ages, the salt street from Bad Reichenhall passed the Gasteig. Here, merchants arriving from the Alps first glanced at Munich, the favourite spot of artists to paint the cityscape.

The eastern slopes of the Isar always suffered from social tension. The city's keep ranged to the hill ridge, today the Innere Wiener Straße. The soil was too loamy and stony to till the earth, and thus the harborages turned into a slum. Only the impoverished settled in Haidhausen who could not afford the right to become a freeman: maidservants, day labourers, workers, prostitutes and the destitute.

During epidemics, the grim reaper sharpened his scythe in Haidhausen. Life in the neighbourhood was oppressing and onerous. On average, a married woman gave birth to 12 children; about one-third perished while still gasping for their first breath. The flowers only blossomed after speculators had insightfully refurbished the district. The mass residences converted to apartment blocks, and beer halls added a homely atmosphere.

Beer halls? Ah yes, the drunken beer halls! During the Weimar Period, the nationalistic ideology fermented at those beer halls into an extreme right-wing brew! In 1923, Adolf Hitler fired his first shot of the Hitler Putsch at the Bürgerbräukeller.

Sixteen years later, the carpenter Georg Elser sought to blow up the Führer at the same spot where the movement had started. The assassination attempt failed, he was detained, and World War II murdered millions.

▲ Haidhausen's Gasteig is Munich's cultural epicentre, currently closed.

Location: Rosenheimer Straße 5 **Entrance:** Closed for refurbishment. HP8 hosts the events.
Internet: https://www.gasteig.de **Münchner Volkshochschule:** https://www.mvhs.de
Münchner Philharmoniker: https://www.mphil.de

The Assassination Attempt at the Bürgerbräukeller

Georg Elser was not the only one who saw; many sensed that the radicalisation of the Nazi regime would lead to war. When Adolf Hitler seized power, the cabinetmaker was afraid too, but his fear inspired him to act: *the terror must end before it can break forth*. Night after night, he locked himself into the Bürgerbräukeller, a beer hall at the Gasteig, and he painstakingly hollowed out a supporting pillar. On 3 November 1939, the resistance fighter deposited a self-made bomb. Three days later, he added the time fuse. Shortly after, the Führer grated a speech at the beer hall, the air trembling with his squeaking voice. At 9:15 pm, the detonator went off, but Adolf Hitler survived. For no reason, he had left the beer hall early, a quarter-hour before the bomb exploded. Georg Elser was not the only one who saw, but he was the only one who acted.

81 Müllersches Volksbad

Facts & Figures

The engineer Karl von Müller commissioned the Art Nouveau building that houses the Müllersche Volksbad, a bathhouse with a steam room and sauna. In 1901, the architect Carl Hocheder completed Munich's public pool, the only one in the city centre. He decorated the complex with vivid frescoes and stuccoes. Wall paintings, gargoyles and bronze statues accentuate the style of the turn of the century. At its water tower, the Münchner Arbeitsgemeinschaft für Psychiatrie supports trauma victims. Until 1989, the bath strictly segregated the genders. The men splashed around in the larger swimming pool, measuring 31 by 12 metres; in the smaller one, extending over 18 by 11 metres, the women swung their arms rhythmically. The Auer Mühlbach once provided the water, which the neighbouring Muffatwerk heated. In 1999, the Jugendstil jewel was modernised, and the latest technology was installed.

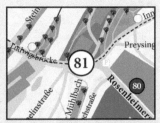

At the turn of the century, only a minority could afford the luxury of fresh water; Haidhausen even lacked public fountains. The workers and day labourers, the court officials and travelling artisans went to public bathhouses to find refreshment from the mud. Typically, they dived into the tubs once a week. The Middle Ages knew of water's benefits on health, and Munich provided several bathhouses; many had funny names, like Eselsbad (bathhouse of the donkeys) or Herzogbad (the Duke's bathhouse).

The head of the household would lead the family and servants to the bath, and a custodian safeguarded the clothing and watched the hearth. During the Middle Ages, the barber also worked as a surgeon and healer. He oversaw small invasions, and performed bloodlettings. The Munichers knew and trusted him.

By the dawn of the 20th century, life had changed little for Munich's day labourers, maids, and workers, who lived hand to mouth. The forgotten dwelled in Haidhausen, in simple harborages, crammed into collective accommodations where the sanitation was dire.

At last, the engineer Karl von Müller felt moved by the suffering and turned from entrepreneur to social reformer. He compassionately designed

▲ The Müllersche Volksbad is the world's most beautiful art nouveau bathhouse.

a bathhouse at the Isar for Haidhausen's impoverished.

The **Müllersche Volksbad** became Europe's most splendid bathhouse: bronze water faucets decorated in Art Nouveau, a Roman steam bath, 86 bathtubs and 22 shower baths, marble fountains in the shape of cascades, two swimming pools, a sauna - Karl von Müller made sure that the complex fell short of nothing. He even installed a tub for dogs. The engineer took the water from the Auer Mühlbach and the steam from the Muffatwerk.

A dream come true, the day labourers rejoiced, but on the opening day, they quickly realised none could afford the splendour.

Location: Rosenheimer Straße 1 **Entrance:** Adults 5 €, Concession 3.50 €
Opening Times: Mon - Sun 7.30 - 23.00
Internet: https://www.swm.de/baeder/schwimmen-sauna/muellersches-volksbad

The Day the Ludwigsbrücke Collapsed

It was the *13 September 1813*, and it was *high tide;* the citizens stood along the Ludwigsbrücke to marvel at the Isar's rapids. The waters from the Alps voraciously pushed against the river banks - what a spectacle - what power - nature! Then a trembling - horror struck - the bridge wavered. A pier lost its grip - the piling collapsed, washed out by the gushing waters. A second pillar flushed away - a third. Within minutes, eight hundred curious onlookers fell into the Isar, and the raging waters devoured the helpless. Nearly 100 burghers died on that day. Until the construction of the Sylvensteinspeicher in the 1950s, which today regulates the seasonal waves, floods often devastated Munich's crossings over the Isar, like in 1899, when both the Luitpoldbrücke and the Max-Joseph-Brücke collapsed.

(82) Deutsches Museum

Facts & Figures

During the 19th century, Munich embanked the former coal island, once Europe's largest raft port. Today, the Museum for Technology founded by the engineer Oskar von Miller in 1925, introduces the splendour of the natural sciences. The curators present across 5000 square metres well-designed dioramas and historical instruments, steaming engines and rattling machines. Interactive models invite to experiment at the push of a button, to investigate and wonder about our world. By following the 16-kilometre-long leading line, young and old may explore maritime navigation, airship aviation, the mining industry, manufacturing, and the boundless vastness of the cosmos. A library stores more than 750,000 volumes and 4300 magazines. Historians delight in notes scribbled by scientists, in sketches and hand-written records. Currently, the museum is undergoing refurbishment, and some sections are closed.

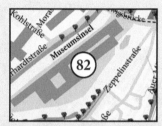

Once, Europe's largest raft port was at the **Museumsinsel.** Here, traders unloaded their precious merchandise from Italy during the Middle Ages, which they embarked on at the foothills of the Alps - the last leg of an arduous journey. The city repurposed the tree trunks of the floats as building material or smoulded them into wood charcoal for their kilns. The Frauenkirche's roof, for instance, had demanded more than 1500 tree trunks in the 15th century.

Until the 19th century, more than 12,000 floats landed at the Museumsinsel annually. The island was strategically significant. During the reign of Kurfürst Max Emanuel, the infantry maintained barracks, which Kurfürst Max III Joseph rebuilt after a devastating fire in 1762. The military base defended the city not only against a foreign foe but also guarded Munich's nobility against the ragtag of the slums in Haidhausen, preventing a revolt. Day labourers and migrant workers were too poor to obtain the liberty of the city, so they settled on the eastern side of the Isar outside the city wall. The bourgeoisie dreaded the proletariat: they could swim across the Isar, dagger in mouth, and stab Munich's patriarchal order!

Finally, the soldiers faded out at the turn of the 19th century. Dams

▲ The tower of the Deutsche Museum, 55 metres tall, offers a panoramic view.

turned the island into a Parisian *Île de la Cité*, a valuable building land close to the city centre.

At that time, the engineer Oskar von Miller inspired Munich to the sciences, and the magistrate agreed to the construction of a technology museum. Even the Prussian Emperor Wilhelm II participated in the festivities that laid the founding stone. The stately building, constructed in a functional style, was finished in 1925.

About 1 ½ million enthusiasts visit the island annually, seeking inspiration at the world's largest temple of technology, where the curators make the machines arc and snarl, the flying wheels fume and pong, the transmission lines rumble and hiss. ➡

Location: Museumsinsel 1 **Entrance:** Adults 14 €, Concession 4,50 €
Opening Times: daily 9.00 - 17.00 **Internet:** https://www.deutsches-museum.de
Sudetendeutsches Museum: https://www.sudetendeutsches-museum.de

The Planetenweg - a Road to the Planets

A walk along the Isar's eastern banks from the Deutsche Museum southwards mirrors the solar system to a scale of one to 1.29 million: one footstep roughly corresponds to one million kilometres. The first step is taken at the sun, a golden sphere in the centre of the inner courtyard. The first planet waves at a distance of 45 metres: Mercury. He dangles at a column sheltered by the passage to the patio. 39 metres further, Venus awaits the space traveller under a streetlamp - of course. Planet Earth follows at a distance of 32 metres at the corner of Zeppelinstraße. Mars makes his rounds at the banks of the Isar, a further 61 metres to the south. Jupiter shows its splendour at the Corneliusbrücke. Finally, at a distance of 4 ½ kilometres, Pluto welcomes the adventurer close to the entrance of the Tierpark Hellabrunn.

Highlights of the Deutsche Museum

The Deutsche Museum illuminates the wonders of natural science and technology in 28 thematic areas on 25,000 square metres. The curators discuss everything from the intricate technology of mining to extract raw materials to the evolution of mobility, communication technology, and the vastness of space and time. *Where do we come from? How does the world that surrounds us function? Where are we headed?*

A 500-metre-long path leads through a replica of a tunnel, where the curators explain the *history of mining*. Life-size dioramas show shaft construction, salt production, coal mining and the processing of raw materials.

The *shipping department* presents the still dangerous conquest of the seas. A simulator allows one to experience the journey through the port of Hamburg from the wheelhouse of a ship - even the ground trembles. The history of shipbuilding is linked to the development of international trade.

The *aviation department* dreams of flying. Balloons, Otto Lilienthal's flying machine and historical biplanes awaken the longing to disappear into the sky like birds. A flight simulator gives the impression of being a pilot.

The *high current department* explains the history of electricity generation, its distribution and use. The high-voltage demonstrations are exciting: the electrical discharges crack and hiss and shine brightly in red and blue.

In the *physics department*, experiments invite to become a scientist. Stations explain the laws of pulleys, the conservation of angular momentum, the physics of waves, thermodynamics and magnetism. Galileo Galilei's workroom points to the beginnings of the scientific revolution.

The extensive *Astronomy* Section introduces the discovery of the cosmos and space travel. The museum presents instruments used by astrophysicists, explains the ageing of stars and provides an overview of our current understanding of the origin of the cosmos. The planetarium uses a Zeiss Skymaster ZKP4 to show the constellations seen from Munich. Modern technology allows to travel to the limit of the observable universe. At the observatories, visitors can take a look through telescopes.

▲ The Deutsche Museum introduces the history of the sciences.

The *Pharmacy department* shows how people are embedded in the environment. The curators present the development of pharmacy, explain how blood circulates and take a journey into the microcosm of life. The focus is on biochemical processes in cells.

A replica of the *Altamira Cave* shows reconstructions of the paintings that people immortalized on cave walls some 15,000 years ago in the Upper Paleolithic. One can spot bison, horses, deer and shamans.

In the section *People and Environment*, the museum discusses the interaction between people and nature: How do we change our planet? What is the impact of global population growth? Why do we pollute our environment? Where are we heading as a planet?

The Sudetendeutsche Museum

Just around the corner from the Deutsche Museum at Hochstraße 10, a museum opened in 2020 that highlights the culture of the Germans in the former Czechoslovakia (now the Czech Republic). On five floors, the curators present the 1,100-year history of the ethnic group in Bohemia, Moravia and Silesia, ranging from immigration to expulsion. The museum discusses the agriculture, mining and religion of the Sudeten Germans. Insights into the period of National Socialism and the expulsion after World War II illuminate the recent history. Databases make it possible to track individual places; they allow interested to get in contact with the past. Temporary exhibitions highlight specific topics.

(**Location**: Hochstraße 10, **Opening Times**: Tue - Sun 10.00 - 18.00, **Entry** € 5)

(83) Mariahilfplatz

Facts & Figures

The parish Church of Mariahilf, commissioned by King Ludwig I, puts on the frills as the first of Bavaria's neo-Gothic buildings; the inventive design caused a stir when it was finished. The architect Joseph Daniel Ohlmüller constructed the church in 1839. The 90-metre-tall tower mirrors the Dome of Freising; the facade also reminds of French cathedrals. In 1944, an Allied air raid destroyed the church. After World War II, the clerics redesigned the interior and merged the three naves of the prayer house into one. They covered the nave with a concrete ceiling accentuated by a slightly elevated sanctuary. The southern extension is home to a *Shrine to Our Lady*, presenting a figurine of the Virgin Mary. Kurfürst Maximilian I donated the image in 1600. At the front yard, the Auer Dult delights young and old several times a year - a market with a carousel.

The *Auer Dult* is as irresistibly Munich as the charming neighbourhood. At the spacious piazza, Kurfürst Wilhelm IV blew the horn at Schloss Neudeck, a hunting lodge. In 1660, the Paulaner purchased the property to brew beer. Today, the office building houses the district administration. In this neighbourhood, the Auer Mühlbach passes old townhouses and the humorist Karl Valentin was born and raised. Three times a year, the burghers of this former slum stage a market that could not be more quaint: the *Auer Dult*.

In 1796, Kurfürst Karl Theodor granted the Auer people the right to organise a market at the Isar in spring and autumn as a financial compensation for the annual flood damages during the thawing period.

In the 20th century, the magistrate relocated the *Jacobidult* from the Am Anger to the **Mariahilfplatz**. Ever since, the Auer organise a *Dult* around the Parish Church of Mariahilf three times a year, respectively for nine days. The townspeople frolic at the *Maidult* in May. The *Jacobidult* dances into the summer in July, and the *Herbstdult* spreads joy the week before the parish fair.

A *Bavarian Dult* is a traditional funfair. In the past, simple people

▲ The first church at the Mariahilfplatz dates from 1466.

acquired unusual items at a Dult, merchandise which local traders did not offer. By and by, the aspect of the market was sidelined, and the folk festival gained in importance.

Today's Auer Dult rocks with busy cosiness. Amusement rides enchant children while their older brothers thrust speedsters as a preparation for life. Merchants present corroded antiques; mountebanks offer saucepans, rummage, wooden decoration and household items. As night falls, the dirndl twist and the lederhosen dance the Schuhplattler. And above all! Bavarian recipes water the mouth: candyfloss, roasted almonds, fried sausages, grilled chickens and pork knuckles.

Location: Mariahilfplatz **Entrance:** Without charge **Opening Times:** during the day
Internet: https://www.erzbistum-muenchen.de
Auer Dult: https://www.facebook.com/auerdult // https://www.auerdult.de

The Chapel of the Cross in the Au

The Isar lost its power as a torrential mountain river after the construction of the Sylvensteinspeicher. Until then, the waters used to press against the banks during spring's thawing period. In 1463, the flooding destroyed many farms and dwellings along the Isar, and the desperate Auer cajoled the Blessed Mother with prayers for help. They had hardly launched their solemn vows when a crucifix paddled along the Isar, rocked a little, hither, then thither, and finally settled gleefully on a sandbank. The faithful burghers immediately pledged to build a chapel at this spot - and - what a miracle - the waters receded quickly. Holy waters! Waters of grace! Since 1466, the *Chapel of the Cross* has offered hope to all believers. And in the 19th century, the splendid Church of Mariahilf replaced the prayer house.

(84) Nockherberg

Facts & Figures

Off the Rosenheimer Straße, the Hochstraße runs through the neighbourhood Au. Below the foothills, the meandering Auer Mühlbach brings freshness to the district. The Isar regularly flooded the region during the Middle Ages. When the city embanked the river, the neighbourhood became an idyllic suburb, covered by an alluvial forest, a residential area for families with young children. The picturesque elevation stretches as far as Giesing to the south and embraces the Maximiliansanlagen to the North. Taverns conduct the rhythm of the quarter. The *Wirtshaus in der Au* and the *Paulaner am Nockherberg* are popular amongst the locals. The *Starkbierfest* bawls out a drinking spree for 17 days in March. During Munich's 5th season, cabaret artists lampoon their parliamentarians and politicians of all colours; the poor statesmen are obliged to smile at even the cheapest jokes.

The **Au** is a tranquil neighbourhood where everyone knows everyone and where rumours spread quickly. Regular drinking companions on a pub crawl had to consent to the innkeeper's jokes. Humour digests misfortunes publicly without losing the community's support as long as everyone laughs heartily.

If an innkeeper was rhetorically talented, people flocked to his tavern. Those who failed to master the art of jesting engaged musicians and singers to enliven festivities - the birth of Munich's 5th season: the annual *Strong beer festival* in March, heralded by the tapping of the delectable Salvator barrel. It is at this time that comedians would satirise the wealthy, powerful, and politicians of all shades.

The Order of Paulaner inherited the license to brew strong beer in 1634 when the commoner Lerchl took the vows. The bulbous friars concocted, suckled, donated and sold the liquid bread to the Munichers, adding entertainment. According to legend, the pope authorised the strong beer as nourishment during Lent after a barrel, carted by the pious monks across the Alps for trial, arrived in Rome spoiled - it was jolted to vinegar during the rocky way.

▲ A personification of the Au splutters at the Nockherberg.

In the 18th century, the monk Barnabas honed the recipe, creating a dark beer with a hint of sweetness. The Munichers called the formula Saint-Father's Beer - in short, *Salvator*.

The innkeeper Franz Xaver Zacherl bought the license of the strong beer after the dissolution of the monasteries. The clever entrepreneur quickly organised an annual fair to celebrate the tapping of the Salvator. By 1858, musicians and singers performed at the festival, and in 1891, the first public lampooning inaugurated Munich's tradition of satire and political cabaret - jolly are the laughs that swish across the crowd dressed in lederhosen and dirndl.

Location: Au **Entrance:** Without charge **Opening Times:** Always accessible
Strong beer festival: https://paulaner-nockherberg.com/starkbierfest
See also: https://www.brauchwiki.de/nockherberg

The Battle of Salvator in the Au

Whenever Munich's beer prices rise, a social uprising is the consequence - so it happened on 23 March 1888. A difference of opinion between a regular drinking companion and a gendarme sufficed to ignite the most violent punch-up Munich had ever experienced: the police drew their truncheons, the drunkards threw their beer mugs; the vigilantes swung their sabres, the boozers their fists. The gendarmerie was helpless because the news of the scrap spread like wildfire across town, and Munich was ready for it. The more units the police mobilised, the more paunches came running. The annals report of about 4000 lederhosen who drubbed the *Battle of Salvator* into the Bavarian history books. Only mounted police ended the fighting after a bloody night and only in the early morning hours.

Gärtnerplatz

Facts & Figures

In 1806, Bavaria became a kingdom, and immigrants from the new regions sought their home in Munich. During the late 19th century, the city expanded towards the open fields in the southwest, a district known as Isarvorstadt, sandwiched between the old town and the river. There, the Jewish merchant Baron von Eichthal designed a neighbourhood for the affluent bourgeoisie. In the heart of the Gärtnerplatz, the centre of the development area, a fountain throws calming water, and flower beds invite for a rest. Like the rays of the sun, alleyways run towards the cardinal points. An opera house, founded as a stock company, adds charm to the quarter. The Staatsschauspiel am Gärtnerplatz stages operetta and musicals. After World War II, the Gärtnerplatzviertel turned into an artist's demesne. Bohemian Munich feels at home here.

The architects designed the **Gärtnerplatzviertel** at the drawing table, just like the Maxvorstadt. At its centre rests the Gärnterplatz, spreading its tentacles like an octopus, clamping one arm to the Isar and suspending itself at the Viktualienmarkt with another leg.

At the turn of the century, many well-to-do Jewish citizens settled at the housing development, and thus, Kristallnacht furrowed deep wounds into the neighbourhood.

The vicinity of the *Staatstheater am Gärtnerplatz* enticed writers and actors to live at the demolished houses after World War II. When the suburb gradually mutated from a bourgeoisie neighbourhood to the epicentre of bohemian Munich, it discovered the rainbow. During the 1980s, the Isar-chaps crested not the Alps to pick the gentian but stepped onto the winners' rostrum of the gay liberation movement. Only the *Hotel Deutsche Eiche*, Germany's first homo-hotel, survived the cleansing, though - a relic of bygone times. The renowned film director Rainer Werner Fassbinder lived opposite the hotel during the 1970s. He had fallen head over heels in love with a steward and languished - love is love.

Freddie Mercury, the lead vocalist of the rock band *Queen*, staged

▲ The Gärtnerplatz is named after the architect Friedrich von Gärtner.

his 39th birthday at the Reichenbachstraße. According to the BBC, it was the most outrageous party of the century.

Munich's *homosexual community* was a thorn in the flesh of conservative Bavarians, and they pestered the magistrate until strict regulations forced the nighthawks out. Those still glued to Munich's bittersweet honey relocated to the Glockenbachviertel.

At last, art galleries and boutiques slurped to the piazza to rub shoulders with the state theatre. The visionary architect Franz Michael Reiffenstuel had constructed the opera house in 1865. Munich's second most significant stage presents light opera, musicals and dance theatre.

Location: Gärtnerplatz **Entrance:** Without charge **Opening Times:** Always accessible
Münchner Schwulenzentrum (gay centre): https://www.subonline.org
Hotel Deutsche Eiche: https://www.deutsche-eiche.de

Freddie Mercury Conquered Munich

In the 1980s, Munich gloated over its vibrant gay liberation movement - just like Amsterdam, New York and San Francisco. Then, the magistrate cut the rainbow into pieces. Freddie Mercury was a regular at the *Hotel Deutsche Eiche*. He felt so much at home in Munich that he staged his 39th birthday party at the club *Mr Henderson* in 1985. According to BBC commentators, it was the largest celebration of the century - *The Mother of All Parties* - and all the stars of showbiz came running. The sojourners dressed in latex and leather, wore make-up from top to toe, or proudly showed off their chest hair. The birthday boy splashed champagne and caviar, and the camera ran down film spools. The video clip *Living on my Own* shows the sumptuous hustle - and to marvel at the spectacle - well, one must.

86 Gärtnerplatztheater

Facts & Figures

The pioneering architect Franz Michael Reiffenstuel built Munich's beautiful, 2nd most prominent opera house in the style of the Italian Neo-Renaissance. King Ludwig II inaugurated it in 1865. The directors mainly present operettas, dance theatre and musicals. The design of the Gärtnerplatztheater resembles a folk theatre with a courtly character. The auditorium mirrors the Nationaltheater but on a smaller scale. The last Allied air raid on Munich (April 21, 1945) also hit the theatre and destroyed it. On that day, the Temple of Music went up in flames. The stage reopened in 1948 with the operetta *Eine Nacht in Venedig* (One Night in Venice) by Johann Strauss. The Gärtnerplatztheater is the cultural centre of the neighbourhoods Ludwigsvorstadt-Isarvorstadt, including the district Glockenbachviertel, where the Gärtnerplatzviertel is located.

Munich is a city steeped in classical music. The audience is experienced and well-educated. The list of composers and singers who have lived in Munich or given guest performances at the Isar is long; they have left an indelible mark on the city's musical landscape. Notable figures such as Hans Knappertsbusch, Wolfgang Sawallisch and Sir Peter Jonas have served as artistic directors at the Nationaltheater.

When Herzog Albrecht V invited Orlando di Lasso to his humanist court in 1556, he laid the foundation for 450 years of music history in Munich. The Belgian maestro, who lived and composed at the Isar for almost 42 years, is widely regarded as the greatest composer of the Renaissance. At the Alps, he developed his famous vocal polyphony; he is still celebrated for his motets and madrigals.

The composer Agostino Steffani, who has recently experienced a revival, served as Munich's court music director for several years during the late 17th century. At the Isar, he devoted himself to opera.

Wolfgang Amadeus Mozart also stayed in Munich - but only briefly. Here, he composed the opera Idomeneo for Carnival 1781, which premiered at the Cuvilliés Theater.

▲ The Gärtnerplatztheater stages mostly operettas and musicals.

King Ludwig II, who opened the Gärtnerplatztheater in 1865, admired Richard Wagner. The premieres of the operas *Tristan and Isolde, Die Meistersinger, Das Rheingold* and *Die Walküre* were staged in Munich.

The composer Richard Strauss was a son of the city. He was born in Munich in 1864. His mother was a daughter of the Pschorr beer brewing dynasty. In 1886, Richard Strauss was appointed the third conductor of the Munich Court Opera. He later moved to Weimar, Berlin and Wien. In Munich, he found his unique style with the symphonic poems *Don Juan* and *Tod und Verklärung* (Death and Transfiguration). His last opera, *Capriccio*, premiered at the Nationaltheater in 1942.

Location: Gärtnerplatz 3 **Entrance:** Depending on performance
Internet: https://www.gaertnerplatztheater.de See also facebook
Tickets: https://www.theage-muenchen.de

When the souls rise at the Alter Südfriedhof

When the living envied the dead in the plague year 1563, the Munichers unearthed another cemetery outside the city walls, so enormous was the suffering. In 1788, Kurfürst Karl Theodor sealed all graves inside the city wall and moved the remains to the Südfriedhof. Since Friedrich von Gärtner had expanded the complex into a *Campo Santo* in 1840, the immediate residents have used the wild ivy lung as a local recreation area. Here, one finds time to relax, strolling by the graves. However, on All Saints Day, the clouds darken. Then the souls haunt and rattle between the crosses for one night. Anyone who glimpses over the fence at the stroke of midnight will see the shadows of all those the year will take. And the bones of those buried far from home will return for one night on All Saints Day to clatter in Bavarian style.

⑧⑦ Glockenbachviertel

Facts & Figures

The Glockenbachviertel derives its name from the blacksmith who cast Munich's church bells. When a horrific epidemic decimated the Munichers in 1563, the grave diggers stacked the penniless in mass graves at the Südfriedhof (Old Southern Cemetery). In the 19th century, God's Acre was converted into a resting place for the rich, where the influential performed their eternal dance macabre with maggots and worms. Today, the graveyard enjoys the atmosphere of a Gothic park. The rainbow throws its colours along the Hans-Sachs-Straße, especially on Christopher Street Day at the end of July, when the crackers explode into a shower of exuberant confetti. A lovingly restored Marionettentheater (puppetry) welcomes all young-at-heart at the Blumenstraße, and the Feuerwehrmuseum (fire-brigade museum) squirts with traditional rubber hoses at the main sentry, just like in the olden days.

Conservatives fear the image of execution, death and prostitution. Still, the cocktail of black ghosts wraps the **Glockenbachviertel** between the Südfriedhof and the Blumenstraße into a blanket of humility, celebrating the Puritans' repressed phantasies.

Where today the main sentry of Munich's fire brigade rescues black cats from shaggy trees, the hangman's maidens once quenched the thirst of bachelors. Around 1436, a brothel with twelve rooms beautified the executioner's dosshouse. An ivy-covered wall enclosed the bordello, fencing in a garden and two parlours, a medieval Disneyland for temporary love. Here, the unmarried found relief, hidden from the watchful eyes of the clerics.

When Herzog Wilhelm V spearheaded the Counter Reformation, the devout Catholics locked the house of pleasure and donated it to the gravedigger. The duke prohibited the game of cards and the throwing of the dice, he stigmatised the *dolly daughters* to witches and brewed beer at the Hofbräuhaus to level the loss of taxes from his horizontal enterprise. Later, a hospice moved in, and in 1902, the fire brigade took over.

Fifteen brothels spread across the Glockenbachviertel at the turn of

▲ The Marionettentheater delights young and old with the play of puppets.

the century, and the poorest maidens offered their services in private quarters. Later, high-class prostitutes sat in ambush at the dance bar *Kolosseum* to angle a sapless, well-to-do older gentleman for a long-term liaison of mutual benefit.

Recently, the rainbow carried its treasure box to the Glockenbachviertel to enmesh the district in its charm and fasten a pink ribbon at its forehead.

However, taverns, bars and the best Tango Milonga in town have attracted too many Munichers by now. Gourmet restaurants already dilute the 500-year-old wickedness of the neighbourhood. And the marginalised wonder if the time has come to move quarters again.

Location: Glockenbachviertel **Entrance:** Without charge **Opening Times:** Always accessible
Marionettentheater: https://www.muema-theater.de
Feuerwehrmuseum: https://www.muenchen.de/sehenswuerdigkeiten/orte/119232.html

The Ochsengarten - the first leather bar in Germany

Penal Code § 175 - it was the year 1872. Sexual acts between males are prohibited - any act is punished. Homosexuality is fornication, unnatural, a perversion, pathological - thus the authorities - what verdict! Around 140,000 men were sentenced - up to ten years in prison for aggravated cases - imagine! The Ochsengarten (Ox-Garden, Müllerstraße 47) was a restaurant with a beer garden. The innkeeper sold roast oxen, hence the name. After World War II, the bar became a prominent meeting place in the red-light district. In 1966 came the contract for the Olympic Games - the magistrate restricted the area - the end of the rainbow. 1969 - the bar is waiting in the starting blocks. Decriminalisation of same-sex love - a deep sigh! And the Ochsengarten? It reopened as a leather bar - the first in Germany. Freddie Mercury was a regular: Killer Queen!

St Maximilian

Facts & Figures
The architect Heinrich von Schmidt designed the neo-Romanesque Church of St Maximilian at the Wittelsbacherstraße in 1901 - the *Notre Dame at the Isar*. Allied air raids demolished the building, but in 1949, the Munichers rebuilt the colossus of the Glockenbachviertel. The mighty twin towers at the southwestern side, visible from afar, overlook riverbanks and avenue trees. The three-aisled basilica awaits with an incredible abundance of space. At the stony main altar, designed by the artist B. Schmitt and resembling a Celtic megalithic tomb, Saint Maximilian heals the bleeding hearts of pagans. Bavarian missionaries encircle him. At the sidewalls, David fights Goliath, and Saint Christopher carries the cross of the world, both works of J. Bergmann. The artist also created the Last Judgement at the nave. (Currently, access is limited because of refurbishment.)

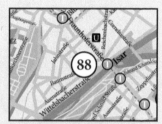

Contradictions bring the neo-Romanesque Church of **St Maximilian** to life. The architect Heinrich von Schmidt reintroduced the Romanesque to Munich. The barely adorned stone-ashlar beguiles the mind to knights' games and the chanting of troubadours. The church is wanting, however, the rough burliness of its medieval predecessors.

The orientation of the church surprises: St Maximilian follows the flow of the Isar from south to north; it is not casting its eternal flame towards the East. The temple enchants like a bulwark, a castle to the Lord, visible from afar - a slap in the face of the Biedermeier who sought to remain inconspicuous.

St Maximilian symbolises the contradictions of the times. During the late 19th century, society simmered in history's saucepan, an ongoing process. The bourgeoisie glanced from behind its shadow, pointed the finger at the monarchy, spurred on democracy and gave capitalism the bridle, but when the stallion tottered, stabbed to death by the blades of the Weimar Period, it fell on the detonator that ignited fascism.

St Maximilian was a counterweight to the Ludwigskirche in the Maxvorstadt, commissioned by King Ludwig I. The giant at the Isar

▲ The Church of St Maximilian follows the flow of the Isar from south to north.

wanted to pay homage to King Maximilian I, but instead, the architects established a monument to the aspiring middle class. The burghers romanticised medieval values such as courtship and heroic feats - in search of a damsel in distress that beguilingly required saving.

St Maximilian's main altar equally astonishes: no Virgin Mary with child, no crucified admonishes the believer, but a group of sturdy statues gather around a Celtic cross - a sublime image! The council of the wise embraces those Saints who planted the Catholic faith into Bavaria's thorny soil - after AD 700, during the Irish-Anglo-Saxon phase of conversion to Christianity.

Location: Deutingerstraße 4 **Entrance:** Without charge
Opening Times: Limited access due to refurbishment
Internet: https://www.st-maximilian.de

Bavarians are Pious People

Bavaria required three attempts to convert the lands to Christianity: First! Roman soldiers smuggled a Bible into Noricum, the province to the north of the Alps, but the Bavarians were illiterate, and words alone never appealed. Instead, the pagans burnt Saint Afra in 304, and they drowned Saint Florian, the patron of firemen, in the Ems. The second shot fared only slightly better: Franconian overlords dispatched Irish missionaries - the Kilian, the Kolonat and the three Bavarian apostles Rupert, Korbinian and Emmeran - and yes, they survived, but hardly anyone remembers them. Finally, success! The Anglo-Saxons rolled in their might! They sent Saint Boniface in 738, a papal legate. He founded the bishoprics Regensburg, Freising and Passau. Now, the cross had arrived, rammed upright into Bavaria's rocky soil, to stay and to suffer.

Flaucher

Facts & Figures

The Isar upstream to the South of Munich crosses an area called Flaucher. The innkeeper Johann Flaucher administered a tavern at this location in 1871, thus naming the meadows. During the first half of the 19th century, the magistrate embanked the waters with dams to regulate the raging billows.  The first tree nursery operated at the Flaucher in 1845, and in 1875, the first women's only bathhouse opened, today a children's playground. Since the turn of the millennia, countryside campaigners gradually liberated the Isar from its concrete corset; prickly bushes, grasslands, alluvial forests, birds and snakes returned, and ever since, naturalists defended their habitat against the planning hand of the government. On weekends, however, the spiders and salamanders lose the battle when sizzling grill stations and daring nudists flood the gravel banks.

Munich exists only because of the Isar. The 283-kilometre-long mountain river sources its water in the Karwendel and flows into the Danube at Deggendorf. Its rapids at Munich stretch over 14 kilometres. The waters enter the city in Grünwald, float along the **Flaucher**, and leave the town at the meadows of Garching.

The river is omnipresent in Munich. Already the Celts conquered the torrents and used the stream as a crucial trading route. During the late Medieval period, the Alpine people constructed the first crossing. Until then, they passed the flow at fords. In addition, watermills powered machines.

Mountain minerals colour the Isar green. Along its way, the water washes seeds from the Alpine foreland ashore, determining the character of the river banks: poplars, ashes, maple and birches splendidly thrive along the meadows. After sewage treatment, again plants enjoy the purity of the jingling waters - and our feathered friends returned, too - singing and quacking: ducks, water ouzels, kingfishers, loons and Canada geese; the Isar has turned into a mecca for wildlife and bird lovers.

The stream alternates its bed regularly; the gravel banks rock from one side to the other, altering the course of the meandering arms, branching

▲ Nudists enjoy the beach along the Auer Mühlbach at the Marienklausenbrücke.

out, interweaving and dancing. At the Flaucher, the Isar's green belt transforms into a local recreation area. The river is an inspiring example of how nature and culture may flourish aside - in practice and not on paper. Rumours have it that even Isar-mermaids and goblins have returned, whispering and groaning under bushes at night (*Attention! Hazardous! Do not disturb!*)

It may seem impossible, but several sources have independently confirmed it: around midnight, the snore-manikin from the Bavarian Uplands rings out, sleeping off a drinking spree. The troll is good-natured, but only when chanting, laughter, and clapping do not rouse him.

Location: Flaucher **Entrance:** Without charge **Opening Times:** Always accessible
Isar-Floß-Event: https://www.isar-floss-event.de
Beergarden Flaucher: https://www.zumflaucher.de

Sliding Along the River

The raftsmen fire the starting gun at the picturesque village of Wolfratshausen early in the morning. The excited screamers slide across the Isar on tree trunks, targeting the Flaucher in Hellabrunn, just like the beer barrels once washed to Munich from the Alps. At the Mühltaler-Isarwehr, a weir, the raft tumbles down eighteen metres. After passing Schäftlarn Abbey and Grünwald Tower, the journey ends at the raft canal in Thalkirchen, where Bavaria's canoeists train for the Olympic Games. Along the 25-kilometre-long route, more than 50,000 adventurers dash annually, braving the waves and avoiding going overboard. The strong, who can keep their stomach, may nourish their belly with golden manna and sausages. A traditional band thunders with a tuba, and a thunderbox promises relief. The idea is to experience the Isar like in bygone times, vivid and wild.

(90) Tierpark Hellabrunn

Facts & Figures

The Hellenpron estate was once owned by the geometer Franz Anton von Paur, where he tilled the soil until 1754. Today, it is an animal lodge. Next door, the Harlachinger Mill harvested the power of the Isar at the Auer Mühlbach. In 1911, the Munichers constructed their first zoological garden, and the many beasts of our planet, wild or domesticated, booked into the heathen landscape, straw and breakfast included. By 1914, Emanuel von Seidl had constructed an elephant house in Byzantine style. During World War II, the animal park was closed to the public but again opened its gates shortly after Germany's surrender. Since the 1970s, donations have modernised the animal lodge by and by. The Zoo created an arctic landscape in 1975, an aviary in 1980, a monkey house in 1983, a jungle hall in 1995, and a polar bear slide in 2010. An enchanting savannah is the latest addition.

Munich's **Hellabrunn Zoo** rightly claims to manage one of the best-equipped zoological gardens in the world. Species-appropriate animal keeping under authentic conditions and thoughtful nursing is the doctrine of the institution, which is hailed by staff and visitors alike.

The animal park reports astounding results in the rescue of endangered animals and the back breeding of species. Thanks to the keepers' dedication, the aurochs and the wild horse stomp again over grasslands.

The 40-hectares state-of-the-art geo-zoo, one of the largest in the world, presents its *four-legged hotel guests* separated by continent. About 1.3 Million nature enthusiasts and animal lovers visit the hairy quadrupeds annually. And the guided moon adventures pluck the stars from the sky: at night, judicious keepers skilfully lead a small group of visitors across the compound to introduce with night-vision devices the breathtaking activity of the owls among the animals.

Hellabrunn tirelessly presents new enclosures: the 2800-square-metre-large Polar World, for example, introduces Munich to the freezing world of polar bears, penguins, seals and sea lions. The 5000-square-metre-large aviary, designed by the architect Frei Paul Otto, is home to black storks.

▲ Ibexes welcome the visitors at the entrance to Munich's zoological garden.

Bourgeois gorillas bustle at the enchanting jungle house and chimpanzees amuse beside coral fish and Mississippi alligators. Lions roar, leopards hiss and flying foxes bark at their enclosure. Even parrots and iguanas have found their home in the corral.

At the big bat grotto, the ghosts of the night whoosh through the aether. A 10,000-square-metre savannah is a home to African reticulated giraffes, porcupines and meerkats.

Last but not least, horned rhinoceroses whistle at the rhino house and bearded pigs trot across the artificial steppe; in the world of the aquariums, sea horses splash about, hiding from sharks.

Location: Tierparkstraße 30 **Entrance:** Adults 15 €, Concession 4,50 €, Families 19 €
Opening Times: daily 9.00 - 18.00
Internet: https://www.hellabrunn.de

The feedings at Tierpark Hellabrunn

Like our domestic cats, the Siberian tigers sleep all day, but at noon, they wake up from their dreams and lick their teeth: they are being fed! Knowledgeable keepers explain their species and describe their everyday life at the Zoo. The Asian elephants receive their ration at 14.15. The children are particularly enthusiastic about the training of sea lions. Domestic animals can be petted in the Hellabrunn-Arena; among the child-friendly are goats, ponies, alpacas and llamas. Close by, a grandstand awaits guests for a demonstration of the birds of prey. The princes of the skies are truly breathtaking. *How do they hunt? Why don't they fly away?* The well-trained keepers know all the answers to these and all other questions. The feeding of the anaconda snakes and the crocodiles is also impressive.

(91) Bavaria Filmstadt

Facts & Figures

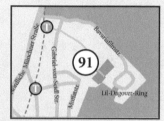

Around 350,000 curious film enthusiasts pilgrimage to the Bavaria Filmstadt in Geiselgasteig every year. The Bavaria Film GmbH found its home on this vast site outside Munich. The studios made such pioneering films as *Die unendliche Geschichte* (The Neverending Story) after the book by Michael Ende, *Krabat* by Otfried Preußler and most recently *Die Zauberflöte* (The Magic Flute) directed by Florian Sigl. The 14-part series *Berlin Alexanderplatz* (Rainer Werner Fassbinder) was also recorded here. The Bavaria Filmstadt invites cineastes to take a 90-minute tour across the studios. Original backdrops include the submarine U96 from the film *Das Boot* (The Boat). A 4D adventure cinema shows enchanting animated clips enlivened with surprising mechanical effects. An interesting exhibition presents the company's 100-year history.

On December 28, 1895, the Lumière brothers showed ten short films to a paying audience at the Grand Café in Paris - it was the day film as a medium was born. In Munich, the curtain opened ten years later when Peter Ostermayr launched his travelling cinema Original-Physograph Company in 1907; he recorded short documentaries and presented them to the public. The Bavaria Film GmbH emerged from his Münchner Lichtspielkunst AG (founded in 1919 shortly after World War I).

After World War II, the company produced numerous film and television classics in their studios. Until the fall of the Berlin Wall, Geiselgasteig was the largest film studio in West Germany. Episodes of the crime series *Derrick*, *Tatort* and *Der Fahnder* were recorded here. The Schimanski thriller *Zabou* was also filmed in Grünwald.

Like the medium, so is the Bavaria Filmstadt: It is dynamic and changes its program year by year. Stuntmen and stuntwomen showed their skills until 2010. The Bullyverse introduced the world of 3D effects, and on *Storm of Love* Fan Day, visitors marvelled at the backdrop of the series and shook hands with the actors.

Munich is a stronghold of the film industry. The Hochschule für

▲ The Bavaria Filmstadt shows numerous sets from past films.

Fernsehen und Film München (University of Television & Film) on Gabelsbergerstraße (Maxvorstadt) offers training courses for 400 students.

The Filmmuseum München (Munich Film Museum), located next to the Stadtmuseum, collects, archives, and restores historical productions, from silent films to New German Films and shows them to the public.

The Filmfest München (Munich Film Festival) invites cinephiles to a festival at the end of June, focusing on feature films, documentaries and short films.

The Filmtheater at the Sendlinger Tor is traditionally the home of Munich's film premieres.

Location: Bavariafilmplatz 7, 82031 Geiselgasteig bei Grünwald
Entrance: Adults 20 €, Concession 18 € **Opening Times:** see Internet
Internet: https://www.filmstadt.de

Orion space patrol

The top-rated series had ratings of up to 56%. The streets were empty when the first science fiction television series flickered on the screen; everybody was glued to their TV. The Bavaria Film GmbH production was shot in black and white and still enjoys cult status. The episodes were called *Attack from Space*, *The Battle for the Sun* and *Invasion: Humanity Colonises Space*. The spaceship Orion whizzes across the Milky Way at unimaginable speed. It protects the Earth from threats by aliens from outer space. The evil characters were called Frogs, their control centre was on a planetoid in the Vesta group, and the heroes were attacked by robots called Alpha Ce Fe. It was the 1960s and 1970s - German-French co-production - many scenes were reminiscent of the Cold War - the climax of the East-West conflict.

92 Burg Grünwald

Facts & Figures

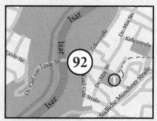

At the hills near Grünwald, a castle has towered over the Isar since the 12th century; the Wittelsbacher dynasty once maintained a hunting lodge there. Today, a branch museum of the Archäologische Staatssammlung presents the exhibition *Burgen in Bayern* (Castles in Bavaria). The curators explain the history of the fortresses in southern Germany. The focus is on Burg Grünwald, but the museum also presents other complexes along the Isar and Bavaria: knight's castles, escape castles and princely castles. Participatory stations introduce the Middle Ages. The castle also produces honey throughout spring and summer; the sweet delight can be purchased in the museum shop. Scenic Burg Grünwald is located in an upscale neighbourhood. The posh district, home to entrepreneurs, actors and footballers, is a popular destination for bikers and hikers.

Already during the Bronze Age, Grünwald was inhabited. Vases, urns and weapons from that period displayed at the Burg Grünwald give a testimonial of the first people in the region. Excavations in Grünwald also unearthed a Roman settlement with workshops and a guard station. In the Middle Ages, the lands were handed over to the Wittelsbacher dynasty as a Hofmark, a region with independent jurisdiction. In 1288, documents mention a village in Grünwald for the first time.

There is evidence of a well-fortified castle in Grünwald as early as the 12th century. It was subordinate to the Grafen von Andechs, and in 1270, it passed to the Wittelsbacher dynasty. Herzog Albrecht IV expanded the castle around 1486. Ever since, the complex served the Bavarian regents as a hunting lodge. A fresco in the Antiquarium of the Münchner Residenz, commissioned by Herzog Wilhelm V in 1590, depicts the adventurous pleasure place.

In February 1522, Herzog Wilhelm IV and Herzog Ludwig X convened at the Grünwalder Konferenz with the criticism of Martin Luther. The talks were held at Burg Grünwald. On Ash Wednesday, the regents proclaimed the ban on his teachings: "*Anyone following his ideas is punished.*" Munich took

▲ An exhibition in the former hunting lodge introduces the castles of Bavaria.

the first step of the Counter Reformation early, but it was not until Herzog Albrecht V invited the Jesuits to Munich in 1559 that the ban had any effect.

The castle fell into disrepair under Kurfürst Max Emanuel; his focus was on Schloss Nymphenburg and Schloss Schleißheim. At that time, the former hunting lodge served as a prison and an armoury. In the 18th century, the Isar eroded the hill so much that parts of the castle had to be demolished.

In 1879, the hunting lodge became a private property, and in 1977, the Bavarian state took over the complex, refurbished it and housed a well-informed branch museum of the Archäologische Staatssammlung in its rooms.

Location: Zeillerstraße 3 **Entrance:** Adults 4 €, Concession 1 €, Sundays 3 €
Opening Times: Wed – Sun 10.00 – 17.00
Internet: http://www.archaeologie-bayern.de/de/zweigmuseen/gruenwald

The Mermaid of Grünwald

A knight lilted the bagpipe at Herzog Albrecht IV's wedding. Amongst the eavesdroppers was a mademoiselle from the Grünwald Castle, craning her neck and pushing her bodice into sight. She was beautiful - without a doubt - her hooking nose and her eyes ignited fiery passions. Soon, the two met again at the Isar by chance, where the musician confessed his love, falling on his knees. "*I only accept a man who is willing to die for me.*" The woman lisped and threw her jewellery into the rapids of the river. The youth, blinded by love, jumped into the surge - neither he nor the gilded chain was ever seen again. Three days later, the damsel disappeared, and ever since, the billows of the Isar are haunted. The chanting of the Isar-Mermaid tempts, and many a raftsman drowned in the floods of the imprecated currents.

Greater Munich

Insiders Know ...

Floating around in Lady Bavaria's Head
Who wants to investigate the mind of Bavaria's ageless beauty? One may climb her cast-iron statue and view the world from the perspective of her eyes. What an idea!

Roaring with Bavaria's Stags
Bavaria's stags yodel in their native tongue, and in the past, they even romped around the beer tables; today, an open-air enclosure fences them in. Our four-legged friends can be experienced at the Hirschgarten.

About Beauties and Bathhouses
Schloss Nymphenburg offers the bizarre. Here, Lola Montez smiles and shows her bosom. And Munich's first warm-water paddling pool awaits at the garden palace Badenburg.

Munich's Hunting Lodge
Schloss Blutenburg presents Bavaria's lively history, built in the Gothic style, imprecated. Agnes Bernauer, the barber's daughter, bewitched the Duke, and panel paintings by the artist Jan Polak eternalise the castle.

Magnificent Baroque
During the Age of Absolutism, Bavaria envisioned an empire. A regent requires a castle, and thus Bavaria's sovereigns commissioned Schloss Schleißheim, a palace in Baroque style, Munich's Versailles.

Catholicism Unadulterated
Ora & Labora and a stein - one enjoys living under the wings of Freising's crosier - because of the brewery in Weihenstephan, which pours out liquid gold. The spectacular dome is worth a visit, too.

Climbing onto the Roof of Munich
The two-hour guided tour around the Olympic Stadium's pavilion roof ends with an abseil. The visit offers a sporty perspective of the Olympic Stadium - for the adventurous only.

The Most Beautiful Timber Ceiling North of the Alps
The world knows Dachau because of its concentration camp. What a pity, because Bavaria's first Wittelsbacher castle awaits on an elevation, offering a magnificent timber ceiling and an incredible view of the Alps.

◄ The central station is Munich's main hub.

93	Hauptbahnhof	284
94	Oktoberfest	286
95	Bavaria	288
96	Ruhmeshalle	290
97	St Paul	292
98	Donnersbergerbrücke	294
99	Hirschgarten	296
100	Nymphenburger Kanal	298
101	Schloss Nymphenburg	300
102	Botanischer Garten	306
103	Schloss Blutenburg	308
104	Olympiazentrum	310
105	BMW Zentrum	314
106	Dachau Altstadt	316
107	Schloss Dachau	318
108	Gedenkstätte KZ Dachau	320
109	Schloss Schleißheim	322
110	Freising	328
111	St Maria & St Korbinian	330
112	Weihenstephan	334
113	Allianz Arena	336

▶ Freising's Mariensäule resembles the one at the Marienplatz in Munich.

Beer gardens, baroque castles and pious monasteries pile up in Greater Munich. People sing, dance, and celebrate life - in lederhosen and dirndl - of course!

Schwanthalerhöhe

Every year, at the Schwanthalerhöhe to the west of Munich, the *Oktoberfest* surrenders to traditional cosiness on the Theresienwiese, where the *Ruhmeshalle* and the *Bavaria* are enthroned. Towards the end of the 19th century, the Munichers built the Parish Church of *St Paul*.

After World War II, the immigrants to Germany arrived at the *Münchner Hauptbahnhof* (Central Station) as their first stop, and Munich's gallows once stood at the *Donnersberger Brücke*.

Nymphenburger Schloss

The *Schloss Nymphenburg* scatters royal golden dust. From the nearby *Hirschgarten*, one arrives at the graceful castle following the *Nymphenburger Kanal*. The extensive garden attracts swans and deer. Numerous small palaces hide enchanted princesses, and a flower girl welcomes visitors to the *Botanischer Garten*.

Schloss Blutenburg

The *Blutenburg castle* appears mystical, enchanted, protected by its wall, and medieval. The lodge waits to be kissed awake.

Schloss Schleißheim

The heart of absolutism beats calmly and self-aware at the gates of Munich. *Schloss Schleissheim* extends over the Alte Schloss (Old Castle), the baroque Neue Schloss (New Castle) and Schloss Lustheim. The complex symbolises power in the style of Versailles. The garden is preserved almost in the original style.

Olympiazentrum

In 1972, the athletes competed at Munich's *Olympiazentrum* for medals during the Games of the XX Summer Olympiad. The architecture is defined by the roof of the stadium, and from the *Olympiaturm*, the view reaches the Alps. The technology of tomorrow is presented at the *BMW Zentrum,* and in the *Allianz Arena*, the FC Bayern München disqualifies the league.

Dachau

The world shudders with disbelief at the *Gedenkstätte KZ-Dachau*, but the city offers more. The *Schloss Dachau*, the first summer residence of the Wittelsbacher dynasty, shines above the old town.

Freising

The prince-bishop city of *Freising* is home to one of the most interesting monasteries in Bavaria, located above the old town on the Domberg. Once the bishops ruled over vast lands. They were the spiritual counterpart to the secular regents at the Münchner Residenz. Nearby, the university town of *Weihenstephan* brews the tasty beer of the scholars.

(93) Hauptbahnhof

Facts & Figures

Investors rolled out Munich's first train line in 1839. It terminated at today's Maffeistraße close to the Hackerbrücke, where the trains from Augsburg squealed into Munich. When the central building caught fire in 1847, the architect Friedrich Bürklein, commissioned by King Ludwig I, extended the tracks to the Karlstor. The 19th century enjoyed a new form of mobility; people's wanderlust brought success to the central train station. During World War II, the Allied air raids heavily targeted the Nazi transport infrastructure, and when Germany surrendered, the terminus was a heap of rubble - unrecoverable. During the 1950s, the architect Heinrich Gerbl rebuilt the airy hall close to the city centre. Most recently, in 2024, the hall was extensively refurbished. Today, nearly half a million visitors arrive daily, change trains or leave Munich's transport hub to explore the world.

The year is 1955, **Münchner Hauptbahnhof** (central station), platform 11! A train arrives from Italy. Germany experienced an economic miracle; the country was short of labourers. The Germanic machinery pounded, the conveyor belts turned - the bleeding wounds cut by the Nazi regime were repressed. Munich had its eyes fixated on the future!

Germany had just signed its first bilateral labour recruitment program with Italy and paid 50 Deutschmarks as a reward for any migrating worker. With time, an army of Italian, Turkish, Portuguese and Spanish families streamed from the South to the beating heart of Europe. And Munich's central station transshipped them across the country.

Munich was the final destination for many. Two million workers buzzed through the central station with two suitcases and a bag full of hope. The foreign workforce had to slave away in Germany and was to return home after years of hard labour. Some followed the call and returned to the sun - too chilly are the long winters north of the Alps. Many stayed, however, started a family, gave birth to children, picked up the language and integrated. The technical jargon calls them *Germans with a migrant background*.

▲ In 1839, the first train left the Hauptbahnhof on its way to Augsburg.

Integration means to accept the cultural roots of migrants and embrace the idea of multiculturalism. Only around the central station, however, along the Schillerstraße and the Goethestraße where the arrivals spent their first night in Munich, emerged a little-Istanbul, with a pizzeria, bazaar and kebab-house. The migrant workers opened hidden mosques in backyards and showed the Munichers how to enjoy life - pasta, pizza and Chinese noodle pots. At least gastronomically, the Bavarians embraced the alien cultures, those who once arrived at Munich's central station on platform 11 with two suitcases and a bag full of dreams on their back.

Location: Bayerstraße 10A **Entrance:** Without charge **Opening Times:** Always accessible
Deutsche Bahn: https://www.bahn.de
Münchner Verkehrsverbund MVV: https://www.mvv-muenchen.de

About Eagles and Steam Engines

On 26 August 1839, Bavaria's first locomotive hissed from Munich to Augsburg. Top speed: 60 km/hr. *"Too fast to my taste"*, King Ludwig I proclaimed. *"At that speed, the people see none of the wonders!"* And he added: *"Wrapped and will-less parcels like men shoot through pristine lands."* However, clouds steaming progress never volatilize. In 1835, the Eagle, Germany's first locomotive, rattled from Nürnberg to Fürth. Newcastle in northern England had manufactured the flying cauldron, but soon, the engineer Josef von Maffei welded much better trains - and they rolled onto the tracks at the Hirschau in the north of Munich. Already in 1803, Georg von Reichenbach had put the first Bavarian steam engine into operation at the Alte Münze - to run the embossing machine of the country.

(94) Oktoberfest

Facts & Figures

Does any public festival in the world frolic wetter, funnier and more passionately than Munich's Oktoberfest? Hardly! For two weeks in September, about 6 million jolly visitors make a pilgrimage to the beer mugs at the Theresienwiese, quenching their bellowing thirst, drowning in 60,000 hectolitres beer, dancing on tables to Bavarian brass band music. The party greedily devours 500,000 grilled chickens and slaughters more than 100 oxen. The Oktoberfest opens with the parade of the innkeepers, and Munich's mayor taps the first barrel. On the first Sunday, a costume procession introduces Bavaria's traditional way of life. The city organises the Bavarian Central Agricultural Festival every fourth year, presenting the country's animal husbandry and agricultural machinery. Since 2010, the *Historical Wiesn* calmly invites traditional amusement rides, which are popular with families.

Over five days, Munich celebrated the wedding of the heir apparent Ludwig I with his spouse, Princess Therese von Saxony-Hildburghausen, in 1810. Sergeant Franz Baumgartner suggested a horse race to conclude the festivities at the Schwanthalerhöhe, and the King agreed - everyone was up and about. More than 40,000 onlookers enthusiastically accompanied the horses speeding across the track. Surprise, surprise: Franz Baumgarten won the race on a seven-year-old mule. The townspeople socialised after the race, and they celebrated, and they boozed, and they called the grassland *Theresienwiese* in honour of their Queen. To this day, the oval racetrack is imprinted on the Bavariaring.

The horse race delighted many, and many wanted the show repeated the following year. Where people gather cheerfully, profit awaits, and in 1818, amusement rides attended the festivities - show booths, carousels and street artists. A magical swing followed in 1894, the toboggan in 1908, and the devil's wheel in 1910. In 1896, the innkeeper Michael Schottenhammel installed a tent - the horse race evolved into a folk festival.

As with any traditional event, the Nazi regime abused the **Oktoberfest** for their ideology, too; during World War II, the leadership had to cancel

▲ The monument reminds of the 1980 Oktoberfest terror attack.

the festivities, however.

In 1950, Munich's ingenious mayor Thomas Wimmer reopened the spectacle, this time without a horse race. The amusement was to distract the citizens from their grey reality, offering days of joy and hope instead.

When tourists streamed to the festival in the thousands, bawling out and dancing on beer tables, many locals longed for tranquillity. Since the year 2010, the Münchner Stadtmuseum organises the Historical Wiesn, a family-focused event on a small scale, separated and with traditional rides, with carnies built at the turn of the century, with street-artists and pantomime, quiet too - a good thing.

Location: Theresienwiese **Entrane:** Without charge **Time:** Last two weeks in September
Oktoberfest: https://www.oktoberfest.de
Oktberfestattentat: https://dokumentation-oktoberfestattentat.de

Bombs at the Oktoberfest

It is the 26 September 1980, 22:19: the Oktoberfest bustled when an explosion shook the cheerfulness. A pipe bomb, filled with 1 ½ kg TNT, bedded in nails and screws, detonated at the main entrance to the Theresienwiese. The basket where the assassin had deposited the bomb burst ino a thousand pieces, and the horrific shreds killed and injured many innocent victims. Thirteen died on this day, and the metal splinters caused life-threatening injuries to more than 200 visitors. Amongst the dead was the assassin, the right-wing extremist Gundolf Köhler, a 21-year-old student from Donaueschingen who had been radicalised. The police investigated, interrogated witnesses, and concluded that the youth had acted alone! *Who believes that!* And the carousel of investigation turns and turns and turns - unsuccessful to this day.

(95) Bavaria

Facts & Figures

After New York's Statue of Liberty, *Lady Bavaria* is the most giant bronze statue in the world. She gracefully thrones above the Theresienwiese on an elevation. Ludwig von Schwanthaler designed the matron, and the Erzgießerei Ferdinand von Miller cast the 18-metre-tall and 80-tonnes massive Bavarian Madonna. Munich unveiled the statue during the Oktoberfest in 1850. In 1610, Kurfürst Maximilian I had pronounced the *Patrona Bavaria* as the country's patron saint. Catholic and Greek-Pagan symbolism merge emblematically in her archetypal design: she dresses in a bearskin; she fastens the blade of war and peace at her belt; she lifts a Greek laurel wreath with her left arm, and a lion roars to her right, the country's avatar. Visitors may climb Lady Bavaria along a spiral staircase in her belly. Inside her head, viewing hatches allow to glance at the Schwanthalerhöhe.

At the beginning of the 19th century, Bavaria longed for a symbol to unify the country. The nation had doubled its territory when it ascended to a kingdom by annexing Swabia and Franconia. All should be proud of the monarchy and feel at home. A hall of fame was to honour past achievements and spur Bavaria into the future! The pantheon had to be in Greek style because its originator was King Ludwig I, the patron of the Königsplatz and the Ludwigstraße - the Bavarian Greek on the throne, a lettered humanist.

Since the Early Renaissance, ambitious regents were restless to outperform classical antiquity. Europe's artists had matched their idols in music, architecture, painting and sculpting, but Phidias' legendary *Statue of Zeus* and the *Colossus of Rhodes* were still unrivalled. For the first time in modern history, the Bavarians ambitiously attempted to measure up to the glorified past.

At last, the Munichers erected the **Patrona Bavaria** at the Theresienwiese, an amalgam of Blessed Mother and Patron Saint of Bavaria. Leo von Klenze designed the Iron Lady, and Ludwig von Schwanthaler fleshed out the details.

▲ King Ludwig I commissioned the Patrona Bavaria to unite the country.

With the King's preferences in mind, the artists embellished the Colossus with attributes of the lands and added a lion, the spirit animal of the country. The ancients contributed with a sword and a laurel wreath, turning the Patrona into a Goddess of Victory. Even the Germanic past entered the design - gifting the statue a bearskin, covering her breasts.

Munich's passionate gossip factory speculated that the artist's lover posed naked, and thus, the unrivalled beauty of Munich's maidens also entered into the design. Ever since, the matron has symbolised the unity of the country and watches, cast in bronze, over the fate of the lands with an iron fist.

Location: Theresienhöhe 16 **Entrance:** Without charge **Opening Times:** Always accessible
Internet: https://www.br.de (Weltwunder über der Theresienwiese)
https://www.schloesser.bayern.de/deutsch/schloss/objekte/mu_ruhm.htm

The Casting of the Lady Bavaria

It whooshed, it reeked, it fumed when the iron caster Ferdinand von Miller poured the blistering metal into the mould - then - trembling - the hollow concrete block cracked under the weight of the metal - ore leaked out. At last, the bronze had solidified. And the cast? It was a success! The workers called for the King because Ludwig I wanted to witness the birth of the head. The iron casters polished the metal and attached the cable winches. Cleverly, thirty labourers climbed into the hollow head to welcome the regent. The King stood silently, waiting, enthralled for the cast to appear. First, the hairline was seen as the workers pulled, then the eyes and suddenly - a *"Hurray Hurray Hurray"* from inside the Lady - the tempters hailed! The King was moved to tears when the men squeezed through the lips of the statue. A glorious day!

(96) Ruhmeshalle

Facts & Figures

The architect Leo von Klenze designed King Ludwig I's *Hall of Fame* at the Theresienwiese in 1853. The regent wanted a lasting monument to the most notable Bavarian scientists, artists and politicians, and thereby unite the country in spirit to demand his subjects to be committed to the monarchy. The three-winged Dorian marble hall exhibited 74 busts of famous Bavarians at the time of inauguration. By the turn of the millennia, the number had increased to 115. In the year 2000, the actress Clara Ziegler and the authoress Lena Christ were the first women to enter the pantheon. And Munich added a bust of King Ludwig I in 1888. During World War II, the complex suffered substantial damage from the many Allied air raids, but the city rebuilt the Ruhmeshalle in 1972. Nevertheless, access to the hall is strictly prohibited for the risk of safety.

People and not monuments shape the history of a country. Ludwig I commissioned the **Bavarian Hall of Fame** at the Theresienwiese as a counterpart to the Walhalla in Regensburg, where the busts of eminent German authorities represent the country. Three days after the King ascended to the throne in 1825, the architect Leo von Klenze worked on the temple's design - no time to waste. Today, 115 scientists, inventors, artists, religious leaders and politicians populate the Ruhmeshalle; their innovative work dates from the 16th to the 20th century.

The list of Bavarian heroes is long, ranging from Wolfgang Miller, the 16th-century master-builder of St Michael, to Werner Heisenberg, the founder of quantum mechanics. The statues honour Balthasar Neumann, the mastermind of the Royal Palace, Friedrich von Gärtner and Leo von Klenze. Johann Graf von Tilly commanded the Bavarian troops during the Thirty Years' War, and Graf Rumford reformed the country's encrusted structures, just like Maximilian Graf von Montgelas one hundred years later.

In Munich, musicians swung the baton, including Orlando di Lasso and Karl Orff. Martin Schongauer mastered the Gothic, and Hans Holbein carved the Isenheimer Altar. Albrecht Altdorfer founded the Danube

▲ The Ruhmeshalle, designed by Leo von Klenze, presents Bavarian dignitaries.

School, and Franz Mark the group *Der Blaue Reiter*.

During the 16th century, Hans Sachs cobbled rhymes, and four hundred years later, the dialect poet Ludwig Thoma put his tongue on paper. Simon Schmidt invented the lithography, and Joseph von Frauenhofer investigated the optics. Franz Xaver Gabelsberger came up with the shorthand, and Georg Simon Ohm formulated the law of electrical resistance. The engines of Rudolf Diesel still burn oil, and Oskar von Miller found the Deutsche Museum. Sigmund Count of Haimhausen established the Academy of Science, Lorenz von Westenrieder explored history, and Arnold Sommerfeld worked on quantum mechanics.

Location: Theresienhöhe 16 **Entrance:** Not accessible
Verkehrszentrum Deutsches Museum: https://www.deutsches-museum.de/verkehrszentrum
Location: Am Bavariapark 5, Opening Times: daily 9.00 - 17.00, Entrance: Adults 7 €

Das Verkehrszentrum Deutsches Museum

At the Isar in Haidhausen, the inspiring collection of the Deutsche Museum grows day by day. As the showrooms were bursting at the seams, the city council decided to make Munich's former exhibition grounds available to the museum as an extension. In 2003, the magistrate inaugurated the Museum of Transport and opened its gates to the public. The branch museum presents the exciting world of mobility in three listed buildings designed by Wilhelm Bertsch. The curators explain the social, political and economic significance of mass transportation during the 19th and 20th centuries. The collection focuses on the urban commuter service through time. The exhibits show horse-drawn carriages, old-timer cars, locomotives, saloon cars, busses, mountain railways and electric trams.

(97) St Paul

Facts & Figures

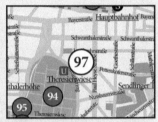

The Church of St Paul floats like a Hanging Jewel above the Theresienwiese. Georg von Hauberrisser, the architect of the Neue Rathaus, completed the prayer house in 1906. A 97-metre-tall central tower overtops the neo-Gothic building, modelled after the cathedral in Frankfurt. Two 76-metre-tall side towers flank the main entrance. The three-nave church, constructed from grey-brown sandstone, impresses with its abundance of space. At the entrance to the filigree stair tower, a statue of the architect welcomes marvelling visitors with a smile. The altar of *Our Lady* by Gabriel Hackl at the southern side chapel and the altar of *St Joseph* in the northern transept amaze with their delicate execution. The tabernacle originates from the workshop of August Hartle, and the benediction monstrance keeps a splinter of the cross. The central tower can be climbed, an option during the Oktoberfest.

When the Munichers persuaded the King to step down in 1848, Ludwig I had already left his mark on the city by designing the Maxvorstadt, an effort that was not to beat. At the turn of the century, the *Age of Industrialisation* presented the magistrate with a new challenge: the population growth, a consequence of centralising the administration on Munich, threatened to overrun the city, and the middle class demanded new living space. Eventually, the city expanded to the south, constructing the Isarvorstadt and the Ludwigsvorstadt close to the Isar.

In the 20th century, new building developers entered the stage. Silently, Munich's bourgeoisie had turned wealthy in the wake of the Industrial Revolution. Villas and apartment blocks were built around the Theresienwiese; today, they serve solicitors and private physicians as offices. The clinical complex of Munich's university added solicitude to the neighbourhood in 1823; the compound was designed by the architect Leo von Klenze. The bourgeoise creativity climaxed in 1906 when Munich constructed the neo-Gothic Parish Church of **St Paul** - the upper-middle-class had erected a lasting monument to itself.

The Theresienwiese remained, however, shielded from speculators.

▲ The neo-Gothic Church of St Paul enthrones the Theresienwiese.

Here, the annual Oktoberfest fills the coffers of the treasury. The spring festival and the Africa Days fund the city equally. The paved rubble area is an attractive base for travelling circuses visiting Munich.

The Theresienwiese made history: here, on 7 November 1918, the Munichers - workers, soldiers, and farmers - enforced the abdication of the monarchy. Today, the unions march their members to the bronze statue of the *Lady Bavaria* during their May Day rally.

Of course, Adolf Hitler paraded here, too - during a celebration of the annexation of Austria on 2 April 1938. At the square, he swore in the soldiers - a blood-oath to the Führer.

Location: St.-Pauls-Platz 11 Entrance: Without charge Opening Times: 9.00 - 19.00
Internet: https://www.erzbistum-muenchen.de/pfarrei/pv-westend/st-paul/104606
see also: http://www.pfarrverband-muenchen-westend.de

An Air Crash with Consequences

On 17 December 1960, a grey autumn day, Munich's trams were overcrowded. Shoppers lined the streets and prepared for Christmas. At Munich's airport, shortly after 14.00, a twin-engined American courier plane took off: model Convair 240. The pilots steered towards Norfolk in England. Seven crew members and sixteen passengers surrendered to the weather. Shortly after takeoff, the pilot reported engine failure, and the aircraft dropped rapidly. Panic alarmed the fire department, which prepared for an emergency landing at the airport. The pilot intended a loop when the wing brushed against the tower of St Paul. Like a plucked fowl, the glob crashed into the darkness of nirvana, where it smashed into a tram. Fifty-two people died on this grey autumn day, and many more were injured.

(98) Donnersbergerbrücke

Facts & Figures
The gibbet strangled Munich's convicts between the Hackerbrücke and the Donnersbergerbrücke, where the ghosts of the hung rattled during the 16th century. At the Marienplatz, only politically motivated executions were showcased. After opening the railway route from Munich to Augsburg in 1839, entrepreneurs and the city administration moved into the neighbourhood. The 180-metre-wide central customs office opened in 1912. In 1919, the winter house of the Zirkus Krone, a travelling circus during summers, settled at the Marsstraße. Since 2002, the Central Tower - an office building - overlooks the area. That year, the carmaker Mercedes-Benz opened its customer centre at the Arnulfstraße. Management consulting companies that have pitched their offices in the district appreciate the mobility provided by the train connection at Pasing Bahnhof.

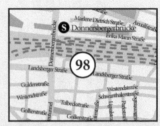

Adolf Hitler envisioned a grand architectural design for Munich: excavators were to demolish the central station and relocate the tracks to Laim. The Führer wanted a 120-metre-wide and six-kilometre-long boulevard instead. Similarly to the Rosenheimer Straße, soldiers in uniform were to march at the **Donnersbergerbrücke,** too, parading their standards to the city centre, goose-stepping to reverberating chants, torchlight in hand, worshipping the *God of Fascism*, ready to spill their blood in sacrifice.

At today's central station, the Führer demanded a temple to honour his movement, and by 1938, chief architect Hermann Giesler submitted proposals. The sketches envisaged a rotunda of vast dimensions: a dome in the style of a pantheon, 250 metres wide and 136 metres high.

To the west, serving as the conclusion of the avenue, a 100-metre-broad pedestal was to idolise the Aryan race, carrying a 175-metre-tall obelisk. At its top, the fascists planned an over-dimensioned imperial eagle clawing its bitterish talons into a weeping globe. Inside, the Führer envisioned keeping the blood standard he carried during the failed 1923 Hitler Putsch.

Underground train lines were to skid the Munichers into the centre; the city planners proposed to lay the tracks seven metres below ground in a

▲ The Central Tower rises tall at the Donnersbergerbrücke.

tunnel - which could serve as a bunker, too. Adolf Hitler also demanded human hatcheries on the outskirts to ensure the supply of cannon fodder.

To the east, at the Haus der Kunst, the blueprint envisaged museums, halls and exhibition rooms. The Königsplatz, where the Braune Haus had orchestrated the beginnings, was to be turned into a centre of power. It was there where Adolf Hitler planned his mausoleum, the resting place of his petty mortal remains, a monument to his quirky bones.

When the Allied Forces rained bombs onto Munich, the fascists clapped into their hands: *"Excellent! Excellent! The Allied air raids make space for our vision. Not our fault - not our fault!"*

Location: Donnersbergerbrücke **Entrance:** Without charge **Opening Times:** Always accessible
Literature: Hans-Peter Rasp: Eine Stadt für tausend Jahre.
Zirkus Krone: https://www.circus-krone.com

Munich Executes

On 9 November 1861, Munich bowed out a spectacle that had amused the people for centuries: public executions. Only then, the hangman fastened the last delinquent into a barge to prod him across the Jordan. The sword decapitated criminals at the Scharfrichterplatz until 1854. When the blade required seven strokes to cut a head off, Munich introduced the guillotine. To be sure, Freiherr von Kreittmayr introduced the *Codex Maximilianeus Bavaricus Criminalis* in 1751, the Bavarian criminal and civil code, but law enforcement remained harsh. Offenders continued to be hung (at the Galgenberg until 1804) and beheaded (until 1861). Their limbs were broken on the wheel (until 1805), and confessions were extracted under torture (until 1806). Even witchcraft remained a criminal offence during most of the 19th century.

⑨⑨ Hirschgarten

Facts & Figures

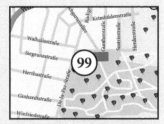

Bavaria quenches its thirst and hunger at the Hirschgarten, the most extensive beer garden in the world. The open park is a part of Munich's green lung between the train line Munich-Augsburg and the castle Schloss Nymphenburg. Up to 8000 visitors wallow in the shadow of 150-year-old oak trees, beeches and chestnuts; a children's playground provides swings and slides. The restaurant *Zum Königlichen Hirschgarten* entertains about 500 guests in its six halls, offering groups of regulars, wedding receptions, corporate events and Christmas parties a delightful ambience. Fallow bucks and deer pasture in a 2 hectares outdoor enclosure; the Forstenrieder Park once was a hunting ground for the aristocracy, and the animals remind of these bygone times. To the south, the beer garden borders a 27-hectare local recreation area popular among sun worshippers during Bavaria's pleasant summers.

Bavaria distinguished between the royal hunt and the commoners' hunt during the Middle Ages. The royal hunt chases bears, wolves, stags, pheasants, swans, and eagles - a privilege open only to the nobility. The ordinary people had to be content with small game - doves, hares, and rabbits.

The aristocracy fenced their hunting grounds in; guardians kept a watchful eye on the wetlands and woodlands to discourage poachers. Munich's nobility enclosed the forested **Hirschgarten** in 1720 and reared pheasants at the nearby Fasanengarten. Once fully fledged, the breeders released the birds at the Amalienburg in the park of Schloss Nymphenburg, and the nobility shot the fowls conveniently from the chateau's roof-top - the one who had shed most feathers had won the day.

During the late 18th century, the Hirschgarten farmed hops. Later, the aristocracy planted 17,000 mulberries to grow silk, but the grubs disliked the climate, disobeyed their masters, sulked, and refused to produce silk. Finally, the huntsman *Johann Theodor Freiherr von Waldkirch* fenced in a game reserve 135 hectares in size, planted oak trees and bred deer.

Kurfürst Karl Theodor had granted the Munichers access to the Englischer Garten, and opened the Hirschgarten to the public.

▲ The world's largest beer garden is located at the Hirschgarten.

Additionally, he constructed a hunting lodge with a tavern, where his stags roamed at large, strolling between tankards and beer tables, slurping remains and delighting in the fattening.

The railway line from Munich to Augsburg, constructed during the early 19th century, trimmed the southern part of the garden. After World War II, the magistrate turned the greenery into a local recreation area.

Today, a two-hectare game enclosure reminds of the former royal hunting grounds, hosting deer and stag. For Munich's city kids, the furry vegetarians are often their first encounter with nature, feeding the animals with fallen twigs from trees.

Location: Hirschgarten 1 **Entrance:** Without charge **Opening Times:** Always accessible
Hirschgarten: https://hirschgarten.de
see also: https://www.biergartenguide.com

About Physicists and Beer Gardens

In Munich, notable physicists lived, worked and frolicked. The city of the golden manna frothed the new sciences of the first half of the 20th century across the world. Albert Einstein spent his youth at the Adlzreiterstraße 12, where he playfully experienced the thrill of technology as a child at the rear of a residential building where his father operated a dynamo factory. Later, he bestowed the marvelling world with the theories of relativity. Werner Heisenberg, one of the originators of quantum mechanics, formulated his thesis in Munich; he had studied physics under Arnold Sommerfeld at the Ludwig-Maximilians-Universität. Max Planck spent his school days in the regional capital and returned as a private lecturer. The first Noble Prize honoured Wilhelm Conrad Röntgen, who meditated at the Friedensengel.

100 Nymphenburger Kanal

Facts & Figures

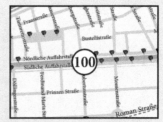

The Nymphenburger Kanal branches off romantically at a brook called Würm. Kurfürst Max Emanuel excavated the canal to connect his magnificent castle to the freshness of the billows. The Würm feeds its waters from the Starnberger See and meanders 40 kilometres across Bavaria. In Pasing, the Nymphenburger Kanal siphons off about one-third of the brook's flow. The canal first cascades into the palace garden at a waterfall and then quietly journeys to the castle. Later, the waves dance across the district Neuhausen until the Hubertusbrunnen. A second canal flows from the palace to the Olympiapark, where the rapids disembogue into the artificial Olympiasee. Ice skaters pirouette between Schloss Nymphenburg and the Hubertusbrunnen on cold winter days. An exclusive residential area sandwiches the idyllic canal, home of the affluent middle class.

Hunting is a traditional sport in Bavaria, and Hubertus is its patron saint. Legends tell that Graf von Lüttich, born around 655 in Toulouse, encountered a magnificent stag with a crucifix between its antlers on a hunting trip; overwhelmed, he converted to Christianity. A painting at the northwestern pillar of St Peter depicts the encounter.

The story arrived in Bavaria with Kurfürst Karl Theodor, who founded the Alpine **Order of Hubertus**. Prince Regent Luitpold was a passionate huntsman, too. At the Bayerische Nationalmuseum, Munich commemorated the sovereign with a monument to Hubertus, which the magistrate moved to the neighbourhood Gern/Neuhausen in 1954. Today, the memorial concludes the Nymphenburger Kanal.

The lands dedicated the enchanting temple to Bavaria's wild stags, grazing and bawling - but only those who carry a shining crucifix between their antlers. Prince Rupprecht donated the four bronze sculptures at the corners of the monument in 1916. They idolise nature and the chase: an energetic young Amazon roams the meadows, an aged witch collects drugs, a bearded huntsman shoulders a prey, and a youngling stalks game with bow and arrow.

▲ Adolf Hildebrand completed the Hubertusbrunnen in 1907.

During the Middle Ages, the archetype of Saint Hubertus brought pagan wisdom to the Christian doctrine. The new teachings thus preserved the ancient knowledge of nature - about the phases of the moon, about life and death, medical herbs and remedies, prey and predators.

Already neolithic cave paintings depicted shamans dancing and singing to the rhythm of nature. A reproduction of the Cave of Altamira at the Deutsche Museum presents the ancient priest, and the legends of Saint Hubertus have preserved the wild man, too; he was a son of the Great Mother Goddess, who now submitted to the Christian cross.

Location: Neuhausen/Gern **Entrance:** Without charge **Opening Times:** Always accessible
Literature: KulturGeschichtsPfad: Neuhausen-Nymphenburg
Hubertusorden: http://www.int-st-hubertus-orden.de

The Bavarian Order of Hubertus

Saint Hubertus conquered Bavaria under Kurfürst Karl Theodor. The knightly order originated on 3 November 1444; Herzog Gerhard II von Jülich-Berg had triumphed in the Battle of Linnich on the birthday of Saint Hubertus. Lost under a veil of obscurity, the year 1609 remembered the Order of the Knights, and in 1744, Kurfürst Karl Theodor formulated the statutes. Under Kurfürst Maximilian I, the brotherhood ascended to the highest gentlemen's club of the country. According to legend, Graf Hubertus von Lüttich was converted to Christianity in the 7th century by a stag with a crucifix between his antlers, which he encountered during a hunt. The count renounced all earthly duties, became a hermit, and ascended to the rank of a bishop. After his death, the pope canonised him.

Schloss Nymphenburg

Facts & Figures

The enchanting Schloss Nymphenburg sprays Baroque lightness and *joie de vivre* across the park. In 1664, the architect Agostino Barelli constructed on behalf of Kurfürst Ferdinand Maria the cubic central pavilion as an Italian cottage. His son Kurfürst Max Emanuel commissioned the two lateral buildings and connected them to the central lodge by galleries. One generation later, Emperor Karl Albrecht finished the side wings and the complex at the fountain. Finally, the Age of Absolutism dressed the compound in Baroque style. At its centre flaunts the Steinerner Saal, a dining hall and ballroom richly decorated with frescoes and paintings. The legendary Gallery of Beauties, commissioned by King Ludwig I, eternalises Bavarian charm at the southern wing. At the Blauer Saal (blue saloon), King Ludwig II was born in the year 1845.

Schloss Nymphenburg was the gift of Kurfürst Ferdinand Maria to his beloved wife Henriette Adelaide von Savoyen when she gave birth to a long-awaited son on 11 July 1662, the later Kurfürst Max Emanuel. The Palazzo Reale in Turin stood as a model - the splendid Italian country villa where Adelaide had spent her childhood. Kurfürst Ferdinand Maria adored his wife; he wanted her to feel at home in Bavaria. At the time of construction, the handsome country house was surrounded by a baroque pleasure garden, which reached as far as today's water jet.

Kurfürst Max Emanuel desired a castle to affirm his aspirations for the imperial crown. He expanded his mother's hide-out by two lateral pavilions in 1704, connecting them to the central compound by galleries. During a stay in Brussels, Max Emanuel discovered Dutch canals, which the Elector introduced at Schloss Nymphenburg. He aspired to connect all castles in and around Munich by waterways. After his surrender at the decisive Battle of Blenheim in 1704, the building work on the castle was halted as the Elector had to flee. The construction continued after the sovereign returned from his exile in Paris. Finally, Emperor Karl Albrecht added a row of houses in the shape of a half-ring in 1730, which encircles

▲ The historic façade stretches over an impressive length of 630 Metres.

the forecourt; he also enlarged the garden.

In 1719, Kurfürst Max Emanuel built the Pagodenburg, a pavilion in the park. The Badenburg followed in 1722 and the Magdalenenklause in 1728. The Amalienburg, the latest addition to the garden palaces, was constructed under Emperor Karl Albrecht.

As fashion changed, King Maximilian I transformed the garden compound in the year 1800, commissioning Friedrich Ludwig von Sckell to create an English landscape park. The royal gardener replaced the geometric baroque splendour with spaciously laid-out meadows, where the art magically hides man's interference in nature.

Location: Schloss Nymphenburg 1 **Opening Times:** daily 9.00 - 18.00
Entrance: Adults 19 € Concession 16 €   https://www.schloss-nymphenburg.de
Museum Mensch und Natur: https://www.mmn-muenchen.de

The Museum Mensch und Natur

The northern wing of Schloss Nymphenburg houses the inspiring *Museum of Man and Nature*. The exhibition summarises the genesis and evolution of life on Earth. The insightful curators present with dioramas, diagrams and three-dimensional models the origin of the solar system, the geophysical structure of our place in the universe, the emergence of the first life forms, the evolution of humans, and societies' changing relationship with nature. Humans have substantially altered the environment over the past century - contaminating the soil upon which culture rests - as outlined in the sections *Food & Nourishment, Growth of Human Population* and *Climate & Environment*. The sections *Human Organs, Nervous System* and *The Brain* explain the structure of our human biology.

Highlights of Schloss Nympenburg - Castle

The story of Schloss Nymphenburg, the summer residence of the Wittelsbacher dynasty, began under Kurfürst Ferdinand Maria. The Elector commissioned an Italian country villa in 1664. By 1679, the architect Agostino Barelli had constructed the central compound, which was later converted into a banquet hall. During the reign of Kurfürst Max Emanuel and Emperor Karl Albrecht, court architect Enrico Zuccalli expanded the complex into an extensive baroque complex during the 18th century.

The **Steinerne Saal** in the central pavilion is the heart of the complex. The hall was designed by Johann Baptist Zimmermann and François Cuvilliés the Elder from 1755 to 1757. It is decorated in the Rococo style with a cycle of frescoes depicting the pantheon of the Olympus: nymphs pay homage to Flora, Venus sits on a cloud and worries about her beauty, and Orpheus teaches Muses the art of music. The glazed windows and doors in the west facing the setting sun offer an impressive view of the large parterre and the castle garden.

The **northern rooms** are dedicated to the Elector, and the southern rooms to the Electress. The suits are divided into anteroom, bedroom and gallery. The portraits and frescoes show scenes from Greco-Roman mythology and the Bavarian nobility. Portraits of French ladies-in-waiting entice with sensuality (Pierre Gobert, 1715). The Wappenzimmer (coat of arms room) and the Karl-Theodor-Zimmer refer to Kurfürst Karl Theodor; in 1778, he reluctantly took over the regency of Bavaria. The paintings in the northern gallery depict the building projects of Kurfürst Max Emanuel (Franz Joachim Beich, 1722/23).

The **southern rooms** began under Henriette Adelaide von Savoyen. They are decorated with a cycle of nature goddesses. In the Gazebo, the ceiling fresco by Antonio Triva shows the nymph Arethusa. The anteroom is dedicated to Mother Earth Cybele. In the bedroom, the flower goddess Flora floats above the bed; she gave Nymphenburg its name. Portraits of the electoral family decorate the walls of the rooms. The Chinese cabinet, created by François Cuvilliés the Elder, appears exotic; it was designed in 1763/64. The southern gallery presents paintings from Schloss Dachau and Schloss Schleißheim (Franz Joachim Beich, Franz Lorenz Stuber, Joseph Stephan).

▲ The view along the garden canal to the castle is enchanting.

The spacious Queen's apartment was located in the **southern pavilion**. The rooms were furnished for Princess Karoline Friederike Wilhelmine, the second wife of King Maximilian I. Lola Montez, the royal mistress, stands out in King Ludwig I's beauty gallery. (Joseph Stieler, 1827 to 1850.)

The Queen's study, decorated with exotic precious woods in blue, shows portraits of the royal couple. The Queen's audience room is representative but comfortably furnished. Its Empire style refers to Bavaria's political alliance with Napoleon, the then master of Europe. The future King Ludwig II was born on August 25, 1845 in the adjacent Queen's bedroom. The luxurious mahogany furniture was made in Munich around 1815.

English Ladies in Nymphenburg

The Maria-Ward-Straße leads from the Botanischer Garten to Schloss Nymphenburg. The street is named after a nun born in the County of York on January 23, 1585, during Elizabethan England. It was the time of the Reformation and the persecution of Catholics. At 24, Maria Ward founded an order dedicated to educating young girls. In 1627, she arrived in Munich, where Kurfürst Maximilian I entrusted her with the Paradeiserhaus on Weinstraße. There, the God-fearing young ladies ran Munich's first girls' school with a boarding facility. Maria Ward died in England in 1645. Four hundred years later, the Nazi regime banned the Congregation of Jesus. A year after World War II, the Maria Ward School opened in Nymphenburg. The church can be visited; it is Munich's most innovative place of worship.

Highlights of Schloss Nympenburg - Park

The castle garden covers an area of 180 hectares. From north to south, it measures two kilometres. It is surprising how a park of the extent of Schloss Nymphenburg could survive into the present. It is also surprising that the gardeners hid the city's silhouette entirely behind the 200-year-old trees. Strolling through the castle park from the large parterre to the cascade, the visitor becomes aware of the various elements with which the creators had designed the garden.

On the **large parterre**, a baroque garden from the absolutist period decorates the complex. Here, the flowerbeds line up strictly in rows. Sculptures of Greek gods and goddesses watch over tulips and daffodils. Already in 1671, under Henriette Adelaide von Savoyen, the country villa was surrounded by a lovely garden; the Piedmontese hunting lodge La Venaria Reale stood as a model. The first instalment reached up to the fountain. In the geranium house, an exhibition presents the park's history with documents and maps.

From 1701, Charles Carbonet, under Kurfürst Max Emanuel, laid a branch canal from the **Würm** eastward to supply the castle with water. The French designer Dominique Girard restructured the baroque garden in 1715. The axially symmetrical complex was surrounded in the west by a **forest** with clearings where the nobility could pass their time. Additionally, the regents commissioned park castles: Amalienburg and Badenburg in the south, Pagodenburg and Magdalenenklause in the north.

Joseph Effner designed the **Badenburg** at Badenburger See. Kurfürst Max Emanuel had the lodge built between 1718 and 1722. A water basin gurgles in the basement. The frescoes in the ballroom show mythological scenes about the element water. The **Pagodenburg** was built between 1716 and 1719 after a design by Joseph Effner. Here, the nobility played ball games. In 1739, François Cuvilliés the Elder designed the **Amalienburg** under Emperor Karl Albrecht in the Rococo style. The central hall of mirrors impresses with silver and delicate tones of blue. The cabinet and the hunting rooms are richly decorated.

In the 19th century, the zeitgeist changed. Friedrich Ludwig von Sckell, commissioned by King Maximilian I, transformed the baroque splendour into an English landscape garden. The gardeners completed the southern part of the **Prinzengarten** in 1807, and the northern part followed until

▲ The rulers once had fun splashing about at the Badenburg.

1823. Winding paths meander furtively along lovely lakes and gentle canals, through delicate forests, and across bright vistas. The stroller constantly enjoys new elements, which turns the joy of walking into a voluptuous experience.

Friedrich Ludwig von Sckell designed the **park** with sensibility. His spirit was less radical than his Londoner contemporaries; he retained parts of the Baroque garden and included them in the redesign of the complex, and thus, the central canal, the cascade and the large parterre were preserved. To compensate, he created wild forests where deer graze to this day.

The philosopher Cay Lorenz Hirschfeld aptly summed up the ideology of landscape gardening: "Everything seems to be nature; art so happily is hidden."

The Magdalenendult at the Hirschgarten

Shortly before he died in 1725, Kurfürst Max Emanuel commissioned a chapel at Schloss Nymphenburg in honour of the sinner Mary Magdalene. It was designed as a ruin to exaggerate the atmosphere. On Magdalen Day (22 July), pious believers pilgrimage to her shrine to beg for relief from their sins and pain. According to biblical tradition, Mary Magdalene was Jesus's companion and a witness to his resurrection. She is the patron saint of Schloss Nymphenburg. Since 1728, the Munichers have held the Magdalenendult at the Hirschgarten during the week of Magdalen Day. The fair invites showmen, traders, and travelling journeymen who show their skills and goods: the mishmash of swingboats, shooting galleries, and sales stands mainly attracts families with young children.

102 Botanischer Garten

Facts & Figures

Munich's botanical garden cultivates flowers, bushes and woods; its area stretches over 22 hectares and covers 4500 square metres of greenhouses. The biologists maintain more than 14,000 plant species, groomed after scientific and artistic considerations. The range of  colours includes orchids and water lilies, fruit trees, medical herbs and crops. Rose bushes, rhododendrons and mangroves lift the spirit on grey days. The garden simulates, by strictly dividing into sectors, different ecosystems. Along a dark gorge grow ferns, mosses and mushrooms. An artificial lake splashes about at the Alpinum, overgrown with encroaching reeds. Here, the inconspicuous gentian grows, the *open sesame* to the neckline of the maiden's dirndl. A bank of peonies tantalises the nose during the early summer, intense but pleasant, invoking a belated spring fever.

The **botanical garden** in Nymphenburg throws its colourful peddles with bliss into the landscape. Ritter Karl von Goebel, a professor at the Ludwig-Maximilians-Universität, created the garden with love and dedication in 1914. By the end of World War I, the flowerbeds replaced the meagre fields at the Alter Botanischer Garten close to the Karlstor. Filigree Art Nouveau greenhouses shelter protected plants at the eastern corner of the compound, whereby the greenery's tallness determines the height of the glasshouse for thermal-energetic reasons.

Munich's botanical garden operates with a dual brain. On the one hand, the scholars' scientific curiosity has to be satisfied. On the other hand, the garden must convey aesthetic well-being; not one horticultural technique alone should dominate the compound.

The **Schmuckhof,** close to the entrance, is the gem of the garden. Flowers, shrubs, and bushes encircle a water lily pool. The gardeners adjust the greening throughout the year.

The **Hortus Conclusus**, designed by the English landscape artist Bardly Hole, presents an award-winning rose garden.

The woods of the world grow in the park-like region to the west, the

▲ Munich's Botanischer Garten introduces the most splendid Alpine flora.

so-called **Arboteum**, where conifers, beeches, tulip and magnolia trees blossom.

At the **Alpinum**, an artificial mountain region, mosses and alpine flowers thrive next to the plants of the Himalayas and the Andes. At the foothill, an artificial lake wets the reeds of grassland; the lough is covered with water and marsh plants. The gardeners separate the flora by continent and height above sea level.

Additionally, fourteen spacious glasshouses cultivate delicate plants from all over the world, simulating different climates, from hot and humid to arid and temperate. Inside the ample compound grow palm trees, orchids, water lilies and ferns.

Location: Menzinger Straße 65 **Opening Times:** daily 9.00 - 16.30
Entrance: Adults 5 €, Concession 4 € **Internet:** https://www.botmuc.de
Literature: Botanischer Garten München (Herausgeber): Botanischer Garten München

An Edelweiß to Die for

Many stories in Bavaria tell of the magical blue gentian. Even operators of rides at the Oktoberfest call their business Enzian. The medicinal herb is applied as a seasoning in liquor production, but otherwise, it has little gastronomic importance. The gentian is a flower that grows in the high regions of the Alps. To pluck the plant is dangerous (and forbidden); it thrives only in impassably rough terrain. The deep blue colour turns the Edelweiß into a symbol of loyalty. Many younglings had to go to get the frightful messenger of death - before the wedding bells would ring, they had to present the flower to their lovers. Yes, the lustful gentian demanded many lives, wretched by tempting promises. The herb divides, according to common parlance, the timid Prussian tourist from the dreaded Bavarian fellow.

Schloss Blutenburg

Facts & Figures

The Blutenburg, the regents' enchanting hunting lodge, is one of Bavaria's few authentic late-Gothic castles. Herzog Sigismund and Herzog Albrecht III commissioned the fortress between 1430 and 1490, the first stronghold of the Wittelsbacher dynasty. The mighty walls 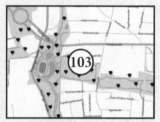 and the four massive towers guard bewitching damsels at the manor house. At the Burgkapelle, Jan Polack's panel paintings decorating the central altar and the two side chapels convert any atheist with their beauty. They are an artistic culmination of the Bavarian Gothic. A comprehensive children's library moved into the castle in 1983; the Jewish immigrant Jella Leppman collected the mountain of books after World War II, counting over 350,000 titles. Annually, the lodge's banqueting hall delights with the well-received Blutenburger Konzerte, a series of performances focusing on chamber music.

The enchanting **Schloss Blutenburg** is one of Bavaria's few late Gothic secular buildings that survived the ravages of time unadulterated. A wooden building had served the Menzinger gentry at this location already during the 12th century. In 1432, documents referenced the lodge; Herzog Sigismund commissioned the fortress' refurbishment in 1490.

Sigismund was the third son of Herzog Albrecht III. In 1467, he renounced his entitlement to co-regency and received Schloss Blutenburg as an offset. Henceforward, the youthful Duke indulged in the arts, worshipped fair women, played music and staged fiery festivities. Like Orpheus, he surrounded himself with animals. Peacocks and other birds ran around freely at Schloss Blutenburg. Like his feathered friends, the Bavarian troubadour wheeled wisdom around his tail. Although he was never married, he fathered four children - most progressive for his time. Bavaria's first princely art collection emerged at his instigation. Infected by the minstrel of Schloss Blutenburg, his brother, Herzog Albrecht IV, started to collect art during the 16th century.

Sigismund was Munich's patron of churches and monasteries. He laid the founding stone for the Frauenkirche. After he had passed away,

▲ The tranquil castle enchants like a Bavarian fairy tale since 1430.

Bavaria's building mania exhausted Munich, and Schloss Blutenburg fell into oblivion. In 1676, Anton Freiherr von Berchem purchased the crumbling complex and revitalised the joyful fountain of youth.

In 1702, the fortress returned to the Wittelsbacher dynasty when Kurfürst Max Emanuel bestowed the castle to his wife, Therese Kunigunde.

On 12 February 1848, Lola Montez, the seductively charming lover of King Ludwig I, spent her final night in Bavaria at Schloss Blutenburg before the country deported her. Today, the castle is under the administration of the non-profit organisation *Staatliche Seen & Schlösser*.

Location: Seldweg 15 **Entrance:** Adults 3 € **Opening Times:** daily 10.00 - 16.00
Internet: https://www.blutenburg.de
Blutenburger Schlosskonzerte: https://schlosskonzerte-blutenburg.de

The Tail of Agnes Bernauer

Herzog Albrecht III had surrendered to his fate. As the sovereign to be, he must not fall in love with Bavaria's charming Ladies, and he promised his hand to Herzogin Anna von Brunswick-Grubenhagen-Einbeck on 6 November 1436. The prince fell in love nevertheless, but with another, with the daughter of a barber from Augsburg. Her name was Agnes Bernauer. Historians believe the youngster had married her secretly, keeping her at Schloss Blutenburg. When his father Herzog Ernst learnt about his son's passion, he denounced the maiden of sorcery and drowned her in the Danube. A woman who kept his son from his duties must be a witch. The story moved many poets, and even Karl Orff drew the quill. The site of their romance was at Schloss Blutenburg on the outskirts of Munich.

Olympiazentrum

Facts & Figures

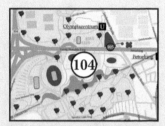

In 1972, the world enthusiastically celebrated the Games of the XX Summer Olympiads in Munich. Competition arenas, stadiums, an indoor swimming pool, a television tower, the Museum Sea Life and event arenas are scattered over three square kilometres. The architectural company Behnisch & Partner from Stuttgart designed the complex. Fifteen thousand workers excavated the soil over four years. They laid bricks, installed fountains and connected lights; they glazed the ceilings and paved the roads. After the games, the magistrate transformed the site into a recreation area enjoyed by residents and tourists alike. The artificial lake feeds from the Nymphenburger Kanal, and the 5000 trees have converted the urban space into a landscape park. Markets and cultural events enliven the former Olympic compound: the Tollwood Festival bongs during July and the Lilalu Festival in August.

On 26 April 1966, during its 64th meeting in Rome, the International Olympic Committee accepted Munich's bid to host the 1972 Summer Olympics. The global community had sent out a signal of wisdom: *After the fascists had shattered humanity during World War II, Germany had returned to the federation of peace-loving nations* - what tremendous honour!

When the Alps prevailed against their competitors Madrid, Montreal and Detroit, the Munichers danced excitedly. Once lost as the *Capital of the Movement*, Munich was now spreading joy and not air raids across all nations. The celebrations were accompanied by a fanfare of peace and a message of brotherhood.

Not even King Ludwig I had as feverishly constructed as Munich was now putting on the frills. No disharmony was to spoil the atmosphere. In less than four years and a feat of strength evolved out of nothing the **Olympiapark** (Olympic Centre). The magistrate pressed ahead to build the public transport system and to convert the Neuhauser Straße between the Marienplatz and the Karlstor into a pedestrian area. Most importantly, a new beer garden welcomed visitors at the Viktualienmarkt.

Munich happily anticipated peaceloving, innovative and sophisticated

▲ The roof of the Olympiastadion follows the ideas of bionic architecture.

games, embellished with the idea of a world-brotherhood. Only the attack on the Israeli Olympic squad by a Palestinian terrorist group left a mark on the otherwise vibrant presentation.

After the games, the Munichers cheerfully embraced their Olympiapark (Olympic Park) as a multifunctional sports and recreation centre. Today, the racecourses run, swim and cycle under the wing of a privately run operating company, and the athletes' anthems have turned into pop concerts, opera spectacles and funfairs, like the Tollwood Festival in July. In contrast to Schloss Nymphenburg, the park of the Olympiazentrum still suffers from an artificial ➡

Location: Olympiapark **Entrance:** Without charge **Opening Times:** Always accessible
Internet: https://www.olympiapark.de/de/olympiapark-muenchen
Olympiaturm: daily 10.00 - 22.00. Entrance Adults 11 €

Munich's First Zeppelin Landing

On 2 April 1909, the first travel-to-target of Zeppelin LZ 3 landed at the Oberwiesenfeld where today sports enthusiasts hail their athletes. A military training ground occupied the area in 1887; the Bavarian infantry and horsemen were drilled there. The demonstration of a Zeppelin flight impressed the officials, and the army's high command voiced interest in supporting the invention. In 1912/1925, Bavaria added a military airport. The airfields relocated to Riem in 1939 when commercial airliners took off from the runway. After World War I, the now Olympic site was utilised as a refugee camp; later, it became a dumping ground. The 60-metre-tall Olympiaberg (a hill), referred to by the Munichers as *Monte Scherblino*, was erected from fermenting waste and the rubble of the houses destroyed during World War II.

taste - a flaw that the decades will iron out.

The delicate Olympiastadion (Olympic Stadium) evolved into Munich's widely recognised landmark. Its filigree tent extends to the Olympiahalle (Olympic Hall) and the indoor swimming pool; its style borrows from bionic architecture. The surface of soap bubbles served as a model for the ingenious rooftop. The sky shines through translucent acryl-glass panels into the stadium; the clouds enchant like wearing diving goggles. The architects Behnisch & Partner built the arena low into the ground; the upper tiers thus cheer the athletes at street level - the architectonic masterstroke harmoniously embeds the colossus into its surroundings without hinting at its monumentality.

Until 2005, the Olympic Stadium hosted the challenges of the football club FC Bayern München. Germany's elite footballers moved to Fröttmaning when the Allianz Arena was completed. The Olympic Stadium hosted the 1974 Football World Cup final; in 1987, Pope John Paul II beatified Padre Rupert Mayer SJ at the stadium during a moving service.

Opera, pop concerts, musicals, and other large-scale events rock at the neighbouring Olympiahalle (Olympic Hall), which hosts up to 14,000 visitors. At the Olympic swimming pool, families splash with laughter on a grey and rainy day. Dancers pirouette at the ice rink, and hockey players learn from their masters at the EHC Red Bull München.

Anyone ambitious must climb the Olympiaturm (Olympic Tower). Its viewing platform, 200 metres above ground, offers a breathtaking panoramic view over Munich and the Bavarian Alps. The small exhibition of Rock & Pop at the lower platform presents guitars signed by Frank Zappa, Pink Floyd, and the Rolling Stones. Golden vinyl and rare phonograms spin their music alongside. At 181 metres, an exquisite restaurant serves connoisseurs' culinary delights. At the foot of the tower, the busy takeout restaurant with a terrace offers an affordable alternative.

Munich's Walk of Fame plods along the bank of the Olympic Lake, where the organisers immortalised those musicians whose concerts have repeatedly filled the Olympic Stadium. The mix of feet and hands includes the Austrian crooner Udo Jürgens - and international luminaries, such as Elton John, Metallica and Die Toten Hosen. A lake stage, the Theatron, delights its audience during the summer by allowing emerging local bands a chance to rock the waters.

▲ The Olympiaturm offers a sensational view over Munich and its surroundings.

The Olympic village nearby, constructed for the 11,500 participants of the 1972 Summer Olympics, harbours the past spirits to the north of the Olympic Tower. There, the terrorist group *Black September* assassinated the Israeli Olympic squad on 5 September. After the games, the city transformed the spacious athletes' village into a residential complex and a hall of residence for students.

At the neighbouring Museum Sea Life, delightfully designed by Greenpeace, more than 10,000 flippers bustle through a 750,000-litre water tank. Water creatures from Bavaria's rivers and lakes, from the Mediterranean and the Baltic Sea parade their enticing colours. A well-presented replica of the raging Isar enchants with the beauty of the Bavarian alpine upland.

Games of Sorrow, Games of Joy

Eight activists of the group Black September slipped through the barbwire of the Olympic Village on 5 September 1972 - hiding Kalashnikovs under their coats. At the quarters of the Israeli Olympic squad, they assassinated two athletes and took nine as hostages. Their demands: *the release of 200 prisoners, among them members of the RAF*. When the negotiations failed, the terrorists requested a private jet to escape to Cairo. On their way to the military airfield in Fürstenfeldbruck, a sniper lost his nerves, Bavaria played Wild West, and the terrorists blew their helicopter up with a hand grenade. The explosion tore all hostages, a policeman and the five assassins into pieces. Munich wept salty tears, but the games had to continue. A wailing beam at the Olympiazentrum reminds of the massacre.

BMW Zentrum

Facts & Figures

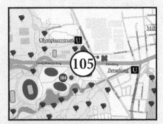

The Bayerische Motorenwerke assemble their luxury speedsters in factory plants behind the Olympic Centre. Since 1972, the headquarters of Munich's car manufacturer brood over the future of mobility at the BMW four-cylinder skyscraper. The architect Karl Schwanzer constructed the 100-metre-tall building; four towers rise on cantilever arms, interconnected, forming a cross-shaped engine cylinder. The adjacent *BMW Museum* opened in 1973; in a windowless futuristic building, it presents the enticing history of the company. Common parlance lovingly compares its shape with a salad bowl. The distribution warehouse *BMW Welt*, constructed by the architects Coop Himmelb(l)au in 2007, delivers the company's high-tech vehicles to end customers. Already in 2013, it had handed the keys of the one-hundred thousandth car to a proud new owner.

Technology meets eroticism when it merges the power of the cylinder with the curving lash of a whip; the **Bayerische Motorenwerke** are the masters of seductive design. The customers receive their commercial vehicles at the futuristic *BMW Welt* - a feeling that reminds many of a wedding night. The impressive temple is covered in glass and designed as a wave that radiates the elegance of a flashing thundercloud. Turrets and ramps intermingle in ordered chaos. They host showrooms, presentation halls, restaurants and bars. BMW's strategists made a mark with their distribution warehouse, underpinning their market position as the worldwide leading producer of high-class vehicles.

The history of the Bayerische Motorenwerke started in 1916 when the Rapp Motorenwerke AG and the Gustav Otto Flugmaschinenfabrik merged. Initially, the company constructed aeroplanes. The first motorcycle rolled off the assembly line in 1923, the R 32. When management took over the Fahrzeugfabrik Eisenach in 1928, the company expanded its offering to vehicles; shortly after, the engineers launched the BMW Dixi.

Under the Nazi regime, the enterprise became the country's leading engine manufacturer. The number of employees sky-rocketed from 8000

▲ The BMW-headquarters are located next to the Olympic Centre.

in 1933 to 180,000 within five years.

World War II destroyed BMW's construction facilities, and the Berlin Wall separated the Eisenacher Automobilwerke from its headquarters. Then, Munich's management team attempted a new beginning. The engineers designed the first motorcycle of the post-war years in 1948 - the R 24; in 1952, the speedy BMW 501 chugged across the country. After the economic crises of the 1970s, the construction of the prolific BMW 1500 gave the company new hope. Later, the engineers manufactured sports cars, the BMW 3, 5 & 7 series, took over Rover and researched hybrid and hydrogen engines.

Location: Am Olympiapark 2 **BMW Museum:** Opening Times Tue - Sun 10.00 - 18.00 Entrance: Adults 9 €, Concession 6 € Internet: https://www.bmw-welt.com
Guided tours through the manufacturing facilities: see Internet

BMW and the World of Tomorrow

Fossil resources become sparse, the climate changes and the future belongs to hydrogen and electric engines, not fossil fuels. At the Expo 2000, BMW presented an innovative hydrogen car, the 750i, which the Bavarian engineers upgraded to the BMW Hydrogen 7 shortly after. However, the infrastructure is still lacking and a hydrogen filling station operates only at the company's test course because the liquefaction process is challenging and expensive. More promising are the BMW electric vehicles marked with the letter *i*. The first vehicle went into series production in 2013. With a reach of 200 kilometres and a battery charging time of 6-8 hours, they are perfect for cities. And BMW announces with pride that *innovation means reflecting today on the world of tomorrow* - a philosophy that inspires.

(106) Dachau Altstadt

Facts & Figures

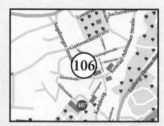

Dachau, idyllically located at an elevation above the stream Amper, suffers from the staining fame having invented the template of the Nazi concentration camps. However, the city's moving history stretches back to medieval times. At the Schlossberg, the Wittelsbacher dynasty erected its first summer residence. Dachau's upper city is one of Bavaria's most attractive market towns, offering a panoramic view of the Bavarian highlands. Its character was engraved during the 16th and 17th centuries; its irresistible charm survived unaltered into the modern era. Picturesque bourgeois facades from the 19th century complement the urban landscape, and the beauty of the nearby Dachauer Moos, a marshland, attracted an artists' colony. The baroque parish Church of St Jakob is one of the few countryside temples in Bavaria that has preserved its traditional magic through the centuries.

Dachau, the city at the Amper (a creek), is 350 years older than Munich; documents mention the settlement in 805 - at a time when Charlemagne ruled the Frankish Kingdom. Archaeologists unearthed many treasures in Dachau, just like in Freising. The lands from Munich's gravel plains to the climatically benevolent hills in the north were inhabited by humans during the Stone Age. Findings from the *La Tène Culture* prove a Celtic settlement.

By the time of Christ, a Roman road crossed Rhaetia, passing Dachau on its way from Salzburg to Augsburg. The Grafen von Scheyern erected a fortress at the nearby Giglberg in the early 12th century. In 1182, when Konrad III, a member of the dynasty Grafen von Dachau, died without an heir, the Wittelsbacher Herzog Otto I inherited the lands.

During the 13th century, Bavaria's sovereigns fortified the Schlossberg, and in 1240, they granted Dachau the right to hold a market. Finally, Herzog Wilhelm IV and Herzog Albrecht V expanded the castle into a summer palace. The court defined the rhythm of Dachau until the construction of Schloss Nymphenburg and Schloss Schleißheim; then, the city fell into a deep sleep.

▲ Dachau's historic city centre has preserved its character into modern times.

During the 19th century, attracted by the romantic location and the idyllic palace, artists from Munich settled in Dachau, founding an artists' colony to harvest the brilliant light of the moorlands.

In 1933, the Nazi regime appreciated Dachau as a city, and the town hosted Germany's first concentration camp. Later, Adolf Hitler appointed Dachau's commanding officer, Theodor Eicke, to the head of the Third Reich's gas chambers - in short, he became the regime's chief executioner.

After World War II, Dachau digested its history, and today, with a sad voice, the town warns against right-wing populists, tyrants and crimes against humanity.

Location: Dachau **Entrance:** Without charge **Opening Times:** Always accessible
Internet: https://www.dachau.de   see also: https://www.verein-dachauer-moos.de
Künstlerkolonie Dachau: https://dachauer-galerien-museen.de

Die Künstlerkolonie Dachau (Artists' Colony Dachau)

During the 19th century, the painters Simon Warnberger, Wilhelm von Kobell, Johann Georg von Dillis and Eduard Schleich discovered the brilliant lights at the Dachauer Moos, a marshland. The Dachauer also stood as a model for their paintings and posed with their traditional costumes. At the turn of the century, many artists flocked to the village, and the painters founded the vibrant Artists' Colony Dachau. The group was widely appreciated across Germany for its solidarity rooted in the archetype of brotherhood. Dachau promoted and encouraged their creative struggles, and they offered living space and ateliers - often for free. The two world wars, however, put an end to their endeavours. Today, the artists' colony prospers again, encouraged by the recent inauguration of the Dachauer Art Gallery.

Schloss Dachau

Facts & Figures

The Schloss Dachau, a contemporary of Munich's Neuveste, was the first summer residence of the Bavarian regents. Herzog Wilhelm IV and Herzog Albrecht V commissioned the palace in the 16th century. The castle, visible from far, has survived the ravages of time only in parts. The enchanting Renaissance facade attracts the eye, and the richly decorated festival hall provides a beautiful ambience for classical concerts. A magnificent coffered wooden ceiling vaults the banqueting hall; Hans Wisreutter timbered it in 1566. The fruit trees at the inviting court garden overlook Munich and the Bavarian uplands; one may catch a sight of the Alps when the Föhn-wind blows. In 1823, Friedrich Ludwig von Sckell added an English landscape garden. The woodlands run along the picturesque Fürstenweg, which connects uptown Dachau with the farmsteads below.

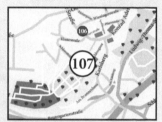

Schloss Dachau in the old town is an eye-catcher. The bird's-eye view from the palace catches the sight of the Alps on sunny days. During the 16th century, the Bavarian regents overlooked most of their lands from the Schlossberg, and thus, they constructed their summer palace at this elevation, designed in the Italian Renaissance style.

In 1403, documents mention a fortress subordinated to Herzog Ernst. Neglected and overgrown, the building became dilapidated in the 16th century, and the complex had to be destroyed. On behalf of Herzog Wilhelm IV, the master builder Heinrich Schöttl laid the founding stone to a four-wing complex in 1546. Thirty years later, Wilhelm Egkl finished the building under Herzog Albrecht V.

The castle served the Bavarian regents as a summer palace since the Counter Reformation. On the day of the capstone, the country estate housed 108 rooms, lightened by 350 windows. Finally, the regents consecrated the chapel to Saint Nicholas, a church demolished by now.

The spacious court garden magically includes many fruit trees. It is a jewel of the Baroque, delightfully hidden behind the walls, enchantingly protected, with chirping birds and apples so sweet. The impressive

▲ Schloss Dachau was the first summer residence of the Wittelsbacher dynasty.

Renaissance coffered wooden ceiling at the banqueting hall dates from the 16th century.

Kurfürst Max Emanuel refurbished the castle in 1715 and commissioned the architect Joseph Effner to redecorate the saloon wing in the Baroque style. Ever since, the hoof-shaped staircase twists from the drab ground floor to the bright ballroom on the upper level.

When construction work shifted from Dachau to Schloss Nymphenburg, the summer residence declined, and when the Bavarian sovereigns felt the squeeze, King Maximilian I sold its brick stones to a housing project. Only the festive saloon wing survived the onslaught; the magnificent Great Hall is still worth a visit.

Location: Kurfürst-Max-Emanuel-Platz 2, 85221 Dachau **Entrance:** Adults 2 €
Opening Times: Wed - Sun 12.00 - 16.00 (tickets at the Café)
Internet: https://www.schloesser.bayern.de/deutsch/schloss/objekte/dachau.htm

Knight Arnold of the Giglberg

A fortress towered over the Giglberg long before the Wittelsbacher dynasty had built their summer palace in Dachau. Knight Arnold dwelled at the castle, a rotten egg who squeezed the blood out of his vassals. The fast liver led a nasty life; he was addicted to feasting, drinking and the maidens. Above all, he mocked God. One day, a dreadful thunderstorm settled on the hill, and a stroke of lightning fissured the Giglberg into halves. His fortress crashed into the crack and disappeared without a trace, swallowed by Mother Earth. Ever since, ghosts haunt the hill at midnight. Common parlance tells of fire-red wolfhounds roaming the mountain and devouring maidens. The people know: this is why the Wittelsbacher erected the castle in Dachau and not on the Giglberg - they were also terrified of the devil's beasts.

(108) Gedenkstätte KZ Dachau

Facts & Figures

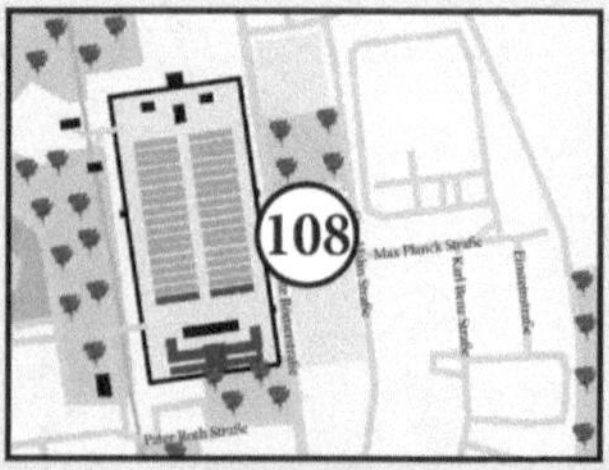

The Dachau Concentration Camp Memorial Site commemorates the 200,000 victims who were incarcerated here under inhuman conditions during World War II. The memorial site reminds the world of the 40,000 helpless brutally murdered by the Nazi regime in Dachau. Former detainees instigated the memorial site in 1965. Annually, more than one million visitors tiptoe with a bleeding heart across the terrifying barracks. The holocaust memorial site alerts all generations to the brutalities man is capable of inflicting on the human soul. The circular route, best navigated with an (audio)guide, illustrates what cannot be described in words. An extensive specialist bookstore offers help and further literature. The discussions and presentations at the conference rooms strive to render the carnage tangible, the cruelties, which must never be forgotten. The world weeps - the world mourns - with caution, we face absolute evil.

On 22 March 1933, shortly after Adolf Hitler had seized power in Germany, Heinrich Himmler opened the gates to the regime's first **concentration camp** at Dachau's former *Royal Ammunition Factory*. In the first phase of terror, the fascists silenced the political opposition. They detained critics or anyone who had voiced concerns about right-wing ideology: communists, social democrats and trade union officials.

In June 1933, the Führer appointed Theodor Eicke as the head of the compound. The devil's henchman drew up the camp statues, which he later imposed across the Reich. Bypassing the judiciary, he mandated the camp commander the power over life and death.

Dachau quickly matured into a prime example of oppression and turned into a training centre of the *Totenkopf-SS* (Death's Head Unit: a task force which administered the Reich's concentration camps). The sadists practised the execution of prisoners until the pulling of the trigger evoked no emotion. The *School of Terror* taught that *tolerance is weakness,* and the teachers ordered their students to aim at the neck - and fire.

In 1934, the Führer promoted Theodor Eicke to the Reich's Chief Inspector of Concentration Camps and Commander of the SS-Guards,

▲ The Dachau Concentration Camp Memorial Site remembers the victims of fascism.

a career only suitable for psychopaths who enjoy watching over gas chambers.

Since 1935, the Nazi regime imprisoned Sinti & Roma, beggars, the homeless, homosexuals, and clerics.

In the spring of 1938, the Nazis initiated the next phase: the annihilation of races. During Kristallnacht, they incarcerated 11,000 Jews in Dachau; after the annexation of Austria, they cooped up the Jews in Vienna, and after the outbreak of World War II, it was the turn of the Polish, Dutch and French. During the 12 years of violence, the Dachau Concentration Camp mutilated the souls of 200,000 victims and sacrificed more than 40,000 innocent souls.

Location: Alte Römerstraße 75 **Entrance:** Without charge **Opening Times:** daily 9.00 - 17.00
Internet: https://www.kz-gedenkstaette-dachau.de
Literature: Biografisches Gedenkbuch der Münchner Juden 1933–1945

Freedom!

In April 1945, US-American troops marched into Bavaria and liberated the concentration camp. As the Allied forces advanced, the Nazis evacuated the gas chambers and sent the prisoners on a death march. More than half of the detained succumbed to the hardship before the survivors were freed. Forty-eight hours into the advance, Major General Max Ulich recalled the guards from Dachau; the sound of isolated gunfire snarled through the air. On 29 April 1945, Colonel Sparks and the Seventh United States Army assumed control of the barbwire. The GIs witnessed the atrocities; in a fury, they assassinated some of the remaining guards. However, Obersturmbannführer Eduard Weiter and Martin Weiß, the camp commanders, had escaped. Weiter shot himself days later; Weiß was captured in Mühldorf am Inn and brought to justice.

(109) Schloss Schleißheim

Facts & Figures

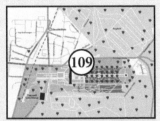

The castle in Oberschleißheim, *Munich's Versailles*, served the Bavarian sovereigns as an idyllic summer residence during the Age of Absolutism. The complex covers three areas: a farmstead with a country house, the new palace, and a garden with a pavilion. Kurfürst Maximilian I had the rustic *Alte Schloss* constructed during the late Renaissance, modelled in the style of Italian country villas; the manor and hermitage is the oldest part of the compound. In the years 1701-1726, Enrico Zuccalli built the *Neue Schloss*, an elaborate royal seat in Baroque style; Joseph Effner and François Cuvilliés expanded the palace and decorated it in French Rococo. Towards the east, Kurfürst Max Emanuel erected Schloss Lustheim in 1684 - a wedding gift for his wife Maria Antonia von Österreich, the daughter of the Hapsburg Emperor Leopold I. Fountains with water jets and Greek statues decorate the palace garden.

When Herzog Wilhelm V constructed the Jesuit Church of St Michael in the 16th century, he overspent Bavaria's feeble treasury and had to step down, leaving empty coffers. His ambitious son, Kurfürst Maximilian I, followed him on the throne in 1597. The ageing father purchased land from the bishops in Freising, and - seeking solitude - he retreated as an eremite to the Dachauer Moos, a marshland. In his final days, he immersed himself in prayers and contemplation.

His manor house had included a farmstead and some hiking paths - trails in a rough landscape - with chapels along the way and a secluded hermitage, where Wilhelm V repented his many sins. At his farm, the retired sovereign bred sturdy horses for the regent's stables; he brewed flavourful beer and operated a dairy farm. The economic success of the estate impressed Maximilian I; the son purchased the estate in 1616, promising his father an annuity for life in return. One year later, the Elector demolished the old manor house and replaced it with an Italian-style country villa - the **Alte Schloss**. From the times of Wilhelm V, only the clock tower remained, still beating the hour at the entrance to the inner courtyard.

▲ The Neue Schloss in Oberschleißheim outshines Versailles in grandeur.

The rustic palace had quadrupled the size of the estate; the single-storey building, constructed in late Renaissance style, impresses by its outside staircase, centred along a symmetrical facade. The large hall, the museum's foyer, hints at the compound's former splendour.

Some 100 years later, Kurfürst Ferdinand Maria died at the southern wing, today the Schlosswirtschaft, a restaurant. The regent had retreated to the marshes of the Dachauer Moos after his wife, Henriette Adelaide von Savoyen, had passed away.

During the 17th century, after Kurfürst Max Emanuel had expelled the Turks from Europe, the Bavarian sovereign

Location: 85764 Oberschleißheim **Entrance:** Adults 10 €, Concession 8 €
Opening Times: 9.00 - 18.00 **Internet:** https://www.schloesser-schleissheim.de
see also: https://www.oberschleissheim.de/Schleissheimer-Schloesser.n15.html

Popular Piety Brought to Life

The northern wing of the Alte Schloss exhibits an ecumenical collection that is unique in the world: six thousand items of popular piety document the Christian festivals of the church calendar. Professor Gertrud Weinhold had collected the objects during her journeys across the globe and donated them to the Bayerische Nationalmuseum. The branch museum in Oberschleißheim exhibits crucifixes, nativity scenes, rosaries, mannequins of the devil, statues of the Madonna, wooden figurines of saints and dioramas of the miracle of Pentecost. The mascots once embellished private homes, or the believers carried them as charms under their shirts. The collection presents the faith of everyday people; the museum introduces the items lovingly to bring the anthropology of Christian piety to life.

received the hand of Maria Antonia von Österreich, the Emperor's daughter. On 15 June, Europe celebrated the wedding in Vienna. Three years later, the Hapsburg dynasty confided in him the supreme command of the imperial troops, and the Elector took Belgrade by storm. Finally, Austria had overcome the Turkish danger.

At the climax of Bavarian power, the lands drained in the blood of its people - more than 40,000 soldiers had lost their lives on the battlefield, and Kurfürst Max Emanuel wanted more: royal dignities were close at hand! Maria Antonia, his wife, was the rightful heir to the Spanish crown should her brother, Carlos II, pass away without an heir. Meanwhile, Max Emanuel had finished **Schloss Lustheim** in Munich and inaugurated the garden palace with a banquet. Even Emperor Leopold I was present to honour the newlywed couple and their imperial splendour.

When Maria Antonia gave birth to Joseph Ferdinand in 1692, her spark of life had faded, and she rested her eyes - forever. Six years later, Carlos II of Spain nominated the Bavarian prince as his heir, but one year later, the frail boy died, too. And the *Goddess of Fate* grinned at Bavaria ungraciously with a mischievous smile.

When Max Emanuel had constructed Schloss Lustheim, he still harboured hopes for royal dignities, but ten years later, when Carlos II passed away, he stood at the abyss empty-handed. At last, the Sun King Louis XIV of France unexpectedly promised Bavaria a royal crown, and Max Emanuel switched sides. The *Goddess of War*, however, had deserted him, too, and in the Battle of Blenheim 1704, he lost his country; the Austrians marched into Bavaria; Max Emanuel had to flee, but the Elector still dreamt of royal dignities - at night.

After the Treaty of Rastatt, which ended the War of the Spanish Succession, Max Emanuel returned from his exile in Paris. Two years later, he resumed building at the **Neue Schloss** in Oberschleißheim. The portraits showcased at the castle depict him as the conqueror of the Turks; they originate from this period. Max Emanuel still envisioned glory: Emperor Karl VI had not fathered an heir, and Europe prepared for another war of succession.

Austria altered its laws in 1713 to allow princesses to ascend to the throne, but would the incrusted European nobility respect the decree? Eagerly, Max Emanuel expanded Schloss Schleißheim and Schloss Nymphenburg, added gardens and tapestry, and prayed to the *Goddess of Fortune* to mercifully smile on Bavaria's diplomatic adventure.

▲ The manor at the Alte Schloss is the oldest part of the compound.

In the year 1726, Kurfürst Max Emanuel passed away, and his son Karl Albrecht bashfully followed in his footsteps. In 1740, Emperor Karl IV embarked on his final journey, and Bavaria opened its arms to welcome what the diplomacy had seeded for more than 50 years.

To be sure, the Pragmatic Sanction of 1713 envisaged Maria Theresia of Austria as the heir to the imperial crown, but Karl Albrecht convinced the delegates, and Frankfurt crowned the Bavarian Emperor on 24 January 1742.

Two days later, the Austrians occupied Munich, and the Emperor fled. He returned to the Alps two years later - in October 1744. And six months later, he succumbed to gouty arthritis. Bavaria's dream to steal the imperial crown from the Austrians had vanished into thin air.

Bavaria's First Military Airfield

Schloss Schleißheim was struck hard by the Allied air raids during World War II because, close by, Adolf Hitler commanded a German military airport. Already in 1912, Prince Regent Luitpold inaugurated in Oberschleißheim the first Bavarian flying squadron; King Ludwig III added motorists. The Führer strengthened the compound with bunkers and control rooms; the operators coordinated the aerial battles over South Germany. By 1939, a prisoner-of-war camp confined French and Russian soldiers captured during combat. After the war and until 1981, a military training centre drilled soldiers, first US-American GIs and later recruits of the German Bundeswehr. Today, the hangar houses a Museum of Aircraft, exhibiting planes and spacecraft. It is a branch of the Deutsche Museum.

Highlights of Schloss Schleißheim

The Versailles of Munich was born before its brother, Schloss Nymphenburg. At the end of the 16th century, Herzog Wilhelm V set up a contemplation room in Oberschleißheim and relocated at the age of 50 in 1598. He lived in seclusion at the moor for another 28 years. The **Alte Schloss** (Old Castle) originated with the introverted regent, but most parts had been refurbished. Only the authentic gate tower dates from his time. The current complex was built under Herzog Maximilian I from 1617 to 1623. The middle hall and the southern rooms had to be reconstructed after World War II. Peter Candid designed the stuccos and frescoes. In addition to the *Museum religiöser Volkskunst* (Museum of Religious Folk Art), the Alte Schloss also houses the *Sammlung zur Landeskunde Ost- und Westpreußens* (a collection depicting East and West Prussia).

Between 1701 and 1726, the court architects Enrico Zuccalli and Joseph Effner built on behalf of Kurfürst Max Emanuel the **Neue Schloss** (New Palace), separated from the Alte Schloss by a parterre. The palace was originally planned as a four-wing complex, but only the eastern wing was finished. The baroque castle is unusually located west of the garden; the morning sun, not the evening sun shines over the garden. Alte Schloss and Neue Schloss were to form a unit, which is why. Johann Baptist Zimmermann, Charles Dubut, Cosmas Damian Asam and Jacopo Amigoni were involved in the interior design.

The vestibule made of Tergernsee marble and the staircase testify to the monumentality of the complex. The impressive ceiling fresco (Cosmas Damian Asam) shows *Venus in the forge of Volcano*. The Great Hall is kept in white. It glorifies Kurfürst Max Emanuel as the *Victorious leader in the fight against the Turkish army* (Franz Joachim Beich). The ceiling painting depicts the *Fight of Aeneas* (Jacopo Amigoni). The Victorian Hall served as a dining room. Its ceiling painting shows the scene in which *Dido receives Aeneas*. Paintings refer to Max Emanuel's victorious battles. The Elector's apartments extend to the south, that of the Electress to the north. They include an anteroom, an audience room, a bedroom and a cabinet; many are luxuriously decorated with carpets and paintings. The documentation room illustrates the history of the castle. On the ground floor, a model of the castle as it was planned (date:1725) shows the impressive overall complex. However, the ambition was never realised.

▲ The Flugwerft Schleißheim presents the history of aviation and spacecraft.

The **castle garden** is one of the most beautiful in Germany. Enrico Zuccalli designed the baroque splendour in 1684. By 1689, an extensive canal system crossed the complex. A fountain system allows for impressive jets. The parterre is decorated with statues of the Goddess Minerva and the Greek hero Hercules (Giuseppe Volpini 1717/23).

The central canal leads to **Schloss Lustheim**, which Enrico Zuccalli built 1,300 metres from the Neue Schloss. The ballroom and the electoral apartments were designed by the painters Francesco Rosa, Giovanni Trubillio and Johann Anton Gumpp. The scenes show the goddess of the hunt, Diana.

Flugwerft Schleißheim: Effnerstraße 18, 85764 Oberschleißheim
Opening Times: daily 9.00 - 17.00, Entrance: Adults 7 €, Concession 3 €
Internet: https://www.deutsches-museum.de/flugwerft-schleissheim

Deutsches Museum Flugwerft Schleißheim

In 1992, near Schloss Schleißheim, a branch of the Deutsche Museum opened at a former hangar of the army. It covers an area of 8,000 square metres and explores the history of aviation and spacecraft. In the spacious halls, the museum presents aircraft, helicopters, military equipment and the evolution of civil aviation. Gliders (DFS Olympia Meise) show their technical brilliance alongside bombers from the German Air Force (Henkel HE 111). Launch vehicles, satellites, a replica of the Mercury space capsule, a model of the Helios space probe and a copy of the Spacelab space station are on display. A historical outline leads from the beginnings of aviation to the present. The Königlich-Bayerische Fliegertruppe (Royal Bavarian Air Force) was stationed at the former airport between 1912 and 1919.

Freising

Facts & Figures

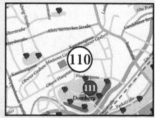

The Episcopalian Freising is a medieval town; its roots are more profound than Munich's. During the 8th century, a village tilled the fertile soils of the Erdinger Moos at the transition from Munich's gravel planes to the Lower Bavarian hilly region. Two elevations, the Domberg and the Weihenstephaner Berg, protected the citizens from flooding and assault. Shortly after Herzog Heinrich der Löwe had founded Munich, Freising burnt down in 1159. The burgess rebuilt their town during the late 12th century; the urban layout is still imprinted on the enclosure, and the morphology is still visible in today's streets. Until the expropriation of church property in 1803, Freising was Bavaria's most splendid diocesan town, commissioned mainly by the bishops. To this day, the Catholic faith defines the rhythm of life, although a wave of immigration has recently added to its diverse charm.

Archaeological finds at the Domberg and the Weihenstephaner Berg tell of **Freising's** strategic importance throughout the ages. Excavations near the municipal school unearthed ceramics and hornstone weapons from the Neolithic period; the region must have been populated as early as 1000 BC. Artefacts from the Early Bronze Age document a settlement since the Urnfield Period.

Around 715 AD, after the great migration of the 5th century, the Agilolfings, Bavaria's first tribal leaders, constructed a wooden fortress at today's Domberg. As no other city foundation by these Bajuwaric settlers is known, Freising must be the oldest town in Upper Bavaria.

Documents mention *Castrum Freisinga* for the first time in 744 when Herzog Hugibert and Herzog Odilo reigned. After Charlemagne had banished the last Agilolfinger Herzog Tassilo III in 788, Bavaria fell under the Carolingian dynasty.

Towards the middle of the 8th century, Saint Boniface appointed Freising to a bishopric. At that time, the people still prayed to a pantheon of gods, but the monastery gradually united the ethnic groups under one faith. Without a unifying religion, no sovereign was to reign.

▲ The Marienplatz in Freising hosts a market since 996.

Since the 8th century, Freising has lived and grown under the power of the crosier, a bishop's seat. The influence of the monastery stretched from Landshut in the north to Garmisch at the Alpine foothills.

The expropriation of church property in 1803 hit the town hard; the reformers closed the monastery and Freising's population declined rapidly. Soon, the city was only half its previous size.

However, the *Goddess of Vitality* returned in recent years; immigrants refreshed the genetic pool, and the nearby agricultural university has attracted many students. By now, enthusiasm carries the citizens again.

Location: Freising **Entrance:** Without charge **Opening Times:** Always accessible
Internet: https://www.freising.de // https://www.kreis-freising.de
see also: https://www.erzbistum-muenchen.de

The Hallertauer Hop Production

The region north of Freising is called the Hallertau where farmers have wired hops to long poles since the 8th century. Hops are the only condiment that brewers may apply to the golden manna in Bavaria. Its flavour is created upon heating while sterilising the beer. The Middle Ages escaped epidemics by drowning the bacteria in beer. Historically, the frothy beverage contained only a little alcohol, and mothers offered a cup to children with the morning porridge - the lesser of two evils and thus worry-free. Talented historians argue that the hops farming in the Hallertau is proof enough for the existence of breweries in Freising in the Early Middle Ages. During the 20th century, the Hallertau became the largest hop-growing area in Germany; still today, the hops are produced by medium-sized farms in a traditional way.

⑪ St Maria & St Korbinian

Facts & Figures

Freising's history is intertwined with the Bishop's seat. Bavaria's most striking temple settled at an elevation. The clerics constructed the compound at the Domberg for more than a thousand years; their efforts terminated only with the expropriation of church property in the early 19th century, initiated by Napoleon. Monasteries reclaimed the lands during the Early Middle Ages, and equally, Freising to the north of Munich tilled the lands after it was born. The initial impulse of our culture emanated from pious monks long before secular rulers reigned. The comprehensive library of Bavaria's first theological-philosophical academia, founded in the 9th century, testifies to this early revolution. Throughout the centuries, the best artists of the time expressed their vision at the Freising Minster, the spiritual power base of the bishops playing many political games.

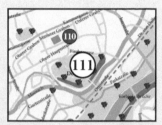

The bishops of Freising pitched their mighty cross at the **Domberg** thirty metres above the historic city; they organised society according to the rules of Saint Benedict, who had passed away in 547.

When Munich constructed the Frauenkirche during the 15th century, the anxious patricians wanted to relocate the bishop's seat to the Isar; the endeavour was only successful when King Maximilian I established the Archdiocese of Munich & Freising in 1821.

Ora et Labora was cumbersome, and the diplomacy of the powerful was a dangerous game. Until the 19th century, indulgences, donations and cessions empowered the bishops. Just like Munich's Electors had expanded the Münchner Residenz in the city centre to assert their power, the bishops in Freising fortified their Dome to a spiritual citadel, too - a manifestation of their ecclesiastic authority.

By and by, Bavaria's clerics gained in influence, and a political correction was inevitable. Maximilian Graf von Montgelas relentlessly advanced the expropriation of church property, striking hard at the diocesan town Freising. The dissolution of the abbey broke up the monastic library; the holy books were relocated to the Bayerische Staatsbibliothek. The

▲ The Domberg housed for more than 1000 years the power of the crosier.

Count even barricaded the training centre of the diocese to limit the bishop's leverage. One generation later, King Ludwig I reopened the Dome of Freising, but the crosier was broken.

In no other Bavarian city had the expropriation of church property left deeper wounds than in Freising. The cathedral, where generations of artists had expressed the divine wisdom of the New Testament, was degraded to a parish church. Glory only returned when Pope Benedict XVI appointed the temple to a procathedral. The Domberg, once Bavaria's spiritual and cultural centre, could, however, never fully recover its former historical significance.

Location: Domberg **Entrance:** Without charge **Opening Times:** daily 8.00 - 17.00
Internet: https://www.freisinger-dom.de
Literature: Verein für Diözesangeschichte: Geschichte des Erzbistums München und Freising

Saint Corbinian and the Bear

The itinerant preacher Corbinian, born around 680 in Paris, stretches his protective hand over the lands as the patron saint of the archbishopric; the Domberg safeguards his holy relics in a neo-Romanesque shrine at the crypt. Corbinian, who died in 730, embellishes Freising's coat of arms; a bear carries his belongings. According to legend, the beast killed the saint's pack animal during a pilgrimage to Rome. At that point Corbinian flogged the hairy symbol of motherhood into repentance and forced him to carry his possessions to Italy instead. Corbinian is said to have rammed his stick into the soil of the Weihenstephaner Berg at the southern slope and discovered a water spring. Ever since, the local breweries have fed their fountains from a divine source, brewing the golden manna with sacred water - the secret of the recipe.

Highlights of St Maria & St Korbinian

The bishops of Freising expanded their cathedral into a spiritual power house, just as the Bavarian Electors and Kings expanded the Münchner Residenz into a secular fortress. By 715, a Lady Chapel on the Domberg protected the lands. From 724 onwards, Saint Corbinian was Freising's first cleric to celebrate mass in the chapel. A monastery with a school and a library was established as early as the 8th century. After a devastating fire, Bishop Adalbert rebuilt the complex in the late 12th century. The master builder Jörg von Halspach added Gothic elements. Egid Quirin and Cosmas Damian Asam redesigned the interior in the Baroque style from 1724 onwards. After secularisation in 1802 and with the founding of the Erzbistum München-Freising (Archdiocese of Munich & Freising) in 1821, the spiritual centre moved from Freising to the Frauenkirche in Munich.

The simple **courtyard** with a fountain was designed in the late 17th century based on the prince-bishop's complex in Salzburg. The **vestibule** is the oldest surviving part of the compound. It was built between 1314 and 1480. The **main portal** was part of a previous Romanesque building. On the left is Emperor Friedrich I Barbarossa with Bishop Otto von Freising. On the right, the Emperor's wife, Beatrix of Burgundy, shines. The toad below is a symbol of fertility; it refers to the birth of a son.

The interior is striking because the **nave** is lowered. Here, the Freisinger take part in the services. The **ceiling fresco** depicts the virtues of Saint Corbinian: piety, wisdom, love and devotion. In the middle part, God holds his benevolent hand over the monastery. Christ crowns Corbinian. The **high altar** shows *The Apocalyptic Woman*. The painter Peter Paul Rubens created the picture around 1624. The Archangel Michael triumphs over the evil forces. With her tender foot, Mary overcomes the tempting serpent. The contrast between dark (bottom left) and light (top right) symbolizes the battle between good and evil.

The **side chapels** of the five-aisled church are a journey through art history. The paintings in between depict the Virgin's life from conception to ascension. They were created by Peter Candid, Hans Rottenhammer, Joachim Sadrart and others. In the **sacrament chapel**, Erasmus Grasser depicts the Holy Sepulchre with a group of mourners (1492). Egid Quirin

Asam designed the **Johann Nepomuk Chapel** around 1738.

The octagonal Maximilian Chapel, built by Giovanni Antonio Viscardi in 1710, is a highlight. The Bishops Rupert, Maximilian, Corbinian and Boniface decorate the niches; they brought the Gospel to Bavaria. The ceiling frescoes are by Hans Georg Asam.

The **cloister** encircles a garden. It was set up as a burial place in the 15th century. Johann Baptist Zimmermann stuccoed the walls. The pictures tell the history of the monastery from the 14th to the 18th century. The reading room of the **library** is above the cloister.

▲ Freising recently explored the archetype of the Great Mother Goddess.

The **Benedictus Church** was built in 1347; its Gothic glass windows were created around 1412. Corbinian's first burial site was located here.

Freising's Bestiensäule (Beast Column)

In the crypt of Freising Cathedral, a supporting pillar in the middle shows three-dimensional depictions of fighting soldiers and animals. It is the only one of its kind in Germany and was probably carved in the 12th century. Valiant knights fight voracious dragons that closely resemble crocodiles. Some succeed to stab the monsters, while others are swallowed by them - only the legs are still visible. On the east side, a graceful woman with long braids welcomes the light of the rising sun, a moving symbol of resurrection. Three rows of columns divide the oldest part of Freising Cathedral. The crypt houses a shrine to Saint Corbinian; it contains the bones of the itinerant bishop. The Munich goldsmith Ferdinand Harrach created the shrine based on an ingenious design by Caspar von Zumbusch.

(112) Weihenstephan

Facts & Figures

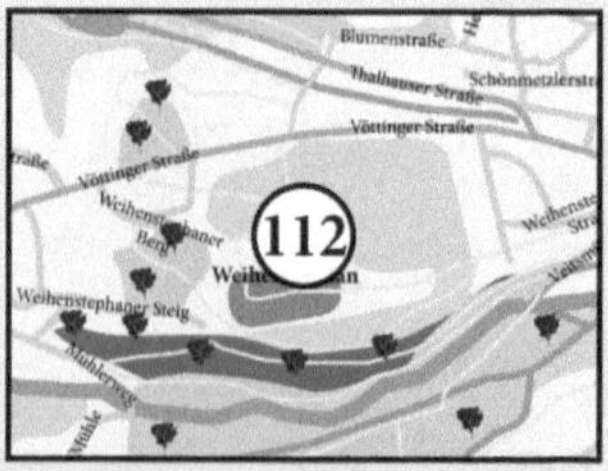

The University of Weihenstephan investigates the process of nature close to Freising. Seven thousand students are enrolled in the *Department of Environment, Food and Rural Affairs*. The former Benedictine monastery offers the lettered a playground for their aspirations in the life sciences. The Korbinians-Quelle at the southern slope, a water spring, reminds of Freising's first itinerant preacher, who discovered the bubbling source at the Weihenstephaner Berg; the freshwater enabled the beer brewing at the hill. Pleasure gardens and a romantic castle with a park sweeten the life of the professors and students alike. Most importantly, the Bräustüberl, a tavern, spices up the lectures. A museum at the water tower and the brewery's chimneys introduces the art of fermented liquid bread; the guided tour indulges with beer tasting.

When Saint Corbinian waded through Freising's alluvial forest in 720, he discovered a chapel at the Domberg, so he settled at the **Weihenstephaner Berg** instead, building a hermitage dedicated to Saint Stephan. Bishop Hitto von Freising consecrated the monastery one hundred years later, and around 1020, a Benedictine order moved in, bringing the art of brewing beer to Weihenstephan.

Despite some critics questioning the authenticity of the documents, for Bavaria, there is no doubt: Weihenstephan is home to the oldest continuously running brewery in the world. The abbots gained the right to splash about in 1040, enlightening the public with their potable mixture. Beer must have been brewed here centuries earlier because no other use for the hops growing in the Hallertau is known. During medieval times, the abbots conjured different types of beer in their cauldrons: a small beer for pilgrims, farmhands and beggars, a dark beer for the clerics and a strong beer for the abbot.

The expropriation of church property dissolved Weihenstephan's monastery, and the Bavarian Government confiscated the brewery. Under the new administration, the homestead transformed into a model farm

▲ Weihenstephan's meadows and forests invite hikers to enjoy a stroll.

where local peasants learned about the latest ideas.

When Schleißheim's agricultural school relocated to Weihenstephan in 1852, the founding stone for the *University of Environment, Food and Rural Affairs* was laid. In 1930, the Technische Universität München joined the endeavour, and Karl Lintner authored the first book on the art of brewing.

Today, Weihenstephan's dairy plant is again under private ownership, but the brewery still drafts its beer as a state enterprise, filling the coffers of the Bavarian treasury. Many master brewers learned their craft at the university - a vocation to cosiness, science, and art.

Location: Weihenstephan **Entrance**: Without charge **Opening times**: Always accessible
Universität Weihenstephan: https://www.hswt.de
https://www.braeustueberl-weihenstephan.de // https://www.weihenstephaner.de

Bavaria's Green Centre

Investigating environmentally friendly diets is a pressing debate of the third millennium. In a rapidly changing world, the battle of calories must be won. More than seven billion people bustle about on our blue planet. The anticipated change in climate will move the cultivation zones northwards; the world requires new plant types to combat the changing weather. The researchers at the *Centre of Life Sciences* in Weihenstephan focus on the survival of the human race in a post-industrial society: *providing the world's nutrition, avoiding resources becoming scarce and protecting the globe against the impact of climate change.* The international team and their students work together with interdisciplinary scientists; silently, they may save the world by providing us with the food of tomorrow.

(113) Allianz Arena

Facts & Figures

Since May 2005, the elite football club FC Bayern München has harvested success after success at the Allianz Arena; the team regularly declassifies the German premier league. The executive board argued for a football melting pot, and finally, they got it! At the Allianz Arena, the spectators chant, glued to the playing field; their cheers heat the atmosphere to the flashpoint. The Swiss architects Herzog & Meuron designed the innovative arena. Its exceptional inclination imparts the feeling of being immersed in the action, even at the uppermost stalls. The 1400 VIPs at the cosy 100 boxes pop their champagne corks, intoxicated by the vibrant atmosphere. The stadium's 2800 membrane airframes light up in red, blue or white during a match, depending on the team playing: the *FC Bayern München*, the club *1860 München* or the *National Football Team*.

Any fan on a pilgrimage to Fröttmaning to witness a game of the **FC Bayern München** quickly forgets that other spectacles in the vicinity attract, too. Not only the € 285 Million Eur **Allianz Arena,** with a capacity of 66,000 spectators, is worth a visit.

The tireless enthusiast will enjoy the best view of the stadium from the 75-metre-tall Fröttmaninger Mülldeponie. The landfill is a child of Germany's economic miracle, where the city deposited the waste of the economic recovery after World War II.

The debris mountain does not permit a glimpse of the playing field, but the parking lot at the wind turbine, erected in 1999 by the Stadtwerke München, offers a panoramic view of Munich and the Alps. The wind turbine is a symbol of Germany, which decided after the 2011 nuclear accident in Fukushima to bow nuclear power out and to switch coal-fired power plants off. Today, the country aspires to rely on alternative energy sources, predominantly harvested inland. The effort is substantial, but only a few years into the project, renewable energy covered a quarter of the annual electricity demand.

The heathen landscape to the north of Munich enjoys a long history:

▲ The wind turbine contributes to satisfy Munich's electricity demand.

a farmstead settled at today's motorway junction München-Fröttmaning in 815. The Heilig-Geist-Kirche at the foothill of the elevation is one of Munich's oldest prayer houses. However, after World War II, the feeder road chased the village away.

The artist Timm Ulrichs unveils the structural transformation with his art installation *Sunken Village*.

Fans who nevertheless prefer to succumb to the passion of the ball may visit the *FC Bayern Erlebniswelt*, a theme park that presents the history of the traditional lederhosen team - a club cheered with enthusiasm by followers all around the world - from Chicago to Hong Kong.

Location: Werner-Heisenberg-Allee 25 **Internet:** https://allianz-arena.com
FC Bayern Erlebniswelt: https://fcbayern.com/museum
ESO Supernova: https://supernova.eso.org/

The ESO Supernova Planetarium & Visitor Centre

In 2018, the ESO Supernova Visitor Centre opened at the research park in Garching in the north of Munich; the initiative was financed thanks to a donation from the Klaus Tschira Foundation. The architects Bernhardt & Partner built the futuristic House of Astronomy; a binary system inspired the design - two stars rotating around each other. In a planetarium, scientists present the world of the starry sky. They introduce the latest scientific findings in astrophysics on over 2000 square metres of exhibition space. Interactive media, video installations and hands-on exhibits bring the wonderful world of the cosmos to Munich. The journey leads from our solar system to distant stars and galaxies. In the section of cosmology, scientists discuss the beginning and the end of the universe.

Index

A

Academica Platonica 117
Adalbertstraße 201
Adlzreiterstraße 297
Africa Days 293
Agilolfinger dynasty 16, 213, 328
AIDS epidemic 102, 103
Aids-Hilfe München 103
Akademie der Bildenden Künste 50, 202
Akademie der Wissenschaften 20
Akademiestraße 202, 203
Akademietheater 233
Aktionsforum Praterinsel 240, 241
Albert, Josef 205
Albrechtinische Gärten 142
Alemanni 5, 16
Allerheiligen Hofkirche 11, 47, 147, 148, 152
Allianz Arena 14, 25, 312, 336, 337
Allianz Versicherung 132
Allied air raids 24, 37, 65, 78, 81, 95, 111, 120, 126, 132, 143, 146, 168, 181, 183, 189, 192, 198, 201, 205, 230, 260, 266, 270, 284, 290, 295, 325
Alpine Museum 29, 240, 241
Alpinum 31
Alte Akademie 19, 117, 200, 202
Alte Münze 81, 188, 285
Alte Pinakothek 11, 12, 33, 49, 173, 185, 188, 189, 190, 191, 192, 194
Alte Rathaus 6, 17, 24, 44, 53, 60, 61, 62, 63, 67, 72, 93, 98, 165, 181
Alter Botanischer Garten 33, 95, 166, 306
Alter Hof 7, 28, 44, 45, 68, 72, 76, 78, 79, 80, 81, 93, 142, 148
Alte Römerstraße 321
Alter Simpl 51, 193
Altötting 8, 102, 175
Altstadtring 102, 222
Amalienburg 30, 296, 301, 304
Am Anger 96, 260
Am Bavariapark 291
Amerikahaus 33, 183
Amigoni, Jacopo 326
Am Olympiapark 315
Amper 316
Am Platzl 45, 82, 83, 85
Amsterdam 265
Anabaptists 18

Andersen, Hans Christian 1
Antikensammlung 11, 33, 49, 172, 176, 177
Antiquarium 18, 46, 47, 148, 152, 278
Apothekenhof 5, 16
Archaeopteryx Bavarica 179
Archangel Michael 36, 45, 116, 117, 118, 119
Archäologische Staatssammlung 29, 212, 213
Archdiocese of Munich & Freising 21, 89, 120, 330, 332
Arcisstraße 186
ARD Music Contest 252
Armeemuseum 22
Arnulfstraße 294
Asam, Cosmas Damian 36, 39, 45, 46, 88, 90, 104, 106, 107, 326, 332
Asam, Egid Quirin 39, 46, 66, 88, 104, 106, 107, 332
Asam, Hans Georg 333
Asamkirche 20, 36, 46, 104, 105, 106, 107
Au 51, 71, 199, 260, 262, 263
Auer Dult 39, 42, 260, 261
Auer Mühlbach 239, 240, 255, 260, 262, 273, 274
Augsburg 5, 16, 18, 20, 70, 71, 104, 121, 249, 284, 285, 297, 309, 316
Augsburger Schied 16
Augustinergasse 16
Augustinerstraße 44, 108, 115

B

Baader, Andreas 197
Bachmann, Josef 197
Badenburg 30, 301, 304, 305
Badenburger See 304
Bad Reichenhall 45, 91, 252
Bad Urach 89
Baker, Josephine 169
Barelli, Agostino 37, 138, 140, 300, 302
Barer Straße 189, 193, 195
Barlow, Willy 182
Barnabas 263
Baron von Eichthal 264
basilisk 70
Basilisk 61
Battle of Austerlitz 10
Battle of Blenheim 300, 324
Battle of Haidhausen 249
Battle of Leipzig 10
Battle of Linnich 299

Battle of Mühldorf 87
Battle of Navarino 171, 182
Battle of Salvator 263
Battle of Vienna 133
Battle of White Mountain 8, 19, 110
Bauer, Ignaz 91
Baumgartner, Franz 286
Bavaria Film GmbH 276, 277
Bavariafilmplatz 277
Bavaria Filmstadt 30, 276, 277
Bavarian Radio State Orchestra 147
Bavarian State Opera 42
Bavarian State Orchestra 147
Bavariaring 286
Bayerische Landesbank 131
Bayerische Motorenwerke 23, 133, 314
Bayerische Nationalmuseum 12, 22, 34, 80, 214, 216, 217, 298, 323
Bayerischer Alpenverein 26, 29, 115
Bayerischer Hof 124
Bayerisches Reinheitsgebot 18
Bayerische Staatsbibliothek 196, 197, 330
Bayerische Staatskanzlei 22, 142, 144, 145
Bayerische Staatsoper 35
Bayerische Staatssammlung Paläontologie 29, 179
Bayerische Theaterakademie 233
Bayerstraße 285
Bayreuth 232
Bayreuther Festspielhaus 232
Bayrhammer, Gustl 221
Becker-Gundahl, Carl 220
Beich, Franz Joachim 302, 326
Berchem, Anton Freiherr von 309
Berg am Laim 24, 130
Berger, Abraham Albert 83
Berger, Matthias 38, 246
Berlin Wall 132, 133, 167, 224, 276, 315
Bern 71
Bernauer, Agnes 309
Bestelmeyer, German 186, 200
Bestiensäule 39, 333
Bier- & Oktoberfestmuseum 28
Bishop Adalbert 332
Bishop Hitto von Freising 334
Bishop Otto von Freising 332
Bishop Waldo 16
Black Death 17, 19, 71, 74, 75, 87
Black Madonna 8, 102
Black September 197, 313
Blumenstraße 36, 268
Blutenburger Schlosskonzerte 31, 308, 309
BMW Museum 314, 315
BMW Welt 314

BMW Zentrum 31, 314
Bogenhausen 16, 34, 49, 215, 230, 231, 236, 246
Bogenhausener Vertrag 230
Bogenhausen Treaty 21
Bohemia 144
Böhm, Peter 184, 185
Bollert, Gerhart 217
Bologna, Giovanni da 91
Boos, Roman Anton 112
Borofsky, Jonathan 206, 207
Börse München 183
Botanischer Garten 23, 31, 283, 303, 306, 307
Brabant, Maria von 69
Brancas, Alexander von 192
Brandhorst, Anette & Udo 194
Braune Haus 24, 53, 173, 180, 182, 295
Braunfels, Stephan 194
Brecht, Bertolt 24, 35, 223
Brienner Straße 130, 131, 133, 134, 182
Bronze Age 16
Bruchsal 106
Brunner, Friedrich 204
Bühlmann, Josef 236
Bürgerbräukeller 24, 52, 53, 137, 180, 181, 253
Bürgersaalkirche 37, 108, 120, 121
Burg Grünwald 30, 278
Burgstraße 45, 76, 77, 146
Burkart, Peter 48, 168
Bürklein, Friedrich 49, 222, 238, 250, 284

C

Café Luitpold 51, 133
Café & Restaurant Isarlust 241
Café Tambosi 135
Café Wiener Platz 245
Candid, Peter 39, 110, 113, 326, 332
Carbonet, Charles 304
Castrum Freisinga 328
Catholic League 8, 9, 19, 70
Celibidache, Sergiu 252
Cenova, Antonio 174
Central Tower 294, 295
Chamberlain, Neville 233
Chiemsee 83
Chinesischer Turm 47, 208, 209, 210, 211
cholera epidemic 60, 162, 167
Christkindlmarkt 43
Christopher Street Day 39, 51, 268
Cignani, C. 140
Codex Maximilianeus Bavaricus Criminalis 295
Cologne War 96
Colonel Sparks 321
Columbus, Christopher 7

Commedia dell'arte 164
Congregation of Jesus 303
Congress of Vienna 10
Corinth, Lovis 206
Corneliusbrücke 257
Cornelius, Peter 38, 49, 142, 175, 198
Corps Franconia München 82
Corps Macaria 82
Corso Leopold 207
Cosimastraße 230
Cosima Wellenbad 230
Counter Reformation 18, 70, 111, 114, 116, 117, 118, 148, 152, 205, 268, 279, 318
COVID-19 pandemic 25
Crayer, Gaspar de 138, 140
Crisensus Bavaricus 115
Cuvilliés, François 322
Cuvilliés Theater 20, 29, 35, 46, 47, 104, 148, 150, 153, 156, 266
Cuvilliés the Elder, François 32, 76, 138, 140, 302, 304
Czechoslovakia 24, 53

D

Dachau 53, 121, 236, 316, 317, 318, 319, 320
Dachau Concentration Camp 14, 24, 32, 52, 53, 131, 320
Dachauer Art Gallery 317
Dachauer Moos 316, 317, 322, 323
Danube 5, 7, 179, 212, 272, 290, 309
Danzig 18
Deggendorf 272
Der Blaue Reiter 23, 50, 133, 178, 179, 188, 202, 203, 218
Deutingerstraße 271
Deutsche Industrieausstellung 22
Deutsches Museum 23, 30, 32, 256, 257, 258, 291, 299, 325, 327
Deutsches Museum Flugwerft 32
Deutsches Museum Verkehrszentrum 30, 291
Deutsches Theater 23, 35, 169
Deutsche Theatermuseum 147
Dienerstraße 73, 74
Diesel, Rudolf 49, 186
Dietl, Helmut 1
Dillingen 121
Dillis, Johann Georg von 317
displaced people 144, 237
Döllgast, Hans 189
Domberg 39, 328, 330, 331, 332, 334
Donaueschingen 287
Donauschwaben 144
Donnersbergerbrücke 294, 295

Dornier, Claude 49, 186
Dreifaltigkeitskapelle 91
Dreifaltigkeitsplatz 91
Drückebergergasse 137
Dubut, Charles 326
Dutschke, Rudi 197

E

Ebendorfer, Thomas 107
Eberding, August 157
Eckart, Werner 250
Edelweiß 307
Effner, Carl von 238
Effner, Joseph 32, 304, 319, 322, 326
Effnerstraße 327
Egkl, Wilhelm 318
EHC Red Bull München 312
Eicke, Theodor 53, 317, 320
Einstein, Albert 237, 297
Eisbach 47, 208
Eisenach 133
Eisner, Kurt 23, 126, 127
Elisenstraße 166
Elser, Georg 24, 53, 55, 181, 253
Emperor Ferdinand II 117
Emperor Friedrich I Barbarossa 16, 67, 332
Emperor Karl Albrecht 8, 20, 30, 46, 47, 104, 105, 148, 149, 152, 300, 301, 302, 304, 325
Emperor Karl IV 325
Emperor Karl V 18, 68, 249
Emperor Karl VI 324
Emperor Leopold I 19, 322, 324
Emperor Leopold II 208
Emperor Ludwig der Bayer 17, 36, 45, 60, 61, 65, 78, 79, 80, 81, 87, 96, 102, 110, 111, 112, 113, 149, 247
Emperor Romulus Augustulus 16
Emperor Taikosama 119
Emperor Wilhelm II 257
Ende, Michael 276
Englischer Garten 9, 20, 42, 47, 147, 171, 199, 206, 207, 208, 209, 210, 211, 238, 296
Ensslin, Gudrun 197
Erding 5
Erdinger Moos 14, 145, 328
Erhard, Hans 144
Erzherzog Ferdinand 68
Eselsbad 91, 254
ESO Supernova 32, 337
Ettenhofer, Johann Georg 88, 120
Ettlingen 106
Ettstraße 115
Evangelische Akademie in Tutzing 243

Everding, August 233

F

Fahrzeugfabrik Eisenach 314
Fasanengarten 296
Fassbinder, Rainer Werner 264, 276
Faustürmchen 101
FC Bayern Erlebniswelt 32, 337
FC Bayern München 14, 23, 25, 32, 60, 312, 336
Feistenberger, A. 141
Feldherrnhalle 21, 24, 52, 53, 134, 136, 137, 180, 196, 197, 204, 205, 214
Feuerwehrmuseum 30, 268, 269
Fiehler, Karl 164, 165, 181
Filmfest München 42, 252, 277
Filmmuseum München 277
Filmpalast 103
Filmtheater 102, 277
Finessensepperl 122
Fischbrunnen 61, 122
Fischer, Johann Michael 38, 220
Fischer, Karl von 21, 156, 172, 182
Flaucher 5, 238, 272, 273
Flaucher, Johann 272
Flugwerft Schleißheim 32, 327
Föhring 6, 16
Forstenrieder Park 296
Foster, Sir Norman 178
Frankfurt 8, 71
Franz-Joseph-Straße 206
Fränzl, Ferdinand 156
Frauenkirche 17, 18, 36, 37, 44, 45, 66, 69, 70, 98, 108, 110, 111, 112, 113, 120, 128, 129, 140, 247, 256, 308, 330, 332
Frauenplatz 111
Freising 6, 16, 21, 39, 110, 112, 206, 230, 260, 316, 322, 328, 329, 330, 331, 332, 333, 334
French Revolution 9, 105, 124
Friedensengel 11, 214, 215, 234, 236, 238, 297
Friedensengel Sommerfest 237
Friedensstraße 250
Frings, Klaus 197
Fröttmaning 312, 336
Fröttmaninger Mülldeponie 336
Frühlingsfest 42
Fugger 126
Fünf-Höfe 141
Fürstenfeldbruck 313
Fürst von Wrede, Carl Philipp 136
Fürth 21, 285

G

Gabelsbergerstraße 185, 277
Galgenberg 295
Galilei, Galileo 7
Galileiplatz 231
Games of the XX Summer Olympiads 14, 25, 72, 310
Gansser, Reto 144
Garching 5, 186, 187, 211, 272
Gärtner, Friedrich von 21, 136, 192, 196, 200, 201, 204, 205, 265, 267
Gärtnerplatz 36, 264, 265, 267
Gärtnerplatztheater 36, 266, 267
Gärtnerplatzviertel 51, 264
Gasteig 6, 14, 17, 25, 35, 60, 64, 70, 146, 147, 230, 238, 246, 248, 252, 253
Gebsattel, Lothar von 243
Geiselgasteig 23, 276, 277
General Eisenhower 25, 180
Gerbl, Heinrich 284
Gerhard, Hubert 71, 116, 118, 143
German Marian Congregation 120, 121
Geschwister-Scholl-Platz 200, 201
Gestapo 131, 201, 203, 236, 368
Giesing 262
Giesler, Hermann 294
Giglberg 316, 319
Girard, Dominique 304
Glockenbachviertel 36, 50, 51, 265, 266, 268, 269, 270
Glockenspiel 18, 68, 69, 70
Gluck, Christoph Willibald Ritter von 124
Glyptothek 11, 21, 33, 49, 169, 172, 174, 175, 176, 184
Gobert, Pierre 302
Goebel, Ritter Karl von 306
Goethe, Johann Wolfgang von 102, 170
Goethestraße 285
Goldberg, Gustav 242
Golden Bull 17
Graf Arco-Zinnenberg 23, 114, 127
Grafen von Andechs 278
Grafen von Dachau 316
Grafen von Scheyern 316
Grafinger Straße 251
Graf Rumford 9, 20, 171, 209
Graf Schack, Adolf Friedrich von 215
Graf Shcherbatov 2
Graf von Lüttich, Hubertus 298, 299
Graf von Metternich 125
Graf von Montgelas, Maximilian 10, 20, 88, 124, 155, 172, 230, 242, 330
Graf von Pocci, Franz 127

Graf von Tilly, Johann 70, 136
Graf von Törring-Jettenbach, August 230
Grasser, Erasmus 36, 45, 63, 64, 66, 98, 112, 332
Graz 73
Greiff, Johann Georg 66
Grimmelshausen, Hans von 191
Große Deutsche Kunstausstellung 53, 218, 219
Großhesseloher Brücke 95
Grünwald 272, 273, 276, 278
Grünwalder Konferenz 278
Gsaenger, Gustav 103
Gunetzrhainerhaus 124
Gustav Otto Flugmaschinenfabrik 314

H

Haberfeld 114
Hackenviertel 103
Hackerbrücke 284, 294
Hackl, Gabriel 39, 292
Hagenbeck 135
Haidhausen 14, 35, 51, 71, 146, 147, 162, 199, 233, 243, 244, 245, 246, 247, 248, 249, 252, 253, 255, 256, 291
Haidhausen-Museum 248
Hallertau 84, 329, 334
Halspach, Jörg von 18, 36, 39, 45, 62, 63, 98, 110, 332
Hammerthaler Muttergottes 36, 45, 90, 91, 114
Hans-Sachs-Straße 51, 268
Hapsburg dynasty 104, 105, 154, 249, 322, 324
Harlachinger Mill 274
Harrach, Ferdinand 333
Hartle, August 292
Hauberrisser, Georg von 39, 72, 73, 74, 292
Hauptbahnhof 124, 169, 284, 285
Hauptstadt der Bewegung 24, 52
Haus der Kunst 34, 53, 193, 208, 218, 219, 295
Heilig-Geist-Kirche 36, 44, 45, 65, 88, 89, 90, 91, 92, 108, 114
Heilig-Geist-Liberty 88
Heilig-Geist-Spital 16, 21, 88, 89, 92, 168
Heilsbronn 217
Heimeran von Straubing 113
Heinrichsstadt 16, 44, 62, 108, 122, 124
Heinrich von Straubing 110
Heisenberg, Werner 237, 297
Hellabrunn 273, 274
Henselmann, Josef 96, 97
Herigoyen, Emanuel Joseph von 124, 166
Herkulessaal 47, 142, 146, 147, 149, 153
Herzog Albrecht III 18, 308, 309
Herzog Albrecht IV 18, 78, 84, 110, 148, 151, 278, 279
Herzog Albrecht V 7, 18, 31, 82, 112, 117, 142, 146, 148, 184, 188, 202, 266, 279, 316, 318
Herzogbad 254
Herzog Christoph 77, 151
Herzog Ernst 309, 318
Herzog Friedrich 148
Herzog Georg der Reiche 78
Herzog Gerhard II von Jülich-Berg 299
Herzog Heinrich der Löwe 5, 6, 16, 44, 62, 67, 78, 230, 328
Herzog Hugibert 328
Herzogin Anna von Brunswick-Grubenhagen-Einbeck 309
Herzog Johann II 148
Herzog Ludwig der Kelheimer 7, 71
Herzog Ludwig der Reiche 200
Herzog Ludwig I 16, 36, 90
Herzog Ludwig II 7, 45, 69, 78, 79, 80, 224
Herzog Ludwig X 278
Herzog Maximilian I 326
Herzog Odilo 328
Herzog Otto I 16, 316
Herzogpark 231
Herzog Roman 1
Herzog Rudolf 114
Herzog-Rudolf-Straße 165
Herzog Sigismund 110, 308
Herzog Stephan II 84
Herzog Stephan III 148
Herzog Tassilo III 213, 328
Herzog von Leuchtenberg 119
Herzog Wilhelm IV 31, 85, 112, 116, 142, 190, 278, 316, 318
Herzog Wilhelm V 7, 18, 19, 36, 44, 68, 69, 70, 85, 110, 112, 116, 117, 118, 119, 148, 152, 268, 278, 322, 326
Hesseloherstraße 206
Heßstraße 206
Heunischenburg 213
Hildebrand, Adolf 162, 299
Hildebrandhaus 230
Himmler, Heinrich 24, 231, 320
Hingerl, Aloisius 85
Hirschau 208, 211
Hirschfeld, Cay Lorenz 305
Hirschgarten 296, 297, 305
Historical Wiesn 286, 287
Hitler, Adolf 24, 52, 53, 72, 83, 91, 127, 129, 130, 136, 137, 164, 177, 180, 181, 182, 203, 218, 219, 231, 233, 236, 245, 248, 249, 253, 293, 294, 295, 317, 320, 325
Hitler Putsch 24, 53, 63, 137, 173, 181, 182, 183, 253, 294

Hitler Youth 248
Hocheder, Carl 254
Hochschule für Fernsehen und Film 185, 276
Hochstraße 30, 259, 262
Hofbräu 244
Hofbräuhaus 8, 14, 19, 45, 52, 83, 84, 85, 157, 180, 182, 268
Hofbräukeller 244, 245
Hofbrunnenwerk 143
Hofgarten 20, 29, 47, 142, 143, 144, 145, 146, 147, 208, 211, 214, 215, 218
Hofgartentempel 142, 143
Hole, Bardly 306
Holzhausen 382
Horemans, Peter Jacob 36, 88, 90
Hotel Deutsche Eiche 264, 265
Hotterstraße 103
Hubertusbrunnen 14, 298, 299
Hussite War 18
Hypo-Kulturstiftung 33, 141

I

Impler, Johann 149
Industrial Revolution 12, 94, 186, 199, 200, 222, 292
Ingolstadt 5, 116, 117, 200
Inner Council 7, 17, 62, 70, 149
Innere Wiener Straße 244, 252
Innsbruck 7
Isar 5, 7, 11, 14, 17, 25, 51, 60, 64, 67, 77, 78, 82, 86, 93, 95, 110, 114, 133, 208, 210, 211, 222, 230, 238, 239, 240, 241, 244, 246, 252, 255, 257, 260, 261, 264, 272, 273, 274, 279, 291, 313
Isar-Floß-Event 273
Isarphilharmonie 35
Isartor 8, 16, 28, 45, 51, 60, 86, 87, 91, 102, 108, 122
Isarvorstadt 22, 264, 266, 292

J

Jagd- und Fischereimuseum 28, 108, 114, 115
Jakobidult 17
Jakobsplatz 25
Jann, Georg 113
Japanese Teahouse 208
Jawlensky, Alexej von 203
Jewish community 18, 24, 25, 52, 87, 100, 128, 130, 180, 201, 236, 237, 264
Johannisplatz 246, 247
Jonas, Sir Peter 157, 266
Judengasse 16

Judenhäuser 236
Jüdisches Museum 28
Jüdisches Zentrum 100
Jungfernturm 128, 129
Jungfernturmstraße 129

K

Kahr, Gustav von 52, 136
Kaiserhof 19, 148
Kaiserstraße 206
Kandinsky, Wassily 50, 133, 178, 202, 203, 206
Kant, Immanuel 124
Kapellenhof 151
Kardinal Faulhaber 120, 126, 127, 128, 129
Kardinal Faulhaber Straße 126, 127
Karlstadt, Lisl 223
Karlstor 43, 60, 108, 109, 122, 123, 284, 306, 310
Karlstraße 169
Karolinenplatz 10, 53, 135, 171, 172, 182, 183
Kartoffelmuseum 29, 251
Karwendel 272
Kaspar, Hermann 38, 242
Kaufbeuren 217
Kaufingerstraße 108, 109, 114
Kaufmann, Hugo 91
Kaulbach, Friedrich August von 199
Kaulbachvilla 199, 234
Kelheim 105
Keller, Gottfried 1, 206
Kempten 242
Kepler, Johannes 7
King Armleder 87
King Friedrich II 170
King Gustav II Adolf 8, 19, 70, 71, 246
King Louis XIV 152, 324
King Louis XV 104
King Ludwig I 3, 11, 21, 37, 46, 47, 48, 49, 86, 99, 125, 134, 135, 142, 143, 146, 147, 148, 149, 152, 154, 168, 170, 171, 172, 173, 174, 176, 182, 184, 186, 188, 189, 192, 196, 198, 199, 200, 204, 214, 222, 260, 270, 284, 285, 286, 288, 289, 290, 292, 300, 303, 309, 310, 331
King Ludwig II 11, 36, 47, 74, 75, 95, 119, 146, 153, 205, 214, 232, 239, 266, 267, 300, 303
King Ludwig III 12, 23, 113, 126, 150, 325
King Maximilian I 8, 9, 10, 19, 32, 44, 46, 47, 48, 70, 71, 73, 80, 81, 85, 92, 110, 112, 117, 118, 132, 133, 134, 142, 148, 152, 154, 155, 156, 163, 166, 170, 174, 188, 189, 200, 216, 224, 242, 243, 246, 271, 288, 299, 301, 303, 304, 319, 322, 330

King Maximilian II 3, 11, 49, 94, 95, 138, 140, 167, 214, 216, 222, 223, 238, 239
King Otto I 170, 171, 214
King Otto of Bavaria 214
King Rudolf von Hapsburg 17
King Wenceslau 106, 107
King Wilhelm I 205
Kirchenstraße 246
Klee, Paul 50, 133, 178, 202, 203, 206
Kleinhesseloher See 47, 208, 210
Klenze, Leo von 38, 49, 119, 132, 134, 143, 155, 156, 157, 169, 170, 172, 174, 176, 185, 188, 190, 192, 196, 198, 208, 288, 290, 291, 292
Klitzing, Klaus von 237
Kloster Bernried 357
Kloster Ettal 121
Knabel, Joseph 246
Knappertsbusch, Hans 157, 266
Kobell, Wilhelm von 317
Kobus, Kathi 193
Kocherlball 42, 211
Koch, Robert 162
Köhler, Gundolf 287
Koller, Friedrich 48, 168
Köln 18, 71
Königliche Erzgießerei 155
Königliche Pulver- und Munitionsfabrik Dachau 53
Königsbau 149, 152
Königsplatz 3, 11, 24, 48, 53, 135, 169, 170, 172, 173, 177, 178, 179, 183, 201, 288, 295
Korbinians-Quelle 334
Kreittmayr, Freiherr von 295
Krempe 244
Kreppe, Karl 145
Kristallnacht 13, 24, 53, 63, 99, 100, 181, 236, 264, 321
Kronach 213
Kronprinz-Rupprecht-Brunnen 151
Krumpper, Hans 36, 45, 67, 110, 111, 112, 114, 143
Kultureinrichtung Lothringer 13 249
Kunsthalle München 141
Künstlerhaus 23, 35, 164, 165
Künstlerkolonie Dachau 317
Kunstpavillon 33, 166, 167
Kurfürstenplatz 183
Kurfürst Ferdinand Maria 8, 19, 30, 37, 47, 138, 139, 140, 141, 150, 300, 302
Kurfürst Karl Theodor 9, 20, 65, 66, 86, 102, 122, 123, 128, 134, 142, 154, 170, 171, 172, 184, 188, 208, 209, 210, 260, 267, 296, 298, 299, 302
Kurfürst Max Emanuel 8, 19, 20, 30, 32, 37, 46, 47, 124, 138, 139, 141, 188, 195, 256, 279, 298, 300, 301, 302, 304, 305, 309, 319, 322, 323, 324, 325, 326
Kurfürst-Max-Emanuel-Platz 319
Kurfürst Max III Joseph 9, 20, 113, 140, 141, 142, 170, 202, 256
Kurfürst Wilhelm IV 249, 260

L

Laim 294
Landsberg am Lech 52, 91, 108, 114, 122, 180
Landshut 78, 200
Landshut War of Succession 18
Lange Nacht der Museen 43
Lange Nacht der Musik 42
Langen, Albert 191
Lasso, Orlando di 18, 68, 82, 83, 124, 146, 266
Lederer, Jörg 217
Lehel 199, 220, 221
Leibnitz, Hans-Maier 186
Leipold, Karl 219
Lenbach, Franz von 50, 164, 178, 179, 188, 199, 202
Lenbachhaus 33, 50, 178, 179, 234
Lenbachplatz 164, 165
Lenin, Vladimir Ilyich 206
Leopoldstraße 132, 183, 197, 205, 206, 207
Leppman, Jella 308
leprosarium 249
Lerchenfeldstraße 213
Lessing, Gotthold Ephraim 170
Leutstetten 5
Liebfrauenstraße 109
Lilalu Festival 310
Lilienthal, Otto 258
Linde, Carl von 49, 186
Lindwurmstraße 183
Lintner, Karl 335
Linz 136
Literaturhaus München 135
Littmann, Max 49, 223, 232
Loggia dei Lanzi 136
Lorraine, Renata of 44, 68, 69, 70
Loth, Ulrich 90
Löwel, Friedrich 89
Löwenturm 96, 97
Loyola, Ignatius 7, 116, 121
Ludwig-Maximilians-Universität 21, 49, 200, 297, 306
Ludwigsbrücke 238, 255
Ludwigskirche 11, 38, 49, 198, 199, 270

345

Ludwigstraße 11, 21, 49, 134, 135, 172, 173, 196, 197, 198, 199, 200, 204, 205, 206, 207, 214, 288
Ludwigsvorstadt 266, 292
Luisenstraße 179
Luise, Therese Charlotte 11
Luitpoldbrücke 255
Luther, Martin 7, 114, 118, 243, 278

M

Macke, August 178, 203
Madame de Pompadour 104
Madame Dubarry 104
Maerz, Franz Borgias 91
Maffei, Josef von 285
Maffeistraße 284
Magdalen Day 305
Magdalenendult 305
Magdalenenklause 301, 304
Magdeburg 70
Mahler, Gustav 146, 157
Maidult 42
Mailinger, Josef 98
Mainz 71
Mangfalltal 162
Mangoldstein 69
Mannheim 9, 20, 106, 170, 172, 188
Manninger, Karl 89
Mann, Thomas 1, 231
Marc, Franz 50, 178, 202, 203
Maria Anna von Österreich 163
Maria Anna von Sachsen 140
Maria Antonia von Österreich 322, 324
Mariahilf 39, 260, 261
Mariahilfplatz 39, 42, 260, 261
Maria Theresa 105
Maria-Theresia-Straße 230
Maria Ward School 303
Maria-Ward-Straße 303
Marie Friederike von Preußen 138, 140
Marienhof 16, 44, 71
Marienklausenbrücke 273
Marienplatz 6, 7, 8, 16, 19, 21, 42, 43, 44, 45, 60, 61, 62, 66, 69, 71, 74, 75, 89, 91, 92, 93, 94, 96, 102, 108, 122, 124, 131, 162, 294, 310
Mariensäule 6, 8, 19, 44, 55, 60, 61, 70, 71, 98, 162
Marionettentheater 36, 268, 269
Marsstraße 294
Marstallplatz 142, 157
Martius, Carl Friedrich Phillip 166
Marx, Karl 120

Master Eder 221
Mathilde von Hapsburg 80
Matteo, Antonio 88
Maximilian Chapel 333
Maximilianeum 49, 222, 238, 239
Maximiliansanlagen 238, 262
Maximiliansbrücke 239
Maximilianstil 11, 222, 238, 246
Maximilianstraße 11, 35, 49, 222, 223, 224, 225, 238
Maximilianswerk 240
Max-Joseph-Brücke 255
Max-Joseph-Platz 35, 154, 157, 222
Max-Mannheimer-Platz 181
Max-Planck-Straße 239
Maxvorstadt 3, 10, 11, 21, 48, 52, 132, 134, 135, 172, 173, 182, 183, 186, 187, 194, 195, 200, 206, 224, 264, 270, 277, 292
Mayer, Hans 76
Mayer SJ, Rupert 25, 29, 37, 120, 121, 312
May, Karl 233
Mehta, Zubin 157
Mehul, Étienne-Nicolas 157
Meier, Richard 133
Meinhof, Ulrike 197
Mein Kampf 52
Meiser, Hans 103
Menzinger Straße 307
Mercury, Freddie 51, 264, 265
Messerschmidt, Willy 49, 186
Metten 106
Michel, Johann B. 20
Mielich, Hans 76
Milbertshofen 24, 130
Miller, Ferdinand von 288, 289
Miller, Konrad 89
Miller, Oskar von 23, 186, 256, 257
Mittelalterliche Kriminalmuseum 129
Mittenwald 7
Möhlstraße 236, 237
Monacensia 34, 230, 231
Monopteros 47, 208
Monte Scherblino 311
Montez, Lola 21, 47, 99, 125, 173, 303, 309
Montgelasstraße 231
Moriscan Dancer 45, 63, 98
Mößbauer, Rudolf 187
Mössel, Julius 164, 232
Mozart, Wolfgang Amadeus 76, 77, 146, 266
Mr Henderson 51, 265
Muffat, Karl 94
Muffatwerk 255
Mühldorf am Inn 179, 321
Mühltaler-Isarwehr 273

Müller, Karl von 51, 254, 255
Müllersches Volksbad 23, 51, 254, 255
Müllerstraße 269
Münchner Bücherschau 252
Münchner Freiheit 206
Münchner Kammerspiele 23, 35, 223
Münchner Kindl 28, 45, 69, 74, 98
Münchner Lach- und Schießgesellschaft 25, 51
Münchner Lichtspielkunst AG 276
Münchner Neueste Nachrichten 21
Münchner Opernfestspiele 35, 42
Münchner Philharmoniker 35, 252, 253
Münchner Residenz 5, 8, 11, 17, 18, 19, 20, 29, 35, 45, 46, 69, 78, 80, 82, 119, 124, 126, 134, 135, 137, 146, 147, 148, 149, 151, 153, 154, 156, 170, 195, 222, 232, 278, 330, 332
Münchner Rückversicherung 22, 197, 206, 211
Münchner Schwulenzentrum 265
Münchner Stadtbibliothek 230, 252
Münchner Stadtgeburtstag 42
Münchner Stadtmuseum 28, 45, 63, 98, 277, 287
Münchner Symphoniker 146, 147
Münchner Volkshochschule 23
Munich Agreement 24, 53, 177
Münzmuseum 29, 148, 151
Museum Ägyptischer Kunst 25, 33, 49, 184, 185
Museum Brandhorst 25
Museum Bürgersaalkirche 29
Museum infopoint 28, 45, 78, 79, 81
Museum Mensch und Natur 301
Museum of Jewish History 100
Museum of Urban and Contemporary Art 33, 103
Museum Sea Life 31, 310, 313
Museumsinsel 240, 256, 257
Mussolini 233

N

Napoleon 9, 10, 21, 64, 105, 125, 134, 154, 155, 172, 182, 183, 204, 242, 330
Napoleonic Wars 9, 136, 247
Nationaltheater 21, 35, 146, 147, 154, 156, 157, 232
Nazi regime 14, 24, 29, 32, 34, 37, 48, 52, 53, 63, 72, 99, 100, 103, 114, 120, 121, 128, 129, 130, 131, 137, 170, 173, 177, 180, 181, 182, 193, 201, 203, 218, 219, 231, 233, 236, 248, 253, 284, 286, 303, 314, 317, 320, 321
Neptunbrunnen 167
Neue Pinakothek 11, 33, 49, 173, 188, 192, 193, 194, 199

Neue Rathaus 10, 12, 18, 22, 44, 68, 71, 72, 73, 74, 292
Neuhausen 298
Neuhauser Straße 14, 108, 109, 115, 117, 118, 119, 122, 147, 200, 202, 310
Neureuther, Gottfried von 186, 202, 203
Neuveste 17, 18, 28, 46, 80, 142, 148, 149, 318
Newcastle 285
New York 265
Night of the Long Knives 24
Nockherberg 262, 263
Nördlingen 212
Noricum 271
November Revolution 23
NS-Dokumentationszentrum 29, 52, 53, 173, 180, 181, 182
Nürnberg 18, 20, 21, 70, 198, 216, 242, 285
Nymphenburger Festspiele 30
Nymphenburger Kanal 14, 298, 310
Nymphenburger Porzellanmanufaktur 20, 221

O

Obatzter 41
Oberföhring 16
Oberhaching 5
Oberlandesgericht 166
Oberlauterbach group 5
Oberschleißheim 323, 324, 325, 326, 327
Oberstleutnant Menzel 247
Oberwiesenfeld 23, 311
Occamstraße 206
Ochsengarten 269
Odeon 132, 134, 146
Odeonsplatz 8, 19, 42, 46, 47, 53, 60, 122, 134, 135, 136, 137, 139, 142, 146, 172, 196
Ohel Jakob 100, 101
Ohlmüller, Joseph Daniel 39, 260
Oktoberfest 11, 21, 25, 43, 49, 286, 288, 292, 293, 307
Oktoberfest terror attack 25, 287
Olympiaberg 311
Olympiagelände 25
Olympiahalle 36, 312
Olympiapark 31, 43, 298, 310, 311
Olympiasee 298
Olympiastadion 121, 311, 312
Olympiaturm 25, 31, 312, 313
Olympiazentrum 31, 42, 310, 311
Oppidum Manching 5, 16, 213
Oranienburg 120
Order of Augustinians 17, 90, 114
Order of Benedictines 6, 37, 168, 169, 334
Order of Cistercians 80

Order of Franciscans 17, 157, 220
Order of Hubertus 119, 298, 299
Order of Jesuits 8, 18, 19, 47, 108, 116, 117, 120, 139, 200, 279, 322
Order of Paulaner 260
Order of Poor Clares 65
Order of Theatines 19, 138, 139, 141
Order of the Holy Ghost 88
Orff, Karl 309
Original-Physograph Company 276
Orlandohaus 82, 83
Orleansplatz 251
Oskar-von-Miller-Ring 133
Ostbahnhof 29, 248, 250, 251
Ostermayr, Peter 23, 276
Otto, Frei Paul 274
Ottoman Empire 171, 195
Outer Council 17, 62

P

Pacher, August 246
Pagodenburg 30, 301, 304
Palais Arco-Zinneberg 132
Palais Barlow 182
Palais Holnstein 126
Palais Ludwig Ferdinand 132, 133
Palais Pinakothek 194
Palais Porcia 126
Palais Sensheim 126
Palais Törring-Jettenbach 154
Papagei Bar 83
Paradeiserhaus 303
Pariser Platz 248
partition of Bavaria 7, 17, 78
Pasing 16, 298
Passow, Beate 189
Patrona Bavaria 8, 49, 288, 289, 293
Paulaner am Nockherberg 262
Pauli, Wolfgang 237
Paur, Franz Anton von 274
Peace of Augsburg 7, 8, 18
Peace of Pressburg 10
Peace of Westphalia 8, 19
Peiker, Hermenegild 66
Peiner, Werner 219
Perlach 245
Petersbergl 44, 64, 69
Petersplatz 65
Pettenkofer, Max von 162
Pfaffenhofen 5
Pferdebändiger 12
Pinakothek der Moderne 25, 34, 49, 188, 194, 195

Planck, Max 237, 297
Planetenweg 257
Platz der Opfer des Nationalsozialismus 130
Platzlgasse 82
Polack, Jan 31, 66, 308
Pope Benedict XIII 107
Pope Benedict XVI 111, 331
Pope Clemens VII 249
Pope Innocent IV 88
Pope John Paul II 25, 121, 312
Pope Pius XI 129
Possart, Ernst von 232
Pragmatic Sanction 325
Prague Defenestration 8
Prangl, Georg 122
Prannerstraße 126
Praterinsel 240, 241
Praterwerk 240
Preis, Toni 130
Present Continuous 3
Preußler, Otfried 276
Preysingplatz 38, 246
Preysingstraße 247
primogeniture law 18, 78
Prince Regent Luitpold 11, 49, 51, 74, 109, 119, 135, 136, 140, 202, 214, 215, 225, 232, 234, 298, 325
Prince Regent period 214
Prince Rupprecht 298
Princess Caroline of Baden 242, 243
Princess Therese von Saxony-Hildburghausen 21, 286
Prinz-Carl-Palais 214, 215, 218
Prinzregentenbad 230
Prinzregentenplatz 53, 214, 233
Prinzregentenstraße 11, 22, 35, 49, 145, 164, 193, 209, 214, 215, 216, 217, 218, 219, 230, 233, 234, 235, 236, 237
Prinzregententheater 23, 35, 49, 231, 232, 233
Promenadeplatz 60, 124, 125
Propyläen 48, 135, 170, 172, 173
Prunkhof 10, 72, 75
Pumuckl 221

Q

Queen 51

R

Raetia Province 16
Rama Dama 131
Rangierbahnhof München Ost 250
Rapp Motorenwerke AG 23, 314

Rationaltheater 51, 206
Rauch, Christian Daniel 155
Reformation 7, 45, 68, 249, 303
Regensburg 5, 11, 78, 105, 113, 212, 290
Reger, Max 246
Regierung von Oberbayern 223
Regulierungswehr 240
Reichenbach, Georg von 285
Reichenbachstraße 265
Reichsdeputationshauptschluss 21
Reiffenstuel, Franz Michael 36, 265, 266
Reithalle München 206
Renata of Lorraine 18
Residenzmuseum 29, 46, 148, 152
Residenzstraße 137, 149, 154
Residenztheater 35
Richard Strauss Brunnen 108
Richard Strauss Conservatory 252
Riedl, Adrian von 210
Riem Airport 24
Riemenschneider, Tilman 216, 217
Riemerschmid, Richard 223, 240
Rindermarkt 16, 44, 96, 122, 165
Rindermarktbrunnen 97
Robert, Eugen 223
Rohr 106
Roman Empire 5, 16
Röntgen, Wilhelm Conrad 237, 297
Rosenheim 250
Rosenheimer Straße 52, 248, 251, 253, 255, 262, 294
Rosenkavalierplatz 230
Rosenlehner 123
Rosenstraße 96
Rossschwemmbach 93
Rothenburg ob der Tauber 129, 242
Rottaler, Lukas 98, 128
Rottenhammer, Hans 332
Rottmann, Carl 192
Rudolfinische Handfeste 17
Ruhmeshalle 11, 49, 290, 291

S

Sadrart, Joachim 332
Saint Afra 271
Saint Aloysius of Gonzaga 119
Saint Anna 38, 220, 221
Saint Benedict 330
Saint Benno 73, 74
Saint Boniface 271, 328
Saint Christopher 270
Saint Corbinian 6, 39, 331, 332, 333, 334
Saint Florian 271
Saint George 74
Saint Hubertus 298, 299
Saint John the Evangelist 246
Saint Kajetan 141
Saint Maximilian 270
Saint Nepomuk 46, 104, 105, 106, 107
Saint Nicholas 318
Saint Peter 36, 44, 45, 64, 66
Saint Stephan 334
Salvator 263
Salvatorkirche 37, 128, 129
Salvatorplatz 128, 156
Salvatortheater 19
Salzburg 16, 24, 70, 73, 146, 316, 332
Sammlung Bollert 34, 217
Sammlung Brandhorst 34, 194
Sandrart, Joachim von 141
Sandtner, Jakob 45, 98
San Francisco 265
Savoyen, Henriette Adelaide von 8, 19, 37, 47, 138, 139, 140, 141, 300, 302, 304, 323
Sawallisch, Wolfgang 266
Schack-Galerie 34, 215
Schäffler 68, 74
Schäftlarn 6, 64, 230, 273, 367
Scharfrichterplatz 295
Scharnagl, Karl 130, 181
Schatzkammer 29, 47, 148
Schauburg 206
Schäzlerpalais Augsburg 104
Schedel, Hartmann 2
Schedelsche Weltchronik 18
Scheinerstraße 230
Schillerstraße 285
Schleich, Eduard 317
Schleich, Erwin 115, 198
Schloss Blutenburg 18, 31, 66, 147, 308, 309
Schloss Dachau 31, 146, 147, 302, 318, 319
Schloss Lustheim 19, 32, 47, 322, 324
Schloss Neuburghausen 230
Schloss Neudeck 260
Schloss Nymphenburg 3, 8, 19, 23, 30, 46, 47, 114, 135, 147, 166, 172, 279, 296, 298, 300, 301, 303, 304, 305, 311, 316, 319, 324, 326
Schloss Possenhofen 353
Schloss Schleißheim 3, 8, 19, 32, 46, 47, 147, 195, 208, 279, 302, 316, 322, 324, 325, 326, 327
Schloss Steppburg 230
Schmid, Jakob 201
Schmidt, Albert 38, 242, 246
Schmidt, Heinrich von 270
Schmidt, Johann Baptist 38, 246

Schmidt, Ludwig 243
Schmidt, Veit 114
Scholl, Hans 201
Scholl, Sophie 201
Schöner Turm 108, 109, 122
Schönfeldwiese 208
Schottenhammel, Michael 286
Schöttl, Heinrich 318
Schrannenhalle 94, 95
Schrannenplatz 60, 162
Schrenk Altar 45, 66
Schuhbeck, Alfons 83
Schwabing 16, 50, 51, 206, 208
Schwabinger Bach 197, 208
Schwabinger Krawalle 25
Schwabinger Tor 122, 134, 208
Schwanthalerhöhe 286, 288
Schwanthaler, Jakob 209
Schwanthaler, Ludwig von 156, 198, 204, 288
Schwanthalerstraße 23, 35, 169
Schwanzer, Karl 314
Schwartz, Christoph 45, 116, 118
Sckell, Friedrich Ludwig von 21, 30, 102, 166, 172, 208, 231, 301, 304, 305, 318
secularisation 10, 20, 80, 88, 92, 112, 332
Sedlmayr, Walter 95
Seidl, Claudius von 122
Seidl, Emanuel von 274
Seidl, Gabriel von 23, 38, 96, 164, 178, 210, 216, 217, 220
Seitz, Rudolf von 220, 221
Seldweg 309
Semper, Gottfried 232
Sendling 92
Sendlinger Straße 36, 96, 105
Sendlinger Tor 8, 46, 60, 101, 102, 122, 169, 243, 277
Sendlinger-Tor-Platz 103
Senefelder, Alois 20
Separeé XX 83
Siegert, Diethard 144
Siegestor 136, 196, 197, 204, 205
Siemens 132, 133
Siemens Forum 133
Sigl, Florian 276
Simbach 250
Simplicissimus 51, 133, 191, 193, 231
Sinti & Roma 130, 131, 321
Sobeck, Andreas 130
Solnhofen 179
Sommerfeld, Arnold 297
Sonnenstraße 102, 103
Sophienstraße 167
Spanish flu 23

Spielzeugmuseum 28, 62, 63
Spix, Johann Baptist 166
Staatschauspiel am Gärtnerplatz 264
Stachus 123
Stadler, Christine 48, 168
Stadtschreiberhaus 45, 76, 77
Stadtwerke München 240, 336
Stahl, Friedrich 219
St Anna 38, 220, 221
St. Anna Platz 38, 220
St.-Anna-Straße 221
Starkbierzeit 43
Starnberg 5, 349
Starnberger See 119, 153, 214, 243, 298
St Bonifaz 11, 37, 48, 168, 169, 172, 175
Steffani, Agostino 266
Steiger, Ivan 63
Stephan, Joseph 302
Sterneckerbräu 91
St George 231
Stieler, Joseph 303
Stiftung Maximilianeum 239
St Jakob Anger 65
St.-Jakobs-Platz 45, 98, 99, 100, 101
St Johann Baptist 38, 246
St Johannes 38, 243, 246, 247
St John relic 246
St Lorenz 78, 80
St Lukas 38, 242, 243
St Maria & St Korbinian 39, 330, 332
St Markus 243
St Matthäus 103, 243
St Maximilian 12, 39, 270
St Michael 7, 19, 36, 44, 45, 108, 116, 117, 118, 119, 140, 322
St Nikolai 17, 39, 249
Stöberl, Wilhelm 107
Stoss, Veit 217
St Paul 12, 39, 292, 293
St Peter 6, 16, 36, 44, 45, 64, 65, 66, 67, 88, 92, 108, 298
Strasbourg 71
Strauß, Franz Joseph 145
Strauss, Johann 266
Strauss, Richard 108, 146, 156, 157, 267
Stritter, Max 65
Stuber, Franz Lorenz 302
Stuber, Nikolaus Gottfried 64, 66, 90
Stuck, Franz von 35, 50, 51, 188, 199, 234, 235
Studentenwerk München 201
Stuttgart 71
Sudeten crisis 53, 177
Sudetendeutsche Museum 30, 259
Sudetenland 144, 177

Südfriedhof 128, 268
Sunken Village 337
Sustris, Friedrich 117
Sylvensteinspeicher 240, 255, 261

T

Tal 91, 93
Talburgtor 6, 16, 28, 44, 62, 122
Tambosi 20
Tanz der Marktweiber 43, 92
Taschner, Ignatius 244
Technische Universität München 22, 49, 186, 187
Tehran Conference 132
Tellus Bavarica 143
Thalkirchen 273
Theatermuseum 29, 218
Theatinerkirche 8, 19, 37, 47, 134, 138, 139, 140, 141, 243
Theatinerstraße 137, 141
Theatron 43, 312
Theresienhöhe 289, 291
Theresienstadt 130
Theresienstraße 196
Theresienwiese 42, 43, 49, 126, 286, 287, 288, 290, 292, 293
The Walking Man 197, 207
Thiersch, Friedrich von 91
Thierschstraße 243
Thirty Years' War 8, 44, 46, 47, 64, 68, 70, 71, 73, 110, 116, 118, 136, 138, 139, 140, 163, 242, 243, 246, 252
Thoma, Ludwig 85
Thomas-Mann-Allee 231
Thorvaldsen, Bertel 132
Tierpark Hellabrunn 23, 30, 257, 274, 275
Tierparkstraße 275
Tollwood Festival 42, 43, 310, 311
Totenkopf-SS 320
Toulouse 298
Treaty of Frankfurt 236
Treaty of Rastatt 324
Treaty of Versailles 180
Triva, Antonio 302
Troost, Paul Ludwig 34, 53, 218
Tschudi, Hugo von 192
Türkenkaserne 194
Türkenstraße 51, 193, 194, 195
Tutzing 243

U

Uhlfelder Department Store 53, 99, 165
Uhlfelder, Heinrich 99
Uhlfelder, Max 99
Ulich, Max 321
Ulrichs, Timm 337
Umadum Riesenrad 251
Universitäts-Sternwarte München 231
Ursulastraße 206
Utz, Christian & Stephanie 103

V

Valentin, Karl 51, 169, 193, 223, 260
Valentinmusäum 28, 51, 86, 87
Vereinigung Münchner Secession 22
Verona 7, 67
Viani, Anton Maria 119
Viktualienmarkt 21, 43, 45, 60, 66, 88, 92, 93, 95, 168, 264, 310
Villa Stuck 35, 50, 51, 234
Vindelics 5
Viscardigasse 53, 137
Viscardi, Giovanni Antonio 333
Voit, August 167
Völkerkundemuseum Fünf Kontinente 29, 224
Volkssternwarte München 29, 248, 251
Volpini, Giuseppe 327
Volunteer Corps Lützow 245

W

Wackerle, Josef 166, 167
Waderé, Heinrich 232
Wadler 89
Wagner, Adolf 181
Wagner, Johann Martin von 204
Wagner, Richard 68, 146, 157, 232, 233, 267
Waldkirch, Johann Theodor Freiherr von 296
Walhalla 11, 290
Walter, Bruno 157
Wandel, Hoefer & Lorch 100
Wank, Bruno 137
Ward, Maria 303
War in Ukraine 25
Warnberger, Simon 317
War of Succession of Landshut 78, 82
War of the Austrian Succession 20
War of the Spanish Succession 19, 324
Weber, Christian 114
Wechs & Finsterwalder 145
Wedekind, Frank 1
Weihenstephan 213, 334, 335
Weihenstephaner Berg 328, 331, 334
Weimar Period 72, 83, 253
Weingarten 106

Weinhold, Gertrud 323
Weinstadl 18
Weinstraße 61, 74, 75, 303
Weißenburg 242
Weißenburger Platz 248
Weiße Rose 24, 201
Weiß, Martin 321
Weißwürste 22, 40
Weiter, Eduard 321
Weizsäcker, Andreas von 189
Weltenburg 105
Werneckerwiese 211
Werner-Heisenberg-Allee 337
Westenrieder, Lorenz von 124
White Guards 245
Widenmayerstraße 221
Wien 18, 133, 146
Wiener Platz 244, 245
Wieskirche 104
Wilhelmina-Busch-Woods-Park 345
Wilhelminische Veste 163
Wimmer, Hans 108
Wimmer, Thomas 25, 131, 287
Wirtshaus in der Au 262
Wisreutter, Hans 318
Wittelsbacher Brunnen 162, 163
Wittelsbacher dynasty 9, 12, 17, 20, 29, 30, 31, 32, 37, 45, 46, 72, 74, 78, 81, 110, 111, 113, 126, 138, 140, 142, 148, 149, 152, 170, 202, 208, 209, 216, 232, 278, 302, 308, 309, 316, 319
Wittelsbacher Palais 131
Wittelsbacher Platz 9, 51, 132, 133, 243
Wittelsbacherstraße 270
Wolfratshausen 273, 367
Wolpertinger 115
World War I 12, 23, 52, 72, 73, 136, 145, 150, 179, 180, 205, 210, 245, 306
World War II 12, 14, 24, 30, 37, 45, 48, 62, 65, 66, 72, 78, 81, 83, 91, 95, 96, 102, 111, 114, 115, 120, 121, 122, 126, 130, 131, 132, 133, 134, 140, 143, 144, 145, 146, 147, 156, 164, 167, 168, 169, 175, 177, 181, 182, 185, 189, 192, 196, 198, 201, 210, 218, 224, 230, 232, 236, 241, 242, 249, 253, 260, 264, 269, 274, 276, 284, 286, 290, 297, 303, 308, 310, 311, 315, 317, 320, 321, 325, 326, 336, 337
Wörthsee 372
Würm 298, 304
Wurmeck 74, 75
Würzburg 237

Z

Zacherl, Franz Xaver 263
Zeillerstraße 279
Zenetti, Arnold 92, 122
Zeppelin Landing 311
Zeppelinstraße 257
Zeughaus 18, 45, 98, 99
Ziebland, Georg Friedrich 37, 48, 49, 168, 169, 176, 177
Ziegler, Clara 147
Zimmermann, Johann Baptist 36, 39, 45, 64, 66, 302, 326, 333
Zimmermann, Wilhelm 238
Zistl, Max 65
Zuccalli, Enrico 32, 37, 126, 138, 140, 302, 322, 326, 327
Zumbusch, Caspar von 223, 333
Zum Königlichen Hirschgarten 296

The Author

Rudolf is a widely travelled cosmopolitan. He was born in Munich, graduated in physics with distinction at the Ludwig-Maximilians Universität and completed his doctorate on star formation at the Max Planck Institute for Astrophysics. He then followed the call to become a senior management consultant in London, where he advised the leaders of the financial services industry for nearly ten years. His passion for the Tango tempted him to Buenos Aires. There, he studied psychology and sociology at the Universidad de Palermo. Rudolf is drawn to the analytical school of Carl Gustav Jung. His travels across the globe carried him to the Middle East, to Asia and Africa; in Latin America, he feels at home. The globetrotter speaks three languages fluently, and he is convinced that the tongue of the heart is the most important one. Rudolf is a passionate photographer and never at a loss for a story.

The Book

Munich: Strictly Confidential is more than just an ordinary travel guide. It describes a journey through town to discover the culturally rich city in 113 travel points with the eyes of a local. The author presents Munich's historical background in an engaging and informative manner; from emotional experience and intuitive understanding to hard facts, the book provides never-ending insight into Munich and the life of its burghers. The focus is not on individual sights, but the author delves into the historical development of the city. "It is only when we look at the whole," says Rudolf, "that the detail makes sense." Just flipping through the pages enthrals to adventure. With the guide *Munich: Strictly Confidential*, the world-traveller feels the excitement of exploring the cultures of this marvellous blue planet called home to all earthlings.

Rudolf H. Stehle

MUNICH
STRICTLY CONFIDENTIAL

Phekaruma Travel Guide

Phekaruma is an indie project that aims to enrich the niche market of culturally interested globetrotters using cutting-edge PoD technologies.

Since the turn of the millennium, the psychological energy of globalization has overshadowed that of nationalistic trends. The conflict between regional and global dynamics defines our time. In the chain of ancestry, the task of the 21st century is to bring the world's cultures together without reducing them to the lowest common denominator. Diversity in unity is only achieved through understanding and through emotional openness. The Phekaruma Travel Guides want to help outgrow this challenge.